Coordination Failure

STUDIES IN POSTWAR AMERICAN POLITICAL DEVELOPMENT

Steven Teles, *Series Editor*

The Delegated Welfare State: Medicare, Markets, and the Governance of Social Policy
Kimberly J. Morgan and Andrea Louise Campbell

Rule and Ruin: The Downfall of Moderation and the Destruction of the Republican Party, From Eisenhower to the Tea Party
Geoffrey Kabaservice

Engines of Change: Party Factions in American Politics, 1868–2010
Daniel DiSalvo

Follow the Money: How Foundation Dollars Change Public School Politics
Sarah Reckhow

The Allure of Order: High Hopes, Dashed Expectations, and the Troubled Quest to Remake American Schooling
Jal Mehta

Rich People's Movements: Grassroots Campaigns to Untax the One Percent
Isaac William Martin

The Outrage Industry: Political Opinion Media and the New Incivility
Jeffrey M. Berry and Sarah Sobieraj

Artists of the Possible: Governing Networks and American Policy since 1945
Matt Grossman

Building the Federal Schoolhouse: Localism and the American Education State
Douglas S. Reed

The First Civil Right: How Liberals Built Prison America
Naomi Murakawa

How Policy Shapes Politics: Rights, Courts, Litigation, and the Struggle Over Injury Compensation
Jeb Barnes and Thomas F. Burke

No Day in Court: Access to Justice and the Politics of Judicial Retrenchment
Sarah Staszak

Ideas with Consequences: The Federalist Society and the Conservative Counterrevolution
Amanda Hollis-Brusky

The Business of America is Lobbying: How Corporations Became Politicized and Politics Became More Corporate
Lee Drutman

Below the Radar: How Silence Can Save Civil Rights
Alison L. Gash

Building a Business of Politics: The Rise of Political Consulting and the Transformation of American Democracy
Adam Sheingate

Prison Break: Why Conservatives Turned Against Mass Incarceration
David Dagan and Steven Teles

The Other Rights Revolution: Conservative Lawyers and the Remaking of American Government
Jefferson Decker

When Bad Policy Makes Good Politics: Running the Numbers on Health Reform
Robert P. Saldin

Citizens By Degree: Higher Education Policy and the Changing Gender Dynamics of American Citizenship
Deondra Rose

Politics at Work: How Companies Turn Their Workers into Lobbyists
Alexander Hertel-Fernandez

The Cities on the Hill: How Urban Institutions Transformed National Politics
Thomas K. Ogorzalek

Framing Inequality: News Media, Public Opinion, and the Neoliberal Turn in U.S. Public Policy
Matt Guardino

Mobilized by Injustice: Criminal Justice Contact, Political Participation, and Race
Hannah L. Walker

Short Circuiting Policy: Interest Groups and the Battle Over Clean Energy and Climate Policy in the American States
Leah Cardamore Stokes

The Rise of Political Action Committees: Interest Group Electioneering and the Transformation of American Politics
Emily J. Charnock

Separate But Faithful: The Christian Right's Radical Struggle to Transform Law & Legal Culture
Amanda Hollis-Brusky and Joshua C. Wilson

Captive Market: Accountability and State Prison Privatization
Anna Gunderson

The Myth of Left and Right: How the Political Spectrum Misleads and Harms America
Hyrum Lewis and Verlan Lewis

Why Congress
Philip A. Wallach

Privatizing Justice: Arbitration and the Decline of Public Governance in the US
Sarah Staszak

The Power of Black Excellence: HBCUs and the Fight for American Democracy
Deondra Rose

The Thinkers: The Rise of Partisan Think Tanks and the Polarization of American Politics
E.J. Fagan

Agents of Justice: How the American Bureaucracy Mobilizes Private Lawsuits to Make Policy Work
Quinn Mulroy

Liberalism and the Reinvention of the Modern Corporation
Kathleen J. Frydl

The Republican Civil War: What Liz Cheney's Wyoming Tells Us About a Divided American Right
Stephanie Muravchik and Jon A. Shields

Coordination Failure

State Taxation and National Response from the New Deal to Today

ADAM S. MYERS

OXFORD
UNIVERSITY PRESS

Oxford University Press is a department of the University of Oxford.
It furthers the University's objective of excellence in research, scholarship,
and education by publishing worldwide. Oxford is a registered trade mark of
Oxford University Press in the UK and in certain other countries.

Published in the United States of America by Oxford University Press
198 Madison Avenue, New York, NY 10016, United States of America.

CIP data is on file at the Library of Congress.

ISBN 9780197831847

ISBN 9780197831830 (hbk.)

DOI: 10.1093/9780197831878.001.0001

Paperback printed by Integrated Books International, United States of America

The manufacturer's authorized representative in the EU for product safety is
Oxford University Press España S.A. of Parque Empresarial San Fernando de Henares,
Avenida de Castilla, 2 – 28830 Madrid (www.oup.es/en or product.safety@oup.com).
OUP España S.A. also acts as importer into Spain of products made by the manufacturer.

MIX
Paper
FSC FSC® C183721

For my parents

Contents

Acknowledgments

This book began many years ago, when I was a newly minted Ph.D., thinking about my next big academic project. All I knew at that point was that I wanted to write a historical monograph on American state politics, one that would lie at the intersection of the state politics and American Political Development literatures in political science. Having long been fascinated by the New Deal, I initially decided to write a book about the state-level politics of that period, but my research revealed that one issue consumed a disproportionate share of the attention of New Deal–era state politicians: taxation. Noticing interesting through-lines between that period's taxation debates and those of today, I eventually broadened the project to examine how state taxation and fiscal federalism in the United States developed from the 1930s onward. Looking back at how the project evolved (a story that involved many more twists and turns than just the ones listed above), I am amazed that I finished this book, and feel nothing but deep gratitude to the many, many people and institutions who assisted me along the way.

To begin, I must thank Providence College, which has provided me with a job I love and a convivial academic home for eleven years now. More than that, the College provided this project with important financial support, particularly in its early stages in 2015–2016, when I received a Committee on Aid to Faculty Research (CAFR) grant to visit archives around the country. In later years, I also relied on the College's generous Faculty Discretionary Fund to finance additional travels. Also important in this regard was the American Political Science Association's Small Research Grant, which was generously awarded to me in 2016.

The staff at the many archives I visited over the years were invariably kind and helpful. I am particularly appreciative of those archivists who helped facilitate my visits under the difficult circumstances posed by the COVID-19 pandemic. These include the staff at the National Archives in Washington, D.C., the University of North Carolina Special Collections, and the Hagley Library in Wilmington, Delaware. And lest I forget, the staff at Providence College's Phillips Memorial Library have always located whatever obscure mid-twentieth-century report I've asked them to find and gotten it to me via interlibrary loan. Many thanks to all of you.

In addition to extensive archival work, the research for this book involved putting together a large dataset of state tax actions from 1930 to the present day. In this, I was assisted by a number of excellent student research assistants from years past, including Max Seferian, Mike DeBarge, and Andrew Balmer. I also wish to thank Mandy Rafool from the National Conference of State Legislatures for providing me with early editions of the NCSL's Annual State Tax Actions reports, which were invaluable in completing the dataset.

A number of fellow scholars, both political scientists and historians, have read various chapters of this work and provided useful feedback. I wish to thank Shanna Pearson-Merkowitz, Ryan LaRochelle, Vlad Kogan, Ajay Mehrotra, John Kincaid, Nick Jacobs, Tim Conlan, and Monty Hindman. Shanna merits special thanks for inviting me to give a talk on the project at the University of Maryland School of Public Policy, and Ajay deserves credit for suggesting that I submit my manuscript to Oxford's Studies in Postwar American Political Development book series.

Speaking of Oxford: publishing this book there has been a refreshingly smooth process, for which I am very thankful. Dave McBride, Andrea Smith, and Phoebe Aldridge-Turner have been a pleasure to work with. I thank the book's two anonymous reviewers, who gave it a very incisive read and made several crucial recommendations. I also thank Swetha Kodimari of Integra for seamlessly facilitating the book's production.

Two faculty from my graduate school days at the University of Texas at Austin—Bryan Jones and Andrew Karch—have continued to offer valuable guidance and assistance to me as a professor. In the years immediately after I finished my Ph.D., Bryan pushed me to publish my dissertation as a book. Since he was disappointed that it didn't happen, I am hoping that the culmination of this book project will bring him a bit of joy. Bryan just retired last year, I should add, and his many former students and colleagues—not to mention other political scientists throughout the world—know just how big a loss for the discipline that is.

My colleagues in the Political Science Department at Providence College have all been wonderful, but since there are eighteen of them, I will single out a few who merit special recognition as far as this book is concerned. There are relatively few people out there with whom one can have a robust and scintillating conversation about federalism, but Paul Herron is one of them, and his insights helped make the book better. In addition to being a good friend and an excellent department chair, Matt Guardino read and provided comments on several book chapters and talked me off a (proverbial) ledge at the tail end of this project. Likewise, Bill Hudson has encouraged me on numerous occasions—as a chair, as a colleague, and now as a friend. Discussing this project on his podcast helped me think about how to present it to a non-academic audience. Joe Cammarano has helped me out many times over the years, including at some very difficult moments; he's probably not aware of it, but he played an important role in facilitating my completion of this book.

My broader community of friends in Providence has helped push this book along in various ways. Members of "The Salon"—Cynthia Scheinberg, Eliahu Klein, Rebecca Schorsch, Shai Afsai, and Ronnie Ben-Zion—listened to me give a whole presentation on this project and responded with numerous questions and comments. The vibrant, hours-long conversation on the book that we had reassured me that (some) non-political scientists will find it interesting. I also wish to thank Elissa and Michael Felder, Mark and Gail Rubenstein, Yosef and Ruchama Szendro, Yochanan Ellis, John Marion, Ken Mattingly, Caroline Stanley, Randy Uang, Emily Meehan, and the whole pub trivia gang at McBride's, who have heard me talk about this project on many occasions. Lisa Tenasco in particular deserves credit for suggesting an image of the U.S. in which the states are represented as gears for the book cover. Two folks involved in Rhode Island fiscal policy—Mike DiBiase and Alan Krinsky—have also been useful sounding boards. I especially want to thank Mike for organizing a presentation I gave on this project to various tax policy experts in the Ocean State.

Lastly, of course, I must thank my immediate family. I can always count on my two sisters, Talia and Naomi, to be there for me when I need them. Talia followed me to Providence in 2017, and having her build a life here alongside me has been an unexpected gift. Finally, my parents, Jamie and Leika Myers, to whom this book is dedicated. It is impossible for me to convey how much they mean to me and how much I owe them. They have been anxiously awaiting the completion of this book for many years now, and I can't wait to give them a hard copy.

Note to the Reader

Books and articles on American federalism and intergovernmental relations often confusingly alternate between referring to America's central government as the country's "national government" and referring to it as the "federal government." In this book, I make the pragmatic choice to use the term "national government" rather than "federal government" whenever possible to avoid confusion with the term "federalism," which broadly refers to the American system of divided power between its central and regional (state) governments. However, I also generally refer to those taxes levied by the American national government as "federal taxes" and not "national taxes," and to the American national government's tax policies more broadly as "federal taxation" and not "national taxation," since the former are the more widely used terms in this context.

Many of the figures in this book will list their data source as the State Tax Actions Dataset. This is the main dataset I put together in my research for the book. It includes tax rates as well as dates of adoption and dates of rate change enactments for major state taxes from 1930 to the present day. The actual sources for the data in the dataset are too numerous to list here, but they will be included in an online appendix along with the dataset itself.

Introduction

America's Peculiar Intergovernmental Taxation Relationship

> "A student should enter the field of intergovernmental fiscal relations with modesty and even humility. It is a large field cutting well across four or five of the social sciences and including in its scope some of the major problems of about 165,000 American governments of all shapes, sizes, populations, and degrees of sovereignty...It is a field mined with explosives; beneath a placid surface lie some very deep emotions ready to burst into flame at the slightest provocation."
>
> —Short excerpt from *Federal, State, and Local Government Fiscal Relations* (special report to the U.S. Treasury Department), 1943

To understand how state taxation and national fiscal policy are intertwined in modern American politics, consider two policy stories from the past decade.

In 2017, as part of their landmark tax-cutting package called the Tax Cuts and Jobs Act, congressional Republicans included a highly controversial provision limiting the State and Local Tax Deduction (SALT)—the amount of taxes paid to state and local governments which taxpayers could deduct from their federal taxable income—to $10,000. GOP leaders argued that the SALT cap was necessary to reduce the impact of their tax cut on the national government's annual deficits, but observers noticed that it had a political side benefit: in adversely affecting wealthy taxpayers from high-tax states like California, New York, and New Jersey, the SALT cap would put tremendous pressure on these Democrat-controlled states to reduce their

Coordination Failure. Adam S. Myers, Oxford University Press. © Oxford University Press (2026).
DOI: 10.1093/9780197831878.003.0001

tax burdens, lest their wealthy taxpayers flee to less-taxed and usually redder jurisdictions.[1]

Despite diligent efforts by a small cadre of Republican lawmakers from high-tax states to remove the SALT cap from the tax package, the cap emerged intact when the package was passed by Congress and signed into law by President Trump in December 2017. The implementation of the SALT cap did not cause debate over the issue to subside, however. In addition to being successfully deployed by several Democratic challengers to Republican incumbents in wealthy, blue-state districts during the 2018 midterm elections, the SALT issue stayed on the congressional agenda thanks to a bipartisan group of lawmakers who came together to form a congressional caucus dedicated to the singular goal of restoring the full SALT deduction.[2] After Democrats took full control of the national government in 2021, the obstinacy of Democrats in the so-called "SALT caucus" proved to be a major obstacle for the party's congressional leaders as they sought intraparty unity on Build Back Better, President Biden's large-scale taxing and spending proposal.[3] And upon the return of President Trump and congressional Republicans to power in 2025, the SALT issue reared its head yet again. At this point, a small but persistent band of House Republicans from the SALT Caucus demanded that the SALT cap be raised in exchange for their votes on the One Big Beautiful Bill Act, Trump's signature piece of legislation that would (among many other things) make his 2017 tax cuts permanent.[4] After multiple rounds of negotiation (and much to the consternation of many congressional Republicans from low-tax states), GOP leaders ultimately agreed to raise the cap to $40,000 for a five-year period, paving the way for the bill's passage.[5]

[1] Jesse McKinley and Nick Corasaniti, "If the G.O.P. Tax Plan Hurts You, Congressmen Say It's Your State's Fault," *New York Times*, December 7, 2018, https://www.nytimes.com/2017/12/07/nyregion/republican-tax-plan-new-york.html

[2] Noah Zwiefel, "Did SALT-y Voters Punish Republicans in 2018," *Tax Policy Center*, October 8, 2021, https://www.taxpolicycenter.org/taxvox/did-salt-y-voters-punish-republicans-2018; Naomi Jagoda, "Lawmakers Launch Bipartisan Caucus on SALT Deduction," *The Hill*, April 15, 2021, https://thehill.com/policy/finance/548493-lawmakers-launch-bipartisan-caucus-on-salt-deduction

[3] Alan Rappeport and Patrick McGeehan, "Tax Deduction that Benefits the Rich Divides Democrats before Vote," *New York Times*, November 18, 2021, https://www.nytimes.com/2021/11/18/us/politics/salt-tax-deduction-democrats.html

[4] Andrew Duehren, "Republican Agenda Hits Familiar Obstacle: State and Local Taxes," *New York Times*, May 9, 2025, https://www.nytimes.com/2025/05/09/us/politics/republicans-salt-cap.html

[5] Ashlea Ebeling, "Where the Megabill Landed on the SALT Deduction," *Wall Street Journal*, July 3, 2025, https://tinyurl.com/w4hc6uvw

The SALT cap has not been the only controversial provision of a recent congressional budget bill that was a direct reaction to state-level taxation politics. In 2022, congressional Democrats passed and President Biden signed the American Rescue Plan (ARP), a large-scale relief package in response to the COVID pandemic. Included within ARP was $350 billion in special funds to state governments whose tax revenues had plummeted because of the pandemic-induced economic downturn.[6] Usage of these funds, while largely unrestricted, came with one major caveat: states could not pad their coffers with the funds at the same time as they cut their own taxes. This provision, obviously intended to stymie Republican-controlled state legislatures eager to use the COVID funds to facilitate income tax cuts, prompted large cries of protest from red-state officials who accused Congress of unconstitutionally interfering in state fiscal choices. Many of these officials eventually sued, and the resulting litigation fights allowed red states to enact tax cuts at the same time as the national government funneled huge sums of money into their coffers.[7]

The foregoing vignettes demonstrate the important role that state taxation plays in American politics and the American political economy more generally. Upon closer examination, it becomes clear that the stories display both an old dynamic as well as a newer one. The old dynamic is the way in which the ability of state governments to make their own taxation policies, while theoretically limited by only a few provisions of the U.S. Constitution, is more significantly affected by the reality of interstate competition for people and capital.[8] The new dynamic is the way in which interstate economic competition has taken on a clear partisan cast: as high-tax states have become increasingly Democratic while low-tax states have become increasingly Republican, state taxation politics has become integrated into the national partisan divide, with important consequences for federal tax policy.

From a broader perspective, the vignettes point to a distinctive aspect of the American federal system that has been largely (though not entirely)

[6] "Assistance to State, Local, and Tribal Governments," U.S. Department of Treasury, https://home.treasury.gov/policy-issues/coronavirus/assistance-for-state-local-and-tribal-governments, accessed January 8, 2024.

[7] Tony Romm, "Republican States Are Trying to Use Federal COVID Aid To Cut Taxes," *Washington Post*, July 5, 2022, https://www.washingtonpost.com/us-policy/2022/07/05/republicans-tax-cuts-stimulus/

[8] By shifting the burden of state taxation onto the national government, the SALT deduction has limited this competitive dynamic to some degree.

overlooked by students of American federalism: the multi-level nature of American taxation. Scholarship on American fiscal federalism (i.e., the relationship between the national government and the states in the area of fiscal policy) has focused overwhelmingly on the spending side of the ledger, with many articles and books examining how the massive system of conditional grants from the national government to the states that emerged during the mid-twentieth century altered intergovernmental relations.[9] But very few studies have examined the revenue-generating side of the ledger—the way in which the growth of government at both the national *and* state levels beginning in the mid-twentieth century fostered a new and complicated interplay between state taxation and national fiscal policy. This book will show that the evolving state-federal taxation relationship from the 1930s to today constitutes an untold story of American intergovernmental relations. Over the course of the period covered in this study, the size of state government budgets underwent a decades-long (if uneven) growth spurt, prompting regular battles in state capitals over state-level tax policy throughout the twentieth and early twenty-first centuries.[10] State taxation during these decades was not exclusively a state politics issue, however. To the contrary, and as this study will show, the rise of the states as centers of fiscal policy made their taxation systems matters of national concern.

The goal of this study is therefore twofold: to trace and explain the evolution of state tax systems (in particular, the politics behind state taxation choices) over the past ninety years, and to examine the national debate over the intergovernmental dimension of tax policy that emerged in response. The book's title, *Coordination Failure*, refers to the fact that, in contrast to the world's other federal democracies, the United States has largely eschewed major efforts to coordinate state and federal taxation and avoided establishing programs designed to equalize state fiscal conditions. As a result, intergovernmental relations in the realm of taxation have exhibited a cyclical dynamic in which state taxation decisions trigger national debates and

[9] A few of the many important works in this area include: Martha Derthick, *The Influence of Federal Grants: Public Assistance in Massachusetts* (Cambridge, MA: Harvard University Press, 1970); John E. Chubb, "The Political Economy of Federalism," *American Political Science Review* 79, no. 4 (1985): 994–1015; Valentino Larcinese, Leonzio Rizzo, and Cecilia Testa, "Allocating the US Federal Budget to the States: The Impact of the President," *Journal of Politics* 68, no. 2 (2006): 447–456; Sean Nicholson-Crotty, *Governors, Grants, and Elections: Fiscal Federalism in the American States* (Baltimore, MD: Johns Hopkins University Press, 2015).

[10] As will be shown, prior to the 1930s, state governments raised and spent little revenue compared to both local governments and the national government.

policy choices, which in turn shape state taxation decisions at a later point, which in turn shape later national decisions, and so forth. The result is a constantly evolving national-state taxation relationship whose key characteristics are closely linked to broader, more politically salient debates and dilemmas.

As the study moves from the 1930s to the present day, it focuses on key moments (the 1930s, 1960s, 1980s, and 2010s) in which major changes in state-level tax policy occurred alongside major debate (and, occasionally, action) on intergovernmental fiscal relations in the nation's capital. Moving back and forth between developments in statehouses and in Washington, D.C., the book sheds light on the interplay between activity at both levels of government. Along the way, the study demonstrates how key features of state-level taxation in the United States (i.e., the state-level tax burden, the degree of state tax progressivity, etc.) have been shaped as much by national political forces as by internal state politics. It also demonstrates why and how American national policymakers, at a series of critical junctures, established a dramatically different form of fiscal federalism from that which exists in every other advanced federal democracy in the world.

Federalism and Taxation: Key Concepts

Prior to laying out the book's key themes and contributions, it is worth spending some time describing what is meant by several concepts at its heart: tax coordination, tax autonomy, and tax competition. Defining these concepts is no easy task, as the literature on them is beset by a large number of ambiguities and contradictions. Nonetheless, the importance of precision in social scientific analysis necessitates that I at least try to map the key concepts of this study at its outset.

Intergovernmental Tax Coordination

The essence of any type of coordination involves the arrangement of the constituent parts of a system so that they can work properly to achieve a common goal. Intergovernmental coordination is a special type of coordination involving two basic parts of a common constitutional system: a national government, and multiple subnational governments. Bakvis and Brown understand the basic goals of intergovernmental coordination to be "[facilitating] the likelihood of achieving horizontal objectives, [reducing] overlap and duplication, and...[ensuring] that horizontal objectives are not impeded by the actions of one or more units."[11]

Schnabel and Hegele helpfully point out that intergovernmental coordination can be conceptualized as either a process or a policy outcome.[12] A coordinated intergovernmental process involves a designated forum in which representatives of various governments—national, state, and perhaps local—come together to hash out differences and assign responsibilities regarding a particular policy problem. A coordinated intergovernmental outcome, on the other hand, is a policy or arrangement that is "characterized by minimal [intergovernmental] redundancy, incoherence, and lacunae."[13] This study will examine some efforts to create coordinated intergovernmental processes (i.e., intergovernmental councils in which taxation issues are discussed and differences ironed out, etc.) in the United States, but it will pay greater attention to efforts to create coordinated taxation outcomes through congressional action. This is largely because, unlike in other federal systems, most intergovernmental coordination efforts in the United States occur via laws passed by Congress rather than through designated intergovernmental processes.[14] It is important to bear in mind, however, that Congress is itself a forum in which subnational governments exercise indirect influence through their lobbying activities; indeed, as we will see, congressional debates over intergovernmental taxation questions have always been shaped by the interests and agendas of state and local governments.

Intergovernmental coordination in the area of taxation, sometimes called "tax harmonization" but hereinafter referred to simply as "tax coordination," involves answering a fundamental policy question famously articulated by

[11] Herman Bakvis and Douglas Brown, "Policy Coordination in Federal Systems: Comparing Intergovernmental Processes and Outcomes in Canada and the United States," *Publius* 40, no. 3 (2010), 484.

[12] Johanna Schnabel and Yvonne Hegele, "Explaining Intergovernmental Coordination during the COVID-19 Pandemic: Responses in Australia, Canada, Germany, and Switzerland," *Publius* 51, no. 4 (2021), 539.

[13] Schnabel and Hegele, "Explaining Intergovernmental Coordination during the COVID-19 Pandemic," 539, quoting B. Guy Peters, "Managing Horizontal Government: The Politics of Co-Ordination," *Publius* 17, no. 3 (1998), 296.

[14] Bakvis and Brown, "Policy Coordination in Federal Systems," 488.

the economist Richard Musgraves as: "Who should tax, where, and what?"[15] Whether conceived as a process or an outcome, tax coordination is an effort to tackle the many problems that can emerge when a national government and multiple subnational governments each seek to use their tax authority simultaneously and independently of each other. These problems include: inefficiencies and costs associated with duplicative taxation, the harmful effects of tax competition between subnational governments (often referred to as a "race to the bottom"), a mismatch between revenue needs and revenue-raising capacities across levels of government, and disparities in fiscal capacity among subnational governments.[16]As a policy outcome, tax coordination can take a variety of forms, including the separation of tax fields across national and subnational government (so that each level generates its revenue from different sources), the sharing of national tax revenue with subnational governments in lieu of subnational taxation, and the use of national tax policy to facilitate or incentivize certain forms of subnational taxation (resulting in less tax policy variation across subnational jurisdictions).

There are also a wide array of additional, more technical tax policy challenges demanding intergovernmental coordination, including the reconciliation of national and subnational tax codes, the determination of rules for the taxation of goods or services that cross subnational borders (i.e., interstate commerce taxation), and others. Though important, these challenges are not the focus of this study.[17] The question of how to reconcile national and state tax codes involves a litany of complex and arcane legal issues, rendering it a poor fit for a study that focuses primarily on the changing *politics* of taxation. Similarly, controversies over interstate commerce taxation have tended to involve questions of constitutional interpretation in which the judicial branches of state and especially national government have been the central actors. This book, however, focuses primarily on taxation politics inside America's state and national *legislatures*, not its courts.

[15] Richard A. Musgrave, "Who Should Tax, Where and What?" in *Tax Assignment in Federal Countries*, ed. Charles E. McLure, Jr. (Canberra: Centre for Research on Federal Financial Relations, Australian National University, 1983).

[16] George Anderson, *Fiscal Federalism: A Comparative Introduction* (Don Mills, Ontario: Oxford University Press, 2010), 26–27.

[17] Both these issues do, however, receive some tangential consideration in the book. Interstate commerce taxation is discussed in Chapter 6, which recounts the challenges states faced in taxing internet sales in the early twenty-first century, and the issue of federal-state code conformity is discussed briefly in the conclusion.

Subnational Tax Autonomy

The autonomy of subnational governments can be defined as the extent to which they "have a sovereign political power...for general choices in their area of competence."[18] In the realm of taxation, then, subnational autonomy refers to how much authority subnational governments have to set their own tax policies independently of national government directives or intergovernmental agreements. Public finance economists have identified several dimensions of subnational tax autonomy, including autonomy in the choice of which taxes to levy, in the setting of bases and rates, and in the administration of the taxes that are imposed.[19]

Generally speaking, subnational tax autonomy is negatively associated with intergovernmental tax coordination: the more coordinated the intergovernmental taxation relationship of a country, the less tax autonomy subnational governments of that country tend to have. This is because tax coordination, as a policy outcome, usually entails some sort of reduction in the discretion that subnational governments have in their taxation choices. But this is not always the case. One can imagine a tax system in which tax fields are strictly separated across levels of government, so that only one level of government can tax a particular part of the economy, but little interaction exists between state and federal taxation otherwise. This sort of tax system would be one in which coordination coexists with a very high level of subnational tax autonomy.

Subnational Tax Competition

Tax competition refers to the dynamic that ensues when taxpayers (either people or businesses) enjoy mobility across subnational boundaries, giving them the option of relocating from one jurisdiction to another in response to subnational tax policies.[20] This very possibility, it is thought, causes subnational governments in a federal system to assess their competitive positions vis-à-vis other jurisdictions when making tax policy decisions. The effects of

[18] Claudio Sacchetto, "Analysis of Fiscal Federalism from a Comparative Tax Law Perspective," in *Tax Aspects of Fiscal Federalism: A Comparative Analysis*, ed. G. Bizioli and C. Sacchetto (Amsterdam: IBFD Press, 2011).

[19] Jorge Martinez-Vazquez, "Revenue Assignments in the Practice of Fiscal Decentralization," in *Fiscal Federalism and Political Decentralization: Lessons from Spain, Germany and Canada*, eds. Nuria Bosch and Jose M. Duran (Cheltenham, UK: Edward Elgar, 2008), 32–35.

[20] Robin Boadway and Anwar Shah, *Fiscal Federalism: Principles and Practice of Multiorder Governance* (New York: Cambridge, 2009), 38.

such a competitive dynamic have long been debated by political economists. While the literature on these effects is too vast to review here, much of it can be summarized as falling into one of two opposing camps.[21] One camp (generally composed of left-leaning economists) holds that tax competition causes subnational governments to keep their taxes at sub-optimally low levels, leading to the undersupply of basic public goods in a way that harms citizens of all jurisdictions.[22] The other camp (generally composed of right-leaning or libertarian economists) holds that tax competition prevents government exploitation of taxpayers through disciplining subnational politicians into providing the levels of taxes and services expected by their constituents.[23] As this book will show, American national policymakers have oscillated between these two camps over the past century, affecting the national government's approach to intergovernmental fiscal relations.

The extent of subnational tax competition is directly affected by the degree of subnational tax autonomy: the higher the level of subnational tax autonomy, the greater the extent of subnational tax competition. This is because, in a constitutional system in which people and goods move freely across subnational jurisdictions, limiting the tax choices available to subnational governments is the principal way to prevent the competitive dynamic described above from ensuing. Indeed, most interventions in subnational tax policy by the American national government have been designed, at least in part, to limit subnational tax competition.[24]

Federalism and Taxation in Comparative Perspective

Having described some of the basic concepts at the heart of the study of fiscal federalism, I now move to discussing American fiscal federalism in a comparative global context. The discussion is necessary because, though this

[21] For a good summary of this literature during the twentieth century, see: John Douglas Wilson, "Theories of Tax Competition," *National Tax Journal* 52, no. 2 (1999): 269–304.

[22] See, e.g., Wallace E. Oates, *Fiscal Federalism* (New York: Harcourt Brace Jovanovich, 1972); Joseph E. Stiglitz, "The theory of local public goods twenty-five years after Tiebout: A perspective," in *Local Provision of Public Services: The Tiebout Model after Twenty-Five Years*, ed. G. R. Zodrow (New York: Academic Press, 1983), 17–53; David E. Wildasin, "Interjurisdictional Capital Mobility: Fiscal Externality and a Corrective Subsidy," *Journal of Urban Economics* 25, no. 2 (1989): 193–212; Sam Bucovetsky, "Asymmetric Tax Competition," *Journal of Urban Economics* 30, no. 2 (1991): 167–181.

[23] See, e.g., Geoffrey Brennan and James Buchanan, *The Power to Tax: Analytical Foundations of a Fiscal Constitution* (New York: Cambridge, 1980); Michael L. Marlow, "Fiscal Decentralization and Government Size," *Public Choice* 56, no. 3 (1988): 259–269; Philip J. Grossman, "Fiscal Decentralization and Government Size: An Extension," *Public Choice* 62, no. 1 (1989): 63–69.

[24] Michael S. Greve, *The Upside Down Constitution* (Cambridge, MA: Harvard University Press, 2012).

book is about the United States, it is impossible to understand fiscal federalism in the United States absent a comparative vantage point. As with many other areas of political economy, intergovernmental fiscal relations in the modern United States are highly distinctive when compared to other countries—*including other federal systems.* This is especially true regarding tax policy, where American federalism stands out on several key matters.

First, American federalism is defined by an unusually high level of subnational tax autonomy.[25] Subject to several relatively minor constitutional constraints, the American states can levy whatever taxes they wish on their residents and businesses and can structure these taxes however they see fit. Only two other countries in the world (Canada and Switzerland) rival the United States in the overall degree of autonomous taxation authority that subnational governments enjoy.[26] Of these two countries, only Switzerland matches the United States in giving its subnational governments full discretion in the setting of tax rates and bases.[27] The high amount of tax autonomy enjoyed by the American states has resulted in substantial interstate variation in tax policy, a key topic that this book will examine.

Second, state and federal taxation in the United States occurs in the context of unusually *low* levels of intergovernmental coordination. Unlike most other federal democracies, the United States features no coordinated intergovernmental tax assignment policy, lacks a revenue-sharing program unlinked to national policy objectives, and has implemented relatively few tax instruments designed to influence state tax policy (the SALT deduction being an important exception). Moreover, as discussed above, the United States features no intergovernmental forum designated for the purpose of ironing out conflicts between national and state tax policy.[28]

[25] It is important to emphasize that the degree of subnational tax autonomy does not necessarily correspond to the degree of subnational autonomy on other policy matters. Indeed, there are examples of federal systems in which subnational units enjoy significantly greater autonomy than the American states in many policy areas (particularly cultural policies), but not in taxation.

[26] Jonathan Rodden, "Comparative Federalism and Decentralization: On Meaning and Measurement," *Comparative Politics* 36, no. 4 (2004): 485.

[27] Hansjörg Blöchliger and Josette Rabesona, "The Fiscal Autonomy of Sub-Central Governments: An Update," *OECD Working Papers on Fiscal Federalism*, No. 9 (Paris: OECD Publishing, 2009), http://dx.doi.org/10.1787/5k97b111wb0t-en

[28] This does not mean that other federal democracies have adopted identical approaches to intergovernmental relations in tax policy. Quite to the contrary, there are major differences between, for example, the highly centralized tax system of Australia (where the national government controls nearly all tax sources and the states are largely reliant on the national government for their revenues) and the highly decentralized one of Canada (where a majority of tax revenue is levied at the provincial, not the federal, level). However, decentralized tax systems are not necessarily uncoordinated. In Canada's case, provincial and federal taxation occur mostly separately but their relationship is

The upshot of America's uncoordinated intergovernmental taxation system is that, for the most part, the American states and the national government tax citizens and businesses independently of each other. States make tax policy without formally consulting other states or Congress, and Congress makes tax policy without formally consulting the states. This lack of a formal consultation process does not mean, however, that each taxing jurisdiction in the United States makes its tax policies in a vacuum. Quite to the contrary, American policymakers routinely make tax policy changes in response to tax policy developments in other jurisdictions. For example, states might cut their taxes in response to competitive pressures initiated by tax cuts in neighboring states. Or, they might raise their taxes after a federal tax cut has decreased the federal tax burden on their citizens. For its part, a Congress controlled by progressive Democrats might respond to the large-scale adoption of regressive taxes by states by changing the federal tax code to incentivize state-level progressive taxation. Conversely, a Congress controlled by libertarian Republicans might seek to punish high-tax states by eliminating elements of the federal tax code that help to facilitate higher state taxes. There are many other hypothetical examples. The point here is that, in the United States, intergovernmental relations in the realm of taxation occur via an iterative process that (compared to other countries) results in frequent, short-term changes.

In addition to its unusually low degree of intergovernmental tax coordination, the United States also differs from other federal systems in that it lacks a national program expressly designed to ameliorate fiscal inequalities across subnational governmental units. Such "fiscal equalization" programs are found in all major federal systems in the world besides the United States, regardless of their overall degree of decentralization. As Daniel Béland and André Lecours state, "From Canada to Germany, India to Australia and South Africa to Switzerland, most federal systems feature...stand-alone equalisation programmes aimed at reducing fiscal inequalities between constituent units..."[29] Because of the unique absence of a fiscal equalization

governed by a complex set of intergovernmental agreements, leading to a high level of tax harmonization and relatively lower subnational tax competition than in the United States. The only federal system that might rival the United States in its relative lack of tax coordination is Switzerland. See, e.g., Thomas. O. Hueglin and Alan Fenna, *Comparative Federalism: A Systematic Inquiry*, 2nd edition, (Toronto, ON: University of Toronto Press, 2015), 174–204.

[29] Daniel Béland and Andre Lecours, "Fiscal Federalism and American Exceptionalism: Why is there No Federal Equalisation System in the United States?," *Journal of Public Policy* 34, no. 2 (2014): 304.

program in the United States, state-level tax policies (in combination with other factors, like the diverse tax bases of the various states) have a tremendous impact on the overall fiscal capacities of individual state governments.

The Historical Origins of American Fiscal Federalism

To a significant degree, the differences between the United States and other federal countries in the realm of intergovernmental fiscal relations can be traced to the origins of the regimes themselves. Unlike the United States, the other advanced democracies that have a federal form of government (e.g., Australia, Canada, Germany, and Switzerland) were usually founded between the late nineteenth and mid twentieth centuries, a period when the public sector was growing rapidly in countries around the world.[30] Consequently, the framers of these countries' constitutions anticipated that their central and provincial governments would both have substantial revenue needs, potentially leading to intergovernmental conflict and competition over tax sources. To avoid these problems, the "founding fathers" of these countries inserted provisions into national constitutions designed to coordinate taxation across levels of government, usually via assigning specific taxes to specific levels or via various forms of revenue sharing.[31] These initial provisions blossomed into far more complex tax coordination arrangements over time.

The American constitutional regime is, of course, older than the regimes of countries like Australia or Canada. When the U.S. Constitution was written in 1787, few if any anticipated that the domestic public sector would become such a large part of the American economy. The main fiscal objective of the American Founding Fathers was securing sufficient revenue for the fledgling national government so that it could effectively fight wars against its foreign enemies, not so that it could support an extensive domestic public sector.[32] It was with the goal of national security in mind that the Framers of the U.S. Constitution chose to give Congress a nearly unlimited taxing power. But though their primary interest was in strengthening the national government,

[30] One major exception here is Switzerland, whose founding as a confederation can be traced to 1291. However, the Swiss Constitution in operation throughout much of the twentieth century was ratified in 1874.

[31] Mabel Newcomer, *Reconciling Conflicting Taxes in Federal Governments*, special report prepared for the U.S. Department of Treasury, March 1942 (found in the Luther Gulick Papers, CUNY Baruch College Archives, Box 29, Folder 6).

[32] Max M. Edling, *A Hercules in the Cradle: War, Money, and the American State, 1783–1867* (Chicago: University of Chicago Press, 2014).

the Framers were mindful of the strong allegiances that eighteenth-century Americans had to their states and wary of alienating would-be supporters of the Constitution by reducing the states' fiscal powers too abjectly. Thus, they also chose not to add many explicit limits on the states' taxation powers.[33] Because of these twin decisions, the U.S. Constitution of 1787, in sharp contrast to the constitutions of future federal regimes, created a nearly open field for both the national government and the states in the realm of taxation.

Not everyone was happy with this proposed arrangement, and the Framers' defense of it during the ratification debate in 1788–1789 reveals much about how they expected intergovernmental fiscal relations to work under the Constitution. Of the many fears expressed by opponents of the Constitution during the ratification debates, perhaps the most often repeated was that, under the Constitution, the national government would use its vastly increased taxing powers to colonize all sources of revenue and impoverish the state governments. Over time, the Constitution's critics argued, this would reduce the state governments to irrelevant subordinate units lacking anything approaching sovereign power. As Brutus (perhaps the most incisive writer opposing the Constitution) aptly summarized: "The command of the revenues of [a country]...gives the command of everything in it. He that has the purse will have the sword, and they that have both, have every thing."[34]

In the *Federalist Papers*, Alexander Hamilton offered a convoluted but nonetheless revealing response to these arguments.[35] In *Federalist* 32, Hamilton sought to assure concerned parties that, under the Constitution, the states would "retain the authority to raise their own revenue to supply for their own wants...in the most absolute and unqualified sense."[36] The Constitution, in Hamilton's view (at least as expressed in this paper), would make taxation a true concurrent power. Under this arrangement, Hamilton argued, the most likely outcome would be that the national government and the states would each drift to their own, separate revenue sources over time, with neither level of government interfering with the taxation policies of the other.

[33] The main limit on state taxation in the Constitution is the ban on state taxation of imports and exports.

[34] Brutus, "Brutus, no. 5," in *The Founders' Constitution*, eds. Philip B. Kurland and Ralph Lerner (University of Chicago Press, 1986). https://press-pubs.uchicago.edu/founders/documents/a1_8_1s7.html, accessed October 24, 2021.

[35] These insights about Hamilton's response to Brutus are drawn from Michael Greve's excellent book *The Upside-Down Constitution*. Michael Greve, *The Upside-Down Constitution* (Cambridge, MA: Harvard University Press, 2012), 77 and 423 (footnote 33).

[36] Alexander Hamilton, "Federalist no. 32," National Archives (1788), https://founders.archives.gov/documents/Hamilton/01-04-02-0189, accessed October 25, 2021.

Two papers later, however (in *Federalist* 34), Hamilton further fleshed out his vision for dual taxation under the Constitution in a way that, while consistent with his argument in *Federalist* 32, would be significantly more likely to raise alarm bells among advocates of states' rights. The ultimate reason why state governments need not have any fear that the national government would invade their revenue sources, Hamilton admitted, is that under the Constitution, states would simply not need much revenue. This was because the policies for which they would be responsible (morality legislation and "internal police") would just not require much of it. "What are the chief sources of expense in every Government?" Hamilton asks, to which he replies: "The answer, plainly is, wars and rebellion...The expenses arising from those institutions, which are relative to the mere police of a state...are insignificant, in comparison with those which relate to the National defense."[37]

While it is impossible to know whether the other Constitutional Convention delegates shared Hamilton's views on these matters, his remarks in *Federalist* 32 and 34 suggest both a vision of how fiscal federalism would work under the Constitution and an accompanying rationale for the intergovernmental fiscal arrangements (or lack thereof) that the document set up. Stated simply, the Framers appear to have given wide-ranging taxation powers to both the national government and the states on the assumption that the national government would occasionally use its powers to the fullest while the states would never need to. As long as this was the case, intergovernmental tax conflicts could largely be avoided. And, indeed, this *was* the case throughout much of the nineteenth century, when the national government financed its periodic wars via tariffs and consumption taxes, while the states (and their local units) relied almost exclusively on property taxes for their very minimal revenue needs.

During the twentieth century, however, the American government was transformed in a way that its eighteenth-century Founders simply could not foresee. The domestic public sector grew exponentially, and this growth involved all levels of government—national, state, and local. Because all three levels needed new revenue to fund a vastly enlarged public sector, the potential emerged for regular tax conflicts between the national government

[37] Alexander Hamilton, "Federalist no. 34," National Archives (1988), https://founders.archives.gov/documents/Hamilton/01-04-02-0191, accessed October 25, 2021.

and the states, as well as among the states themselves.[38] Unfortunately for the United States, the absence of provisions in the U.S. Constitution for coordinating taxation and revenue sharing across governments meant that there were very few overarching rules governing the intergovernmental arrangement of American tax policy. Consequently, America's unique form of modern tax-policy federalism developed haphazardly and iteratively rather than via grand design. While numerous expert commissions, committee reports, and think-tank studies made recommendations for large-scale reforms leading to a more coordinated American tax system over the course of the twentieth century, political difficulties (which will be discussed extensively in this book) doomed almost all their recommendations. Thus, much to the dismay of the country's fiscal policy experts, America developed a complex and incoherent intergovernmental taxation arrangement, one that few planners of a tax system would consider ideal.

The Book's Key Themes and Contributions

This book's exploration of state taxation and national-state relations over the past ninety years will highlight several themes embedded in the larger story. It is worth describing each of these themes in some detail at the book's outset.

Path-Dependence and the Development of State Tax Systems

To the extent modern-day Americans know anything about how their state's tax policies compare to those of other states, what they know is often derived from their understanding of their state's electoral characteristics. If their state is "blue" (i.e., Democratic), many will assume that its taxes are high; conversely, if their state is "red" (i.e., Republican), many will assume its taxes are low.[39]

[38] Tax conflicts involving local governments were, of course, also a major feature of twentieth-century tax policy. The role of local governments (particularly involving the property tax) will be occasionally highlighted in this book, but the focus will be on the two levels of government with sovereign taxing powers under the U.S. Constitution: the national government and the states.

[39] In later chapters of the book, states will frequently be described as red or blue without quotations marks around those words. My decision to withhold the quotations marks does not mean that I do not recognize the many problems involved with the use of this simplistic designation in much mainstream American political discourse (where, needless to say, it has been a regular feature for a quarter-century now). Unlike in media discussions of state electoral characteristics, however,

As it turns out, using state partisanship as a heuristic for state tax policy in the absence of other information is not a terrible approach. As I discuss in the book, the association between these two state-level characteristics has become strong in the twenty-first century. However, this is a relatively new development: prior to the 1990s, party control of state government and state tax policy were barely related.[40] Moreover, even today, there remains a substantial amount of variation in state tax policy that cannot be explained by modern partisanship. Perhaps more surprisingly, much of this variation cannot be explained by other contemporary factors (such as a state's economic characteristics, political institutions, or geographic location) either.

In fact, besides state partisanship, the most important factor influencing modern state tax policy is history, or what social scientists call "path dependence." As the books shows, variations in contemporary state taxes can often be traced to the different choices made by state governments at two key junctures: the 1930s (when state governments were forced to completely revamp their tax systems in response to the Great Depression) and the 1960s (when states dramatically increased their revenues to fund rapidly growing education systems and various Great Society programs). States responded to the fiscal pressures of these eras by taking very different paths, creating fiscal regimes featuring unique combinations of sales, income, and other taxes. The state-level taxation outcomes of these periods (especially the 1930s) were highly contingent and based on a complex array of factors that are not easily generalizable. But these outcomes mattered: to a significant degree, modern interstate differences in tax policy are their legacies.

The Rise and Decline of Intergovernmental Fiscal Reform Efforts in Congress

The fact that the intergovernmental fiscal relationship in the United States is highly disorganized and unwieldy, with numerous overlapping taxes and little coordination between national and subnational authorities, might lead

in this book *red* and *blue* mean something very specific: a red state is one whose government is generally controlled by Republicans, and a blue state is one whose government is generally controlled by Democrats. As will be shown, when examining state taxation policy in the modern era, this shorthand designation is both substantively meaningful and analytically useful.

[40] The many studies from earlier periods finding little influence of party control of state government on state tax policy include: Thomas R. Dye, *Politics, Economics, and the Public* (Chicago: Rand McNally, 1966); Ira Sharkansky, *The Politics of Taxing and Spending* (Indianapolis, IN: Bobbs-Merrill, 1969); David Lowery, "The Distribution of Tax Burdens in the American States," *Western Political Review* 40, no. 1: (1987): 137–158; David R. Morgan, "Tax Equity in the American States: A Multivariate Analysis," *Social Science Quarterly* 75, no. 3: 510–523.

some to conclude that American policymakers have been content to leave it this way. But while this may indeed be the case for contemporary policymakers, it was not the case for those involved in fiscal policymaking between the 1930s and 1970s, when the system was coming into being. As this book will show, the fiscal policymakers and other stakeholders of those decades were often profoundly unhappy with the intergovernmental fiscal arrangement that was then emerging, and significant efforts were made to put the system on a different path, particularly during the 1930s and the late 1960s/early 1970s. Such efforts, however, consistently floundered because, in one way or another, they raised difficult questions regarding how national revenue from particular tax sources should be allocated to the states in lieu of the states levying the taxes themselves. As noted earlier, the U.S. Constitution provides no guidelines on intergovernmental fiscal distributions, leaving such questions to the political process.[41] Among the mid-century politicians who debated them, these questions called forth not only divergent state interests but also profoundly different federalism visions, and these differences proved extremely difficult to overcome via traditional legislative compromise. As a result, efforts to overhaul the intergovernmental taxation arrangement between the 1930s and the 1970s either failed or only passed in a highly diluted and ultimately ineffective form.

Relatedly, the steep barriers to intergovernmental fiscal reform in the United States help to explain America's status as the world's only major federal system without an interstate fiscal equalization program. The notable absence of such a program in the United States is a topic that has only recently begun to receive scholarly attention, and existing studies (which have employed a comparatively case-study framework) have provided a rather cursory review of developments in twentieth-century American fiscal federalism.[42] In this book, I present a much more extensive examination of those developments, leading to somewhat different conclusions. In particular, I show that—contra the extant literature—fiscal equalization was very much on the American policy agenda during the mid-twentieth century. In particular, policymakers in the late 1950s and 1960s were highly concerned about state fiscal inequalities resulting from interstate differences in both economic conditions and taxation policies. Viewing such gaps in

[41] On the lack of a "distributional baseline" governing intergovernmental fiscal arrangements in the U.S. Constitution, see: Greve, *The Upside-Down Constitution*, 155, 244, 255.

[42] See, e.g., Béland and Lecours, "Fiscal Federalism and American Exceptionalism: Why is There No Federal Equalisation System in the United States?"; Giorgio Brosio, "Equalization Transfers and Convergence between Federal and Unitary Systems: A Contribution to Their Historical Analysis," *Economia Pubblica: The Italian Journal of Public Economics and Law* 44, no. 3, (2017): 21–66.

state fiscal capacity as contrary to the nation's equal commitment to all its citizens, mid-century policymakers actively considered ways of redistributing resources to the most revenue-strapped state governments so as to equalize state fiscal conditions. But because fiscal equalization was just one goal among many that informed the intergovernmental fiscal reform efforts of the period, it ended up being only weakly integrated into the main outcome of those efforts—the revenue-sharing law that Congress passed in 1972. Thus, the inability to adequately reconcile competing policy goals and visions in the absence of interstate distributional guidelines in the Constitution played a major role in scuttling the adoption of a fiscal equalization program in the United States.

The Evolving Politics of Competitive Federalism

As discussed above, a key feature of American federalism is the high degree of competition among state governments for capital and economic development. American state government officials make many policy decisions with the goal of convincing businesses to set up corporate headquarters or factories in *their* states and not others, and with the attendant fear that employers and taxpayers might leave their states *for* others. Besides Switzerland, no other advanced democracy seems to feature this sort of competitive dynamic as a normal part of the workings of its federal system.[43] The high degree of tax autonomy that the American states enjoy, as well as the absence of an interstate fiscal equalization program, are key reasons why the United States is such an exemplar of what scholars call "competitive federalism."[44]

Interstate economic competition has been a feature of American politics for as long as the U.S. Constitution has been in effect, but the political debate over it has changed substantially over the course of American history. As this study will show, between the 1930s and the 1970s, competitive federalism was widely regarded as a highly problematic feature of the American political system, at least among national leaders. Executive branch officials, policy intellectuals, and members of Congress from both parties

[43] Thomas O. Hueglin and Alan Fenna, *Comparative Federalism: A Systematic Inquiry*, 2nd edition (Toronto: University of Toronto Press, 2015), 200–201.

[44] Daphne A. Kenyon and John Kincaid, eds., *Competition among State and Local Governments: Efficiency and Equity in a Federal System* (Washington, D.C.: Urban Institute, 1991); Daphne Kenyon, "Theories of Interjurisdictional Competition," *New England Economic Review*, March/April (1997): 13–29; Greve, *The Upside-Down Constitution*, 58–59.

routinely lamented the degree to which state governments were influenced by competitive pressures, particularly in tax policy where it was thought that competitive threats induced states to keep their taxes low and rely disproportionately on regressive sales taxes. Bipartisan commissions studying intergovernmental relations during this period regularly issued recommendations that the national government take active steps to reduce interstate economic competition. The federalism watchword of the age was "cooperation," not "competition," and even business groups like the U.S. Chamber of Commerce avoided publicly defending the competitive dynamic (though they were surely aware that business generally benefited from it).

During the 1980s, as with so much else in American politics, the discourse over competitive federalism shifted substantially. Under Ronald Reagan's leadership, the Republican Party embraced a federalism vision that saw interstate economic competition not as an obstacle to be overcome, but rather as an essential component of limiting (and potentially even shrinking) government. Consistent with this new vision, the Reagan administration promoted policies that sought to unwind federal fiscal support to the states and separate national and state fiscal systems. Though to some degree successful, Reagan's efforts spawned opposition from Democrats who sought to preserve the fiscal linkages between national and state government, leading to the emergence of a partisan divide over fiscal federalism at the national level.

The Partisan Polarization of State Tax Policy in the Twenty-first Century and Its Effect on National Politics

The growth of a national partisan divide over fiscal policy in the 1980s did not immediately make its way to state politics; as of the early 1990s, state fiscal choices were still largely unrelated to state government party composition. But over the course of the next three decades, a strong partisan divide in state tax policy took shape. This divide was largely (though not entirely) focused on the personal income tax, with Republican-controlled states regularly cutting top income tax rates and Democrat-controlled states more sporadically raising them. As this book will show, the partisan polarization of state tax policy developed gradually across a series of economic and political events at the end of the twentieth century and the beginning of the twenty-first. Its growth was made possible by the conjunction of a variety of now well-known factors, including the nationalization of state politics and the increased influence of nationally affiliated interest groups in statehouses across the country.[45] Thanks to its rise, the omnipresent red-blue electoral map of the twenty-first century has become an increasingly good indicator of state tax policy, offering Americans a reasonable shortcut for understanding how their state compares to others in the area of taxation. Reasonable does not mean perfect, however: in state after state, governors and legislators have run up against the limits of political possibility in their efforts to reshape their state's tax policy in accordance with their national party's ideological agenda. The basic frameworks of state tax systems, put into place long ago, have proven remarkably durable in the early twenty-first century, notwithstanding the determination of ambitious politicians to transform them.

The partisan polarization of state tax policy has had implications that go well beyond state-level politics. As Democrat-controlled and Republican-controlled states diverged in their tax policies, Republican politicians and right-leaning media pundits in the 2000s and 2010s began promoting the claim that increasingly low-tax red states were winning the interstate competition for businesses and residents over high-tax blue states. The basic ideas of competitive federalism, previously well-known only to conservative policymaking elites, thus found their way (in diluted form, to be sure) into mainstream American political discourse. The growing entanglement of competitive federalism with party politics has influenced many of the recent congressional debates over intergovernmental fiscal policy, including those over the 2017 Tax Cuts and Jobs Act, the 2025 One Big Beautiful Bill Act, and the various COVID-19 relief bills of 2020–2022.

Plan for the Book

The book proceeds chronologically. It begins with two pairs of chapters separately examining state-level taxation politics and the resulting national debate over intergovernmental fiscal relations during two crucial periods: the 1930s and the postwar era. Each of these topics is then addressed jointly

[45] Jacob Grumbach, *Laboratories Against Democracy: How National Parties Transformed State Politics* (Princeton, NJ: Princeton University Press, 2022); Alexander Hertel-Fernandez, *State Capture: How Conservative Activists, Big Businesses, and Wealthy Donors Reshaped the American States—and the Nation* (New York: Oxford University Press, 2019).

in two subsequent chapters examining developments in the late twentieth and early twenty-first centuries, respectively.

The first pair of chapters—Chapters 1 and 2—focus on the 1930s. In Chapter 1, I explore the origins of modern state tax policy in the cauldron of the Great Depression, when a variety of forces converged to force state governments to dramatically remake their tax systems. After describing the politics surrounding state taxation choices during this period, I separately examine adoptions of the three main tax sources of the era: personal and corporate income taxes, general sales taxes, and selective sales taxes on alcohol and tobacco products. Analyzing the adoption of these taxes across states, I show that few of the variables most commonly used by political scientists to explain contemporary state policy choices (such as partisanship or region) can be used to explain New Deal era state tax policy. Instead, state taxation choices during the 1930s were the result of a complex array of idiosyncratic factors that render systematic explanations elusive. I also explore why the general sales tax came to vastly exceed the personal income tax in terms of state tax *reliance* during the 1930s and continuing into the next thirty years.

Chapter 2 maintains a focus on the 1930s but shifts from analyzing tax-related activities in state capitals to considering the response to these developments in Washington, D.C. As I show, state-level taxation outcomes during this period triggered significant concern among many relevant actors, including state government leaders, tax professionals, business leaders, and the farm lobby. The concerns of these actors varied: some were concerned about the complexity and inefficiency of the emerging multilevel structure of American taxation, others were concerned that the growth of state-level sales taxes were harming American tax progressivity, and still others were concerned about emerging inequalities in the fiscal capacities of the states. These worries prompted many political leaders and organizations to promote various efforts at federal-state revenue sharing and other forms of state tax harmonization. These efforts consistently went nowhere in Congress, however, in large part because revenue-sharing schemes required a (re)distributional formula and members of Congress—the majority of whom sought to protect the fiscal interests of their states—consistently failed to agree on one. This is demonstrated through an in-depth case-study of the most prominent fiscal coordination effort in Congress in the 1930s: a proposal to share alcohol sales tax revenue with the states following the repeal of Prohibition in 1933.

In the next pair of chapters—Chapters 3 and 4—the action moves to the postwar era, when state government spending experienced a dramatic growth spurt and Congress renewed its focus on fiscal federalism issues. In Chapter 3, I examine the wave of tax adoptions and increases passed by state governments in the 1950s and 1960s. In doing so, I show how and why an initial period of sales tax expansion during the late 1950s to early 1960s was followed by a sudden growth in state-level income taxation during the late 1960s to early 1970s. Thanks to the latter, state tax systems had become substantially more progressive by the early 1970s, though this progressivity was made possible by greater tax regressivity at the federal level. I also show how postwar state-level taxation politics was highly influenced by the tax systems put into place during the 1930s, leading to path-dependent outcomes that in many cases reinforced the interstate differences that had emerged at the end of the New Deal.

Chapter 4 returns to the national arena and focuses on the robust efforts to adopt a system of revenue-sharing between the national government and the states during the 1960's. Like Chapter 3, which analyzes failed efforts at tax coordination during the 1930s in light of the state tax policy developments of that period, Chapter 5 focuses on the revenue-sharing efforts of the 1960s as a response to contemporaneous state tax activities. More specifically, I examine how liberal policymakers in the Kennedy and Johnson administrations envisioned revenue-sharing as a response to interstate fiscal inequalities and the growing regressivity of state tax systems during the early 1960s, and how conservatives came to embrace revenue-sharing as a devolutionary strategy in the late 1960s. The chapter concludes with a comprehensive analysis of the politics surrounding the passage of the State and Local Fiscal Assistance Act of 1972 (SLFAA, aka "the Revenue-Sharing Law"), the only major, stand-alone effort on the part of the national government to reform the intergovernmental fiscal relationship in the late twentieth century. I argue that the weakness of SLFAA stemmed from the fact that its supporters were motivated by a diverse array of policy goals and federalism visions, leading to major disagreements over how revenue collected by the national government should be distributed to the states. Much as in the 1930s, these ideological disagreements were exacerbated by interstate differences in economic conditions and tax policy. By attempting to integrate as many perspectives as possible into SLFAA, lawmakers ended up diluting its transformative potential, causing it to fall well short of being a robust system of intergovernmental fiscal cooperation akin to those that exist in other federal countries.

Chapter 5 moves to the late 1970s and 1980s, a period when American politics swung sharply in an anti-statist direction, resulting in substantial changes in intergovernmental fiscal relations. After briefly discussing the state-level "Tax Revolt" of the late 1970s and the end of the SLFAA, I turn to examining the fiscal federalism philosophy of President Ronald Reagan and his domestic policy advisors. Consistent with previous scholarship,[46] I argue that the paramount goal of the Reaganites was to shrink the domestic public sector at all levels of government, state and local as well as national. Facilitating a more competitive federalism—particularly by encouraging states to adopt more business-friendly tax policies—was a crucial part of this new emphasis. While Reagan and his congressional allies did successfully advance fiscal devolution via major cuts to intergovernmental grants during Reagan's first term, states responded to these cuts with surprisingly robust tax increases in order to shore up state budgets. The disappointment of the Reaganites with the limited impacts of their first-term reforms on the size of the subnational public sector led to a second attempt at intergovernmental fiscal reform in Reagan's second term, this time via proposed changes to the federal tax code (most notably, by proposing to abolish the SALT Deduction). As I show, however, Congress did not accept Reagan's proposals, instead it adopted a tax reform package in 1986 that actually expanded the capacity of state governments to raise revenue via their own income taxes. Thus, the unexpected outcome of the Reagan presidency was that, as the 1980s drew to a close, state governments had more diversified and capacious revenue systems, and had come to assume a larger fiscal role, than ever before.

The penultimate chapter of the book—Chapter 6—turns to the last decade of the twentieth century and the first two decades of the twenty-first. It was during this thirty-year stretch that, for the first time in modern American history, state tax policy became closely associated with state partisanship. I examine how this process unfolded across a range of economic and political events, including the early 1990s recession, the late 1990s fiscal boom, the Great Recession of 2007–2009, and the post-2010 Republican takeover of numerous state governments. In doing so, I show how the partisan polarization of state tax policy was made possible by the confluence of a variety of trends, including the growth of Republican strength in state governments, the alignment of state parties with their national counterparts' fiscal policy positions, and the increasingly pronounced role of

[46] Richard P. Nathan and Fred C. Doolittle, *Reagan and the States*, (Princeton, NJ: Princeton University Press, 1987); Timothy Conlan, *From New Federalism to Devolution: Twenty-Five Years of Intergovernmental Reform*, (Washington, D.C.: Brookings Institution Press, 1998).

nationally affiliated advocacy groups in setting the agendas of state legislatures. I also carefully consider how the divergence of Democrat-controlled and Republican-controlled states on tax policy helped fuel the rise of a popular discourse on how red states were winning the interstate competition for businesses and residents, with important consequences for national fiscal policy debates. The chapter ends by examining trends in state own-source tax revenue and federal intergovernmental spending over the course of the three-decade period at hand. Demonstrating that these decades witnessed a gradual decline in the former and a rise in the latter, I suggest that the Republican state-level tax-cutting agenda may have, by weakening state fiscal capacity, inadvertently paved the way for a greater federal role in state fiscal affairs.

In the book's concluding chapter, I consider the implications of its findings for the present and future of state taxation politics and American fiscal federalism. Summarizing the book's key contributions, I emphasize how the many competing forces that once influenced state taxation politics and fiscal federalism debates have been gradually superseded by the influence of partisanship. Today, it is, above all else, the party composition of government that influences tax choices at the state level as well as intergovernmental fiscal policy at the national level. Turning to examine the national parties' distinct approaches to fiscal federalism in twenty-first-century America, I argue that the GOP's thoroughgoing embrace of competitive federalism has created a dilemma for Democrats, whose desire to expand the domestic public sector has been (and will continue to be) undermined by red-state tax cuts. I conclude the chapter by discussing the social and political problems exacerbated by the contemporary intergovernmental fiscal system, suggesting modest reforms to create a more coordinated intergovernmental tax arrangement, and arguing that more significant reforms can only be achieved after a national consensus emerges regarding the need to limit the influence of competitive federalism in American politics. Such reforms, I caution, are unlikely to be truly transformational if and when they occur. The enduring presence of the institutional factors that obstructed efforts on behalf of large-scale reform in the past will probably doom similar efforts in the future. Policymakers will therefore have little choice but to implement patches enabling the intergovernmental fiscal system to hobble along, just as they always have.

1
The Emergence of Modern State Tax Systems in the New Deal Era

> "My primary purpose in coming before you with a mid-session message...is to consult with you on an emergency problem, which, if permitted to go unsolved, will retard, if not destroy, the economic development and the social welfare of Washington."
>
> —Gov. Clarence Martin, addressing the Washington State Legislature, February 6, 1933

> "This administration must face and solve problems of present emergency and future policy which will demand of us all the utmost in patience, self-sacrifice, patriotism, and cooperation."
>
> —Gov. William A. Comstock, addressing the Michigan State Legislature, January 5, 1933

> "Nothing short of an emergency of imperative nature would impel me to assemble you at this period in the State's life. Our financial situation is not such as to make it desirable to hold a costly session...But after numerous conferences with our citizens and several with those in charge of affairs at the seat of government in Washington, I have been forced to the conclusion that Legislative action on the part of Montana is absolutely necessary..."
>
> —Gov. Frank H. Cooney, addressing the Montana State Legislature, November 27, 1933

The 1930s witnessed a true revolution in state taxation. When the decade began, the tax systems of most states were primarily composed of property taxes, a host of longstanding fees, and more recently passed automobile-related imposts to fund transportation projects. But the economic collapse of the late 1920s and early 1930s, the ensuing crisis in property tax collections, and the subsequent adoption of numerous federal programs requiring state fiscal cooperation forced all states to go well beyond these revenue sources to

Coordination Failure. Adam S. Myers, Oxford University Press. © Oxford University Press (2026).
DOI: 10.1093/9780197831878.003.0002

meet their fiscal needs. By the end of the decade, states had passed numerous new tax laws, in most cases adopting one or more of the three fiscal instruments (the personal income tax, corporate income tax, and general sales tax) that would become the workhorses of state revenue systems during the mid twentieth century and beyond. Thus, it was during the 1930s that modern state tax systems emerged.

State governments of the 1930s transformed their tax systems in a highly challenging political environment. Public demands for a robust response to the economic crisis meant that states had to generate new revenue quickly, but to do so they needed to overcome difficult institutional barriers as well as organized interests opposing nearly every available tax option. Rather than deliberating carefully on what a fair and efficient tax system might look like, state legislatures often temporized on the tax question until they could no longer do so, at which point they hastily agreed to whatever new tax could get them through the next budget cycle. Hence, in their Depression-era taxation decisions, state lawmakers usually settled on what was possible rather than affirmatively choosing what constituted good public policy.

But what was possible depended upon a complex array of institutional, political, and economic factors that varied substantially from state to state. Thus, the flurry of new state tax adoptions during the New Deal resulted in a rather spectacular divergence of interstate tax policy. States emerged from the 1930s with fiscal regimes featuring distinct combinations of sales, income, and other taxes. These tax differences would prove to be surprisingly durable: to a degree that no one at the time foresaw, the tax systems that states wound up with in the 1930s became the frameworks upon which states continued to build their tax systems during the mid twentieth century and beyond.

The cumulative effect of tax-related developments at the state level during the 1930s was to make American taxation significantly more regressive overall. This fact was frequently glossed over or ignored by mid-twentieth-century scholars who, focusing exclusively on federal tax policy, depicted the New Deal Era as an unqualified triumph for progressive taxation. But while the work of later scholars has largely dispelled the myth that New Deal Era federal taxation had major redistributive consequences, it remains the case that few scholars have paid careful attention to the impact of *state* taxation during this period.[1] Indeed, the gap between image and reality in American

[1] Mark Leff's 1984 book is the authoritative work challenging the claim that the New Deal was a triumph for progressive taxation at the national level. Monty Hindman's 2010 dissertation is perhaps

taxation policy during the 1930s is probably larger for state than federal taxation. While states adopted numerous ostensibly progressive income taxes during the New Deal, the bulk of new revenue they collected came from regressive consumption taxes, most especially the general sales tax.

What follows in this chapter is a rich analytical history of state taxation politics in the New Deal Era, with a focus on explaining why the transformation in state tax systems of this period occurred as it did. After briefly exploring state taxation prior to the New Deal, I examine the circumstances that created a critical juncture in state taxation during the years between 1929 and 1937. From there, I consider the main tax options from which states could choose in their efforts to gain new revenue: motor fuel taxes, tobacco and alcohol taxes, income taxes, and the general sales tax. Next, I look at the complicated coalitional politics underpinning the state taxation fights of this period. I then turn to analyzing state tax adoption and reliance patterns during the 1930s. In doing so, I show how state tax adoption patterns were the result of a complex array of political and institutional factors, leading to otherwise similar states adopting vastly different taxation systems. I also discuss the relative insignificance of party control of state government as a variable explaining state tax outcomes during this period. Lastly, I explain why, despite the apparent growth of state income taxation during the 1930s, sales taxes ended up vastly exceeding income taxes in terms of the amount of revenue they generated for state governments.

Before the Storm: State Taxation in the 1920s

While the 1930s are unique among the decades of the twentieth century in terms of the magnitude of the transformation in state-level taxation that they wrought, the years immediately preceding the 1930s also featured notable developments in state tax policy. The changes of the 1920s, while less significant than those that occurred in the following decade, nonetheless proved durable and thus merit some discussion.

Prior to the 1920s, the dominant state government revenue source had for nearly a century been the general property tax. This tax, which was originally envisioned as a tax on all forms of wealth (rather than simply a tax on real

the only comprehensive modern study examining New Deal Era taxation policy at the subnational level. Mark H. Leff, *The Limits of Symbolic Reform: The New Deal and Taxation, 1933–1939* (New York: Cambridge University Press, 1984); Monty Hindman, "The Rise and Fall of Wealth Taxation: An Inquiry into the Fiscal History of the American States" (Ph.D. Dissertation, University of Michigan, 2010).

estate, as property taxes function today), was usually assessed by local governments but its proceeds were shared between localities and states. By the late nineteenth century, however, the heavy reliance of state governments on property taxation had come to be widely perceived as antiquated and unfair: because local governments did not have the administrative capacity to track and capture the new forms of wealth that had emerged in the industrial age (e.g., stocks, bonds, and salary income), the general property tax ended up disproportionately burdening owners of real estate (often farmers of modest means).[2] Over the course of the late nineteenth and early twentieth centuries, progressive reformers and academic economists in numerous states waged a large-scale campaign to transform the property tax into a real estate tax exclusively for local governments, while locating new sources of revenue for state governments.[3] In the first two decades of the twentieth century, these efforts resulted in the adoption of several new forms of taxation, including the first modern state-level income taxes. The number of states that implemented these new taxes was quite small, however, and in most of the states that adopted them, the amount of revenue they raised was relatively small as well. Thus, the general property tax remained the primary revenue generator of states nationwide.

During the 1920s, however, state fiscal systems underwent a substantial shift. First, after decades of relative stasis, state government spending increased dramatically. This increase was overwhelmingly concentrated in the transportation sector, as states were busy building new roads to facilitate the growing use of automobiles. To fund these new transportation projects, states adopted a set of new excise taxes, including consumer taxes on motor vehicle licenses and business taxes on motor vehicle fuel.[4] The diffusion of both taxes—but especially the fuel tax—during the 1920s occurred at

[2] Ajay K. Mehrotra, "Forging Fiscal Reform: Constitutional Change, Public Policy, and the Creation of Administrative Capacity in Wisconsin, 1880–1920," *Journal of Policy History* 20 (2008): 94–112; Edwin R.A. Seligman, "The General Property Tax," *Political Science Quarterly* 5 (1890): 24–64.

[3] Much has been written about the specific policy proposals and efforts of the Progressive-era reformers and economists, including their ideas about classifying property, separating state and local revenue sources, and using taxation as a tool for social change. See, e.g., W. Elliot Brownlee, "Social Philosophy and Tax Regimes in the United States, 1763 to the Present," *Social Philosophy and Policy* 23 (2006): 1–27; Ajay K. Mehrotra, *Making the Modern American Fiscal State: Law, Politics, and the Rise of Progressive Taxation, 1877–1929* (New York: Cambridge University Press, 2013); Marianne Johnson, "Taxation in the Early Progressive Era: From Revenue to Social Policy," *Review of Political Economy* 36, no. 1 (2024): 59–75.

[4] James T. Patterson, *New Deal and States: Federalism in Transition* (Princeton, NJ: Princeton University Press, 1969).

unprecedented speed: the motor fuel tax was first adopted by Oregon in 1919, but over the course of the next decade all other states in the union adopted the tax.[5] By the end of the 1920s, auto-related taxes had overtaken the general property tax as the most important revenue generator of state government, leading some scholars to claim that the decade—sandwiched between the previous era of property tax dominance and the coming era of sales tax dominance—constitutes "an overlooked tax regime" at the subnational level.[6]

The rising importance of automobile-related taxes over the course of the 1920s can be seen in Figure 1.1 which tracks the amount of state government revenue from six sources between 1923 and 1931 (on the eve of the New Deal revolution in state taxation). As can be seen, over the course of the period at hand, business license taxes (the majority of which were motor fuel taxes) came to account for a major share of state revenues. Revenue for non-business license taxes (of which fees assessed on automobile ownership accounted for the lion's share) also grew steadily (though not as impressively) over the course of the 1920s. Personal and corporate income taxes, on the other hand, continually provided a small share of state tax revenue overall

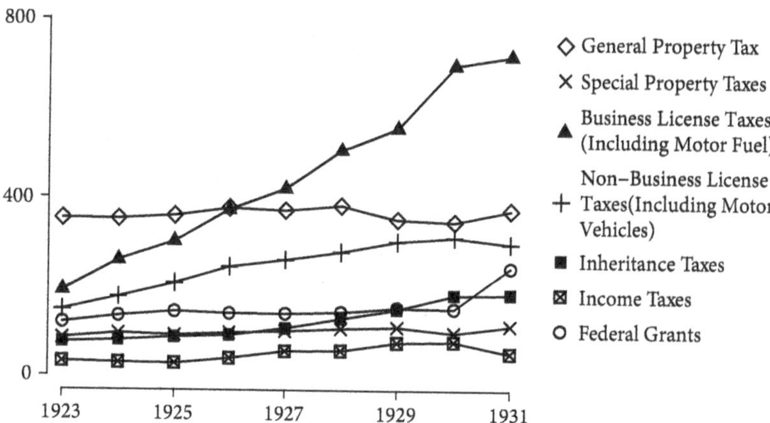

Figure 1.1 Total State Government Revenue (in Millions of USD) from Various Tax Sources, 1923–1931

Sources: U.S. Census, *Financial Statistics of States*, various years

[5] Christopher W. Wells, "Fueling the Boom: Gasoline Taxes, Invisibility, and the Growth of the American Highway Infrastructure, 1919–1956," *Journal of American History* 99, no. 1 (2012): 74.

[6] Hindman, "The Rise and Fall of Wealth Taxation," 400.

(indeed, as of 1929, income taxes accounted for over 10% of revenue in only four states). Perhaps even more importantly, general retail sales taxation—which would come to dominate state revenue collection in the 1930s and beyond—did not yet exist.

The Critical Juncture in State Taxation, 1929–1937

With the arrival of the Great Depression, state governments entered a period that would result in the complete transformation of their tax systems. Whereas the 1900s and 1910s featured incremental adjustments to the property tax-based systems upon which states had relied for decades, and the 1920s witnessed the arrival of automobile-related taxes layered upon the old system, the 1930s was a period in which states would be able to (and ultimately did) thoroughly dismantle their longstanding revenue systems and replace them with something different altogether. For this reason, it is helpful to think of the eight-year period between the stock market crash of 1929 and the economic panic of 1937 as a "critical juncture"—or a moment in which structural barriers to large-scale change weaken and the agency of political actors takes on greater importance.[7]

There were two basic reasons why old barriers to large-scale change declined in strength considerably during the Great Depression. To begin with, state government revenue needs grew dramatically as the national government demanded that states share financial responsibility for providing relief to those who, on account of the Depression, had become unemployed or impoverished. Both emergency relief programs established by the national government (the Reconstruction Finance Corporation from 1930–1932 and the Federal Emergency Relief Administration from 1933–1935) were designed as joint national-state programs financed by a mixture of federal and state funds. During both the Hoover and Roosevelt administrations (but especially the latter), federal officials charged with coordinating relief efforts spent much of their time haranguing recalcitrant states to pony up their share of the funds. Often, these efforts involved

[7] On critical junctures, see: Giovanni Capoccia and R. Daniel Kelemen, "The Study of Critical Junctures: Theory, Narrative and Counterfactuals in Historical Institutionalism," *World Politics* 59, no. 3 (2007): 341–369. Importantly, to say that structural barriers to large-scale change in state taxation policy weakened during the New Deal Era is not to say that they broke down completely. As will be shown, some structural barriers continued to play an important role, while others were far less durable.

threats to cut off federal aid, some of which federal officials made good on.[8] Faced with the possibility (or, in some cases, reality) of the feds turning off the fiscal spigot, reluctant legislators were forced to adopt new state revenue sources. When the worst part of the Great Depression was over in 1935, the national government handed over all responsibility for poor relief to the states and created a variety of new intergovernmental programs (such as unemployment insurance and aid to dependent children) also requiring state financial cooperation, forcing states to maintain their recently adopted taxes and in some cases expand their revenue sources once again.[9]

The fiscal demands for participation in newly established intergovernmental programs only account for part of the reason why the 1930s resulted in the transformation of state revenue systems, however. A second, and perhaps more important, reason involved the weakness of the tax that had buttressed most state revenue systems during the previous century—the general property tax. In the decades prior to the 1930s, progressive reformers worked together with groups representing farmers and real estate interests to decrease states' reliance on the general property tax, resulting in its declining use.[10] With the onset of the Great Depression, the general property tax encountered new problems that gave the tax's longstanding critics the rationale they needed to press for its effective abolition as a state government revenue source. Most importantly, in the wake of the economic collapse, delinquency in property tax payments skyrocketed. In some areas, as many as 25% of taxpayers delayed making their property tax payments, thus putting the spotlight on the inherent deficiencies of the property tax during periods of economic pain.[11] The goals of Progressive-era economists and reformers—to shrink the scope of the general property tax and apply its proceeds purely to local government—thus came into much sharper relief.

[8] John Joseph Wallis, "The Political Economy of New Deal Fiscal Federalism," *Economic Inquiry* 29, no. 3 (1991): 510–524; Patterson, *The New Deal and States: Federalism in Transition*. For case studies of pressure on individual state governments, see: Dwayne Charles Cole, "The Relief Crisis in Illinois during the Depression, 1930–1940," (Ph.D. Dissertation, Saint Louis University, 1974); James F. Wickens, *Colorado in the Great Depression* (New York: Garland Publishing, 1979).

[9] John Joseph Wallis and Wallace E. Oates, "The Impact of the New Deal on American Federalism," in *The Defining Moment: The Great Depression and the American Economy in the Twentieth Century*, eds. Michael D. Bordo, Claudia Goldin, and Eugene N. White (Chicago: University of Chicago Press, 1998), 167–171.

[10] W. Elliot Brownlee, *Federal Taxation in America* (New York: Cambridge University Press, 2016); Hindman, "The Rise and Fall of Wealth Taxation."

[11] Hindman, "The Rise and Fall of Wealth Taxation," 430.

The need to raise revenue to meet new spending obligations and reduce property tax burdens led governors in state after state to pressure state legislators to adopt new taxes. Nearly every governor in the 1932–1933 period delivered an address to his legislature urging the adoption of new forms of taxation. Most governors signaled tremendous flexibility in what forms of revenue generation they would accept. While often pointing to the sales tax as a promising new potential revenue source, they nonetheless emphasized to legislators that designing the state's fiscal policy was ultimately up to them, and that gaining the necessary revenue—from whatever source—was of greater importance than choosing the optimal form of taxation.

State legislators, for their part, routinely dragged their feet in response to gubernatorial pressure. Aware of the urgent need to act but concerned about the political fallout of their choices, they often waited until the last minute to pass major tax legislation. In the interim, legislatures were the sites of intense struggles over numerous tax bills, with their members usually forming blocs that were more closely aligned with the constituencies they represented than with their political parties. The biggest sources of pressure on state legislators were not party leaders but interest groups representing sectors that were influential in a legislator's district.

The Available Tax Options

State legislatures searching for new revenue during the Great Depression explored and ultimately exploited a wide array of tax options. In the late 1920s, their efforts to attain new revenue often focused on increasing rates on non-property taxes already in place, including motor fuel taxes, motor vehicle taxes, inheritance taxes, and poll taxes. By the early 1930s, states were not only raising existing taxes but also adopting numerous new ones. The most common newly adopted taxes during these years tended to be selective sales taxes on specific foods or drinks, including malt drinks, oleomargarine, cigarettes, and (after the end of Prohibition in 1933) alcohol.[12] Then, during the crucial 1933–1937 period, numerous states turned to adopting the three

[12] Beulah Bailey, "Review of Tax Legislation, 1929," *The Bulletin of the National Tax Association* 15, no. 3 (1929): 75–80; Harold M. Groves, "Review of State Tax Legislation, 1931–1932," *Proceedings of the Annual Conference on Taxation under the Auspices of the National Tax Association* 25 (1932): 9–25.

tax instruments that would eventually become the central pillars of modern state tax systems (what I will call the "Big Three" state taxes): the personal income tax, corporate income tax, and general sales tax.[13]

A complete discussion of all the many types of taxes adopted or increased by states during the critical juncture of the 1930s would constitute a book in itself. Rather than discuss each of these taxes in detail, I focus on Depression-era state action regarding four types of taxes that were of particular importance to state governments and/or were especially significant in the national-state taxation relationship: motor fuel taxes, selective sales taxes on tobacco and alcohol, income taxes, and the general sales tax.

Motor Fuel Taxes: Continued Expansion amid Federal Invasion

In comparison to the other tax options on the table during the 1930s, increasing the motor fuel tax rate was a relatively easy political feat for state legislatures. As mentioned previously, the tax experienced unprecedented growth leading to universal state adoption over the previous decade. The rapid ascendancy of the motor fuel tax owed to several features that made it politically attractive: in addition to having low administrative costs and being relatively hidden from public view, it enjoyed the support of politically powerful interests whose tax-related agendas often diverged on other matters, including the business community, real estate interests, and farmers.[14] All these groups favored greater state government spending on transportation, the sector to which motor fuel taxes were originally tied.

[13] It should be noted that the term "Big Three taxes" in relation to state taxation has been used to refer to different sets of taxes in previous studies. For example, in its state taxation reports from the 1960s and 1970s, the Advisory Commission on Intergovernmental Relations used the term to refer to property taxes (rather than corporate income taxes) alongside personal income taxes and general sales taxes. See, e.g., Advisory Commission on Intergovernmental Relations, *State and Local Finances: Significant Features, 1967–1970*, Report #M-50, November 1969. The ACIR studies, however, considered state and local taxes in combination, rather than only examining state taxes. Since property taxes are overwhelmingly a local government tax source in the modern U.S. (they account for a tiny share of modern *state* tax revenue) and since this book is primarily a study of state taxation, I consider the corporate income tax rather than the property tax to be the third of the "Big Three" modern states taxes. I do this while acknowledging that the corporate income tax is a *distant* third (the personal income tax and general sales tax are far more important revenue contributors to state governments), but given the near-ubiquity of the state corporate income tax and its important role in the tax systems of several large states, it is useful to consider it alongside the personal income and general sales tax in analyses of modern state taxation.

[14] Wells, "Fueling the Boom"; Hindman, "The Rise and Fall of Wealth Taxation," 426–427.

With the onset of the Great Depression, the politics surrounding the motor fuel tax changed to some degree. Efforts emerged within numerous states to dedicate motor fuel tax proceeds to spending in areas other than transportation, such as poor relief. This practice, known as "diversion," faced major organized opposition from groups such as the American Automobile Association and local farm lobbies.[15] Not coincidentally, opposition to motor fuel tax increases also grew substantially during this period. Nonetheless, states continued to push through motor fuel tax rate hikes, with eight states increasing rates in 1931 and another seven states doing so in 1932.[16] States also continued to "divert" new motor fuel tax funds to non-transportation programs (despite the fact that, in many states, statutory and constitutional restrictions were put in place to prevent the practice).[17]

The growing reliance of state governments on the motor fuel tax—for building highways and, beginning in the Great Depression, for other purposes as well—meant that, when Congress decided in 1932 that the national government should tax gasoline consumption as well, states responded with alarm. Congress's passage of the first federal motor fuel tax was a response to the national government's own fiscal problems and specifically the fact that federal income tax proceeds had declined precipitously during the nationwide economic downturn. But though the federal tax was originally designed as temporary, it provoked howls of protest from state legislatures and governors, many of which sent resolutions to Congress decrying the invasion of what states saw as their rightful revenue source.[18] As I will discuss in Chapter 2, Congress's decision to enter the motor fuel tax field played a major role in the decision of state governments to organize themselves and begin directly lobbying the national government during the 1930s.

Tobacco and Alcohol Taxes: States Invade a Federal Field

The story of tobacco and alcohol taxes in the 1930s is in some sense the opposite of the story of the motor fuel tax. Whereas the latter story is one of the national government entering an already established field of state taxation,

[15] Finla Goff Crawford, *Motor Fuel Taxation in the United States* (Syracuse, NY: 1939), 71.

[16] Crawford, *Motor Fuel Taxation in the United States*, 4–5.

[17] The percentage of motor fuel tax funds used by states for non-transportation purposes grew from 2% to 16% between 1927 and 1934. Crawford, *Motor Fuel Taxation in the United States*, 69.

[18] See, e.g., North Carolina General Assembly, "A Joint Resolution Requesting Congress to Refrain from a Further Invasion of Sources of Taxation Heretofore Enjoyed by the States, and that the Congress Balance Its Budget Without Further Increase in the Tax Levies," Resolution No. 118, February 20, 1933, Box 177, Robert Doughton Papers, University of North Carolina Archives.

the former is one of the states entering a tax field long occupied by the national government. In this way, it directly defies the Anti-Federalists' predictions (discussed in the book's introduction) that, under the Constitution, the national government would increasingly colonize tax sources previously used by the states but not the other way around.

For the first 130 years of American history, the taxation of alcohol and tobacco products was the exclusive custody of the national government. Federal taxation of both alcohol and tobacco sales originated in the early republic (indeed, a 1791 tax on distilled spirits was the first internal duty Congress ever adopted), but it was during the Civil War that alcohol and tobacco taxes became permanent components of the national government's tax system.[19] By the early twentieth century, they had become important components indeed: in 1916, liquor and tobacco taxes constituted 34% and 12% of federal tax collections, respectively (by comparison, the tariff and the newly adopted income tax constituted 29% and 17%).[20] The onset of Prohibition in 1919 temporarily eliminated the liquor tax as a federal revenue source, but the tobacco tax continued to provide a large amount of federal revenue during the 1920s, when cigarette consumption among the American public increased substantially.

Even as the national government made growing use of them, alcohol and tobacco taxes were not on the radar of state governments as potential revenue sources during the final decades of the nineteenth century or the earliest decades of the twentieth. To be sure, states did charge license fees to alcohol-serving establishments prior to Prohibition, and these fees did produce a significant amount of state revenue. But the taxation of alcohol and tobacco consumption was not seriously considered by states or their local subdivisions. It appears that state policymakers largely agreed with contemporaneous authorities on taxation policy who argued that consumption taxes were better suited for the national government (and who presumed that such taxes would continue to be exclusively levied at the national level in the future).[21]

The inception of state-level tobacco sales taxation occurred in the early 1920s, when ten states in the South and Great Plains (regions where anti-tobacco sentiment was high) enacted tobacco taxes as a way of discouraging

[19] Tun Yuan Hu, *The Liquor Tax in the United States, 1791–1947*, (New York: Columbia University Graduate School of Business, 1950); Warren Aubrey Law, "Tobacco Taxation in the United States" (Ph.D. dissertation, Harvard University, 1953).

[20] ibid., 139.

[21] See, e.g., Fred Fairchild, "The Future of State and Local Taxation," *National Tax Association Bulletin* 3 (1921): 75; Law, "Tobacco Taxation in the United States," 123–124.

tobacco use.[22] Because tobacco consumption in these states was already relatively low, these taxes were largely insignificant as revenue sources. However, when the critical juncture in state taxation opened in the late 1920s, the successful implementation of these early state-level tobacco taxes caught the attention of lawmakers in Northeastern and Great Lakes states, where tobacco consumption levels were far higher. Legislators in these states saw tobacco taxes not as means of discouraging tobacco use but as a way to get much-needed new revenue.[23]

By the early 1930s, almost every state in the Union was considering either adopting a tobacco tax or raising its tobacco tax rates. Tobacco distributors and merchants fought tirelessly against these efforts, and their pushback was often successful: by 1931, they had defeated over 100 tobacco taxation proposals in more than 33 states over the previous few years.[24] In their struggle to derail tobacco tax adoptions, tobacco merchants were likely assisted by the fact that such taxes were broadly unpopular: whenever they were subjected to a statewide voter referendum, they were defeated. Nonetheless, the recurring state-level budget crunches of the 1930s forced state legislatures to reconsider tobacco taxes even after previous attempts at their implementation proved unsuccessful. In New York, a state tobacco tax was finally passed in 1939 after at least eight unsuccessful previous efforts.[25]

The growth of state-level alcohol sales taxation occurred at a different time and pace than the growth of tobacco taxation. This was largely because, between 1919 and 1933, alcohol sales were prohibited under the Eighteenth Amendment of the U.S. Constitution. Thus, in the early years of the critical juncture in state taxation, taxing liquor sales was not an available option for governments at any level. With the impending repeal of Prohibition in 1933, the liquor tax became a tantalizing new potential revenue source for cash-strapped states. Convening in special sessions in late 1933 to craft new alcohol regulation regimes, state legislatures made it known that, in a post-Prohibition America, they would no longer cede the field of alcohol sales taxation to the national government.[26] The liquor tax structure that states ultimately created depended on the system of alcohol regulation that they

[22] Indeed, in several of these states, tobacco taxes were passed as substitutes for outright bans on tobacco products. Law, "Tobacco Taxation in the United States," 123–124.

[23] Law, "Tobacco Taxation in the United States," 125–126.

[24] "State Legislators Are Blowing Tax Rings around Smokers," *Business Week*, March 11, 1931, 30; cited in: Law, "Tobacco Taxation in the United States," 126.

[25] Law, "Tobacco Taxation in the United States," 129.

[26] "$2.60 Tax on Liquor Urged in Report," *New York Times*, December 9, 1933, 10.

adopted. In so-called "liquor monopoly" states (i.e., states where alcohol could only be purchased in state-operated liquor stores), the bulk of new revenue from alcohol sales would come from the net profits of the state-operated stores and stand-alone alcohol excise taxes were low or non-existent. In so-called "private enterprise states" (i.e., states where alcohol would be sold by private retailers), almost all the new alcohol-based revenue would come from excise taxes, whose rates were generally higher.[27]

The states' invasion of the tobacco and alcohol sales tax fields in the early 1930s did not go unnoticed in Washington, D.C. Quite to the contrary, the "double taxation" of alcohol and tobacco became a major cause for concern among a variety of important national political actors, including the alcohol and tobacco industries, federal alcohol regulators concerned about bootlegging in a post-Prohibition America, influential members of Congress, and others. How these actors responded to the actions of the states is discussed in Chapter 2.

Income Taxes: Overcoming Federal Dominance and Constitutional Constraints

The rise of state income taxes alongside the federal income tax is a more complex story than that of either the motor fuel tax or the alcohol and tobacco taxes. Unlike alcohol and tobacco taxation, modern income taxation at the state level preceded modern income taxation at the federal level (though just barely). But unlike the motor fuel tax, the national government came to heavily occupy the income tax space before most states adopted income taxes, and long before most states came to rely on them for a significant share of their revenues.

Income taxes at both the state and national levels first appeared in the United States during the nineteenth century. But unlike modern income taxes, nineteenth-century income taxes were generally insignificant features of American public finance. At the state level, they were infrequently used, poorly administered, and generated little revenue.[28] At the national level, an income tax law enacted by Congress in 1861 played a modestly important role in financing the national government's vast expenses during the Civil

[27] Hu, *Liquor Tax in the United States, 1791–1947*, 121–126.

[28] Edwin R.A. Seligman, *The Income Tax: A Study of the History, Theory, and Practice of Income Taxation at Home and Abroad*, (New York: Macmillan Company, 1914).

War, but the tax was reduced after the war concluded and then allowed to expire in 1871.[29]

Modern income taxation in the United States originated during the Progressive Era, when public finance experts and progressive activists promoted the income tax as a crucial component of large-scale tax reform at both the state and national levels.[30] Progressive-era efforts on behalf of income taxation achieved their breakthrough success in 1911, when the state of Wisconsin enacted a landmark income tax law. In contrast to the state income taxes of the nineteenth century, which were often managed by unskilled, partisan local officials, Wisconsin's personal and corporate income taxes (designed with the Progressive-era principles of neutral, expert administration in mind) were centrally administered by a highly trained state tax commission.[31] They also featured somewhat higher top rates than the earlier taxes. Not surprisingly, the Wisconsin taxes quickly outstripped all previous state income taxes in their revenue-generating abilities. Spurred in part by the success of Wisconsin's income taxes, a corresponding national movement to adopt a federal income tax rapidly picked up steam. The movement culminated in the passage of the 16th Amendment authorizing federal income taxation as well as the enactment of the first modern federal income tax statute in 1913.

In the decade and a half that followed 1913, state-level income taxation experienced limited growth, with only eight states following Wisconsin in adopting a modern, centrally administered income tax. With a few exceptions, all these states adopted top income tax rates of below 5%, severely limiting the ability of these taxes to generate much revenue.[32] Two chief factors seem to account for the limited spread and reach of state-level income taxes during this period. One factor is obvious: states were reluctant to saddle their residents with an income tax burden on top of the new federal income tax, whose rates had risen quickly after it was initially adopted. This was especially the case since, at least during the 1920s, the auto-related taxes states had begun levying were raising plenty of revenue, making additional taxes unnecessary.

[29] Sheldon D. Pollack, "The First National Income Tax, 1861–1872," *The Tax Lawyer* 67, no. 2 (2014): 311–330; Congress passed another income tax in 1894, but it was declared unconstitutional the following year by the U.S. Supreme court in *Pollock v. Farmers' Loan and Trust Company* (157 U.S. 429).

[30] Mehrotra, *Making the Modern American Fiscal State.*

[31] Seligman, *The Income Tax*, 421–422; Mehrotra, "Forging Fiscal Reform," 102–103.

[32] James W. Martin, "Changes in Income Tax Rates, 1930, 1932," *Bulletin of the National Tax Association* 17 (1932): 145–146.

The other reason for the limited growth of state-level income taxation during the 1910s and 1920s had to do with taxation restrictions found in state constitutions. The most important of these restrictions, known as "uniformity clauses," mandated that states tax property in an "equal and uniform" manner.[33] Present in some form within forty-two of the forty-eight state constitutions at the dawn of the twentieth century, uniformity clauses had complex historical origins that need not detain us here.[34] For our purposes, what is important is that, by the late nineteenth century, state high courts were using uniformity clauses as justifications for overruling early taxation schemes perceived to be "confiscatory" or discriminatory against the wealthy. As state legislatures across the country began considering adopting income taxes following the Wisconsin breakthrough, legal experts warned that state high courts could use uniformity clauses to strike down income tax statutes, particularly if they established higher tax rates for higher income levels.[35]

The presence of uniformity clauses in many state constitutions often made income tax adoption a far more complex process than it otherwise would have been. In states whose constitutions clearly authorized income taxation, tax enactment merely involved securing majority support for an income tax bill in both state legislative chambers and a gubernatorial signature after that—not an easy process, to be sure, but a relatively simple one. In the vast bulk of states with uniformity clauses, however, bill passage did not necessarily lead to income tax enactment. Instead, it immediately triggered court challenges by income tax opponents. If these challenges were successful (which they often were), income tax supporters could respond by organizing efforts to pass tax-authorizing constitutional amendments. When such efforts were successful, income tax proponents were not done; they now needed to advocate for passage of an income-tax bill through the standard process involving legislative and then gubernatorial approval.

[33] Wade J. Newhouse, *Constitutional Uniformity and Equality in State Taxation* (Ann Arbor, MI: University of Michigan Press, 1959).

[34] Newhouse, *Constitutional Uniformity and Equality in State Taxation.* For a fascinating account of how uniformity clauses originated in the southern states as a form of protection for slaveowners, but later spread to free states in the Midwest and West, see: Robin L. Einhorn, *American Taxation, American Slavery* (Chicago: University of Chicago Press, 2008).

[35] In issuing these warnings, experts pointed to the U.S. Supreme Court's seminal 1895 decision *Pollock v. Farmers' Loan Trust and Company* (157 US 429), which invalidated the 1894 federal income tax. In that decision, the court ruled that income is a form of property. Using the *Pollock* decision as their basis, constitutional lawyers claimed, state supreme courts could determine that income taxes were inconsistent with uniformity clauses (which tended to mandate uniformity only in the taxation of property).

As it turns out, the political will to work through the most protracted pathway leading to income tax adoption (constitutional amendment followed by legislative statute) was rarely in supply during the 1910s and 1920s. It was only during the critical juncture of 1929–1937, when the need to find new state government revenue sources had reached critical levels, that political actors were willing to take such difficult steps in many states. This is shown in Table 1.1, which presents a chronological listing of personal income tax adoptions by states between 1912 and 1937, along with a classification of the pathway to adoption in each state.[36] States classified as "A" exhibited the simplest pathway: in these states, the pre-1912 constitution clearly authorized personal income taxation, so all that was required for income tax enactment was legislative passage and gubernatorial signature. States classified as "B" exhibited a somewhat more complex pathway in which legislatures passed income tax laws, the laws were subsequently challenged in court, and state supreme courts upheld the laws despite the presence of uniformity clauses in state constitutions. States classified as "C" exhibited the most complex pathway: either because laws establishing a personal income tax were initially overturned by the courts or to preempt such rulings, income tax supporters successfully waged campaigns to amend state constitutions to explicitly authorize income taxation, and state legislatures passed income tax statutes afterward.

As the table shows, between 1911 and 1929, the ten states that adopted personal income taxes usually did so through the two more simple pathways (either Type A or Type B). Income tax adoption via the most complex pathway (Type C) did not become common until the 1930s, when the critical juncture in state taxation arrived. This strongly suggests that, in states whose constitutions included uniformity clauses and with high courts willing to enforce them, pro-income tax forces could only muster the strength to move through the multi-stage process necessary to enact income taxes under crisis conditions. Even then, the Type C process necessarily took several years to bear fruit, and states in the early 1930s needed revenue immediately. This was an important factor in the decisions of numerous states to adopt general

[36] Personal and corporate income tax adoption efforts were subject to similar political dynamics in most states, and state courts generally interpreted uniformity clauses as applying to them in the same way. Additionally, states usually adopted personal and corporate income taxes at the same time, though on occasion states adopted one income tax but not the other. Since personal income taxes were (and are) far more significant to state governments as revenue sources, I have presented data on personal rather than corporate income tax adoption in this table.

Table 1.1 Pathways to Adoption of Personal Income Taxes in the American States, 1911–1937

State	**Year**	**Adoption Pathway Type (see below for descriptions)**
Wisconsin	1911	C
Mississippi	1912	B
Massachusetts	1915	C
Oklahoma	1915	A
Virginia	1916	A
Delaware	1917	B
Missouri	1917	B
North Dakota	1919	B
New York	1919	A
North Carolina	1921	B
South Carolina	1922	A
Arkansas	1929	B
Georgia	1929	B
Oregon	1930	B
Idaho	1931	B
Utah	1931	C
Vermont	1931	C
Alabama	1933	C
Arkansas	1933	B
Kansas	1933	C
Minnesota	1933	B
Montana	1933	C
New Mexico	1933	B
Iowa	1934	A
Louisiana	1934	C
California	1935	C
Kentucky	1936	C
Colorado	1937	C
Maryland	1937	B

Type A: Pre-1911 state constitution clearly authorizes income taxation.
Type B: Income tax statute passes and is subsequently upheld by courts despite constitutional taxation restrictions.
Type C: Statute passes following state constitutional amendment explicitly authorizing income taxation.
Sources: Newhouse, *Constitutional Uniformity and Equality in State Taxation*; New York State Constitutional Convention Committee, *Constitutions of the States and United States* (Albany, NY: J.B. Lyon, 1938).

sales taxes in 1933; unlike income taxes, sales taxes faced few constitutional restrictions, meaning they could be implemented quickly.[37]

It is also important to bear in mind that not all efforts to overcome uniformity clauses were successful, even in the thick of an economic crisis. In four states (Illinois, Pennsylvania, Tennessee, and Washington), statutes establishing personal income taxes that were passed during the 1930s were overturned by state high courts and efforts to amend state constitutions were unsuccessful.[38] Each of these states was thus forced to turn to other taxes (usually the sales tax) for new revenue. In other states like Michigan, the mere threat of judicial nullification caused state legislatures to turn away from the income tax as a potential solution to state revenue problems for decades. Thus, restrictions in state constitutions had a very real impact on tax adoption decisions in a large number of states, usually to the benefit of the sales tax.

The General Sales Tax: Federal Concession Leads to Rapid Interstate Diffusion

The general retail sales tax was the most important state-level tax innovation of the New Deal Era. Like the motor fuel tax of the 1920s, its adoption occurred at an exceedingly fast clip, with the number of sales tax states rising from zero at the beginning of 1932 to twenty-two at the end of 1937.[39] This rapid diffusion was in no small part made possible by the fact that, in 1932, Congress signaled that it would concede the general sales tax field to the states. Thus, unlike the other taxes discussed in this chapter, the general sales tax emerged and developed entirely within state tax systems.

This was not an inevitable development. When the general sales tax first entered the American policy debate, it was envisioned as a federal rather than a state tax. As discussed previously, the consensus among tax experts in the first two decades of the twentieth century was that consumption taxes were better suited to central governments than regional ones, and meetings of the

[37] While the adoption of sales taxes occasionally sparked legal challenges as well, state supreme courts usually ruled that uniformity clauses did not prohibit sales taxation. In the few instances in which sales taxes were struck down by state high courts, legislatures were generally able to respond by altering the language of the statutes to make them pass constitutional muster.

[38] Newhouse, *Constitutional Uniformity and Equality in State Taxation*, 94, 122–123, 530–531, 581–582.

[39] Susan B. Hansen, *The Politics of Taxation: Revenue without Representation*, (New York: Praeger, 1983).

National Tax Association (NTA) during that period examined the sales tax as a potential national rather than subnational policy reform.[40] Interest in a federal sales tax grew following the end of World War I, when numerous European national governments adopted some form of general sales taxation and business leaders were looking for new taxes to replace federal corporate and income taxes (which had become substantially more burdensome to the wealthy over the course of the Woodrow Wilson Presidency).[41] In the early 1920s, business leaders and their Republican allies in Congress proposed a plan to scrap the federal income tax entirely and replace it with a general sales tax. Their efforts were thwarted by a coalition headed by Treasury Secretary Andrew Mellon, a figure who, despite his corporate background and fiscal conservatism, understood that the best way to protect big business and the wealthy from truly confiscatory taxation was to neutralize its appeal by maintaining certain modestly progressive elements within the tax system.[42]

The debate over a federal sales tax awakened state political actors to the possibility of state-level general sales taxation. Their attraction to this idea owed to several factors. To begin with, states' growing reliance on motor fuel taxation and selective sales taxes on tobacco made state legislators and governors increasingly aware of—and comfortable with—the idea of using excise taxes to fill state coffers. Indeed, to many, a general sales tax seemed like a natural extension of the major state tax innovations of the 1920s. Additionally, general sales taxation was becoming an increasingly hot topic in national conferences attended by top state policymakers. For example, at the annual NTA meetings (which were regularly attended by leading state government tax officials), the notion of the general sales tax as a source of state rather than federal revenue was becoming a serious matter of discussion by the mid 1920s. Perhaps more importantly, taxation was the most frequent topic of discussion at the annual meetings of America's governors throughout the 1920s, and by the end of the decade, many of the speeches and lectures in these meetings sang the virtues of the sales tax.[43]

Despite the growing consensus among state political elites around the country that a general sales tax on retail products was an extremely

[40] Meyer D. Rothschild, "The Gross Sales, or Turnover Tax," *Proceedings of the Annual Conference on Taxation under the Auspices of the National Tax Association*, vol. 13 (1920), 180–209.

[41] Leff, *The Limits of Symbolic Reform*; Carl Shoup, *The Sales Tax in the American States* (New York: Columbia University Press, 1934), 6–7.

[42] Brownlee, *Federal Taxation in America*, 112–113.

[43] A summary of the topics discussed in all the Governors' Conferences between 1908 and 1935 can be found in: Governors' Conference, *The Tenth Governors' Bulletin*, October 30, 1936, Box 251, Henry Horner Papers, Abraham Lincoln Presidential Library, Springfield, IL.

promising potential source of additional revenue for state governments, no state adopted such a tax in the 1920s or the first two years of the 1930s. While bills establishing such taxes were proposed in numerous states in the years between 1928 and 1932, none of these bills were passed. The reasons for these failures are not entirely clear, though there are several possibilities. First, as discussed earlier, in the first years of the Great Depression, the most pressing revenue issue for state governments was not how to grow state coffers but rather how to reduce property tax burdens. For the relatively modest goal of replacing state-level property tax revenue, state governments could choose from a wide array of taxes, the vast bulk of which were less controversial than the general retail sales tax. Second, state legislatures likely held off on passing general sales taxes out of concern that the field of sales taxation would soon be invaded by the national government. Given the significant efforts made to establish a federal sales tax in the early 1920s, this possibility seemed quite plausible.

Eventually, however, the deterioration of state finances wrought by the Great Depression forced states to act. The first state to take the plunge into the largely unknown waters of retail sales taxation was Mississippi. The Magnolia State's status as a pioneer in modern state tax policy is surprising given that studies of state policy innovation in the mid twentieth century have consistently rated it one of the least innovative states.[44] Certainly, few in the early twentieth century would have predicted that Mississippi—a poor southern backwater without a professionalized state government—would be a leader in developing fiscal policies emulated by numerous other states in the transformative decade of the 1930s.

Upon closer examination, the fact that Mississippi was a tax policy innovator is less surprising than it initially seems. While nearly all states entered the 1930s in dire financial straits, Mississippi's situation was worse than most: at the beginning of 1932, the state only had $1,326 in the bank, even as it had accrued $6,000,000 in outstanding warrants against it and over $50,000,000 in long-term debt. Government employees, including teachers, had not been paid in full for over a year.[45] Stated simply, the situation in Mississippi was so

[44] Indeed, in a pathbreaking article on policy diffusion among the American states, Jack Walker noted that "Mississippi, which has the lowest average score and ranks last among the states in relative speed of adoption, was nonetheless the first state to adopt a general sales tax." Jack L. Walker, "The Diffusion of Innovations among the American States." *American Political Science Review* 63, no. 3 (1969): 880–899.

[45] William Winter, "Governor Mike Conner and the Sales Tax, 1932," *Journal of Mississippi History* 41 (1979): 215.

bad that it would not allow for temporizing moves, which were common in other states. Additionally, Mississippi had begun experimenting with early forms of sales taxation in the nineteenth century and adopted a limited sales tax law covering a wide range of business activities (including retail sales) in 1930; moving from that tax to a tax on retail sales with rates sufficiently large to generate significant revenue was therefore less of a stretch than in other states.[46] Despite this context, the fight in 1932 over the adoption of what would come to be considered the nation's first modern sales tax was long and intense, involving unusually large public protests (organized primarily by the Mississippi Merchants Association) and multiple defeats prior to eventual success in the state's legislative chambers.[47]

Mississippi's adoption of the retail sales tax had its intended effects: within a very short order, the state's coffers filled with money. The state's successful experiment was covered widely in the nation's newspapers and deeply impressed state policymakers around the country. State politicians became even more convinced that the general sales tax was the solution to their revenue problems after a second major effort to adopt a federal sales tax fizzled in the middle of 1932.[48] Like the effort from ten years earlier, the 1932 effort was backed by powerful supporters (including Treasury Secretary Ogden Mills and House Speaker John Nance Garner), but opponents of a federal sales tax quickly countermobilized. In speeches on the U.S. House floor, opponents of this proposal made a variety of arguments, including that a federal sales tax would disproportionately burden the poor and working classes, but also that it would deprive the states of a revenue source they were on the cusp of claiming.[49] Thus, when the sales tax plan was officially killed in the middle of 1932, governors and state legislators understood its demise as an indication that the national government was permanently ceding general sales taxation to the states. The stage was therefore set for numerous state legislatures to pass sales taxes when they reconvened in early 1933.

Unsurprisingly, the first few months of 1933 were a busy period of travel for Mississippi Governor Conner. His office received invitations from 32 of

[46] Hindman, "The Rise and Fall of Wealth Taxation," 462; Neil H. Jacoby, *Retail Sales Taxation* (Chicago, IL: Commerce Clearing House, 1938), 61–65.

[47] Winter, "Governor Mike Conner and the Sales Tax, 1932."

[48] This effort, spearheaded in early 1932 by Treasury Secretary Ogden Mills and congressional leaders, sparked a rebellion among several powerful House Democrats, including Ways and Means Committee chairman Robert Doughton of North Carolina and Fiorello La Guardia of New York.

[49] Brownlee, *Federal Taxation in America*; Jordan A. Schwarz, "John Nance Garner and the Sales Tax Rebellion of 1932," *The Journal of Southern History* 30, no. 2 (1964): 162–180.

the 48 states to address state legislatures on the benefits of a general sales tax.[50] Flattered by the attention he was receiving but also mindful of his gubernatorial responsibilities in Jackson, Conner chose his speaking engagements carefully. On February 15th, he addressed the Georgia Legislature in Atlanta.[51] A week later, he addresses the Illinois General Assembly in Springfield.[52] In his speeches to policymakers in these states, Conner stressed two themes that were commonly used to convince cautious politicians to embrace the sales tax. First, he emphasized that the retail sales tax was easy to administer and would result in the immediate inflow of revenues, a matter of significance to state legislators searching for ways to fill state coffers quickly. Second, he argued that, because they targeted a wider tax base than property taxes or progressive income taxes, retail sales taxes would be far more stable sources of state government revenue in the long term. In addition to sounding these pragmatic notes, Conner also made a more surprising ideological argument: by facilitating "universality in direct taxation," the retail sales tax would serve as "a powerful antidote for paternalistic and radical socialistic tendencies."[53] At the same time, Conner responded to the common argument that the general sales tax was not levied in accordance with "ability to pay" by claiming that "it is levied on the ability to spend."[54] The pain inflicted by the sales tax on ordinary people was minimal, he added, and paled in comparison to the pain imposed by real estate taxes.

The Coalitional Politics behind Income and Sales Tax Fights

As states considered their many tax options during the critical juncture in state taxation, interest groups began mobilizing in support of, or opposition to, various tax proposals in statehouses across the country. The alignments of these groups (and the corresponding composition of tax policy coalitions) were quite similar across states, particularly in the grueling fights over personal income tax and general sales tax bills that were so common during

[50] "Mississippi Put on Its Financial Feet by Revenue from Levy," *St. Louis Globe-Democrat* (St. Louis, MO), January 29, 1933.

[51] "Mississippi Plan Discussed by Conner," *Atlanta Constitution* (Atlanta, GA), February 16, 1933 (downloaded from newspapers.com).

[52] S. A. Tucker, "Sales Tax 'Painless' Levy, Claim" *Decatur Daily Review* (Decatur, IL), February 22, 1933 (downloaded from newspapers.com).

[53] Press Release from the Office of Governor Henry Horner, February 21, 1933, Box 69, Henry Horner Papers, Abraham Lincoln Presidential Library, Springfield, IL.

[54] ibid.

the five-year stretch between 1933 and 1937. What did differ across states, however, was the relative power of various interest groups, and (as will be discussed in the next section) these power differences did have a substantial impact on tax policy outcomes.

The coalitional configurations underpinning state tax fights in the 1930s were shaped by the two fundamental fiscal realities affecting nearly all states during this period: massive new spending obligations alongside a collapse in the property tax as a source of state and local (but especially state) revenue. The conjunction of these two facts not only forced states to act; it also shaped the alignments of relevant interest groups in the taxation battles that were to come.

To begin with, the state-level interest groups that were the most consistent advocates of new tax adoptions represented those parts of society that stood to benefit the most from property tax reductions. Perhaps chief among these groups were organizations representing farmers, who had long resented bearing a disproportionate share of state tax burdens through the property tax. Having fought for property tax reform throughout the first decades of the twentieth century, state agricultural associations and granges were especially determined to take advantage of the political opening of the 1930s in their quest to end the dominance of the property tax once and for all. The particular tax to be adopted to replace the property tax was less important than ensuring that it *was* replaced. Thus, while farmers' groups tended to support income taxation more than sales taxation, they joined forces on behalf of sales tax adoption efforts whenever they concluded that the sales tax was the most realistic path toward property tax replacement. Similarly, realtor organizations and urban real estate interests also had a major stake in reducing property taxes; like farmers, they found their way to supporting whatever tax stood the best chance of replacing the property tax, even though in their case sales taxes were generally preferred over income taxes.[55]

Other groups that routinely supported the adoptions of both income and sales taxes were motivated by the overarching goal of growing state

[55] Previous scholarship has suggested that urban real estate interests overwhelmingly and enthusiastically supported sales taxes but not income taxes (see, e.g., Shoup et al., *The Sales Tax in the American States*; Hindman, "The Rise and Fall of Wealth Taxation"). However, there are plenty of cases of such groups working on behalf of income taxes as well. For example, in Illinois, the Chicago Real Estate Board joined forces with the Illinois Agricultural Association to promote a plan to levy a state income tax, creating an alliance of urban and rural groups that was highly unusual in the state, particularly on fiscal matters. "Minutes of Illinois Manufacturers Association Directors' Meeting, July 18, 1930," Illinois Manufacturers Association Collection, Chicago History Museum.

revenue coffers, not reducing property taxes. The most important of these groups were state teachers' associations, whose main focus throughout the 1920s and 1930s was securing greater state funds for education (and, more specifically, in having state governments take over the responsibility for funding education from local governments). To be sure, teachers' groups often voiced support for progressive taxation and worked on behalf of income tax adoptions in the initial stages of a state tax debate; however, like farm groups, they often came around to supporting sales tax bills when these bills were tied to their overarching goals (in the case of teachers' groups, increasing school funding). To a lesser extent, the same could be said of labor groups, which often championed income tax bills but could be convinced to support sales tax bills when they were tied to unemployment relief.

Groups representing social and economic sectors that neither stood to gain much from property tax reduction nor had a major interest in increasing state revenue were far more likely to oppose new tax proposals. These groups varied, however, in which proposals they opposed most vociferously. With respect to sales taxes, associations representing retail merchants were the most consistent and fervent opponents. As discussed previously, merchant groups launched a large-scale protest and an aggressive lobbying campaign in an unsuccessful effort to prevent the passage of the first modern retail sales tax in Mississippi.[56] As efforts to adopt sales taxes spread to other states, merchant groups also took the lead in working against them, with varying degrees of success.

With respect to income tax adoptions, opposition was often led by corporate leaders and their representatives in groups such as state Chambers of Commerce. These groups tended to oppose all new state taxes, and in the early years of the 1930s, they often fought against sales taxes as well as income taxes.[57] However, as the inevitability of new taxes of some sort became clear, state business leaders decided to cut their losses and focus on preventing passage of the taxes they feared most: corporate and personal income taxes.

[56] William Winter, "Governor Mike Conner and the Sales Tax, 1932," *Journal of Mississippi History* 41 (1979): 213–230.

[57] In Colorado, for example, the state's leading businessmen created a "taxpayers' committee" explicitly opposing all new taxes during the state legislature's 1933 session. A statement by the committee read: "We are against an income tax. We are against a sales tax...We are against every proposal to lay new burdens upon any group of taxpayers." "Statewide Move on to Fight Every New Tax Proposed in Legislature," *Denver Post*, April 30, 1933, 1. The next year, Colorado's business community launched an initiative petition to change the state constitution to require all non-property taxes to be ratified by the state's voters. The measure ultimately failed at the ballot box. "Chain Store Tax Wins; Amendment 5 Passes but All Others Lose," *Denver Post*, November 7, 1934, 1.

Whenever obstructing passage of income taxes became impossible, business leaders again shifted their focus to ensuring that the rates of these taxes remained low.

When considered in totality, the various alignments described above suggest that sales tax adoption efforts probably enjoyed an easier path to success than income tax adoption efforts during the 1930s. On the one hand, the strength of support for income and sales tax adoptions was roughly equal in numerous states (a product of the fact that governors and many social sectors were primarily interested in securing new revenue and only secondarily concerned with the type of tax used to achieve the revenue growth). But opposition to the taxes was not equal: whereas sales tax opposition was concentrated overwhelmingly in a small segment of the business community (retail merchants), income tax opposition was broadly opposed by business leaders of all types. This extensive opposition often made income tax adoption a heavier lift than sales tax adoption, particularly at rates that would yield significant revenue. Nonetheless, it is crucial to recognize that this observation is only true *on balance across the country*. As alluded to earlier, the matrix of coalitions and alignments on the tax issue varied significantly by state. Influential groups whose tax adoption preferences were inconsistent (e.g., farm associations, teachers' organizations, and labor unions) changed their positions at different times, making the process of coalitional formation highly fluid and tenuous. State-level struggles over New Deal Era taxation policy thus featured many twists and turns, and the ultimate outcomes of these struggles resulted in rejection of the sales tax in favor of the income tax more than once.

Describing and Explaining the State-Level Outcomes

In considering the taxation outcomes in the American states during the 1930s, it is important to distinguish between two different aspects of taxation: tax adoption/usage and tax reliance. As we will see, developments in these two aspects of taxation did not go hand in hand. Particularly among state income taxes, adoption often did not lead to reliance in any meaningful sense. Nonetheless, state adoptions of income taxes during the 1930s mattered even if these taxes did not generate a great deal of revenue in their early years. This is because the enactment of such taxes had path-dependent effects that, over the coming decades, would cause states to rely on them more and more.

Tax Adoption/Usage Patterns

Figure 1.2 is a map depicting usage of the personal income tax, corporate income tax, and general sales tax across the forty-eight states in 1938, following the intensive 1933–1937 period. States are divided into five categories: those that levied only one income tax (usually the personal income tax) but not a sales tax, those that levied both income taxes and no sales tax, those that levied a sales tax but neither income tax, those that levied all three taxes, and those that levied none of the three.

A close examination of the map in Figure 1.2 reveals a variety of imperfect regional patterns. The most noteworthy of these patterns is in the Northeast, where not a single state permanently adopted a sales tax during the 1930s.[58] Also noteworthy is the industrial Midwest, where most states adopted a sales tax but neither type of income tax.[59] Lastly, in many northern states where populism and later progressivism were historically influential, income taxes were used while the sales tax was not. Perhaps most surprisingly, the South—the country's most distinctive region in many other ways—does not evince a unique pattern in terms of state government tax usage during this period.

While regional differences are apparent, it is also clear that they only account for a small percentage of the observed variation. Within each of the

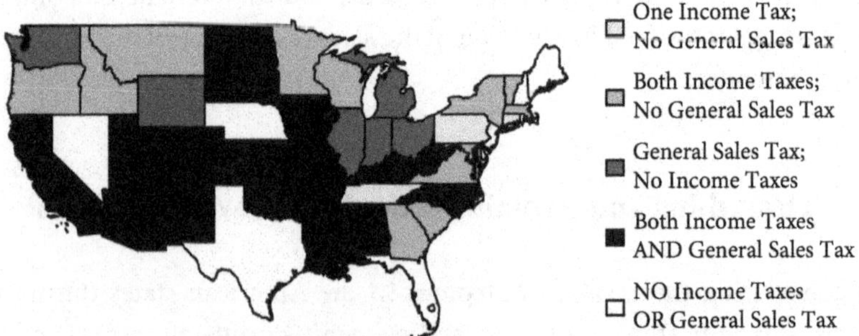

Figure 1.2 Usage of Personal Income Tax, Corporate Income Tax, and Sales Tax by State, 1938

Source: U.S. Census, *Financial Statistics of States: 1938*

[58] Several Northeastern states, including New York and Pennsylvania, adopted temporary sales taxes that were allowed to expire after a few years at most.

[59] One industrial Midwestern states—Illinois—adopted an income tax that was later ruled unconstitutional by the state supreme court.

country's regions, one can see states representing more than one category. Indeed, a close examination of the map reveals pairs of otherwise highly similar states that nonetheless wound up with different tax structures by the end of the 1930s (e.g., Oregon and Washington, North and South Carolina, Wisconsin and Michigan, New York and Pennsylvania). This suggests that explaining state tax adoptions during the 1930s requires something more than a simple, parsimonious account.

Indeed, the few previous scholarly efforts to systematically explain New Deal Era state taxation choices concluded that the complexity of factors influencing these choices render a general account of them elusive. An early such effort, by a team of Columbia University economists who interviewed many involved in sales taxation fights around the country in the early 1930s, observed that these fights featured "every possible combination of fiscal and personal forces," making it difficult to disentangle the most important factors at work in leading to sales tax adoptions.[60] A more recent effort in a 2010 doctoral dissertation opined that, while the politics of taxation across states featured many "common dynamics," the outcomes of state-level taxation fights were "highly contingent" and depended on numerous state-specific factors that are "not easily gauged in a systematic or quantitative way."[61]

Despite the inherent complexity of state taxation politics in the 1930s, several cross-state patterns concerning why states wound up with the taxes that they did can be discerned. These patterns are best expressed by explaining adoption *failures* rather than successes. With regard to income taxes, there are two factors that consistently helped to scuttle adoption efforts. First, as discussed earlier, the constitutional barriers posed by uniformity clauses directly contributed to the failure to adopt personal income taxes in five medium-sized or large states (Illinois, Michigan, Pennsylvania, Tennessee, and Washington). In another soon-to-be-important state (Florida), a constitutional provision explicitly prohibiting income taxation kept the tax off the policy agenda completely. Clearly, then, state constitutions played a big role in shaping state taxation outcomes, largely by precluding income taxes.

The threat posed by capital mobility was a second important factor that prevented income taxes from being adopted in multiple states. As described above, corporations and business leaders were generally the strongest opponents of income taxes and often warned that their enactment would cause

[60] Carl Shoup, *The Sales Tax in the American States*, 22.
[61] Hindman, "The Rise and Fall of Wealth Taxation," 444.

businesses to flee to other states. In a few states, concerns about the possible exit of wealthy taxpayers rather than businesses played a direct role in preventing income tax adoptions. In Rhode Island, for example, state policymakers considering the income tax were keenly aware of what was called "the Newport Situation"—the fact that many of the country's wealthiest citizens resided in the resort city of Newport and would not be happy about being subjected to a Rhode Island income tax.[62] Concerns about alienating the denizens of Newport played a major role in keeping the income tax off Rhode Island's books until the early 1970s (despite the fact that Rhode Island's constitution did not feature a uniformity clause).[63]

Turning to sales taxes, perhaps the strongest factor weighing against sales taxation efforts was the political strength of retail merchants. As discussed above, retail merchants constituted the only economic sector in most states that consistently and unambiguously opposed retail sales taxation. While it is impossible to measure the political power of interest groups across states in the early 1930s, the Columbia University case studies of sales tax adoption efforts during this period suggest that the retail merchant lobby was exceptionally strong in the Northeastern states, and this may well account for the failure of the sales tax to be adopted in this region.[64]

Another factor that occasionally led to the failure of sales tax adoption efforts was the presence of a popular referendum option for nullifying statutes passed by the state legislature. While the opinions of ordinary, unorganized citizens seem to have played a depressingly small role in state taxation policy debates, public opinion became important where it could be marshaled for the purpose of overturning laws at the ballot box. In states where a citizen-initiated voter referendum on sales tax laws could be put on the ballot, such referendums *always* resulted in voters eliminating sales taxes. These nullifications happened in four states (Arkansas, Idaho, Oregon, and North Dakota).[65] In Arkansas and North Dakota, state legislatures eventually found ways of passing sales taxes that avoided another

[62] Rhode Island Advisory Tax Commission, "Report of the Rhode Island Advisory Tax Commission to His Excellency, Robert E. Quinn, Governor of the State of Rhode Island," (Providence, RI, 1938).

[63] Newhouse, *Constitutional Uniformity and Equality in State Taxation*, 11.

[64] Shoup et al., *The Sales Tax in the American States*, 111–134; Hindman, "The Rise and Fall of Wealth Taxation," 502.

[65] Shoup, *The Sales Tax in the American States*, 145–149, 259–264, 298–302; Hindman, "The Rise and Fall of Wealth Taxation," 511. Previous research seems to have missed Idaho voters' nullification of that state's sales tax law in 1936. "Proclamation Ends Idaho Sales Tax," *The Post-Register* (Idaho Falls, ID), November 25, 1936, 1.

popular referendum, but in Idaho and Oregon, the referendum results effectively killed sales tax enactment efforts during the 1930s. Importantly, while income tax statutes were also occasionally nullified via referenda, there were multiple occasions in which voter referenda resulted in income tax *approval*. This suggests that ordinary citizens in the 1930s were more willing to accept income than sales taxation at the state level.

The foregoing variables only get us so far, however; numerous additional factors played an important role in particular states. In Wisconsin and Minnesota, political culture seems to have mattered: the strong progressive tradition of these states made them unusually inhospitable territory for sales tax adoption efforts. In Texas, natural resource wealth mattered: policymakers discovered that they could generate much new revenue via raising that state's crude oil tax and levying a new tax on natural gas, without resorting to either sales or income taxation.[66] Still more factors (too numerous to list here) come through in the histories of individual states; the sheer number of them makes a simple explanation of state tax adoptions in the 1930s unattainable. As we will see, state tax usage during the 1930s is far more easily incorporated into social scientific analyses as an *independent variable* explaining tax usage in later decades than as a *dependent variable* to be explained in the first place.

Tax Reliance Patterns

In contrast to tax adoption/usage, state tax reliance in the 1930s is fairly easy to explain. Before delving into explanation, however, it is necessary to describe the difference between tax usage and tax reliance patterns across the states. This difference can be succinctly summarized as follows: for general sales taxes, adoption almost invariably led to major reliance, but for income taxes it did not.

The much greater reliance on sales taxation than income taxation by states in the 1930s can be clearly seen in Figure 1.3, which presents maps showcasing the percentage of tax revenue received by each state from the personal income tax, corporate income tax, and general sales tax in 1939. As the maps show, states with personal and corporate income taxes generally received

[66] E.T. Miller, "The Historical Development of the Texas State Tax System," *Southwestern Historical Quarterly* 55, no. 1 (1951): 1–29.

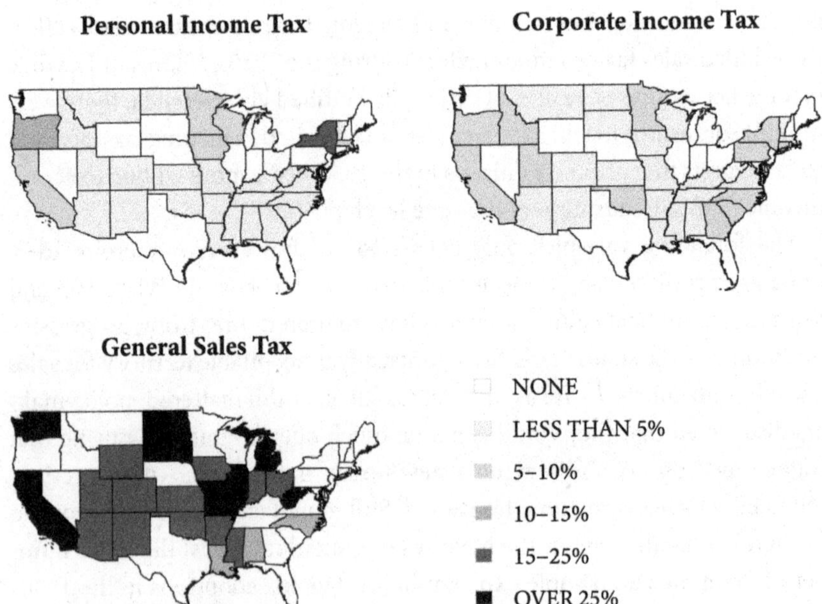

Figure 1.3 Percentage of Tax Revenue from Income and Sales Taxes, 1939
Source: U.S. Census, *Financial Statistics of States: 1939*

small shares of their tax revenue from them, while the sales tax almost always composed much larger shares of tax revenue among those states that had adopted it. Indeed, among the fifteen states that used all three taxes in 1939, the average share of tax revenue raised by the general sales tax in 1939 was 20.0%, while the corresponding percentages for personal and corporate income taxes were only 3.4% and 3.7%, respectively.[67]

What explains why state personal income taxes, whose adoptions were fought for by many throughout the 1920s and 1930s, ended up being relatively unimportant fiscal instruments after they were adopted? A useful way of answering this question is to focus on states that adopted general sales taxes *after* they adopted income taxes. Since it is generally easier to raise rates on an already-existing tax than it is to enact an entirely new tax, one might think that lawmakers in income tax states would have raised income tax rates in response to new revenue demands before seeking to enact a sales tax. And yet, in ten states, legislatures ultimately chose to adopt a sales tax in lieu of

[67] Based on calculations from the U.S. Census, *Financial Statistics of States: 1939.*

expanding income taxes that were already in place. In all these states, the sales tax ended up vastly outstripping the income tax as a source of revenue.

A cursory examination of these states reveals a key factor leading some legislatures to enact a sales tax in lieu of expanding income taxes: because it could be collected year-round, the sales tax was the optimal way to secure new revenue *immediately*. The need for immediate new revenue was particularly pronounced in 1933, when numerous states found themselves on the hook for funds required for participation in FERA, the national government's poor relief program. For example, after FERA chief Harry Hopkins publicly threatened to discontinue the disbursement of federal poor relief expenditures to Missouri until the state's leaders ponied up the state's share of FERA funding, the Missouri legislature mobilized into action. While a few other taxation proposals (including a potential personal income tax increase) were debated, legislative leaders rapidly coalesced around a plan to levy a sales tax for poor relief purposes. As the chief sponsor of the measure in the state senate made clear, the main advantage of the sales tax was that it would allow the state to promptly fulfill its FERA obligations: "If you want revenue, here is a way to get it and get it quickly."[68]

Still, the need to raise immediate funds cannot provide a full explanation for the decisions of numerous states to rely so much more heavily on the sales tax than the income tax during the 1930s. Not all decisions to enact sales taxes following income tax adoptions were made under the same level of pressure that Missouri's leaders faced at the end of 1933. Kansas—Missouri's western neighbor—provides an example of a state that adopted both forms of income taxation and later, following a protracted debate that did not feature a firm deadline, also enacted a sales tax that proved to be a much more significant revenue generator.

Kansas' income taxes were adopted in 1933, capping a decade-long effort to bring income taxation to the state. Prior to 1933, much of that effort was focused on passing a state constitutional amendment to override the constitution's uniformity clause and explicitly authorize graduated income taxation. After several failed attempts, a proposed amendment to this effect was ratified by Kansas voters in the 1932 election. Supporters of the amendment presented a graduated personal income tax as a limited revenue source oriented toward replacing the property tax as a source of state government

[68] "Retailers Oppose Proposed State Income Tax Levy," *St. Louis Globe-Democrat*, November 16, 1933, 4.

revenue, rather than generating additional revenue for the state. When it gathered in Topeka the following year, the Kansas Legislature passed personal and corporate income taxes aligned with this goal; the rates of the taxes were low and money from them would be used to reduce property taxes.

Because the adoption of the income taxes did not result in higher overall revenue levels, few were surprised when the revenue issue reemerged in Kansas just a few years after the income tax enactment. By 1937, the issue was near the top of the agenda for Kansas policymakers, as the legislature was planning to authorize a variety of new programs (including the intergovernmental components of the Social Security Act and an equalization program for education) that would require substantially greater revenue. Having observed numerous other states adopting a variety of taxes in the previous five years, Kansas leaders entered the 1937 legislative session with a clear picture of what the available options for raising revenue were.[69]

In a speech to the legislature at the beginning of the 1937 session, Gov. Walter Huxman endorsed raising revenue through instituting a sales tax along with a severance tax on oil and a modest increase in personal income tax rates. Under Huxman's proposal, 57% of new state revenue would come from the sales tax while only 15% would come from the income tax increase.[70] Huxman stated: "I know that a sales tax is unpopular, but...if we are going to finance old age assistance...it is absolute necessary that we have a sales tax."[71] This claim was challenged by editorialists in Kansas' rural newspapers and by farm organizations, who argued that raising the top rates of the state's income tax to significantly higher levels could yield all the funds necessary to finance the state's new policy responsibilities.[72]

In a report issued to state legislators, the Kansas Legislative Council (the research arm of the legislature) estimated that a retail sales tax of 2% would yield $10,000,000 of additional revenue for the state annually. By contrast, the Council estimated that a comprehensive revamping of the state's income taxes—including an increase in the top personal rate from 4% to 7%, an increase in the corporate income tax rate from 2% to 6%, and the use of personal exemptions instead of credits—would yield just under $4,000,000 annually. To get the same amount of revenue as a 2% sales tax, the legislature

[69] "Howe Discusses Taxation in Kiwanis Club Meeting," *Manhattan Republic* (Manhattan, KS), February 4, 1937, 5.

[70] "Sales Tax to Kansas After All," *Iola Register* (Iola, KS), February 17, 1937, 1

[71] "Sales Tax Proposed by Huxman," *Hutchinson News* (Hutchinson, KS), February 17, 1937.

[72] "Sales Tax It is," *Hutchinson News* (Hutchinson, KS), February 18, 1937.

would have thus had to supplement the income tax increase with the adoption of a variety of new taxes, including an oil severance tax.[73] Legislative leaders likely reasoned that the easiest way to solve Kansas' revenue problems was the adoption of a simple and straightforward tax that would fill up the state's coffers quickly.

Over the course of the next few months of the legislative session, a fight brewed between forces favoring Gov. Huxman's general approach of raising revenue principally through a sales tax and those favoring raising new revenue largely through the income tax. Like in many other states, business groups promoted the first approach, while farm and labor organizations worked on behalf of the latter.[74] Also, like in other states, state legislators dragged their feet, avoiding the tax issue until the last week of the legislative session.[75] In the end, the legislature rejected the governor's recommendation of a multi-pronged approach to taxation, instead adopting a 2% sales tax to meet nearly all the state's new revenue needs.[76]

The legislature's decision to finance the state's new programs almost exclusively through a sales tax (and to impose a 2% rather than a 1% rate) caught Gov. Huxman by surprise. In reaction, the Governor expressed disappointment, saying that he had hoped the legislature would have passed a lower-rate sales tax alongside and oil severance tax to fund the state's obligations.[77] Editorialists in newspapers across the state also criticized the legislature for its last-minute, heavy-handed decision. Calling the 2% sales tax regressive and unfair, they suggested that the legislature could have funded the state's new programs through a mix of income tax increases and new severance taxes instead.[78] Over time, however, it became clear that the legislature's plan worked as intended; within months, the state's coffers filled with enough money to support its new programs, and Kansas citizens gradually became accustomed to the sales tax.

[73] "Potential Sources of Additional Revenue from Taxation," Kansas Legislative Council, Publication #54, January 1937.

[74] "To Fight a Sales Tax," *Emporia Gazette* (Emporia, KS), March 5, 1937, 4; "Nothing Done Yet," *Iola Register*, March 9, 1937, 4e; "State News," *Fairview Enterprise* (Fairview, KS), March 18, 1937, 4.

[75] "Face Tax Conflict in Topeka," *Wichita Eagle* (Wichita, KS), March 22, 1937, 1

[76] "Pass 387 Laws in Session," *Wichita Eagle* (Wichita, KS), April 1, 1937, 1. The legislature also legalized beer and passed a beer tax, which was expected to raise $1 million (in comparison to the $10 million to be raised by the general sales tax).

[77] "Legislators Pass Vital Measures in Last Hours after Dawdling Weeks," *Hutchinson News* (Hutchinson, KS), March 31, 1937, 1.

[78] "The New Laws," *Manhattan Mercury* (Manhattan, KS), April 1, 1937, 10; "The Governor's Job," *Iola Register* (Iola, KS), April 3, 1937, 4.

The Kansas case study demonstrates likely the most important reason for why states came to rely upon the sales tax more than the income tax: doing so was simply the easiest path forward. Sales taxes offered massive new revenue through a single, relatively uncomplicated taxing structure. In Kansas' case, a basic 2% tax on most retail sales solved almost all the state's budget problems in the late 1930s. Despite their greater progressivity (even without graduated rates) and the fact that voters initially seemed more likely to accept them, income taxes posed a host of difficulties that made legislatures less likely to turn to them to finance major new spending programs. The high rates of the federal income tax limited the rate structures of state income taxes, particularly when combined with unrelenting pressure from business interests and wealthy taxpayers to keep rates low. Without high top rates, state income taxes were generally unable to fund large increases in state spending. For this reason, the long processes leading to the adoption of income taxes, often involving state constitutional amendment referenda followed by extensive debates over income tax bills, tended to result in income tax laws whose overall revenue-generating abilities were quite small. These laws were often, as in Kansas' case, aimed at facilitating property tax reductions rather than generating revenue for a more expansive state government. Sales taxes, on the other hand, simultaneously provided a quicker path to adoption and greater revenue post-adoption. As a result, they were a tax that most states could not resist.

The Non-Importance of Party

Readers of the foregoing examinations of state-level taxation politics in the 1930s will perhaps have noticed the absence from the analyses of a factor well-known to observers of twenty-first-century American state politics: partisanship. The reason for this absence is simple: unlike in the modern era, party control of state government played very little role in shaping state tax choices during the New Deal Era. To demonstrate this, I classify state governments based on their partisan compositions during the crucial 1933–1937 period and consider whether states with different patterns of party control were more or less likely to adopt or increase income and sales taxes during these years. States are classified into three categories (primarily Democrat-controlled, primarily Republican-controlled, and primarily exhibiting divided government) based on an average of annual additive scales measuring Democratic party control of state legislative and executive institutions.[79] Additionally, southern states are further separated into their own category because of the unique absence of two-party politics in the South prior to the 1960s.[80]

Figure 1.4 is a bar graph clustered according to each of the four state categories. The bars in the figure indicate, for each category, the total number

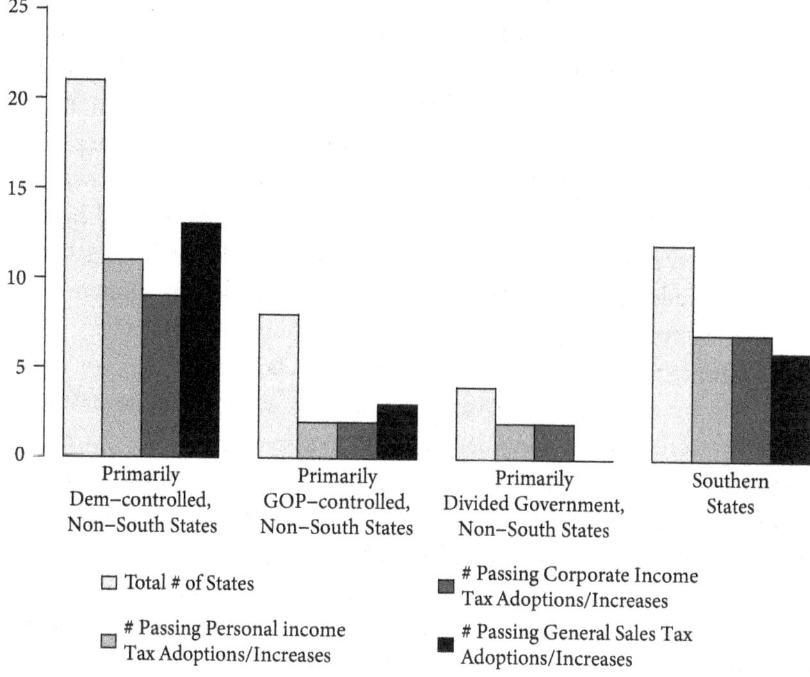

Figure 1.4 The Impact of Party Control of State Government on Income and Sales Tax Adoptions/Increases, 1933–1937

Sources: State Tax Actions Dataset; Walter Dean Burnham, Partisan Division of American State Governments, 1834–1985 (Ann Arbor, MI: Inter-university Consortium for Political and Social Research [producer and distributor], 1992)

[79] For each year between 1933 and 1937, a Democratic governor was worth 0.5 points, a Democrat-controlled lower chamber was worth 0.25 points, and a Democrat-controlled upper chamber was worth 0.25 points, adding up to a high score of 1 (indicating a state under complete Democratic control), a low score of 0 (indicating a state under complete Republican control), and a middle score of 0.5 (indicating a state with a governor from one party and a legislature controlled by the other), etc. Based on a five-year average of the scores, states were classified as "primarily Democrat-controlled" if they had a score above 0.66, "primarily GOP-controlled" if they had a score below 0.33, and "primarily divided government" if they had a score between 0.33 and 0.66. Minnesota and Nebraska were excluded due to their non-partisan legislatures during this period.

[80] The South is defined as all states of the former Confederacy plus Kentucky and Oklahoma.

of states as well as the number that enacted adoptions or rate increases for the personal income tax, corporate income tax, and general sales tax. As the figure shows, part of the reason for why state-level partisanship has such little bearing on state tax outcomes during this period is that there is little variation in the former. In the aftermath of the Democratic landslides in the 1932 and 1934 elections, Republicans controlled very few state governments. Thus, the overwhelming majority of states in this period are either primarily Democrat-controlled non-southern states, or Southern states where the Democratic Party enjoyed complete hegemony. Nonetheless, when either of these categories is compared to the small number of Republican-controlled states and divided-government states, no meaningful differences in income or sales tax policy are apparent. Indeed, rather than inter-category variation in state tax policy, the figure reveals substantial *intra-category* variation: across each of the categories and for nearly all the taxes, around half the states enacted adoptions or rate increases. Clearly, the tax choices state governments made during the New Deal Era were not heavily influenced by whether Democrats or Republicans controlled their institutions.[81]

The weak impact of party control on state tax policy choices in the 1930s can be explained by a variety of factors. First, the state parties of the 1930s were generally not ideological institutions, but rather patronage-based organizations whose leaders and rank-and-file were motivated more by the promise of material gain than by substantive policy considerations.[82] In states where party organizations were weak, the parties were often riven by ideological battles between progressive and conservative factions.[83] Such intraparty factionalism was related to the fact that, in many states, the political parties were not tightly linked to the interest groups that led the charge in statehouse battles over substantive issues like tax policy, as they are today. While Republicans tended to be closer to state business lobbies and Democrats tended to be closer to labor unions, the case studies of the era reveal plenty of examples of interest groups striking alliances with politicians from the party with which they were not usually associated.

[81] For a much more thorough, multivariate statistical analysis demonstrating the non-importance of party on state tax actions during this period, see: Hindman, "The Rise and Fall of Wealth Taxation," Appendix I, 575–633.

[82] David R. Mayhew, *Placing Parties in American Politics: Organization, Electoral Settings, and Government Activity in the United States* (Princeton, NJ: Princeton University Press, 1986).

[83] See Patterson, *The New Deal and the States*, for numerous accounts of intraparty factionalism inside the state parties of the 1930s.

Moreover, a quick scan of the governors of the era reveals tremendous intra-party ideological diversity. Among Democratic governors, for example, the 1930s featured progressive stalwarts like Gov. Herbert Lehman of New York and Gov. Frank Murphy of Michigan, pro-New Deal moderates like Gov. Henry Horner of Illinois and Gov. Paul McNutt of Indiana, and conservative reactionaries like Gov. Charles E. Martin of Oregon and Gov. Eugene Talmadge of Georgia.[84] In short, the New Deal Era politics of taxation in most statehouses was simply not influenced by party conflict in a consistent or predictable way. As this book will show in great detail, the reality inside the statehouses of the postwar era, and even more so in those of the early twenty-first century, would be very different.

The State Taxation Systems at the End of the New Deal

After a decade of major legislative action, how did the patterns of state government taxation change? Figure 1.5 sheds light on this question by comparing total state government tax revenue from seven main sources in 1925, 1930, and 1939. As can be seen, between 1930 and 1939, two types of taxation (property and inheritance) declined as an overall source of state government revenue and a third (motor vehicle taxation) remained quite steady. Motor fuel taxation, which experienced a major growth spurt in the 1920s, continued to grow rapidly as a source of state revenue during the 1930s; by 1939, it was the largest source of state government revenue, accounting for over $700 million raised during that year alone. In second place was the general retail sales tax, whose rise was even more spectacular given that, as of 1930, it had not yet become a permanent feature of any state tax system. By 1939, though, it accounted for nearly $450 million in state revenue. The growing importance of sales taxation is further accentuated by the fact that most of the taxes in the "Other Taxes" category (which also experienced a major increase during the 1930s) were selective sales taxes on alcohol, tobacco, malt beverages, and other products. In addition to adopting sales taxes, states adopted or raised numerous selective sales taxes during this period, thereby buttressing state revenues even more. And, of course, motor fuel taxation was a form of excise taxation as well, since it was passed from businesses (i.e., gas stations) to consumers.

[84] Ibid., 129–167.

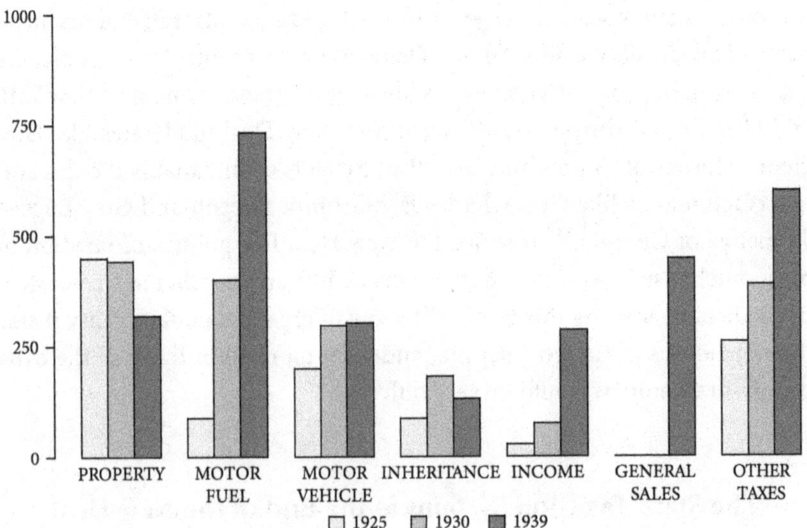

Figure 1.5 Total State Government Tax Revenue from Various Sources: 1925, 1930, 1939 (in Millions of USD)
Source: U.S. Census, *Financial Statistics of States: 1939*

The clear import of Figure 1.5 is that the revolution in state taxation during the 1930s was made possible by the ascendancy of consumption taxes. Whether through taxing motor fuel, general retail sales, or specific sin items and recreational activities, state governments in the 1930s discovered that securing revenue for themselves required tapping into the growing purchasing power of American consumers. This trend would be amplified in the postwar period, but, as this chapter has shown, it began in earnest during the New Deal.

2

The Fiscal Coordination Movement of the New Deal Era

> "It is apparent, I think, to all students of government that there is urgent need for better machinery of cooperation between Federal, State and local governments in many fields ... Two notable instances are the coordination of law enforcement and the interrelation of fields of taxation. The latter question has long seemed to me one of prime importance."
>
> —President Franklin Roosevelt, letter to Henry W. Toll (Chair of the Interstate Assembly), February 18, 1935

The fiscal crises facing the states and the consequent surge in state tax activity during the Great Depression had reverberations that were felt well beyond the sphere of state politics. Although state fiscal policies were formerly matters of primarily local interest, the developments of the late-1920s and early-1930s made them matters of national concern. More than that, the state-federal taxation relationship, which had rarely received much attention from national policymakers, became an important topic of discussion among leading national interest groups and policy intellectuals, and eventually inside the halls of Congress as well. Political actors representing an array of interests and with quite disparate goals were united in their view that the emerging multi-level system of American taxation was highly flawed. More specifically, observers worried that the system was inefficient, that it subjected Americans to double taxation, that it crippled business, and that it threatened the ability of all levels of government to meet their revenue needs. In response to these concerns, numerous plans to create a vastly different national-state tax relationship were proposed. As a 1943 Treasury Department report recounted, "The volume of discussion was so heavy as to almost defy classification."[1]

[1] *Federal, State, and Local Government Fiscal Relations; Letter from the Acting Secretary of the Treasury Transmitting in Response to S. Res. 160*, Senate Document No. 69 (1943), 72.

Coordination Failure. Adam S. Myers, Oxford University Press. © Oxford University Press (2026).
DOI: 10.1093/9780197831878.003.0003

But despite the extensive debate over intergovernmental fiscal reform, the 1930s passed without any major congressional action to revise the state-federal taxation relationship. Instead, the set of conditions that began to emerge in the early-1930s—a progressive federal tax system, generally regressive (though highly diverse) state tax systems, many overlapping federal and state taxes, and little intergovernmental tax coordination—had largely congealed by the end of the decade. That these conditions seemed to please no one made little difference in spurring Congress to act.

The lack of headway made on fiscal coordination efforts in the Depression-Era U.S. is especially noteworthy when compared to action on the same front in the world's other major federal democracies of this period. In many of these countries, the global economic crisis of the 1930s led political leaders to make major changes facilitating greater subnational fiscal uniformity and suppressing subnational tax competition. In Australia, for example, state and national policymakers reached an intergovernmental agreement during the early-1930s establishing near-uniformity in state income taxes, and the national government created the Commonwealth Grants Commission, an agency charged with reducing inequalities in the fiscal capacities of the Australian states.[2] When contrasted with the Australian experience, the lack of progress made in the U.S. toward standardizing the tax systems of the American states and limiting interstate tax competition is striking.

This chapter presents a broad overview of the extensive debate over the intergovernmental taxation relationship that occurred in the nation's capital during the New Deal Era. After briefly discussing fiscal coordination efforts prior to the 1930s, it will show how the state-level fiscal developments discussed in Chapter 1 prompted numerous groups to advocate for major intergovernmental tax reforms in Washington, D.C. Chief among these groups were the state governments themselves, but tax professionals, corporate and business leaders, the farm lobby, and (to a lesser extent) labor unions and left-wing activists were also active. After describing the perspectives and goals of each of these groups, I turn to the tepid reaction inside Congress and examine the one reform plan that came close to passage—a proposal to distribute federal alcohol tax funds to the states

[2] O.J. McDiarmid, "Federal Subsidies to the States in Australia," *Taxes* 17 (1939), 271–272; Robert Murray Haig, "Amalgamated Federal-State Tax Administration in Australia," *Proceedings of the Annual Conference on Taxation under the Auspices of the National Tax Association*, vol. 30 (1937), 370–380.

following the end of Prohibition—to demonstrate why serious efforts at change consistently stalled on Capitol Hill. Stated simply, every proposal to reform the state-federal taxation relationship would have clearly benefited some state governments while negatively impacting others, and members of Congress—wary of provoking regional battles—decided not to address the intergovernmental fiscal relationship head-on.

Fiscal Coordination Efforts before the Great Depression

In the decades prior to the 1930s, the issue of national-state tax coordination began to percolate but was not yet a central matter of debate in American fiscal policy. The two intertwined questions that would dominate the tax coordination debate in later decades—how to distribute taxation authority between the national and state governments, and how much interstate tax competition to countenance within the American federal system—were starting to be discussed, though without much regularity or rigor. Some of the earliest discussions of state tax competition occurred in meetings of the Conference on Uniform State Laws, an organization founded in 1892 with the goal of advancing the standardization of state-level statutes, including in the area of taxation. During the 1910s, concerns about intergovernmental tax conflicts emerged in response to the growth of income taxation at both the state and federal levels. Representatives of forty-four states gathered in 1917 to discuss the threat posed by federal "encroachment" on state tax fields, but decided to delay further action until after the end of World War I.[3]

During the 1920s, national-state tax coordination efforts largely centered on a single tax field—inheritance or "death" taxation—resulting in perhaps the only enactment of a national law explicitly designed to suppress state tax competition in American history. The backdrop to this effort was the widespread adoption of inheritance taxes by states in the late-nineteenth and early-twentieth centuries, resulting in thirty-four states having enacted these taxes by 1916. During this same year, the national government also entered the inheritance tax field. Between 1916 and 1924, several additional states adopted inheritance taxes, so that by 1924, only three states did not have them.[4]

[3] *Federal, State, and Local Government Fiscal Relations*, 70.

[4] Jeffrey A. Cooper, "Interstate Competition and State Death Taxes: A Modern Crisis in Historical Perspective," *Pepperdine Law Review* 33, no. 4 (May 2006): 837.

Despite the increase in the number of states with inheritance taxes, growth in state-level inheritance tax revenue slowed significantly in the early-1920s. This was largely due to competitive pressures unleashed by the actions of the holdout states, most notably Florida, which had adopted a strategy of using tax policy to lure wealthy residents from other states into its borders. Florida's aggressive approach (which included the passage of state constitutional amendments banning inheritance and income taxation) was aided by the rise of the automobile, which allowed wealthy northerners to relocate to the Sunshine State to escape their home states' tax burdens with relative ease. Other states quickly took notice of Florida's actions. A few, most importantly Nevada, sought to imitate Florida by eliminating their inheritance taxes completely, while most merely sought to cut their inheritance tax rates.[5]

Faced with the competitive threat emanating from Florida on the one hand, and the growth of federal inheritance taxation on the other, the leaders of numerous states recognized that their ability to raise revenue from inheritance taxes was imperiled. They thus convened a series of conferences in the mid-1920s to see if they could come up with a unified response. These conferences featured extensive disagreement among state delegates about whether the federal inheritance tax or economic competition from Florida and its potential emulators constituted the larger danger, but eventually a solution to both problems emerged: a credit on state inheritance taxes paid toward the federal inheritance tax. This approach would likely incentivize all states to adopt inheritance taxes with similar rate structures, thereby solving the interstate competition problem. Moreover, if the credit was sufficiently generous, it would allow states to raise significant revenue from the inheritance tax even with a federal tax on top of it. Congress responded to the states' demands by creating a tax credit worth 25% of the federal inheritance tax in 1924, and then raised it to a whopping 80% of the federal tax in 1926. With this incentive in place, every state except Nevada got on board. Even Florida, whose entire economic development strategy rested on its status as a tax haven, repealed its constitutional prohibition on inheritance taxation and passed a law to take advantage of the federal tax credit.

To understand how passage of the state inheritance tax credit—a unique event in the history of American federalism—could occur, it is important to emphasize two factors contributing to this outcome, the convergence of

[5] Cooper, "Interstate Competition and State Death Taxes," 836–837, 849–850.

which would not obtain in the future. The first of these factors was the near-unanimity of state government elites on the inheritance tax issue. To reiterate, state-level inheritance taxation was fully developed by the time the national government adopted its inheritance tax, and the holdout states were few. There were no significant regional or ideological divisions among the states in terms of inheritance tax usage, and state political leaders from every part of the country were sharply critical of Florida's behavior and wanted to put a stop to it. The second factor was the highly favorable fiscal position of the national government in the 1920s. Freed of war-related expenditures and enjoying an influx of revenue thanks to the postwar economic boom, Uncle Sam was flush with money during the twenties and Congress therefore saw little danger in creating a tax credit that would deprive the government of much revenue. It was within this unique context that Congress agreed to create the tax credit. After the critical juncture of state taxation in the early-1930s, state tax systems would permanently diverge, making interstate agreement on tax coordination efforts much harder to come by, even in moments when the national government was relatively unconcerned about its own fiscal condition.

The Great Depression and the Fiscal Coordination Push, 1929–1940

With the onset of the Great Depression and the consequent conjuncture of events described in Chapter 1 (the collapse of state property tax systems, the increase in state revenue needs, and the dramatic growth in new state tax adoptions), the debate over national-state fiscal coordination was transformed in several important ways. First, although before it had been an obscure topic receiving only periodic attention, in the 1930s, it was a significant topic receiving regular attention. Second, although before the focus of coordination efforts was on a few specific taxes (e.g., the inheritance tax), in the 1930s, coordination efforts considered almost all the taxes assessed at the state or federal levels. In this way, the coordination efforts of the 1930s were much more self-consciously systemic in their goals than those of previous decades. Finally, although before the main parties advocating for greater coordination were state governments, in the 1930s, a much larger range of groups were involved. States continued to lead the efforts (indeed, as we will see, they were even more active than before), but they were by no means the only political actors with an interest in the issue.

The result of all these developments was the emergence of a movement, in the sense of "an organization, coalition, or alliance of people working to advance a shared political, social, or artistic objective."[6] Thus, the authors of the 1943 Treasury Department report referenced earlier regularly referred to the "fiscal coordination movement" that took root during the 1930s. In some ways, however, the term "movement" is misleading, since the mélange of groups interested in fiscal coordination—states, business leaders, and farm organizations, among them—were united chiefly in their dissatisfaction with the chaotic, uncoordinated system that was developing and their desire to lend it greater order.[7] These groups did not, however, share a common vision regarding what should replace the nascent system. Indeed, in some cases, the groups were divided internally as well as externally, and the lack of a coherent approach to coordination that they offered was part of what doomed their efforts in Congress.

State Governments and "The Chicago Group" of Intergovernmental Organizations

As mentioned above, the leading proponents of national-state fiscal coordination—both before and during the 1930s—were state governments. However, the nature of their advocacy during the 1930s was much different from what it was in previous decades. To begin with, their advocacy in the 1930s was far more organized: over the course of the 1920s and early-1930s, states built a semi-integrated network of associations whose goals were to foster greater collaboration between state governments and fight for the states' interests in Washington, D.C. This network came to be known by the moniker "The Chicago Group," since the offices of its most significant members were based in the Windy City.[8] The originating entity from which "the Chicago Group" developed was the American Legislators' Association (ALA). Established in 1922 with the goal of fostering greater dialogue among legislators from different states, the ALA rapidly became a forum

[6] "Movement," Oxford English Dictionary, https://www.oed.com/view/Entry/123031?redirectedFrom=movement#eid, accessed December 21, 2021.

[7] Indeed, the authors of the Treasury Department report acknowledged that calling the diverse groups working on intergovernmental fiscal reform in the 1930s a "movement" was a stretch. As they wrote: "The unanimity of purpose usually associated with a *movement* has been hardly discernable [among the groups working on the issue]." *Federal, State, and Local Government Fiscal Relations*, 91.

[8] "Federal, State, and Local Government Fiscal Relations," 75.

for promoting the interests and needs of state governments in the face of expanding national government power.[9] During the early-1930s, the dominant issue in ALA meetings was taxation, specifically the perceived threat that increased federal taxation posed to the vitality of the states. Particularly concerning to the ALA was the national government's adoption of a gasoline tax in 1932. As discussed in Chapter 1, the gasoline tax had been enacted by all forty-eight states during the 1920s and, by the end of the decade, had become the leading source of state government revenue. Congress' invasion of the tax a few years later was widely condemned by state-level politicians, who saw Congress' actions as presaging a future in which the national government colonized an ever-growing number of revenue sources and crowded out state taxes in the process.

Motivated to act by this prospect, the ALA organized a meeting of a broader range of state government officials, called the Interstate Assembly, which took place in Washington, D.C. in February 1933. Meeting attendees received a warm in-person welcome from President Herbert Hoover and an encouraging message from President-elect Franklin Roosevelt, both of whom strongly endorsed the Assembly's goals of establishing greater tax coordination between the national government and the states.[10] They also heard speeches from the country's leading public finance experts, each of which offered different proposals for securing the revenue needs of both levels of government. In response to these speeches, the attendees made two important decisions. First, they established a permanent commission—the Interstate Commission on Conflicting Taxation (ICCT)—whose charge would be to carefully examine the various tax conflicts between the national government and the states and make recommendations regarding how they might be eliminated. Second, they empowered the newly appointed members of the Commission to engage in direct negotiations with members of Congress regarding the proper division of taxation powers between the states and the national government.[11]

The decisions made at the First Interstate Assembly resulted in several promising outcomes. First, members of the ICCT sought and were granted a meeting with leading members of Congress, including Senate Finance

[9] "Chronological History of the Development of the American Legislators' Association/The Council of State Governments," *Book of the States* (Chicago: Council of State Governments, 1937).

[10] Clarence Heer, "The Interstate Commission on Conflicting Taxation," *The Tax Magazine* 11, 218–219.

[11] Heer, "The Interstate Commission on Conflicting Taxation."

Committee Chair Pat Harrison and House Ways and Means Committee Chair Robert Doughton. According to the 1935 Book of the States, this meeting, which took place in April 1933, represented the first time in American history in which "a commission representing officially designated delegates of the various state legislatures conferred with a Congressional group to coordinate federal and state legislative action."[12] At this meeting, attendees agreed upon the creation of yet another permanent organization—the Tax Revision Council—which would be made up of representatives from national, state, and local governments and whose job would be to periodically assess the intergovernmental taxation relationship.[13] Given that the Council was intended to serve as a forum in which policymakers at different levels of government would routinely enter into negotiations—a mode of governance that had very little prior precedent in the United States—its formation was viewed as being of major potential consequence. Also, as a result of this meeting, Sen. Harrison went on record as endorsing the ICCT's recommendation that the national government repeal its gas tax and leave the taxation of motor fuel to the states.[14]

Thus, by the mid-1930s, the activities of the ALA had spawned an array of offshoot organizations, including the Interstate Assembly, the ICCT, and the Tax Revision Council, all of which were advancing the goal of securing greater national-state tax coordination. Particularly productive was the ICCT, which had met seven times in the previous two years and, by the end of 1934, had prepared an extensive report, entitled "Conflicting Taxation," that detailed the scope of the double taxation problem and made recommendations regarding how to resolve it. The report started from the premise that there were three general approaches to addressing tax conflicts between the national government and the states in a way that could be satisfactory to all levels. The most centralizing approach would involve national administration of most taxes alongside the sharing of federal tax revenue with states, a somewhat less centralizing approach would involve credits for state taxes on federal taxes levied on the same source, and the most decentralizing approach would involve intergovernmental agreement for a complete segregation of tax sources between the two levels. Using these three general

[12] "Tax Troubles," *Book of the States* (1935), 86.

[13] "New Attack on Conflicting Taxation Begun by Tax Revision Council," *The Tax Magazine* 13 (1935), 432–433.

[14] *Revenue Revision, 1934, Hearings before the Committee on Ways and Means of the House of Representatives*, 73rd Cong. 834 (1934) (Brief of Mr. Seabury Mastick, of the Legislative Tax Commission of the State of New York).

approaches as guideposts, the ICCT prepared three comprehensive plans of varying degrees of centralization for presentation at the Interstate Assembly's second meeting.[15]

By the late-1930s, however, the tax policy-related activities of the "Chicago Group" organizations slowed considerably. For reasons discussed at the end of the chapter, these organizations began to move on to new priorities (in areas such as transportation and economic regulation) despite having achieved little in the way of fiscal federalism reforms. Thus, the tax coordination "movement" lost its most important backers. But this decline in support was temporary: in the postwar era, state governments joined a larger and more unified movement to reform the country's intergovernmental taxation relationship. The story behind those efforts, whose ultimate outcome was much different from the efforts of the 1930s, is told in Chapter 4.

The National Tax Association

In addition to state governments, tax professionals and experts invested much time and energy on efforts to promote intergovernmental fiscal reform during the 1930s. Many of these efforts occurred within the activities and meetings of the highly influential National Tax Association (NTA). Founded in 1907, the NTA was the pre-eminent national organization focused on fiscal policy in the early-twentieth century U.S. Because of its highly elite membership, which included the nation's top business leaders, tax lawyers, tax administrators, and public-finance academics, the organization held major sway among the country's fiscal policymakers at both the state and national levels when its members could agree on policy proposals.[16] For this reason, the proceedings of NTA conferences provide crucial evidence regarding the substance of elite debates over America's intergovernmental taxation arrangement during the early-twentieth century.

Throughout the Progressive Era, NTA members were largely united around an overarching goal: eliminating the general property tax and replacing it with a host of other state-level taxes.[17] Indeed, numerous panels in the

[15] "Conflicting Taxation: The 1935 Progress Report of the Interstate Commission on Conflicting Taxation," (Chicago: American Legislators' Association/Council of State Governments, 1935).

[16] Albert Luther Ellis III, "The Regressive Era: Progressive Era Tax Reform and the National Tax Association—Roots of the Modern American Tax Structure" (PhD Diss., Rice University, 1991).

[17] Ellis, "The Regressive Era"; Monty Hindman, "The Rise and Fall of Wealth Taxation"; and Mehrotra, *Making the Modern American Fiscal State.*

NTA conferences of the early-twentieth century explored potential new state taxes, the adoptions of which could generate enough new state government revenue to facilitate the transformation of the general property tax into a real estate tax levied by and for local governments. By the late-1920s and early-1930s, however, the NTA's quest to reform property taxation at the state and local levels was nearing completion, and the organization was increasingly moving onto other matters. One of the most important of these matters was the coordination of state and federal taxation. Indeed, a cursory examination of NTA conference proceedings between the 1910s and 1930s reveals a gradual decline in papers concerned with the relationship between state and local taxes and a sharp increase (during the late-1920s and early-1930s) in papers concerned with the relationship between state and federal taxes. As Robert Murray Haig (one of America's most prominent public finance experts in the 1930s) stated in a 1932 NTA conference paper, "After decades of obscurity ..., the subject of the relation of the tax systems of the states and the nation has emerged with startling suddenness into the spot-light ..."[18]

Those who initially put national-state tax coordination at the forefront of the NTA agenda were generally of the view that the NTA needed to advocate on behalf of greater centralization of tax administration at the national level. Two highly regarded academic economists—Haig of Columbia University and Simeon Leland of the University of Chicago—were the most forceful of these advocates. In perhaps the most clear-eyed exposition of the pro-centralization view, Leland argued in a 1930 presentation that the ideal American taxation system would be one "under the control of a single governmental unit—the national government—so as to secure uniformity of laws, administration, and burdens." In Leland's view, the nationalization and even globalization of the economy over the course of the nineteenth and early-twentieth centuries had made decentralized tax administration anachronistic; a vastly preferable system would be one in which "all tax functions save limited local licenses ... and special assessments" were exclusively administered by the national government, with proceeds shared with the states.[19] Acknowledging that the prospects for such a system were "so remote as to be quite visionary," Leland offered several practical ideas for moving in the general direction of his vision,

[18] Robert Murray Haig, "The Coordination of the Federal and State Tax Systems," *Proceedings of the Annual Conference on Taxation under the Auspices of the National Tax Association* 25 (1932): 220–235.

[19] Simeon E. Leland, "The Relations of Federal, State, and Local Finance," *Proceedings of the Annual Conference of Taxation under the Auspices of the National Tax Association* 23 (1930), 104–105.

including transferring existing state income and inheritance taxes to the national government in exchange for promises of shared revenues.[20] For his part, Haig offered a somewhat more nuanced view of the national-state taxation relationship than did Leland. Offering up a metaphor of a stream being fished by one man at each of its pools (the states) along with a more well-resourced fisherman with simultaneous access to all the pools (the national government), Haig suggested that such an arrangement would naturally lead to "the lines [becoming] entangled, the peace ... disturbed, and the two fishermen together [landing] perhaps fewer fish than one fishing alone."[21] While not going so far as to recommend complete national-level centralization like Leland, Haig nonetheless concluded that "expansion of federal administration offers on the whole fewer difficulties and greater rewards" than other available tax coordination schemes.[22]

The growing interest of the NTA membership in national-state tax coordination inevitably led to efforts to unite the organization around a plan that it could recommend to Congress. The most important of these efforts centered on a proposal developed by NTA President Franklin S. Edmonds and New York Tax Commissioner Mark Graves. The so-called Graves-Edmonds plan was introduced during Edmonds' presidential address (entitled "A Taxing Program for the Nation") during the organization's 1933 meeting.[23] It called for the national government to assume collections of all taxes on liquor, gasoline, and cigarettes, as well as for the national government to levy a manufacturers' excise tax (functionally equivalent to a "Value-Added Tax," or VAT) in place of state retail sales taxes. Proceeds from each of these taxes would be shared with the states at varying percentages and according to distinct formulas.

In his address, Edmonds was careful to avoid associating the plan with broader goals for government centralization, such as those espoused by Leland. Revenue-sharing, according to him, was merely a way of rendering the American tax system simpler and more efficient—goals that everyone shared. Edmonds made a point of rejecting the ancient premise (first advanced by the Anti-Federalists during the debates over the ratification of the U.S. Constitution) that the vitality of state governments could only be

20 Ibid., 105.

21 Haig, "The Coordination of Federal and State Tax Systems," 226.

22 Ibid., 232.

23 Franklin S. Edmonds, "[A Taxing Program for the Nation (Presidential Address)]," *Proceedings of the Annual Conference on Taxation under the Auspices of the National Tax Association* 26 (1933): 30–39.

secured via their fiscal autonomy. Pointing to Canada (where proceeds from the federal tariff had been shared with provincial governments since 1858), Edmonds argued that "there has been no decline in the independence of the provinces" since the advent of revenue-sharing.[24] Few details concerning the immediate reaction of NTA members to the Graves-Edmonds plan can be found in the minutes of the 1933 conference; it appears that members agreed to defer discussion of the plan until 1934, when a new organizational committee charged with studying the national-state fiscal relationship would report its findings.

When the NTA convened for its annual conference a year later, the committee chair announced that, due to internal disagreements regarding the Graves-Edmonds Plan, the committee had decided not to issue any recommendations regarding it, opting instead to list arguments both for and against it and let the greater NTA membership voice its thoughts. A lively discussion subsequently ensued, in which opponents of the plan loudly expressed their concerns while others came to the plan's defense. Opponents of the plan were unpersuaded that it posed no threat to state autonomy; sounding Anti-Federalist notes, they argued that transferring taxing powers to the national government would lead to the further subordination of the states over time. Russell Bradford, a tax attorney from New York, argued that nationalizing the administration of taxes "strikes at the heart of our dual government, at our institutions" and that "makes for the selling of their birthright of state and local autonomy and government" for the purpose "securing a less expensive administration."[25] Farwell Knapp of Connecticut similarly predicted that the Graves-Edmonds plan would "inevitably" lead to the "complete absorption of the states by the federal government."[26]

Supporters of the Graves-Edmonds Plan made a variety of counterarguments. Edmonds reiterated his argument that the Plan actually facilitated state autonomy by ensuring that states had the revenue with which to fulfill their traditional functions "without going down to Washington and begging for a bounty."[27] Others argued that the plan was a reasonable way to avoid the many emerging issues with state taxation of interstate commerce. Perhaps the most common refrain of the plan's supporters was that the welfare of individual American taxpayers—rather than government

[24] Ibid., 38.

[25] *Proceedings of the Annual Conference on Taxation under the Auspices of the National Tax Association* 27 (1934), 174.

[26] Ibid., 183.

[27] Ibid., 173.

efficiency or the vitality of the state governments—should be the organization's main focus. Arguing that the organization was giving "insufficient thought to ... the taxpayer ..." and pointing to the large number of new taxation laws passed by national, state, and local governments in 1933 alone, J.W. Oliver of New York argued that the NTA should "[place] expediency ahead of tradition and theory" and endorsed the Graves-Edmonds Plan as a means through which to simplify the tax system for citizens and businesses.[28]

Two years later, at the 1936 NTA conference, the chair of the committee charged with examining the national-state fiscal relationship announced that its members were hopelessly deadlocked on the Graves-Edmonds Plan and that the committee should thus be disbanded. Edmonds made a last-ditch effort on behalf of the plan, couching it once again as a means for securing the autonomy rather than the subordination of the states. The conference rebuffed his pleas, however, and the NTA thus never endorsed a formal plan for intergovernmental fiscal reform.

The Business Community

After the intergovernmental organizations based in Chicago and the NTA, the interest-group community that paid the most attention to the intergovernmental component of taxation policy was the business community. Having spent much of the 1920s focused on a generally successful effort to reduce federal income taxes, the business lobby was caught flat-footed by the unprecedented growth of taxing and spending at both the national and state levels during the Great Depression. But while business organizations in Washington, D.C. had developed an extensive set of strategies for opposing federal tax increases over the prior two decades, they had not previously approached state and local taxation as a matter of national concern, generally preferring to leave the issue to their local affiliates. By the early-1930s, however, these organizations had changed their tune. As a 1931 report published by a Chamber of Commerce committee stated: "There is a distinctly national aspect to most problems of state and local taxation and expenditures. Cumulatively these problems constitute a national question of large proportions ... with the result that nation-wide effort is required."[29]

[28] Ibid., 186–187.

[29] Chamber of Commerce of the United States, Taxation Division, "Taxation Activities: Efforts by Business Associations to Deal with Problems of State and Local Taxation and Expenditures," Box 80, Chamber of Commerce of the United States Records, Hagley Library, Wilmington, DE.

In seeking to craft a coherent response to the new reality of extensive taxation at both the national and state levels, the business community was hampered by internal divisions regarding which intergovernmental relations approach in the area of tax policy would best serve business interests. Broadly speaking, there were two camps of business groups advocating for different approaches in this area. One camp, which included organizations like the U.S. Chamber of Commerce and especially the National Association of Manufacturers (NAM), was displeased with the growth of both federal and state taxation but saw a much greater threat to business interests from the former than the latter. In their published reports, groups within this camp placed the blame for the messy new intergovernmental fiscal reality entirely on an overweening national government that had arrogantly invaded tax fields previously reserved for the states. The solution to this new reality, according to these groups, was for the national government to retreat from many of these fields. NAM, in particular, laid out a program for separating federal and state taxation based largely in the national government ceding inheritance taxation along with the motor fuel tax to the states.[30] NAM strongly opposed tax-sharing proposals emanating from the intergovernmental lobby, suggesting that separating tax authority across the national and state levels provided "a safeguard against the rise of Federal centralization and dictatorship."[31]

The second camp of business interests, which included organizations such as the American Management Association among others, was more concerned with the increasingly decentralized nature of American taxation under the New Deal than with the threat posed by a large national government. These groups worried that the growth of state alongside federal taxation would create an overcomplicated tax system that would vastly raise compliance costs for American businesses, thereby harming their bottom lines.[32] Their perspective was perhaps best encapsulated in a long essay on state and local taxation published in *Fortune Magazine*, the most splashy and

[30] Under this proposal, the states would also agree to cede most income taxes to the national government, but top federal income tax rates were to be vastly reduced. National Association of Manufacturers, "Report of the Committee on Government Finance," December 7–9, 1937, Box 23, National Association of Manufacturers Records, Hagley Library, Wilmington, DE.

[31] National Association of Manufacturers, "Report of the Committee on Government Finance," December 9–10, 1936, Box 23, National Association of Manufacturers Records, Hagley Library, Wilmington, DE.

[32] Robert Murray Haig, "The Costs to Business Concerns of Compliance with Tax Laws," *Management Review*, November 1935, 323–33.

high-profile publication of the country's business elite. The essay (featuring no author byline and thus apparently written by the magazine editors) contended that the American tax system was "the most complicated and disorderly tax system in the world," with disastrous implications for businesses and middle-class Americans.[33] Arguing that the multi-level nature of American taxation was unnecessarily inefficient and burdensome for businesses and taxpayers, the authors charged that Americans interested in lowering their tax burdens must demand intergovernmental fiscal reforms rather than "blindly directing their wrath at rising federal taxes."[34] The authors thus suggested a transformation to an ultra-centralized tax system: with the exception of property taxes, all major taxes (including both income and sales taxes) should be assessed by the national government, with a portion of their proceeds distributed to the states. Dismissing potential complaints that the centralization of taxation would violate state sovereignty, the authors argued that centralizing trends in American society and government had already rendered state sovereignty principles obsolete in all policy areas except taxation. It was high time, the authors argued, for Americans to acknowledge these developments and recalibrate the American tax system accordingly.

These starkly different responses to the new intergovernmental taxation reality in the U.S. limited the ability of the business lobby to craft a unified, coherent approach to the new intergovernmental taxation relationship. On top of that, the national-state relationship in tax policy, while routinely acknowledged as a highly important matter by business groups in all their leading publications and conferences, was ultimately but one of a plethora of issues facing business groups during the 1930s. As various scholars have written, business interests in the 1930s saw threats to their limited-government vision for the U.S. coming from nearly every direction. Given their defensive posture on such a wide array of issues, business groups had to pick their battles carefully. An examination of the records of business groups during the 1930s suggests that they paid a great deal of attention to tax policy (including state tax policy) in the early-1930s but, by the middle of the decade, had moved on to defending their interests on what they likely viewed as more pressing policy fronts.

[33] "U.S. Taxes," *Fortune*, vol. XVI (no. 6), 107.
[34] Ibid, 188.

The Farm Lobby

Another interest-group community that actively engaged in the Depression-Era discussion on intergovernmental fiscal relations in Washington, D.C. was the farm lobby. As discussed in Chapter 1, a central political goal of farmers in the first decades of the twentieth century was reducing property tax burdens, and state-level farm groups expended a tremendous amount of energy advocating on behalf of state property tax reform efforts during this period. By the late-1920s, national farm groups got into the mix as well, issuing calls for the national government to take an active role in helping state and local governments reduce their reliance on property taxes. Chief among these groups was the National Grange, which passed a resolution at its annual convention in 1927 urging Congress to share a portion of federal income tax proceeds with the states, under the assumption that access to the federally shared revenue would allow states to reduce property tax burdens. The Grange also advocated that Congress establish a special tax credit for state income taxes paid as a way of incentivizing states to adopt their own income taxes. In testimony in front of the House Ways and Means Committee, the Grange's chief national lobbyist emphasized that "it is competition between the states to gain industries that prevent so many of our states from passing a law requiring the payment of a personal income tax," and that establishing a generous tax credit for state income taxes would allow states to overcome competitive pressures.[35] Other farm groups likewise advocated for the establishment of a tax credit for state income taxes, and they were even more explicit than the Grange about the ultimate reason for encouraging state income taxation. As the spokesman of the National Farm Bureau Federation stated, "The revenues of the States under State income taxation should be used so as to reduce the property tax especially on farms and homes, not as additions to total expenditures."[36]

The fact that national farm groups were chiefly focused on reducing property tax burdens, and had only a weak commitment to progressive taxation per se, led them to shift their attention away from state tax systems once their paramount goal had been achieved. As explained in Chapter 1, states

[35] *Revenue Revision, 1932, Hearings before the Committee on Ways and Means of the House of Representatives*, 72nd Cong. 139 (1932) (Statement of Fred Brenckman, Washington, D.C., Representing the National Grange).

[36] *Revenue Revision, 1934, Hearings before the Committee on Ways and Means of the House of Representatives*, 73rd Cong. 210 (1933–1934) (Statement of Chester H. Gray, Representative, American Farm Bureau Federation, Washington, D.C.).

vastly reduced the role of property taxes in their tax systems over the course of the 1930s, but this was accomplished primarily via the increased use of regressive consumption taxes, not progressive income taxes. Farm groups at both the state and national levels routinely objected to sales taxes prior to this transition, but after it was complete, they seem to have made their peace with it. Thus, groups such as the National Grange and the National Farm Bureau Federation were no longer strongly advocating for national-state revenue-sharing schemes or pushing for changes in the federal tax code designed to encourage state income tax adoptions by the late-1930s. Because the primary objective of reducing property tax reliance had largely been met, the secondary objective of creating a more equitable tax distribution fell by the wayside.

Indifference from the Left

If the national business community presented a divided and inconsistent approach to the questions posed by New Deal-Era state tax policy, its primary opponents (workers' groups and leftist groups advocating progressive taxation) presented almost no approach at all. While an array of national groups worked hard to make the American taxation system more progressive during the 1930s, it is striking how little interest these groups showed in state tax systems or the national-state taxation relationship.

The most important national group advocating for progressive taxation in the 1930s was the People's Lobby.[37] Led by the eccentric firebrand Benjamin Marsh and famed progressive philosopher John Dewey, the People's Lobby waged a relentless and highly focused battle on behalf of redistributive taxation throughout the 1930s.[38] The group's overarching goal was encapsulated in the first line of the agenda it presented to the House Ways and Means Committee in 1934: "Socialization of the National Income through Taxation."[39] Its specific recommendations included large tax increases on corporate profits, estates, and high incomes alongside the repeal of all regressive "consumption taxes." Marsh tirelessly promoted the Lobby's

[37] Mark H. Leff, *The Limits of Symbolic Reform: The New Deal and Taxation, 1933-1939* (Cambridge University Press, 2003), 104.

[38] Mordecai Lee, *The Philosopher-Lobbyist: John Dewey and the People's Lobby, 1928–1940* (Albany, NY: SUNY Press, 2015)

[39] *Revenue Revision, 1934, Hearings before the Committee on Ways and Means of the House of Representatives*, 73rd Cong. 210 (1933–1934) (Statement of Benjamin C. Marsh, Executive Secretary of the People's Lobby of the Joint Committee on Unemployment, Washington, D.C.)

agenda through numerous congressional testimonies, public speeches, and letters to President Roosevelt. In his efforts, he was supported by allies from the nation's most important labor unions and left-wing organizations, as well as by a long list of public intellectuals who signed his petitions.[40]

Given Marsh's strong support for using taxation as a tool for large-scale wealth redistribution, one might expect that he and his allies would have rapidly noticed and organized against the most important regressive taxation trend of the 1930s: the adoption of retail sales taxes by many states. But evidence from the People's Lobby's publications as well as Marsh's speeches and congressional testimony suggests that the organization was quite slow to recognize the trend and generally unenthusiastic to fight against it. In his 1935 testimony in front of the House Ways and Means Committee, Marsh stated that "I do not think it is my function" to recommend that states change their tax systems. Speaking directly to the Southern Democratic chairman of the committee (Robert Doughton of North Carolina), Marsh further commented that "I do not think a party which is an advocate of States' rights should necessarily interfere with the stupidity of state tax systems."[41] Thus, during the crucial years of the mid-1930s when the New Deal-Era tax regime was being institutionalized, Marsh seemed to view state taxation as largely irrelevant to his goal of establishing a redistributive federal taxation regime, and thus de-emphasized its importance.

By the late-1930s, however, Marsh seemed to have gained a greater appreciation of the magnitude of regressive taxation at the state level, as well as the potential for it to grow even more in the future. Testifying once again in front of the Ways and Means Committee in 1939, he urged that Congress "make Federal aid to any State or local government contingent upon that State or local government also adopting an intelligent system of taxation."[42] He did not go beyond this statement and attempt to explain what "an intelligent system" of state and local taxation might look like. Moreover, proposals for revenue-sharing or fiscal equalization were unmentioned by Marsh or his organization.

[40] Leff, 105.

[41] *Proposed Taxation of Individual and Corporate Incomes, Inheritances, and Gifts, Before the House Ways and Means Committee*, 74th Cong. 107 (1935) (Statement of Benjamin C. Marsh, Washington, D.C., representing the People's Lobby).

[42] *Revenue Revision—1939, Before the House Ways and Means Committee*, 76th Cong. 272–274 (1939) (Statement of Benjamin C. Marsh, Executive Secretary, the People's Lobby, Inc.)

The Congressional Response

Not long after the various sectoral interests described above began their work on intergovernmental fiscal coordination, Congress entered the mix and initiated its own studies of the topic. Congress' decision to tackle the national-state taxation relationship was both a response to the demands of the sectoral interests as well as an affirmative recognition of the fact that, in the modern U.S., creating a comprehensive national tax policy required considering the fiscal situations of state and local governments. This was not the case in previous eras of American history, when, for the most part, Congress could raise taxes without taking other levels of government into account. As discussed in the introductory chapter, the small domestic public sector prior to the New Deal allowed the national and state governments to largely rely on different taxes. While tax duplication did exist and in fact grew substantially during the 1910s and 1920s, one level of government or the other tended to dominate the various tax fields, rendering such duplication inconsequential. The one major effort at tax coordination during the 1920s (that which resulted in the inheritance tax credit discussed earlier) is the exception that proves the rule.

The arrival of the Great Depression changed the relevance of federalism for national taxation policy in a variety of ways. First and foremost, the economic downturn wrought by the Depression, and the consequent need for greater social spending to combat it, caused Congress to abruptly shift its focus from tax reductions to tax increases. Whereas the 1920s were a period in which the national government, freed of its wartime spending obligations, could focus on cutting taxes to stimulate economic growth, the Great Depression forced the Congresses of the early-1930s to raise taxes and search for new revenue sources.[43] In doing so, however, members of Congress quickly recognized that theirs was not the only level of government seeking an infusion of cash: state governments were also on the hunt for new revenue, and their desperation was far greater than that of the national government. After all, the national government's tax system had by the 1930s become firmly based in the income tax, which had proven to be a highly capacious revenue generator and whose top rates had recently been cut. Thus, raising the top rates of the income tax to their previous levels was

[43] W. Elliot Brownlee, *Federal Taxation in America* (Cambridge University Press, 2016), 106–13, 117–19.

an obvious, though controversial, potential solution to the national government's revenue problems. State governments, on the other hand, entered the Great Depression without a stable and relatively uncontroversial tax source to buttress their revenue systems (their previously dominant tax source—the property tax—was under major attack). The solution to their revenue problems was therefore far from obvious.

Amid this context, national policymakers began to assume that the states would soon move to take advantage of a potentially enormous untapped source of revenue: general sales taxation. The need to protect the general sales tax as a potential revenue source for state governments appears to have played a significant role in Congress' rejection of a federal sales tax in the Depression's early years. As discussed in Chapter 1, the 1920s featured periodic efforts by business groups and others to adopt a federal sales tax as a replacement for the income tax, but these efforts routinely failed in Congress. With the onset of the Great Depression and the consequent need for new federal revenue, Treasury Secretary Ogden Mills and House Speaker John Nance Garner collaborated on a plan to adopt a federal sales tax that was designed as a supplement to, rather than a replacement of, the income tax. Given its high-profile backers, this plan represented the most organized, well-supported effort on behalf of federal sales taxation yet. It failed, however, when an eclectic coalition of northern liberal Democrats and southern Democrats united to scuttle it.[44] Among the arguments that congressional opponents of the federal sales tax frequently made was that many states were likely to adopt their own sales taxes and that congressional adoption of a sales tax would amount to national invasion of a state revenue source. This argument is somewhat puzzling when one considers the widespread early-twentieth century view that consumption taxes were better suited for central rather than subnational governments. It appears that changed political circumstances—most notably, the spectacular growth of the income tax as a source of federal revenue and the concomitant decline of the property tax as a source of state revenue—led political actors to reassess their views concerning which level of government should rightfully control general sales taxation.

Congress' decision to cede the general sales tax to the states does not mean that all its Depression-Era taxation decisions were governed by the principle

[44] Jordan A. Schwartz, "John Nance Garner and the Sales Tax Rebellion of 1932," *Journal of Southern History* 30, no. 2 (1964), 162–180.

of intergovernmental comity. As mentioned earlier, shortly before Congress rejected the Mills-Nance proposal for a federal sales tax, it made a highly controversial decision to enact a federal motor fuel tax. The adoption of this tax, which came after motor fuel taxes had been adopted by all forty-eight states and become the leading source of state government revenue, outraged state-level politicians across the country and drove states to focus their intergovernmental lobbying efforts in the 1930s on the tax coordination issue. National leaders who spearheaded the tax's passage seemed to be of two minds regarding the concerns of the states on this matter. Some members of Congress were sympathetic to the states' position; they emphasized that the federal tax was temporary, that it was borne of economic emergency and would sunset once the emergency subsided, and that its rate was considerably lower than those of state motor fuel taxes.[45] But other national leaders were not particularly concerned about the tax's consequences for state governments, with a few even suggesting that the states themselves—through their invasion of the tobacco tax field in the 1920s—were responsible for creating an environment of intergovernmental tax competition that led the national government to adopt its own motor fuel tax. Indeed, shortly before Congress passed the motor fuel tax, Treasury Secretary Ogden Mills made this comment to the House Ways and Means Committee:

> "... if the states continue to trespass on what I've always regarded as taxes that belonged peculiarly to the federal government, the tobacco taxes ... then I say unhesitatingly we are justified in trespassing on state taxes and levying a gasoline tax."[46]

The emergence of intergovernmental conflict over sales, motor fuel, and tobacco taxation, coupled with the growing push for tax coordination described at the beginning of the chapter, spurred Congress to begin seriously investigating the tax coordination issue. Congressional interest in various forms of tax coordination rose in the 72nd Congress and peaked in the 73rd Congress before declining thereafter. The first marked indication that Congress was interested in resolving potential tax conflicts between the national and state governments occurred at the end of 1931, when the House

[45] Robert L. Doughton to Walter Murphy, May 30, 1933, Box 218, Doughton Papers, University of North Carolina-Chapel Hill Special Collections.

[46] *Revenue Revision, 1932*, Hearings before the Committee on Ways and Means of the House of Representatives, 72nd Congress, 1st session, January 13–27, and February 2–4, 1932, 22.

Ways and Means Committee voted to create a special subcommittee for the purpose of studying the overlapping of federal and state taxes. In July 1932, the committee issued its report, which uncovered 326 examples of duplicated taxes between the national and state governments (to be sure, the vast bulk of these taxes yielded an insignificant amount of revenue).[47]

The first few months of the 73rd Congress featured efforts to grapple with the national-state taxation relationship on a number of fronts. To begin with, it opened with the Ways and Means Committee holding hearings on the report of the subcommittee studying double taxation. At around the same time, the two leaders of Congress' tax-writing committees—House Ways and Means Committee Chairman Robert Doughton and Senate Finance Committee Chairman Pat Harrison—met with members of the Interstate Assembly to consider intergovernmental tax policy. Following the meeting, Doughton and Harrison agreed to the creation of the intergovernmental Tax Revision Council and promised to attend its meetings as Congress' representatives. Additionally, Doughton attempted to leverage renewed interest in the tax coordination issue by sponsoring a bill to set up a revenue-sharing system between the national government and the states for tobacco taxes. The bill would have distributed one-sixth of the national government's tobacco tax revenues to the states on the basis of population. In exchange for participating in the revenue-sharing programs, states would have to agree to forego taxing tobacco sales on their own. In letters to constituents, Doughton (who hailed from a district with many tobacco farmers) explained that he hoped that through the program, "we can prevent further encroachment on this source of revenue by the several states. If those states that are now imposing taxes continue this policy, and others also adopt it, I fear it will work an injury to the producer, the manufacturer, and also the revenues of the Federal government."[48]

Thus, the multi-pronged effort to direct Congress' attention to the issue of national-state tax coordination entered the second half of 1933 with a substantial amount of vigor and interest associated with it. But though the initial push for tax coordination in the 73rd Congress was highly wide-ranging, by the end of 1933, attention to the tax coordination issue on Capitol Hill came to center on a single, highly controversial area: liquor taxation.

[47] *Double Taxation: Preliminary Report of a Subcommittee of the Committee on Ways and Means Relative to Federal and State Taxation and Duplications Therein*, 72nd Congress, 2nd session (1932).

[48] Robert Doughton to John R. Morris, February 23, 1933, Box 177, Doughton Papers.

The Failed Effort at Liquor Tax Coordination

The most promising opportunity for national-state tax coordination in the 1930s lay in the realm of liquor taxation, and it was here that efforts probably came closest to fruition. The question of how alcoholic beverages should be taxed (and which level of government should tax them) was at the center of Congress' agenda in the latter half of 1933, when it became clear that America's fourteen-year experiment with alcohol prohibition would soon end. Earlier that year, Congress had proposed the 21st Amendment to the U.S. Constitution, which would repeal the 18th Amendment's prohibition of alcohol sales throughout the U.S. and give states the authority to permit or ban alcohol within their borders as they saw fit. The amendment was quickly ratified by numerous states, and by the fall, it was widely understood that the proposed amendment was on a fast track toward being formally added to the Constitution.

The near-certain repeal of Prohibition thrust the question of how liquor should be taxed to the forefront of the national policy debate. Prior to Prohibition, alcohol taxation in the U.S. was organized according to a longstanding, unofficial intergovernmental compromise: state and local jurisdictions in which alcohol consumption was legal charged occupational taxes to alcohol-serving establishments, while the national government taxed alcohol sales at the points of production or importation (i.e., a "gallonage tax"). The federal and state laws upon which this intergovernmental arrangement was based became inoperative with the onset of Prohibition; following its repeal, they would be in force once again. But with state governments in the 1930s starved for cash and seeking to exploit every new potential revenue source, it seemed likely that they would pass new laws taxing alcohol retail sales on top of the federal gallonage tax as soon as alcohol was legal within their borders.[49]

The impending intrusion of state governments into the field of alcohol sales taxation posed a major quandary for policymakers. To begin with, it would create a new regime of double taxation, a vexing issue in and of itself but one that posed particularly difficult problems when applied to alcohol. A big concern for policymakers in the lead-up to Prohibition's repeal was how to create a system of legal alcohol regulation that would minimize the

[49] *Federal, State, and Local Government Fiscal Relations; Letter from the Acting Secretary of the Treasury Transmitting in Response to S. Res. 160*, S. Doc. No. 69, (1943) 11–513; Charles F. Conlon, "Taxation in the Alcoholic Beverage Field," *Law & Contemporary Problems*, vol. 7 (1940): 728–748.

phenomenon that had bedeviled the country during the Prohibition Era: the bootlegging of illegal alcohol products. The significant expenses inherent in subjecting alcohol sales to separate federal and state taxation systems (including the costs to alcohol distributors in terms of bureaucratic compliance, and the costs to state governments in setting up and staffing new alcohol sales taxation bureaus) seemed likely to be passed onto consumers in the form of higher prices and taxes, thereby making the purchase of bootlegged liquor more attractive and thus potentially undermining the chief goal behind Prohibition's repeal. Creating a streamlined system of alcohol sales taxation that could meet the increased revenue needs of both the national and state governments thus seemed like a paramount objective. A logical way of meeting this objective was to create a system of alcohol sales taxation administered entirely by the national government but part of whose proceeds would be distributed to the states.[50]

As the number of states ratifying the 21st Amendment moved closer to the requisite number for enactment, influential stakeholders released several comprehensive proposals for a new system of alcohol taxation in a post-repeal U.S. The first such proposal was featured in the Fosdick-Scott Report, a highly detailed study of post-Prohibition alcohol policy that was commissioned by John D. Rockefeller, Jr. and publicly released in October 1933 to a great deal of media attention.[51] A month later, the Interstate Commission on Conflicting Taxation released its liquor taxation plan.[52] A month after that, an informal executive branch committee reporting to the U.S. Treasury Secretary transmitted to Congress a report containing its own alcohol regulation and taxation proposals.[53] The three taxation plans offered remarkably similar ideas in the realm of national-state tax coordination. All three plans recommended that alcohol licenses be assessed primarily by the states, that alcohol sales be taxed exclusively by the national government, and that revenues from a nationally administered alcohol sales tax be shared with the

[50] "Report to the Secretary of the Treasury of Recommendations of Informal Inter-Departmental Committee Relative to Taxation and Control of Alcoholic Beverages," Records of the U.S. Senate (RG 46), Sen 73A-E5, Box 51, Folder for HR 6131, National Archives, Washington D.C.

[51] The Fosdick-Scott Report would be highly influential in setting the course of alcohol control in the U.S. in the mid-twentieth century. It is still read and cited today. See, e.g., Harry G. Levine, "The Birth of American Alcohol Control: Prohibition, the Power Elite and the Problem of Lawlessness," *Contemporary Drug Problems* 1985, 63–115.

[52] Clarence Heer, "Splitting the Liquor Taxes," *State Government*, December 1933, pp. 13–17.

[53] Conlon, "Taxation in the Alcoholic Beverage Field."

states in exchange for them agreeing not to levy their own taxes on alcohol sales.[54] On the whole, the unanimity of the economists who worked on these plans concerning the need for a nationally administered, state-shared alcohol sales tax is striking. It could not have been lost on members of Congress' tax-writing committees that this was what the vast bulk of experts were calling for.

But when Congress convened joint House-Senate hearings to consider the issue of post-Prohibition alcohol taxation in mid-December 1933, it became clear that the one significant source of disagreement among the three reports—on the question of the distribution formula used to allocate federal gallonage tax revenue to the states—reflected a profound political difficulty facing proponents of national-state coordination in the area of alcohol taxation. This was because passage of the 21st Amendment would give states near-complete authority over alcohol regulatory policy within their borders, and all signs suggested that states would vary widely in their post-repeal alcohol laws: some states would legalize alcohol sales completely, others would likely devolve alcohol regulation to their municipalities, and still others (mostly in the South and Great Plains) would reinstate longstanding statewide bans on all alcohol sales. Moreover, in a post-Prohibition U.S., states would vary not just in terms of alcohol consumption but also in terms of alcohol production, with the manufacture of alcoholic beverages largely concentrated in a handful of states.

The likely reality of major post-Prohibition variation in the role of alcohol in state economies made the question of how to allocate revenue from a nationally administered alcohol sales tax highly controversial. The three revenue-sharing plans in front of Congress all rejected the idea that gallonage tax funds should be allocated to the states based on their populations and without regard to the amount of state-level alcohol-related economic activity. The reason for their unanimity on this matter was clear: the revenue-sharing program was meant to dissuade "wet" states (i.e., states where alcohol sales were legal) from adopting their own taxes on alcohol sales, but this goal could not be achieved if the program became a mechanism for redistributing money from alcohol consumers and businesses in wet states to the governments of "dry" states (i.e., states where alcohol sales were illegal). The proposals differed, however, in regard to whether funds from the federal

[54] The three plans also differed in the percentage of funds from the nationally administered gallonage tax that they suggested should go to the states. The ICCT plan suggested the highest percentage (50%) while the executive branch committee's plan suggested the lowest (20%).

gallonage tax should be allocated based on state alcohol consumption and production levels, or based on consumption levels alone. The Fosdick-Scott Plan and the Treasury Department plan recommended considering both consumption and production, reasoning that since the federal gallonage tax was assessed at the point of production (even if it was ultimately passed onto consumers), the amount of state-level production should be part of the distribution formula. The ICCT Plan, on the other hand, recommended basing the allocation formula exclusively on state consumption levels, arguing that the revenue-sharing program was specifically designed to prevent the adoption of state taxes on alcohol retail sales and that an inherent feature of such taxes was that they could be assessed only where alcohol was consumed.

During the four-day joint hearing on alcohol taxation, members of Congress subjected witnesses speaking on behalf of the three plans to a barrage of questions about their allocation proposals. These questions revealed that legislators were in many cases more concerned with securing funds for their home states than with either the economic sensibility or social benefits of the revenue-sharing proposals. Prominent legislators from dry states, while remaining somewhat circumspect, repeatedly alluded to their dissatisfaction with any revenue-sharing scheme based on an allocation method from which their states would not benefit. Rep. Fred Vinson of Kentucky—the chairman of the House Subcommittee on Conflicting Taxation—peppered a witness speaking on behalf of the ICCT plan with questions about its proposal to distribute gallonage tax funds to the states exclusively based on consumption. Pointing out that his home state was a leading alcohol producer but could remain dry after Prohibition's repeal, Vinson argued that giving alcohol production "some consideration" in the allocation formula was "certainly ... not unfair." Sen. Pat Harrison of Mississippi, the powerful chairman of the Senate Finance Committee, stated that his home state neither produced nor consumed alcohol and asked a witness testifying on behalf of the Treasury Department plan: "What would it get back out of this proposition?"[55] The committee transcript indicates that his question was greeted with laughter, suggesting that it was asked facetiously and that fellow legislators and the audience understood its political implications.

Legislators from wet states who observed their dry-state colleagues speaking out on their states' behalf had a mixture of reactions. Nodding to political

[55] "Tax on Intoxicating Liquor," 50.

realities, Rep. John W. McCormack of Massachusetts acknowledged that members of Congress from dry states would insist that some of the alcohol-tax funds be distributed to their states, even if such states could not levy the retail sales taxes for which the revenue-sharing plan was meant to act as a substitute. As he said, "we have got to compromise in order to bring about something which will operate nationally" and therefore "it might be well to have a refund to the States on population without regard to production or consumption."[56] To this suggestion, the Treasury Department witness responded with the concern that, under such an allocation scheme, "[there would not be] enough left to offer the States which could impose their own taxes to persuade them not to do it."[57] Reacting to the difficulties involved in getting legislators from different states to agree on an allocation formula, Rep. William Evans of California commented that the revenue-sharing proposal may prove "impractical" due to "the varying conditions of the states and their attitude."[58]

Evans' words proved prophetic. The House Ways and Means Committee did not include a revenue-sharing component in its alcohol taxation plan, opting instead for a national gallonage tax rate that was low enough to, in the words of Committee Chairman Robert Doughton, "leave room for a reasonable state tax."[59] In other words, the Committee adopted a plan that effectively ensured that, in the post-Prohibition U.S., alcohol sales would be subjected to double taxation. During the floor debate on the committee's proposal, committee members provided a simple and straightforward explanation for their decision to reject the various revenue-sharing proposals: as Rep. Samuel B. Hill of Washington said, "the committee gave very serious consideration to that question, and ... was unable to agree upon any basis of allocation."[60] Rep. Frank Crowther of New York added that various difficulties involved in implementing a revenue-sharing system, most notably the allocation issue, proved "insurmountable."[61] The House (and later the

[56] "Tax on Intoxicating Liquor," Joint Hearings before the Committee on Ways and Means (House of Representatives) and the Committee of Finance (United States Senate), December 11–14, 1933, 156 and 53.

[57] "Tax on Intoxicating Liquor," 53.

[58] Ibid., 51.

[59] 78 Cong. Rec. H96 (January 4, 1934) (statement of Rep. Doughton)

[60] 78 Cong. Rec. H99 (January 4, 1934) (statement of Rep. Hill)

[61] 78 Cong. Rec. H123 (January 4, 1934) (statement of Rep. Crowther). Crowther also pointed to potential difficulties in getting states that had already passed alcohol retail sales taxes to give up these taxes, which were already reaping benefits.

Senate) evidently found the committee members' explanation convincing, as they passed the taxation plan overwhelmingly.

Thus, the U.S. entered the post-Prohibition era with a highly uncoordinated alcohol taxation system that resulted in alcohol sales being taxed twice, once at the point of manufacture by the national government and once at the point of retail by the states. Congress' decision not to create a system of shared revenues in alcohol taxation was widely viewed as a missed opportunity by taxation scholars and alcohol control experts in the mid-1930s. The prominent public finance economist Paul Studenski argued that "the whole system of collection of gallonage taxes by state jurisdictions is full of complications and red tape resulting in tremendous waste."[62] Some blamed the lack of coordination of federal and state alcohol taxes on the high cost of alcohol for consumers and thus the persistence of extensive alcohol bootlegging in the post-Prohibition U.S.[63] For better or worse, however, the adoption of alcohol retail sales taxes by numerous states in 1934–1935 created a new status quo that foreclosed the opportunity for greater coordination in this area in the future.

The Failure of Tax Coordination Efforts in the 1930s

In the aftermath of the liquor tax debates, congressional interest in intergovernmental fiscal coordination slowed considerably. Apart from a highly preliminary and quickly aborted effort to replace state sales taxes with a federal sales tax whose proceeds would be shared with the states,[64] almost nothing occurred in Congress during the remainder of the 1930s to advance the tax coordination cause. While direct evidence linking the failure of the liquor-tax revenue-sharing efforts to congressional inaction on intergovernmental fiscal relations in the mid/late 1930s is lacking, the circumstantial evidence strongly suggests that the liquor-tax outcome convinced congressional leaders that tax coordination efforts were futile because all coordination plans would advantage some states and disadvantage others, making it difficult to form the coalitions necessary for passage. Indeed, given the adoption of highly diverse state tax systems between 1933 and 1937, the differential

[62] Paul Studenski, "Liquor Taxes and the Bootlegger," *National Municipal Review* 24, no. 1 (1935), 64–80.

[63] "Statement and Recommendation of the Committee," *National Municipal Review* 24, no. 1 (1935), 63.

[64] "Report Analyzes Federal Sales Impost," *Wall Street Journal*, February 5, 1935, 3.

impact of tax coordination plans on states would have been even larger at the end of the 1930s than in the decade's beginning, rendering the chances of success for tax coordination efforts even lower than they were before. Thus, the failure of tax coordination efforts in the 1930s strongly supports the view that the absence of constitutional rules regarding the distributional impacts of intergovernmental fiscal policy (what Michael Greve calls a "distributional baseline") has impeded the ability of Congress to pass a program designed to coordinate state and federal taxation.[65]

Congress' apparent unwillingness to tackle the country's intergovernmental taxation problem during the mid-1930s demoralized proponents of fiscal coordination, especially the "Chicago Group" organizations that had devoted the most time and energy to the issue. Particularly frustrating to these organizations was Congress' refusal to properly fund the Tax Revision Council, the institution they were counting on to be the site of future intergovernmental negotiations on taxation policy. In the 1937 Book of the States (published by the Council of State Governments, a new addition to the "Chicago Group"), blame was placed squarely on Congress for the failure of the Tax Revision Council to produce a workable proposal to reform intergovernmental fiscal relations. As it stated:

> the federal government has not yet participated financially in the carrying forward of [Tax Revision Council's] work ... The effectiveness of the Tax Revision Council lies in the wholehearted support and participation of those governments which it represents. Accordingly, until the federal government shall bear its share of carrying forward this work, the Tax Revision Council will remain relatively inactive.[66]

With Congress refusing to step up to the plate, the "Chicago Group" organizations began to lose interest in promoting a comprehensive scheme to reorganize the country's intergovernmental taxation arrangement. Their declining interest was also a result of the fact that, by the late-1930s, state tax systems had stabilized as the general sales tax proved its worth as a source of state revenue and efforts to adopt a federal sales tax faded. This made the issue of tax coordination less pressing to state and local governments (for the time being). Stated differently, many state-level fiscal policymakers in the

[65] Greve, *The Upside-Down Constitution*, 244.
[66] Council of State Governments, *Book of the States 1937* (Chicago, 1937), 81.

late-1930s came around to the view that intergovernmental comity in taxation policy had developed organically (i.e., without intervention in the form of a formal national program), even if the arrangement that emerged was far from ideal. Diminished interest in fiscal federalism among state-level actors during the late-1930s can be seen in the programs of the Interstate Assembly and the annual conferences of the nation's governors: in the early-1930s, fiscal federalism was the dominant topic in these meetings, but by the end of the decade, it featured far less prominently in them.[67]

Similarly, other proponents of fiscal coordination during the 1930s had also moved away from the topic by the decade's end. Unable to unite around a coherent approach to fiscal federalism, business groups seem to have put the issue on the backburner, particularly once they became convinced that the New Deal-Era growth of government at both the national and state levels had stalled. Likewise, the NTA gave shorter shrift to fiscal coordination proposals in its meetings during the final years of the decade. Farm groups largely abandoned the fiscal coordination push once they were satisfied that most states had replaced state property tax revenue with other sources. Other sectors that had previously shown some interest in the fiscal coordination issue also appear to have largely given up their minimal efforts.[68] In short, the decline in attention to the problems of intergovernmental fiscal relations at the end of the New Deal was palpable across numerous interest groups and social sectors.

Reflecting on the fiscal coordination efforts of the 1930s, the authors of the 1943 Treasury Department report referenced at the chapter's beginning concluded that the "coordination movement" (as they called it, while acknowledging the inadequacy of the term) suffered from much "wishful thinking" and "an inclination to dodge political issues."[69] In the authors' view, the fundamental flaw behind the decade's tax coordination efforts was that they were led by technocratic elites who were either unable or unwilling to reconcile their idealistic visions of an effective tax system with the hard political realities of the modern U.S. Because of this, the numerous studies, committees, and conference panels on fiscal federalism issues that these

[67] Programs of the meetings of the Interstate Assembly and the national governors' conferences during the 1930s can be found in the Henry Horner Papers, Abraham Lincoln Presidential Library, Springfield, IL (Boxes 43, 251, 299, and 300).

[68] This includes national merchant groups, which briefly sought to replace sales taxes with a national sales tax, and the American Automobile Association, which fought against the national motor fuel tax.

[69] *Federal, State, and Local Government Fiscal Relations*, 91–92.

technocrats convened ended up amounting to little in the way of concrete policy change. Quoting an internal memorandum prepared for their study, the authors wrote:

> Throughout, there seems to have been an abiding faith that acceptable solutions would somehow evolve if enough feet were placed under the same table. There has also been a conviction that a group of specialists could draft a formula or set of specifications to satisfy all parties and resolve all the conflicts, when many of the issues involved are beyond the province of the expert.[70]

This indictment of the New Deal-Era efforts at fiscal federalism reform seems accurate. The large amount of time and energy spent studying the topic of tax coordination was simply no match for the underlying political difficulties and the strong force of political inertia. The intergovernmental taxation arrangement that was in place by the end of the New Deal was no one's idea of a perfect tax system. Rather than being the product of a large-scale intergovernmental fiscal reform formulated by Congress, the arrangement emerged out of the complex interactions between the chaotic spurt of state-level tax actions that occurred in the thick of the Great Depression on the one hand, and the tepid national response to them on the other. By the end of the New Deal, this arrangement had become institutionalized; while it didn't work especially well, it worked well enough to become entrenched. And so it would be until the late-1960s, when a different set of circumstances converged to create a second tax coordination push, one more robust and ultimately more successful than the first.

[70] Ibid., 92.

3

The Growth of State Taxation in the Mid Twentieth Century

Whereas the Depression-era United States witnessed the inception of modern state tax systems, the postwar United States witnessed their growth into maturity. The cause of this growth was a subnational fiscal expansion of greater magnitude than that of any previous era in American history. Because this expansion required substantial new revenue, the same taxation challenges that dominated state politics in the 1930s reappeared throughout the late 1940s, 1950s, and 1960s as states struggled to expand their fiscal capacities. Unlike in the 1930s, however, the menu of tax options available to states in the postwar era was relatively unchanged. The fiscal instruments to which states turned in the 1930s (i.e., general and selective sales taxes, personal and corporate income taxes) continued to be the ones at their disposal in the mid twentieth century.

Examining the record of state taxation outcomes in the thirty-year stretch between 1946 and 1975, one finds a long period of relative continuity followed by a shorter period of major upheaval. The period of continuity occurred between 1946 and 1964, when state taxation grew fairly evenly and usually along the pathways initially carved out during the New Deal. On average, states favored consumption taxes (especially the general sales tax) over income taxes during this period. Between 1965 and 1972, on the other hand, state taxation underwent a transformation that was rapid and momentous enough to be considered a second critical juncture in state taxation (the first being the revolution in state taxation during the 1930s). Like the first critical juncture, the second was precipitated by the convergence of several economic and political trends that burst open the previously constrained arena of state taxation politics. The chief result was the ascendancy of the state personal income tax, which (for the first time) came to assume a nearly equal status with the general sales tax as a source of state revenue in terms of both utilization and reliance.

Coordination Failure. Adam S. Myers, Oxford University Press. © Oxford University Press (2026).
DOI: 10.1093/9780197831878.003.0004

By the end of the second critical juncture, state tax systems looked quite different from how they had looked at the end of the 1930s. To begin with, state tax systems had become much more robust, with a far higher share of states having adopted each of the "Big Three" state taxes (the personal income tax, corporate income tax, and general sales tax). The fact that so many states had adopted these taxes meant that interstate variation in tax policy had declined (though considerable diversity did remain, particularly in tax reliance if not in utilization). Additionally, because of the growth of the personal income tax, the state tax systems that emerged from the second critical juncture were significantly more progressive than those of the past.

This chapter begins by summarizing the unique fiscal challenges facing state governments in the decades following World War II. It then examines the politics of state taxation in the postwar era, demonstrating the ways in which it was similar to and different from the state-level taxation politics of the 1930s (discussed in Chapter 1). In doing so, the chapter emphasizes the increased role of party conflict in shaping state-level taxation politics in the 1950s and 1960s. The nature of this conflict varied substantially across states, however, and was shaped chiefly by the type of tax system that states inherited from the New Deal Era: stated simply, states that had become reliant on a personal income tax differed markedly from states that had become reliant on a general sales tax in the form of taxation politics evident within them. These state-level differences in taxation politics help explain why the tax-policy outcomes of the 1930s had path-dependent effects in the mid twentieth century. The chapter then turns to the second critical juncture of the late 1960s/early 1970s, explaining the factors that led to its emergence and the outcomes that occurred within it. The chapter concludes by describing state tax systems in the mid 1970s (the end of the second critical juncture), emphasizing their greater overall progressivity and diminished interstate variation.

The Context: Fiscal Pressure on the States in the Postwar Era

The revolution in state taxation that was the subject of Chapter 1 ended in 1938, when Republican success in that year's midterm elections led to a halt in progressive policymaking at both the national and state levels.[1] Consistent

[1] On the conservative turn, see: James T. Patterson, *Congressional Conservatism and the New Deal* (Lexington, KY: University Press of Kentucky, 2014); Alan Brinkley, *The End of Reform: New Deal Liberalism in Recession and War* (New York: Vintage, 1996).

with the retrenchment-oriented ideology that pervaded government at that point, 1939 was the first year in over a decade in which most state legislatures were in session but no state adopted a major new general sales or income tax.

At the national level, the anti-government mood that set in during the late 1930s proved to be very short-lived. By 1941, the United States found itself in the middle of a new national crisis—World War II—requiring a much greater fiscal expansion of the national government than the economic crisis of the early 1930s. Congress largely funded this expansion through the Revenue Act of 1942, which dramatically reshaped the federal income tax by simultaneously applying it to the vast bulk of Americans and introducing steeply graduated rates (indeed, the highest marginal rates in the tax's history).[2] The Act's changes caused the percentage of U.S. tax revenue (across all levels of government) generated by the federal income tax to grow from 16% in 1940 to a whopping 51% in 1946.[3] This huge increase in federal income taxation severely constrained state governments, whose own levels of taxation and spending largely plateaued (and in some cases declined) as state policymakers abandoned any expansionary ambitions they may have had in deference to the national government's wartime responsibilities.

After the war ended, however, the national government and the states traded places in terms of their fiscal situations: while the revenue needs of the national government receded, states entered a multi-decade period in which they faced ever-growing fiscal pressures. These pressures were the result of the confluence of two trends: states were becoming the level of government most responsible for service provision at precisely the moment in which the postwar baby boom and the growing affluence of American society created unprecedented demands for government services.

Chief among these demands was greater spending on K-12 education. Fueled by the Baby Boom, total public school enrollment in the United States rose from 25.1 million to 36.1 million—a 43.7% increase—between 1949–1950 and 1959–1960.[4] This sharp increase coincided with both the emergence of a social consensus on the importance of investing in K-12 education as well as the ongoing centralization of education policy in state capitals. The latter was partially a product of the relative inability of

[2] W. Elliot Brownlee, *Federal Taxation in America: A History* (New York: Cambridge University Press, 2016), 142.

[3] Ibid., 147.

[4] National Center for Education Statistics, *120 Years of American Education: A Statistical* Portrait, (Washington, D.C.: 1993), https://nces.ed.gov/pubs93/93442.pdf. Data found in Table 8—Historical Summary of Public Elementary and Secondary School Statistics: 1869–1870 to 1980–1990.

local governments (the traditional centers of education policymaking in the United States) to raise the revenue needed to pay for education spending increases. On numerous occasions throughout the 1950s and 1960s, states were forced to raise more money for education as a way of avoiding major property tax increases at the local level.

Beyond K-12 education, postwar state governments were faced with new demands in a variety of areas. In the wake of the national government's construction of the interstate highway system in the 1950s, state governments became chiefly responsible for the upkeep of thousands of miles of new highways, requiring substantial increases in transportation spending.[5] Large increases in caseloads for the intergovernmental Aid to Dependent Children program required increases in spending on public welfare.[6] And, lastly, a commitment to upgrading state colleges and universities necessitated increased spending in higher education.[7]

Collectively, these new spending needs forced state governments to find lots of additional money, largely from their own sources. As can be seen in Figure 3.1, the amount of money that state and local governments spent from their own sources mushroomed from 5.7% to 10.3% of GDP between 1948 and 1975. While federal assistance to state and local governments experienced a significant increase as well (from 0.6% to 3.1% of GDP), it was nonetheless smaller in overall magnitude. Thus, the increased fiscal burdens on state and local governments were ones that, for the most part, they had to shoulder on their own.

The State-Level Taxation Politics of the Postwar Era

The Postwar Political Context

Given the unprecedented new fiscal burdens they faced, postwar state governments inevitably became the sites of routine and highly contested fights over taxation. These fights occurred in a political context that

[5] Federation of Tax Administrators, *Revenue and Spending Proposals in State Budgets, 1965*, Research Report No. 53, April 1965,18.

[6] Federation of Tax Administrators, *Revenue and Spending Proposals in State Budgets, 1967*, Research Report No. 56, April 1967, 15.

[7] John C. Teaford, *The Rise of the States: Evolution of American State Government* (Johns Hopkins University Press, 2003), 179–187.

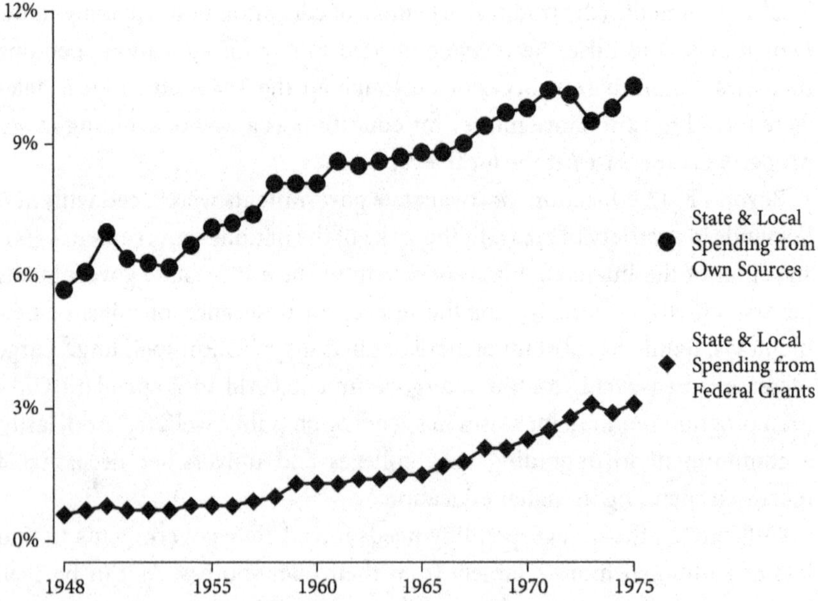

Figure 3.1 State and Local Spending as % of Gross Domestic Product, 1948–1970
Sources: White House Office of Management and Budget (OMB), "Historical Tables," https://whitehouse.gov/omb/historical-tables, Tables 12.1, 14.1, 14.2, 14.5

exhibited various continuities with that of the 1930s, while also reflecting important changes in the American political economy and American politics more generally.

The national-level economic change of greatest importance was the rise of a consumption-oriented mass culture in the 1950s and 1960s.[8] As discussed in Chapter 1, policymakers in the 1930s discovered that tapping into the purchasing power of the American consumer was the most promising way for state governments to generate new revenue quickly. The dramatic growth in American consumer spending during the postwar era led most state policymakers to double down on this strategy, often turning to general and selective sales taxes rather than income taxes to shore up state budgets (at least at first).

The bias of state policymakers toward consumption taxes during the postwar era was amplified by a number of additional factors as well. One

[8] Lizabeth Cohen, *A Consumers' Republic: The Politics of Mass Consumption in Postwar America* (New York: Alfred A. Knopf, 2003).

important such factor was that the mid-twentieth-century federal income tax featured extraordinarily high rates, which limited the ability of states to adopt or raise income taxes of their own. A 1965 report by the Advisory Commission on Intergovernmental Relations described the heavy federal income tax burden as "the single most important deterrent to its expanded use by the States."[9] The constraints that state policymakers felt regarding income taxation was also a product of the large increase in interstate migration (of both people and businesses) in postwar America, which exacerbated the competitive pressures states faced. Because of the widespread perception that income taxes affected residential and business location decisions far more than consumption taxes, increased competitive pressures had the effect of dissuading state-level policymakers from adopting or enhancing income taxes.[10]

Beyond the national political-economic context, state-level conditions also affected the taxation fights that occurred inside statehouses during the postwar era. As in the 1930s, the property tax loomed over the taxation decisions that state legislatures needed to make, though its role was quite different from that of earlier decades. As discussed in Chapter 1, during the early twentieth century, the property tax was a "shared tax" whose proceeds were distributed between local and state governments, and the biggest taxation-related political quandary states faced was how to find new sources of revenue for themselves so that they could afford to turn property tax revenues entirely over to their local sub-units. Moreover, the most outspoken proponents of property tax reform during the early twentieth century were farmers, who resented bearing a disproportionate tax burden due to their real property wealth.

By the end of the 1930s, states had largely achieved their goal of turning the property tax into an exclusively local revenue source, with only a few state governments receiving any revenue from the general property tax as of 1939. In the postwar era, however, it became apparent that the reforms of the 1930s had not solved the problem that property taxation posed for state governments several decades earlier. At best, the reforms had changed the nature of the problem but not its size. Whereas in the early twentieth century the dilemma facing states was how to remove the property tax from the state government revenue stream, in the mid twentieth century the dilemma

[9] Advisory Commission on Intergovernmental Relations, *Federal-State Coordination of Personal Income Taxes*, Report # A-27, October 1965, 111.

[10] Advisory Commission on Intergovernmental Relations, *State-Local Taxation and Industrial Location*, Report # A-30, April 1967.

became how to financially support local governments so that local property tax rates could remain at tolerable levels. This new dilemma had its origins in several interlocking factors. Most prominently, the dramatic increase in public school enrollments following the end of World War II created major fiscal pressures on local governments. Since property taxes were in many cases the only tax source available to localities seeking greater revenues, pressure built on states to increase their support for local governments to forestall property tax increases. Importantly, property taxes in the mid twentieth century were no longer simply a focal point of animus among farmers or wealthy city-dwellers. In an increasingly urbanized (and suburbanized) society where homeownership rates had risen to record-high levels, high property taxes were becoming a palpable burden for middle-class suburban Americans as well. Thus, opposition to property taxation in the postwar era came from a diverse array of social sectors, making it an issue that state governments were unable to ignore.

Postwar Interest Group Alignments

In response to these national and state-level contextual changes, interest group alignments on state taxation policy matters shifted substantially from what they were prior to World War II. To begin with, teacher's groups, who had previously been important though not central advocates of state-level tax increases, became their most ardent supporters. Like the farm groups of the early twentieth century, teacher's groups primarily advocated on behalf of income taxes but would frequently join coalitions in favor of sales tax increases when they concluded such actions were the most viable path toward generating greater state revenue for education.

Unlike teacher's groups, the state-level labor organizations of the mid twentieth century tended to align themselves explicitly in favor of progressive income taxes and against regressive consumption taxes, even when the latter appeared to be the only viable means to raise more state revenue for programs unions favored. This represented something of a shift from the position of unions in the 1930s, when growing tax revenue was the priority and adopting progressive taxation systems was secondary. This shift appears to have been prompted by increased awareness of the economic role of state taxation in the aftermath of World War II. As will be discussed in Chapter 4, national labor organizations in the 1950s began drawing greater attention to the issue of state taxation in their publications, with a particular focus on the regressivity of state sales taxes. This increased attention may have influenced their state-level affiliates to take a more active stand against sales taxes.

As state governments assumed new responsibilities and spent money on a wider range of services over the course of the mid twentieth century, new groups with a vested interest in these services began wading into state taxation fights. Such groups included mental health professionals and administrators of institutions of higher education. Representatives of these groups (to the extent they existed) do not generally appear in accounts of state-level taxation fights in the 1930s, but they are prominent in accounts from the postwar era. Naturally, these groups were in favor of tax increases to fund state services, but they tended to be agnostic about what the best source of tax revenue was.

One group whose position on state-level taxation was nearly unchanged between the 1930s and the 1950s/1960s was the business community. In state after state, business interests and their organizations, including state Chambers of Commerce and National Association of Manufacturers (NAM) affiliates, steadfastly opposed income tax adoptions and increases. Nearly always, business groups favored keeping taxes low and, if raising revenue was inevitable, doing so through mechanisms other than individual or corporate income tax increases. Concerned with attracting businesses to their states during the postwar economic boom, these organizations viewed income taxes as especially damaging to their state's business climate and thus strongly opposed their use.[11]

The Rising Importance of State Parties

The shifts in interest group alignments on state tax policy described above paled in comparison to a far more important change that manifested in the postwar era: the growth in importance of political parties in state taxation struggles. As discussed in Chapter 1, state parties were insignificant actors in the realm of tax policy during the 1930s; sectoral interest groups,

[11] Advisory Commission on Intergovernmental Relations, *State-Local Taxation and Industrial Location*, Report #A-30, April 1967. For a very thorough account of how business groups sought to forestall progressive taxation in one state during this period, see Thomas Julius Anton, *The Politics of State Taxation: A Case Study of Decision-Making in the New Jersey Legislature* (Ph.D. Dissertation, Princeton University, 1961).

not political parties, were the main organizations that influenced tax policy debates during that decade. By the 1950s and 1960s, however, this was no longer the case: while sectoral interest groups continued to play an important role, state parties became significantly more prominent as forces organizing tax policy debates inside statehouses.

The causes of the increased importance of state parties are not entirely clear, but there are several possibilities. One potential explanation is that the sharpening of a national partisan cleavage around issues of economic redistribution during the New Deal Era took time to reach the level of state politics, where parties had traditionally been more patronage-oriented and less programmatic. By this explanation, the national partisan divide over economic policy had finally filtered down to the state level during the mid twentieth century, with state Democratic and Republican Parties increasingly taking positions on tax policy that were ideologically consistent with those of their national affiliates (i.e., support for progressive taxes among Democratic Parties, opposition to all taxes but especially progressive taxes among Republicans).

Another possible explanation is that state party organizations were unprepared for the fiscal crises wrought by the Great Depression and the concomitant rise of tax policy as the premier issue facing state governments during the 1930s, and thus struggled to develop clear platforms on the issue as it unfolded during the New Deal. By the postwar era, however, the range of possible approaches to state tax policy had become clearer, and state parties thus became more comfortable articulating a set of positions on the topic. A third possible explanation relates to changes in the sectoral coalitions underpinning state political parties. As discussed in Chapter 1, alliances between particular interest groups with a stake in tax policy and state-level political parties were tenuous during the 1930s. By the postwar era, it appears that these alliances had become firmer across many states, leading state parties to take stronger stances on substantive issues affecting their sectoral allies (including taxation).

Whatever the reasons, the empirical record is clear: during the mid twentieth century, state parties were adopting and promoting clearer positions on taxation questions, with significant consequences for state tax policy. Importantly, however, the positions of Democratic and Republican parties were by no means consistent across states (a reality that would change dramatically in the late 1990s and early 2000s). State Democratic parties adopted positions ranging from enthusiastic support for ultra-graduated income taxes to tepid and tenuous endorsement of the general principle of progressive taxation. State Republican Parties adopted positions ranging from explicit endorsement of "pro-business" (i.e., regressive) tax policies to a more lukewarm emphasis on low taxes and government efficiency. These positions tended to vary over time in addition to varying across states.

A variety of factors influenced the variation in tax policy positions adopted by mid- twentieth-century state-level Democratic and Republican parties, but one factor stands above the rest: the tax systems states had inherited from the New Deal Era. More specifically, the approach political parties chose on the taxation issue depended greatly on whether their states entered the postwar era with a personal income tax, a general sales tax, both taxes, or neither.

In states that entered the postwar era with a sales tax but no personal income tax, the Republican Party generally took on a stance of unequivocal opposition to income tax adoption. For example, in Illinois (a state where many Republican politicians supported the income tax during the 1930s) all thirty-two GOP members of the state senate co-sponsored a constitutional amendment prohibiting an income tax in the 1956 legislative session.[12] Two years later, the state Republican Party adopted a platform plank clearly opposing a state income tax, and a *Chicago Tribune* survey of state legislative candidates revealed overwhelming opposition to the tax among GOP nominees.[13] Likewise, in Michigan, the Republican-controlled state senate routinely blocked proposals for a state income tax promoted by Gov. Mennen Williams and legislative Democrats.[14] The story was much the same in other sales-tax-only states like Ohio and Washington, where Republicans also stood against income tax adoptions.[15]

The clear and consistent opposition of Republicans to income tax enactments in sales tax states during the 1950s owed to several factors. First, state-level Republicans in the postwar era were allies of business groups, which (as discussed above) almost always preferred sales taxes to income taxes. Additionally, running against the income tax made for a good campaign issue for

[12] O.T. Banton, "Stratton May Propose State Income Tax," *Decatur Daily Review* (Decatur, IL), Apr 12, 1955, 25.

[13] William Anderson, "Demos Hedge, G.O.P. Fights Income Tax," *Chicago Tribune*, October 26, 1958, Part 3, 2.

[14] Richard L. Milliman, "GOP Wins Fight For Sales Tax," *Lansing State Journal*, July 25, 1959, 1.

[15] Harold Hutchings, "Maine to Launch Historic Battle," *Chicago Tribune*, June 16, 1956, 68; John K. Borland, "Conn. GOP Advocates Tax Rise," *Providence Journal*, June 12, 1960, N-50; "Income Tax Plan is Sent to House," *Spokane Chronicle*, Empire Edition, Feb 27, 1961, 1.

the GOP. As Chapter 1 demonstrated, ordinary voters in numerous states seem to have been more opposed to sales taxation than income taxation during the 1930s, but by the 1950s, numerous citizens of states that had adopted a sales tax some two decades earlier had become accustomed to it. Postwar anti-tax sentiment in these states thus centered on opposition to income tax adoptions rather than sales tax increases. Republican politicians understood that state Democratic parties—generally allied with pro-income tax groups like labor and teachers' unions—could be put on the defensive over an issue like the income tax during campaign season.

In contrast to Republicans, Democrats in sales-tax-only states were quite divided on the income tax question. In most of these states, a faction of Democratic legislators worked ardently on behalf of income tax adoption, sponsoring bills to that effect at the beginning of each state legislative session. Many others, however, were wary of the political consequences of promoting such a tax and worked to neutralize GOP attacks on the issue. In Illinois, the anti-income tax forces eventually won out: beginning in 1958, the Illinois Democratic Party added a plank opposing an income tax to its biennial party platform.[16] With both of the state's major parties officially opposed to the income tax, prospects for a major change to the state's tax structure dimmed considerably until the late 1960s. In Pennsylvania, labor-aligned Democrats succeeded in inserting a plank endorsing a graduated income tax into the party platform in the early 1950s, but by the late 1950s the plank was removed in favor of a vague call for new sources of revenue for the state.[17] Similar developments unfolded in other sales-tax-only states, where efforts to authorize or enact income taxes fizzled in the face of near-complete Republican opposition and significant Democratic division.

The political situation in states emerging from World War II with a personal income tax but no sales tax was practically a mirror image of that which existed in sales-tax-only states. In these states, efforts to enact general sales taxes badly split the GOP and attracted unified Democratic opposition. Such was the case in Idaho, where both political parties had adopted platform planks opposing the adoption of a sales tax.[18] Despite these pronouncements, the Idaho business community, concerned that the increasingly high rates

[16] "State Demos Oppose Tax, Rip Downey," *Herald and Review* (Decatur, IL), September 8, 1960, 26.

[17] "Pennsylvania Democrats okay platform of 27 planks," *Philadelphia Inquirer*, September 12, 1958, 10.

[18] "GOP rebukes house Dems for not printing sales tax," *Idaho State Journal* (Pocatello, ID), February 24, 1959, 7.

of the state's income tax were damaging its business climate, began putting pressure on Republicans in the legislature to promote bills establishing a sales tax. By the late 1950s, these bills were introduced at the beginning of every Idaho legislative session, but they badly divided the GOP caucuses while unifying the Democrats in opposition. The state's leading newspapers were mystified by the inability of Idaho legislators to pass a sales tax: in an official editorial, the *Idaho State Journal* wrote: "the reluctance of both Republicans and Democrats...to accept the idea of the state sales tax as at least a partial solution to the state's financial problems, is hard to understand..."[19] Similar dynamics could be seen in other income-tax-only states like Montana, Wisconsin, and New York. In all these states, sales taxes were promoted by business-oriented Republicans, but these proposals were scuttled by a united Democratic Party and a faction of Republicans. Like the income-tax-averse Democrats in sales-tax-only states, these dissident Republicans understood that their states' voters had, over time, accepted a state income tax and were wary of the political consequences of adopting a major new revenue source.

The concerns of these Republicans were well-founded, given the tendency of Democratic candidates in income-tax-only states to use the specter of a sales tax against Republican candidates on the campaign trail. In the 1956 Wisconsin gubernatorial election, for example, Democrat William Proxmire routinely warned voters that the election of his opponent, Republican Vernon Thomson, would lead to the adoption of a sales tax in the state. To defuse Proxmire's attacks, Thomson eventually promised that he would veto any sales tax legislation if elected governor.[20] A half-year later, now-Governor Thomson followed through on his campaign pledge by proposing a state budget that was balanced through significant increases in income tax rates instead of a new sales tax, greatly angering the state's business community in the process.[21] In 1958, Thomson ran for re-election refusing to make the same promise he had made in 1956; perhaps not coincidentally, he ended up losing the race.[22]

In states that had entered the 1950s with both a personal income tax and a sales tax in place, the partisan politics surrounding taxation was considerably

[19] "Why Not a State Sales Tax?," *Idaho State Journal* (Boise, ID), January 30, 1959, 4.

[20] "Sales Tax Looms as Key Issue in 1958 Campaign," *Capital Times* (Madison, WI), August 11, 1958, 34.

[21] "State Chamber Raps Thomson," *Wisconsin State Journal* (Madison, WI), February 2, 1957, 7.

[22] "Sales Tax Looms as Key Issue In 1958 Campaign."

more fluid. Since both taxes had already been implemented and, over time, had achieved a certain level of acceptance from voters, generating more revenue from either one presented political difficulties that were significant but not overwhelming. This gave state political parties considerable flexibility to develop distinct approaches to state tax policy questions. While Democratic parties in these states were generally to the left of Republicans in terms of both support for tax increases and support for greater tax progressivity, they nonetheless varied widely. The most progressive approach was exemplified by the California Democratic Party, which adopted a platform expressly advocating a more progressive state income tax and opposing any increase in the state sales tax throughout much of the 1950s.[23] The party acted on its platform when it attained unified control of state government in 1959; to fund Gov. Edmund G. Brown's large-scale spending program, legislative Democrats muscled through an across-the-board income tax over Republican objections. But Democrats did not always embrace income tax increases over sales tax increases when they were in power: in Missouri, Governor John Dalton united legislative Democrats around a sales tax increase to fund greater state spending on mental health and higher education, despite the fact that the state's labor unions (traditional allies of the Democrats) opposed it.[24] In Arizona, Republican Gov. Paul Fannin cobbled together a coalition of Democrats and Republicans to push a sales tax through the Democrat-controlled legislature.[25]

The Outcomes of the Postwar Era

Having discussed the political context surrounding the state-level tax fights of the postwar era, I next turn to describing the outcomes: which taxes were adopted and/or raised, how state tax choices were affected by the tax systems already in place, and how revenue streams changed overall.

Figure 3.2 presents adoptions and rate increases for the "Big Three" state government tax instruments from shortly after the end of World War II

[23] See California Democratic Party platforms in: Daniel J. Hopkins, Daniel J. Coffey, Daniel J. Galvin, Gerald Gamm, John Henderson, Joel W. Paddock, and Eric Schickler, "Select American State Party Platforms, 1846–2017," Harvard Dataverse. https://doi.org/10.7910/DVN/KNOSHL

[24] Herbert A. Trask, "How Sales Tax Increase Bill Was Enacted," *St. Louis Post-Dispatch*, April 7, 1963, 1.

[25] Jim Cooper, "Legislature Passes School Aid—Sales Tax Increased," *Tucson Daily Citizen*, March 20, 1959, 1.

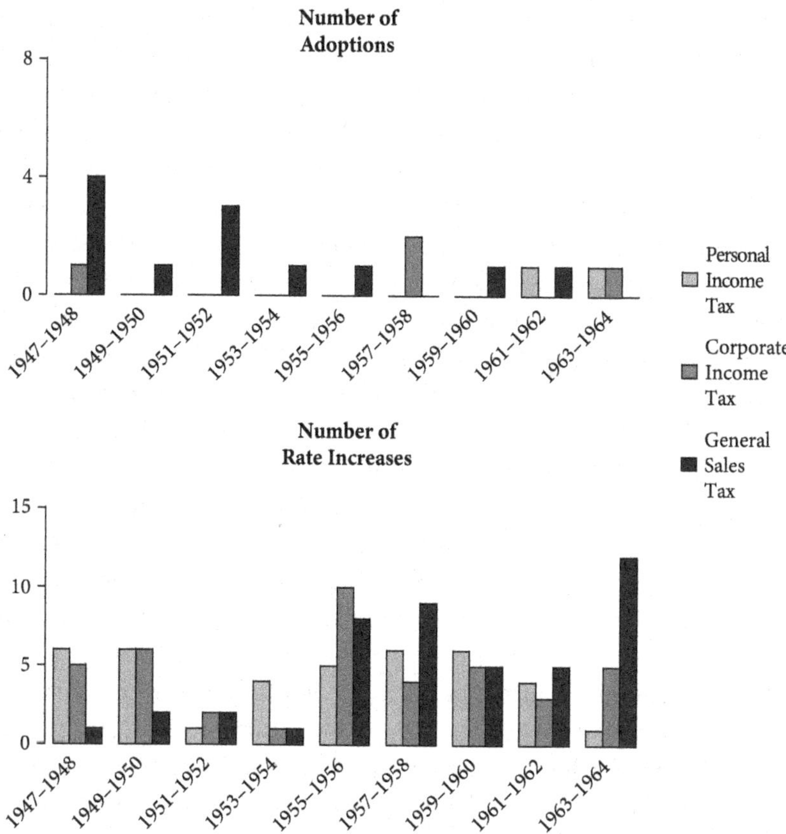

Figure 3.2 Income and Sales Tax Adoptions and Rate Increases, 1947–1964
Source: State Tax Actions Dataset

to the mid 1960s. Data are tracked across two-year intervals beginning in odd years, which corresponds to state legislative biennia for the vast majority of states. As the figure shows, the postwar period featured a fair number of general sales tax adoptions, particularly in the late 1940s and early 1950s, but almost no adoptions of either personal or corporate income taxes. The situation with rate increases is quite different, however; in the late 1940s, rate increases were rare but were more common for income taxes than sales taxes. But by the late 1950s and early 1960s, when numerous states were regularly dealing with budget shortfalls, rate increases for all three taxes became more common and were being passed in between five and ten states in nearly every state legislative biennium.

The findings evident in Figure 3.2 can be further elucidated by considering how adoptions and rate increases in the postwar period were shaped by the tax systems inherited from the 1930s. Table 3.1 compares personal income and sales tax actions between 1946 and 1965 among states that entered the postwar period with a personal income tax but no sales tax, a sales tax but no personal income tax, both taxes, or neither tax. The table's results reveal several important patterns. First, states tended to build on their existing tax structures rather than alter them significantly during the postwar era. This can be seen by comparing the tax-policy records of income-tax-only and sales-tax-only states (the first two lines in the table). As the table shows, among the fourteen states with only an income tax as of 1946, legislatures passed thirty income tax rate increases in the ensuing twenty years, but only seven of these states adopted a sales tax in addition to the income tax during the same period. Likewise, among the eight states with a sales tax but no personal income tax as of 1946, legislatures passed eleven sales tax increases in the next twenty years but only two of these legislatures adopted income taxes.

The tendency of states to work within their existing tax structures indicates that the tax decisions of the 1930s (discussed in Chapter 1) had path-dependent effects in the postwar era. In other words, the outcomes of that earlier period created tax-policy pathways from which states rarely deviated in the decades immediately following World War II. This appears to have been largely due to the ways in which a state's taxation choices

Table 3.1 State Tax Choices in the Postwar Era (1946–1965) by Inherited Tax System

State Tax Structure as of 1946	# of states	# of Personal Income Tax adoptions (1946–1965)	# of Personal Income Tax Rate increases (1946–1965)	# of sSales Tax Adoptions (1946–1965)	# of Sales Tax Rate Increases (1946–1965)
Personal Income Tax Only	14	N/A	30	7	1
General Sales Tax Only	8	2	0	N/A	11
Both Taxes	15	N/A	10	N/A	16
Neither Tax	11	0	0	8	12

Source: State Tax Actions Dataset

in the 1930s altered citizen expectations and partisan politics in future decades. Over time, most citizens had come to accept the taxes that were put into place in their states during the 1930s, but they remained highly resistant to new tax adoptions. As the previous section demonstrated, state political parties responded to these changes in state-level public opinion by adopting policy platforms that reflected both citizen opposition to new taxes (i.e., opposition to income taxes in sales-tax-only states, and opposition to sales taxes in income-tax-only states) as well as support for national party priorities (i.e., high and progressive taxation for Democrats, low and more regressive taxation for Republicans). These distinctive approaches resulted in different forms of taxation politics in income-tax-only states and sales-tax-only states. More than anything else, it is these differences that explain the path-dependent effects in postwar state tax policy.

The second important pattern revealed in Table 3.1 is that, controlling for the type of tax system in place within their states at the end of World War II, state-level policymakers preferred the sales tax over the income tax as a revenue-generating instrument in the postwar era. This is evidenced by the fact that, among states in which *both* taxes were in place, postwar sales tax increases were more common than income tax increases. And it is even more evidenced by the fact that, of the eleven states emerging from World War II with neither a sales tax nor a personal income tax, eight adopted the former while none adopted the latter over the next twenty years. This demonstrates that, when states faced major revenue pressures in the postwar era and had no choice other than to *adopt* a major new tax, they always chose the sales tax over the income tax.

Several factors explain the overall bias toward sales taxation over income taxation among state policymakers during this period. Perhaps the most important factor was the exceedingly high postwar federal income tax, whose top marginal rate had climbed to above 90% for much of the 1950s. Even more than in the 1930s, then, the size and reach of the federal tax severely limited the ability of state governments to generate large sums of money via state income taxes. Beyond the constraining effects of the federal income tax, state policymakers also resisted turning to income taxes for more revenue due to concerns that such taxes would cause businesses and taxpayers to flee to other states. As discussed earlier, the widespread perception that income taxes, in comparison to sales taxes, were more likely to spur interstate tax competition played a big role in causing state policymakers to turn away from income taxes.

An additional and underappreciated factor influencing the advantage of sales taxation over income taxation in this period had to do with the structure of the postwar state governments. More specifically, in many northern states entering the postwar era with neither income nor sales taxes, party politics often interacted with legislative malapportionment to doom income tax adoption efforts. Until the early 1960s, the apportionment of seats in many state legislative chambers was often heavily biased in favor of rural areas. Given that rural areas throughout much of the northern United States were significantly more Republican than urban or suburban areas, high levels of malapportionment tended to give the GOP disproportionate power in these chambers.[26] Republicans, who were consistently more likely to oppose income taxation than Democrats, used their outsized power in malapportioned chambers to quash income tax adoption efforts. Indeed, in states like Connecticut, Pennsylvania, and Rhode Island (all three of which entered the postwar era without a personal income tax or a sales tax), bills establishing personal income taxes would occasionally pass through the less-malapportioned (and therefore more Democratic) legislative chamber, only to die in the more-malapportioned (and therefore more Republican) one.[27] The Republican firewall in the malapportioned legislative chambers of these states proved impossible to overcome, and progressive Democrats eventually sacrificed their secondary goal of implementing a progressive tax system in favor of their primary one: securing more revenue for their state governments. Inevitably, this meant agreeing to the main alternative to the personal income tax (and the one comprehensive new form of taxation that Republicans could accept): the sales tax.

Turning to how the aforementioned tax-policy decisions affected state revenue streams in the postwar era, Figure 3.3 shows the total amount of revenue states raised between 1951 and 1965 from six categories of tax sources: general sales taxes, corporate income taxes, personal income taxes, motor fuel taxes, alcohol and tobacco taxes, and all other taxes. The figure shows that most sources of state revenue, including motor fuel taxes, alcohol/tobacco taxes, and even corporate income taxes, produced fairly

[26] On the effects of malapportionment on party politics in state legislatures, see: Adam S. Myers, "The Reapportionment Revolution and the Decline of Contested State Legislative Elections: The Case of Rhode Island," *New England Journal of Political Science* 11, no. 2 (2019): 130–159.

[27] On failed income tax adoption efforts in Pennsylvania, see: "Graduated Income Tax Amendment is Killed," *Daily American* (Somerset, PA), July 27, 1953, 2; "State Income Tax Bill Killed; Republican Vote Solid for Defeat," *Indiana Evening Gazette* (Indiana, PA), August 5, 1955, 1; "GOP Caucus Rejects State Income Tax, Back 3% Levy," *Philadelphia Inquirer* (Philadelphia, PA), February 27, 1956, 1; Joseph H. Miller, "House Passes State Poll on Income Tax," *Philadelphia Inquirer*, August 11, 1959, 1.

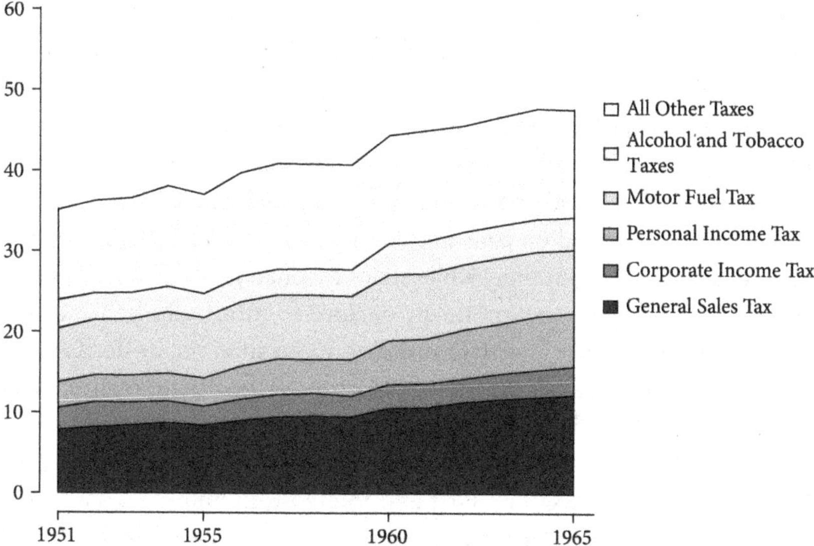

Figure 3.3 Sources of State Tax Revenue (in Billions of $), 1951–1965
Source: U.S. Census, *Historical Finances of State Government* dataset

stable amounts of revenue in the postwar era. The growth in state revenue during these years was almost entirely due to increased receipts from the general sales tax and the personal income tax. The increase in receipts from the latter is particularly striking given the fact that, as demonstrated above, state governments mostly shied away from raising personal income taxes during this period. This growth can be explained by the fact that, in a development unanticipated by economists at earlier periods, the personal income tax turned out to be the state-level tax source that was most responsive to the unprecedented growth in the American economy that followed World War II. As will be shown, it was this greater responsiveness that ultimately convinced many reluctant state governments to finally turn to the personal income tax during the second critical juncture of state taxation.

State Taxation Politics, 1965–1972: The Second Critical Juncture

After a twenty-year period in which state taxation grew continuously and according to the logic of path dependence, the dynamics of state taxation policy shifted substantially in the late 1960s. Suddenly, state taxation policy seemed much more like the wide-open field it had been in the 1930s. Like in the early 1930s, finding new sources of revenue had become imperative for states, old barriers to adopting new taxes fell, and interest groups that had long worked to enact tax policy changes swooped in to take advantage. In other words, a second critical juncture in state taxation policy had begun. As a result of this second critical juncture, states that had for decades built up tax systems centered on consumption taxes found themselves adopting income taxes for the first time, while states that had developed tax systems based around income taxation finally decided to turn to the general sales tax. The result was that interstate variation in taxation policy declined, as many states emerged from the late 1960s/early 1970s with more diversified tax systems that included both sales taxes and personal income taxes.

As in the 1930s, a variety of factors interacted to create the second critical juncture in state taxation. First and foremost, in numerous states, the fiscal problems that had been building up over the course of the 1950s and early 1960s had risen to the level of a true emergency. Fiscal strain came from a variety of sources, including surging school enrollments, increased highway needs, and increased public assistance rolls. The latter issue was compounded in 1969 by a Supreme Court ruling: in *Shapiro v. Thompson*, the court invalidated a Connecticut law that required citizens to live in the state for one year to be eligible for welfare benefits.[28] Due to this ruling, states were required to add recent domestic migrants to their welfare rolls, which further strained state budgets.

The combined impact of all these factors created structural deficits that could not be fixed by simple tweaks to tax systems. Thus, during the late 1960s, nearly all governors called on their legislatures to increase taxes, and in many cases requested major new tax adoptions. The general pattern was that the largest tax system changes were requested by governors in states that lacked one of the "Big Three" fiscal instruments of state government. In other words, sales taxes were promoted in income-tax-only states, and income taxes were promoted in sales-tax-only states.

At the outset of the second critical juncture, efforts to adopt sales taxes enjoyed considerable advantages over efforts to adopt income taxes. The pronounced preference for sales taxation over income taxation that had been such a regular feature of state politics in the postwar era carried over into the beginning of the second critical juncture and resulted in successful

[28] 394 U.S. 618 (1969)

pushes for sales tax adoption in numerous states that had long resisted them. In Massachusetts, for example, Republican Governor John Volpe overcame the strenuous opposition of organized labor in his fourteen-month quest to cajole the overwhelmingly Democratic state legislature to adopt a sales tax.[29] Similar dynamics occurred in New York state, where Governor Nelson Rockefeller cobbled together an unusual legislative coalition composed of Republicans and New York City Democrats on behalf of the sales tax.[30]

By the apex of the critical juncture in the late 1960s, however, movements to adopt income taxes (especially personal income taxes) in sales-tax-only states had gained considerable steam. The rise of these movements across the country is particularly noteworthy given that state income taxes were almost never adopted in the previous thirty years, and existing income taxes were only expanded in states that had come to significantly rely upon them by the end of the New Deal Era. All this changed at the end of the 1960s. Suddenly, serious efforts to adopt income taxes were afoot in nearly all states without them.

The push to adopt income taxes owed to several changed circumstances. To begin with, cuts to the federal income tax implemented during the mid 1960s led state policymakers to feel more comfortable levying state income taxes (as will be discussed in Chapter 4, this was one of the goals of the federal tax cuts). Second, a consensus was emerging that state income taxes had certain economic benefits that sales taxes lacked. In particular, economists were increasingly of the view that income taxes were more "elastic" (i.e., responsive to economic growth) than sales taxes, and thus that states with income taxes on the books were generating more revenue as a result of economic growth than states without them.[31] The view that sales-tax-only states were "missing out" on much revenue automatically accrued through economic growth helped to undermine the deep skepticism among many governors and state legislators regarding the state-level personal income tax.

Third, the growing debate among national policymakers regarding the country's intergovernmental taxation arrangement in the mid-late 1960s (discussed in Chapter 4) helped convince many policymakers in sales-tax-only states that it was time for their states to adopt an income tax. As

[29] Timothy Leland, "Sales Tax War All Over but Final Shouting Today," *Boston Globe*, March 1, 1966, 1.

[30] Sydney H. Schanberg, "Sales Tax Passed," *New York Times*, April 15, 1965, 1.

[31] Advisory Committee on Intergovernmental Relations, *Sources of Increased State Tax Collections: Economic Growth vs. Political Choice*, Report #M-41, October 1968.

Chapter 4 shows, fiscal policymakers in the Kennedy and Johnson administrations widely believed that the reliance of numerous state governments on sales taxes not only made their tax systems unnecessarily regressive, but also unnecessarily rigid and weak. Debates about how to reform the intergovernmental taxation arrangement in Washington, D.C. therefore often centered on the question of how to encourage states without income taxes to adopt them. Sensing that the national government would soon pass tax reforms advantaging states with income taxes over states without them, state-level policymakers moved to ensure their states would be able to benefit from such a reform.

Finally, changes in state government in the early-mid 1960s forced by the Supreme Court's reapportionment decisions led to changes in the politics of state taxation policy. The requirement in *Reynolds v. Sims* that all citizens have an equally weighted vote in all state legislative chambers forced nearly all states to redraw the legislative districts in the mid 1960s in order to give urban areas far greater legislative representation. By the late 1960s, newly apportioned and more progressive legislatures were seated, and these legislatures were far more interested than previous ones in expanding state fiscal capacity to address pressing urban problems.[32]

The most noteworthy political shift wrought by the convergence of these factors was the sudden embrace of income taxes by a large number of Republican governors in sales-tax-only states. In Pennsylvania, Illinois, Michigan, New Jersey, and Rhode Island, all states where top Republicans had long been outspoken opponents of income tax adoption, GOP executives in the late 1960s endorsed enacting personal income taxes as a way of solving state budget problems. In nearly all these cases, the decision to embrace the income tax was reluctant and came at great political risk. Most of these governors had previously been on record as opposing income taxation, and their switch on the issue rendered them vulnerable to being attacked as flip-floppers. This was especially the case for Governors Richard Ogilvie of Illinois and John Chafee of Rhode Island, both of whom had won their seats by campaigning against income taxes and warning that their Democratic opponents would implement them.[33] Eventually, however, exigent

[32] Stephen Ansolabehere and James M. Snyder, *The End of Inequality: One Person, One Vote and the Transformation of American Politics* (New York: Norton, 2008).

[33] George Tagge, "Two Major Issues in Governor's Contest are a State Income Tax and Richard Cain," *Chicago Tribune*, November 2, 1968, 5; John P. Hackett and Paul A. Kelly "The Wider Horizons of John H. Chafee," *Providence Sunday Journal* (Providence, RI), December 24, 1967, N-22.

circumstances forced both governors to revisit their opposition to income taxes. In his 1969 address announcing his income tax proposal, Ogilvie warned that "Illinois was on the brink of bankruptcy" and that "we must have a new revenue source." The income tax was the obvious choice, and Ogilvie concluded that "I have no choice but to recommend the adoption of such a tax (on both individuals and corporations)."[34] Similarly, and in the same year, Republican Governor Raymond Shafer of Pennsylvania explained his newfound support for the personal income tax in his state by saying: "I am convinced... that we must have this kind of a tax program if we are to meet our future needs. This is not politically easy to say, but it must be said."[35]

The decisions of these governors to promote income tax adoption had the effect of altering the alignments of their states' political parties on the issue. In Pennsylvania, Illinois, and Michigan, Republican legislative leaders were caught off guard by their governor's endorsement of income taxation and struggled to put together a legislative coalition to pass income tax proposals. In Pennsylvania, these efforts ultimately failed, while in Illinois and Michigan, leaders were able to cobble together cross-party coalitions composed primarily of Republicans to pass income tax bills.[36] Democrats, on the other hand, turned the tables on Republicans by using the about-faces of the Republican governors on the income tax against them. Indeed, Governors Ogilvie and Chafee ended up losing their re-election bids in 1972 and 1968 largely due to their support of income taxation.[37] The scrambling of state party alignments on the income tax issue had effects that were felt long after the critical juncture in state taxation was over; in some of these states, it was not until the 1990s that a clear party divide over taxation re-emerged.

The policy changes that occurred in the second critical juncture are depicted in Figure 3.4, which shows adoptions and rate increases for the "Big Three" state taxes between 1965 and 1972. The figure confirms that sales tax adoptions tended to occur earlier in the critical juncture while income tax adoptions (especially personal income tax adoptions) occurred later. It also

[34] "Text of Gov. Ogilvie's Budget Address," *Chicago Tribune*, April 2, 1969, 8.

[35] *Pittsburgh Post-Gazette*, January 29, 1969, 4.

[36] On the passage of the income tax in Illinois, see: Taylor Pensoneau, *Governor Richard Ogilvie: In the Interest of the State* (Carbondale, IL: Southern Illinois University Press, 1997), 95–107; on its passage in Michigan, see: Jerry Moskal, "2.6 Income Tax OK'd," *Lansing State Journal*, July 1, 1967, 1; Willard Baird, "Senate Oks Tax Effective Oct. 1st," *Lansing State Journal*, July 2, 1967, 1. For its part, Pennsylvania eventually passed an income tax under a Democratic governor in 1971.

[37] Pensoneau, *In the Interest of the State*, 258; "Chafee Defeat Analyzed," *Providence Journal*, November 22, 1968, 14.

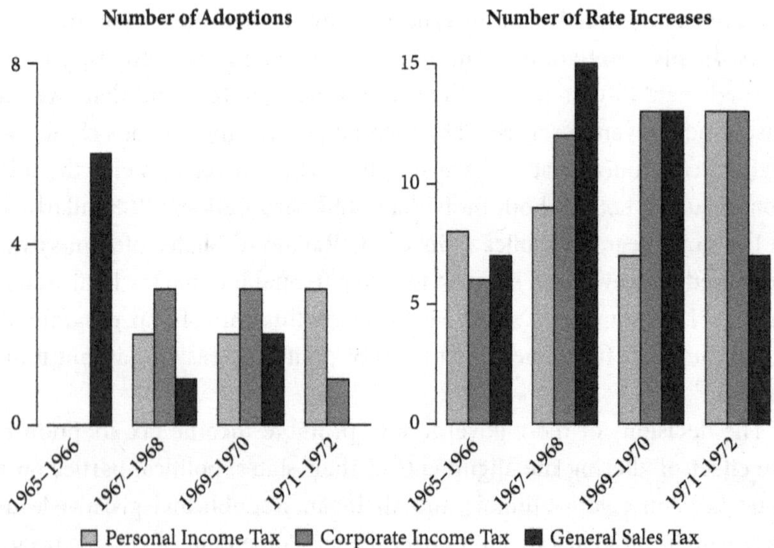

Figure 3.4 Income and Sales Tax Adoptions and Rate Increases, 1965–1972

Source: State Tax Actions Dataset

shows that rate increases for all three taxes were far more common in the 1965–1972 period than in the period immediately after World War II, and that they occurred in large numbers across all the state legislative biennia of the period.

The large number of tax adoptions during the second critical juncture led to a significant increase in the number of states that utilized each of the "Big Three" taxes by its end. Of the seventeen states without a personal income tax and the thirteen states without a corporate income tax as of 1964, only ten and five remained as of 1972 (respectively). Similarly, of the thirteen states without a general sales tax as of 1964, only five remained as of 1973. And whereas in 1964 there were still two states that had not adopted any of the "Big Three" taxes, by 1973 there was no such state.[38] Clearly, then, the second critical juncture led to a major convergence of states in terms of tax utilization.

But the increased utilization of each of the "Big Three" taxes did not lead to major convergence in how the taxes were designed. For example, rates and rate structures continued to differ substantially. For personal income taxes,

[38] The two states were Nebraska and New Hampshire.

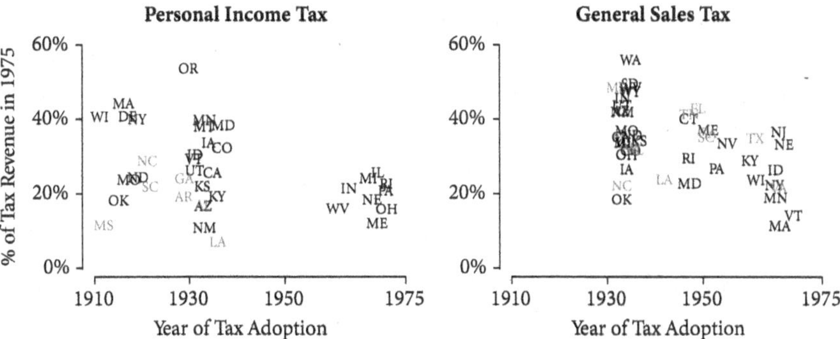

Figure 3.5 The Effect of Year of Adoption on Tax Reliance in 1975 for the Personal Income and General Sales Taxes

Alaska and Hawaii not included; southern states in gray.

Sources: U.S. Census, *Historical Finances of State Government* dataset; State Tax Actions Dataset

top rates ranged from 20.125% (Vermont) to 2% (Indiana) as of 1972.[39] For corporate taxes, top rates ranged from 12% (Minnesota and Pennsylvania) to 2% (Indiana). For general sales taxes, rates ranged from 7% (Connecticut) to 2% (Indiana and Oklahoma). Other important aspects of the taxes differed as well. For personal income taxes, the amount of income exempted varied substantially. For general sales tax, the range of exempted products differed.

Differences in the design of the "Big Three" taxes heavily impacted their ability to generate large amounts of revenue, which in turn influenced the extent to which states relied upon each of them. It is in the area of tax reliance that path-dependent effects continued to leave a major mark on state tax systems past the end of the second critical juncture. This is demonstrated in Figure 3.5, which presents two scatterplots depicting the relationship between the year in which states adopted the personal income tax or general sales tax, and the percentage of tax revenue states gained from each of these sources as of 1975. For both taxes, the scatterplots show a fairly clear if imperfect relationship: states that had adopted each of the taxes at earlier periods generally relied on those taxes more than states that adopted them in later periods. For the personal income tax, this relationship is especially evident when southern states (colored in gray) are excluded from consideration.

[39] Vermont's unusually high top rate was a function of the fact that, between 1967 and 2002, its personal income tax was assessed as a percentage of its citizens' national income tax liability. In 1972, the percentage was 28.75% and the top national income tax rate was 70%; ergo, the top Vermont income tax rate was 20.125% (70% multiplied by 28.75%).

This is because many of the earliest adopters of personal income taxes were southern states. However, due to their relative poverty and the fact that they were especially prone toward keeping taxes low in the mid twentieth century as an economic development strategy, southern states were far less reliant on the personal income tax than non-southern states.

The End of the Second Critical Juncture and the Stabilization of State Tax Systems

The second critical juncture in state taxation ended abruptly in 1973. In sharp contrast to the numerous state-level tax actions of the previous eight years, no state adopted a new income or sales tax during the 1973–1974 state legislative biennium and the number of tax levies declined substantially as well. Several factors were responsible for this waning of state tax activity. First, the many recent tax increases combined with robust economic growth in the early 1970s to yield massive state revenue gains, resulting in state-level budget surpluses for the first time in years. Additionally, states were feeling less pressure to raise new revenue for public education as the effects of the postwar baby boom crested and public school enrollments stabilized. Finally, the influx of new federal funds through the State and Local Fiscal Assistance Act of 1972 (also known as the Federal Revenue-Sharing Law, discussed more extensively in Chapter 4) provided significant new resources to state and especially local governments, which further eased their fiscal pressures.[40]

In the aftermath of the 1965–1972 period, state and local revenue systems became defined by several important new realities. First, unlike in any previous period of American history (save perhaps the early nineteenth century), state governments were now more important fiscal players than local governments. As of the early 1970s, states raised more tax revenue than local governments overall as well as in forty-one of the fifty states (this trend would only grow in the future).[41] This new reality was clearly related to the fact that state tax systems, unlike local tax systems, were now thoroughly diversified. By the mid 1970s, the vast bulk of states were levying each of the "Big Three"

[40] Federation of Tax Administrators, *Trends in State Tax Legislation 1972-1973*, Research Report No. 66, March 1974.

[41] Advisory Commission on Intergovernmental Relations, *Significant Features of Fiscal Federalism, 1976-77 Edition: Vol. II - Revenue and Debt*, Report # M-110, March 1977, 6, 17–18.

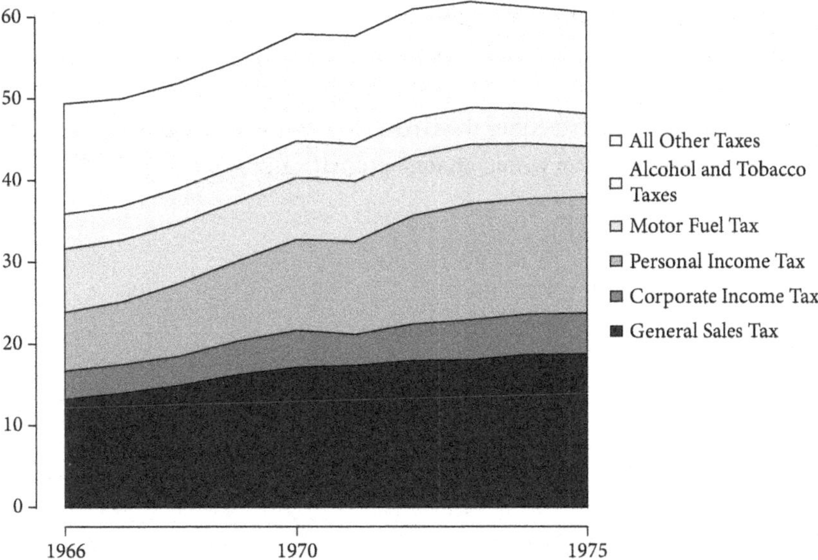

Figure 3.6 Sources of State Tax Revenue (in Billions of $), 1966–1975
Source: U.S. Census, *Historical Finances of State Government* dataset

tax instruments along with numerous selective sales taxes as well as a host of smaller business taxes and fees. Local governments, on the other hand, had become overwhelmingly reliant on property taxes (alongside state and national aid). To a greater extent than ever before, state governments were now the "senior partners" in state and local finance.[42]

But though tax diversification was a key factor behind the rise of the states as fiscal powerhouses in the late 1960s and early 1970s, the bulk of the growth in state tax revenue came from one source: the personal income tax. This can be seen in Figure 3.6, which shows the components of own-source state tax revenue from the beginning of the second critical juncture to slightly after its end. As the figure shows, the ten years between 1966 and 1975 witnessed a shift toward more than half of state own-source revenue coming from the "Big Three" tax sources, but most of this increase came from personal income taxes. Thanks to this growth, by the mid 1970s, states were no longer overwhelmingly reliant on consumption taxes. Income taxes—especially personal income taxes—were assuming increasingly important roles in most state tax systems.

[42] Advisory Commission on Intergovernmental Relations, *Significant Features of Fiscal Federalism, 1976-77 Edition: Vol. II - Revenue and Debt*, Report # M-110, March 1977, 3

The new equilibrium in state finances that was established by the second critical juncture would not last for long, however. By the 1980s, state governments were facing a new set of fiscal challenges, ones that were quite different from those they faced in either the Great Depression or the postwar era. The politics of state taxation would change dramatically as a result.

4

State Taxation Challenges and the National Debate over Fiscal Federalism Reform, 1948–1972

The postwar period was the apogee of national interest in fiscal federalism questions. Unlike the 1930s, when the topic was much discussed among interest groups and advocacy communities but failed to receive regular attention from Congress,[1] the decades after World War II (particularly the 14-year stretch between 1958 and 1972) were a time in which fiscal federalism succeeded in capturing the sustained attention of policymakers in both the national executive and legislative branches. Owing to a convergence of several economic and political developments, the issue of intergovernmental fiscal policymaking was transformed from one that elected officials nodded to and then ignored or set aside for want of an easy solution to one that they regularly and seriously discussed over the course of many years. The dilemma of subnational government finance—in particular, the fact that state (and also local) governments almost continuously found themselves pressed for cash in the 1950s and 1960s, their substantial revenue-raising efforts notwithstanding—was the central topic in these discussions, with numerous congressional committee hearings and joint legislative-executive meetings attending to it. As part of these discussions, proposals for significantly reshaping the national-state taxation relationship were routinely presented and promoted. Eventually, a consensus emerged that the fiscal challenges of subnational government in the mid twentieth century required a robust national response in the form of the general sharing of national revenues with states and localities. The ultimate outcome of this consensus—the State and Local Fiscal Assistance Act of 1972, or SLFAA—represents the only

[1] This was especially the case after the breakdown of the alcohol sales tax revenue-sharing efforts at the end of 1933.

Coordination Failure. Adam S. Myers, Oxford University Press. © Oxford University Press (2026).
DOI: 10.1093/9780197831878.003.0005

major, self-conscious effort on the part of the national government to reform the intergovernmental fiscal relationship in modern American history.

But though SLFAA was undoubtedly a unique breakthrough, in its transformational impact the law fell well short of the intergovernmental fiscal coordination programs adopted by other federal countries like Canada or Australia. As the chapter will show, the chief reason for this was that the forces in mid-century American national politics that demanded intergovernmental fiscal reform had highly different goals in mind. In order to compose a congressional coalition large enough to pass such a reform into law, national leaders thus had to craft a proposal that attempted to achieve not just one of these goals, but many. In the process of doing so, however, they settled on a final product that did not implement any of these goals particularly well, likely dooming SLFAA from the start.

One important goal motivating many supporters of intergovernmental fiscal reform was that of fiscal equalization. As discussed in the introduction, the United States is unique among federal systems in never having implemented a stand-alone program to equalize the fiscal conditions of its subnational governments—an aspect of American public policy that the political scientists Daniel Béland and André Lecours call "a lesser known aspect of 'American exceptionalism.'"[2] As the chapter will show, this was not because significant gaps in fiscal capacity among states did not exist or because such gaps went unacknowledged by the nation's leaders. In fact, the issue of interstate fiscal inequality was widely recognized by top policymakers as a major problem facing the country throughout the 1950s and 1960s, and the man largely responsible for bringing the idea of revenue sharing to the center of the national policy agenda (Walter Heller, the chair of Council of Economic Advisors during the Kennedy and Johnson Administrations) promoted the policy as a way to both revitalize state governments and equalize their resource levels. In the years following Heller's initial proposal, however, a panoply of interests with motivations quite different from those of Heller jumped on the revenue-sharing bandwagon, and the focus on interstate fiscal equalization receded as a result. The final version of SLFAA did include a fiscal equalization component, but equalization was very far from being the main guidepost around which the program was built.

The story of the struggle to shape intergovernmental fiscal relations in the 1960s, and in particular the fight over revenue sharing, has been

[2] Daniel Béland and Andre Lecours, "Fiscal Federalism and American Exceptionalism: Why is there No Federal Equalisation System in the United States?," *Journal of Public Policy* 34, no. 2 (2014): 304.

told before. But previous recountings have only made passing reference to the ways in which it was shaped by state-level developments in taxation policy around the same period. In this examination of mid-century fiscal federalism debates in Washington, D.C., I put state politics and tax policy front and center. In doing so, I show how the concerns over state fiscal conditions that motivated revenue sharing's initial proponents faded as the revenue-sharing coalition grew to include groups with a variety of other concerns (most notably, the bleak fiscal situation facing the nation's largest cities). When revenue sharing finally did make it to the top of the national domestic policy agenda in the early 1970s, its supporters were motivated by a diverse array of competing goals and federalism visions, leading to major disagreements over how revenue collected by the national government should be distributed to states and localities. By integrating as many of these perspectives as possible into the final revenue-sharing bill that passed Congress, lawmakers ended up diluting revenue sharing's long-term effects and transformative potential.

The 1950s: The Fiscal Federalism Discussion Resumes

During World War II, federalism-related questions and concerns took a back seat to the nation's wartime emergency. For the most part, neither Congress nor the executive branch seriously considered questions of intergovernmental fiscal relations while the war was being fought. One important exception was the Treasury Department's Division of Tax Research, which in 1943 completed a massive study of intergovernmental fiscal relations that had been commissioned before the war began. The results of the study were submitted as an extensive report to Congress, which did little in response to the report's findings.[3]

After the war was over, discussions about intergovernmental fiscal relations resumed with vigor. Indeed, the fiscal coordination question was almost certainly more salient in the postwar era than it was in the New Deal Era. For example, between 1945 and 1960, hardly a year went by that did not feature some major study of the fiscal dimension of intergovernmental relations. Like in the New Deal Era, these studies were commissioned by Congress, the executive branch, as well as nonprofit agencies, but the number of studies sponsored by agents of the national government was

[3] *Federal, State, and Local Government Fiscal Relations; Letter from the Acting Secretary of the Treasury Transmitting in Response to S. Res. 160*, S. Doc. No. 69 (1943).

substantially higher than before. Clearly, fiscal federalism was no longer simply capturing the attention of organized interests; it was now a regular cause for concern among policymakers.

The Treasury Department, which did not cease its activities in the realm of intergovernmental fiscal reform during the war, only amplified them after the war was over. In 1949, the Department convened a series of conferences of officials from national, state, and local government to discuss intergovernmental fiscal problems. The main issues discussed in this conference—duplication of taxes between national and state government—were of a piece with the ones expressed by the tax coordination movement during the 1930s.[4] Tax professionals and elite organizations with an interest in tax policy also returned to the issue. In particular, the National Tax Association, American Bar Association, and National Association of Tax Administrators convened a joint committee which, in 1949, produced a comprehensive report examining various tax coordination options.[5]

After a long stretch in which it ignored the issue, Congress, too, began re-engaging with intergovernmental fiscal reform. Under the leadership of its longtime chairman, Robert Doughton, the House Ways and Means Committee restarted its examination of intergovernmental tax conflicts, commissioning the Treasury Department to produce yet another comprehensive study of the topic, which it produced in 1953.[6] Congress also began to hold numerous hearings on the topic, particularly within the Subcommittee of Intergovernmental Relations of the Committee of Government Operations.

By the early 1950s, however, the question of how to reform the nation's intergovernmental taxation arrangement was increasingly being overshadowed by a second fiscal federalism question: how to reform the complex system of conditional grants from the national government to the states and localities that had begun to emerge during the New Deal and exploded in growth following World War II. While the connection between the "taxation side" and the "spending side" of fiscal federalism was widely understood, the tendency of most policymakers was to consider each of these aspects separately. During the 1930s, as described in Chapter 2, organized interests and

[4] Tax Advisory Staff, U.S. Department of Treasury, *Federal-State-Local Tax Coordination: A Treasury Tax Study* (1952).

[5] Joint Committee of the American Bar Association, the National Tax Association, and the National Association of Tax Administrators, The Coordination of Federal, State and Local taxation (1949).

[6] *Coordination of Federal, State, and Local Taxes: Report to the Committee on Ways and Means of the House of Representatives*, 82nd Congress (1953).

policymakers largely focused on the taxation side and gave relatively short shrift to the spending side. By the 1950s, however, the conditional grant system had grown to such levels that a nearly exclusive focus on ironing out the nation's intergovernmental taxation arrangement no longer made much sense to stakeholders. In fact, the fiscal policymakers of this period seem to have overshot in the opposite direction. The Advisory Commission on Intergovernmental Relations, a group that was officially organized by Congress in response to a request from President Eisenhower to study how federalism should work in the mid twentieth century, devoted the bulk of its time to studying the wisdom of various conditional grant programs, giving the question of taxation powers only secondary consideration. When asked to explain the Commission's thinking on this matter, Commission Chair Meyer Kestnbaum argued that determining the appropriate division of labor in substantive policy should take priority over resolving intergovernmental tax conflicts. As he stated to a meeting of state tax commissioners: "I should think that if we can redefine the responsibilities that ought to be exercised by the various levels of government, then our decision with respect to tax resources would follow."[7]

By the late 1950s, however, policymakers seem to have moved into a middle-ground position based on the premise that recalibrating the intergovernmental fiscal relationship should simultaneously involve considering the status of conditional grant programs alongside the relationship between state and federal tax systems. This new view developed from the realization that the taxation and spending components of fiscal federalism were inextricably linked and that addressing both components would necessarily entail making difficult political decisions. From this vantage point, Kestnbaum's assessment that updating the intergovernmental taxation relationship could be easily achieved after questions regarding the appropriate distribution of substantive responsibilities across levels of government were resolved appeared too rosy. Taxation decisions were as controversial as spending decisions and, more importantly, they more squarely implicated the most difficult federalism question of all: which level of government should have the bulk of political power. It was for this reason that members of Congress involved in intergovernmental relations toward the end of the 1950s attempted to take a different approach.

[7] Alfred G. Buehler, "Taxation Aspects of Intergovernmental Fiscal Relations," *Proceedings of the Annual Conference of Taxation under the Auspices of the National Tax Association* 48 (1955), 529–538.

No member of Congress played a bigger role in the effort to reshape fiscal federalism at the end of the 1950s than Representative L. H. Fountain. A North Carolina Democrat, Fountain chaired the Subcommittee on Intergovernmental Relations of the Committee on Government Operations, which regularly held hearings on intergovernmental relations in the decade's final years. Through these hearings, Fountain came to understand that managing America's increasingly complicated federal system in the mid twentieth century required the creation of an intergovernmental body with representatives from all three levels of government that would serve in an "advisory capacity" to the nation's elected leaders.[8] The body Fountain envisioned was thus similar to the ill-fated Tax Revision Council of the 1930s (discussed in Chapter 2), but rather than focusing exclusively on the intergovernmental tax arrangement, it would consider taxation alongside spending and substantive policy responsibilities. As Fountain explained, such a body was needed to "strengthen the ability of our federal system to meet the problems of an increasingly complex society...by promoting greater cooperation, understanding, and coordination of activities between the separate levels of government."[9] His vision thus reflected the new recognition that fiscal federalism needed to be considered holistically rather than via only its taxation or spending components.

Fountain's idea for a new intergovernmental body came into fruition in 1959 when Congress passed and President Eisenhower signed Public Law 86-380.[10] The new law created the Advisory Commission on Intergovernmental Relations (ACIR), a bipartisan body composed of twenty-six members from both the executive and legislative branches of federal, state, and local government. Unlike the Tax Revision Council of the 1930s, ACIR received official blessing from Congress in addition to significant financial resources and a full-time staff of fourteen persons. In the words of Fountain, it was a "political innovation"—the first permanent body dedicated to exploring intergovernmental issues and including representation for officials from all three levels of government.[11] Crucially, of the six charges that Congress gave the Commission, one was "to provide a forum for discussing the

[8] "Statement on H.R. 6904," Undated, Box 4, L. H. Fountain Papers, Louis Round Wilson Special Collections Library, University of North Carolina, Chapel Hill, NC.

[9] "Statement on H.R. 6904," Undated, Box 4, Fountain Papers.

[10] "Public Law 86-380—September 24, 1959," https://www.congress.gov/86/statute/STATUTE-73/STATUTE-73-Pg703.pdf.

[11] Press Release, Office of Congressman L. H. Fountain, September 24, 1959, Box 4, Fountain Papers.

administration and coordination of Federal grant and other programs" and another was "to recommend methods of coordinating and simplifying tax laws...to achieve a more orderly and less competitive fiscal relationship..."[12]

Soon after its official creation, the ACIR got to work, and its early agenda heavily emphasized the importance of considering intergovernmental taxation policy alongside (rather than after) conditional grant decisions and substantive policy responsibilities. Four of the ten items on its original work program—property tax reform, estate tax reform, equalizing state fiscal capacity and/or tax effort, and cooperative tax administration—related to taxation.[13] Additionally, not long after its inception, the ACIR began producing informational papers related to the relationship between national and state/local tax policy. Thus, the ACIR clearly did not view the taxation side of fiscal federalism as being of secondary importance to the spending side. Quite to the contrary, its members understood intergovernmental taxation reforms and intergovernmental spending reforms as being of equal importance.

Closely related to, though not entirely overlapping with, the ACIR's early work on subnational tax policy was its attention to disparities in state fiscal conditions. Though the commission strove to "[maintain] an objective point of view" in its analysis of the issues facing American federalism,[14] its publications reflected the then-common view that such disparities were a significant obstacle to the establishment of a cooperative, low-competition intergovernmental fiscal relationship. For example, in 1962, the ACIR published a report demonstrating the existence of large-scale differences in fiscal capacity (defined as "the resources a taxing jurisdiction can tax to raise revenue for public purposes") across states, with poor southern states generally ranking far lower in fiscal capacity than wealthy northeastern and West Coast states.[15] Soon thereafter, ACIR published another report examining the extent to which existing intergovernmental grants from the national government to the states had an equalizing effect on state finances. The report found that such grants had begun to have an equalization component

[12] 108 Cong. Rec. S10623 (Jun 15, 1962) (statement of Sen. Muskie).

[13] "Summary of Actions Taken by the Advisory Commission on Intergovernmental Relations: June 1964," Box 4340, Sam Ervin Papers, Louis Round Wilson Special Collections Library, University of North Carolina, Chapel Hill, NC.

[14] "Tentative Draft: Suggested Work Plan for the Advisory Commission on Intergovernmental Relations," February 10, 1960, Box 5, Fountain Papers.

[15] Advisory Commission on Intergovernmental Relations, *Measures of State and Local Fiscal Capacity and Tax Effort*, Report # M-16, October 1962.

only in recent years, and that their overall effect was "not yet significant."[16] Acknowledging the politically sensitive nature of equalization discussions, the report nonetheless recommended that Congress take further account of state fiscal capacity in structuring grant programs so as to facilitate greater interstate uniformity in public services (while also emphasizing that complete uniformity was not necessarily desirable).[17] The possibility of a grant program specifically designed to ameliorate subnational fiscal inequalities went unaddressed in this report.

Business, Labor, and the Fiscal Federalism Question

As the discussion over how to reform America's federal system heated up among policymakers in the postwar era, leading social sectors with a stake in the discussion's outcome began to mobilize. The two sectors that took the most active interest in the fiscal federalism debate were the business community and its principal opponents: organized labor. Not surprisingly, these two interest-group communities promoted divergent approaches to the question of how to reform intergovernmental fiscal relations in the mid twentieth century. Importantly, the relative merits of placing greater tax authority at the national level versus the state/local level played a crucial role in shaping the approaches of both communities.

Unlike in the 1930s, when (as discussed in Chapter 2) the business community was divided over the question of how to foster greater intergovernmental tax coordination, business organizations largely united around a common agenda of fiscal federalism reform in the 1950s and 1960s. The overarching goal motivating business groups during the postwar era was a reduction of the size and power of the national government, whose growth over the course of the mid twentieth century they had come to view with alarm. In their many publications of this period, business groups made the case that a robust, decentralized federal system served as an essential constitutional safeguard against tyranny, and that the growth of the national government at the supposed expense of the states was thus a trend that portended not just the end of the free-enterprise system but the eventual rise of authoritarianism itself. Business groups shared a unified understanding

[16] Advisory Commission on Intergovernmental Relations, *The Role of Equalization in Federal Grants*, Report # A-19, January 1964, 72.

[17] Ibid., 73

of what facilitated the aggrandizement of the national government and the eclipse of the states: the growth of federal conditional grant programs, which had run roughshod over state autonomy and turned state governments into "mendicants" depending on the federal trough. Rolling back the grants-in-aid system and returning responsibility in key areas of domestic policy to the states was thus understood as a crucial step in reestablishing a balanced federal system and reinforcing the concept of "government close to and under control of the people."

But though their chief mid twentieth century goal was scaling back conditional grants from the national government to the states, business groups understood that recalibrating fiscal federalism according to their vision required reforming the intergovernmental taxation relationship as well as the intergovernmental spending relationship. The former was important for two reasons. First, for states to reassume control over functions in which the national government had intervened, they needed greater access to revenue. But perhaps more importantly, giving states greater tax authority was an important vehicle for ensuring that American government would remain limited; due to the competitive threats they faced, states would be far more likely than the national government to keep their taxes low, thereby leading to less tax revenue and a less expansive administrative state overall.

With the foregoing goals in mind, business groups developed comprehensive plans for fiscal federalism reform that paid equal attention to "the allocation of tax resources and the allocation of service responsibilities." During congressional hearings on intergovernmental relations, the nation's business lobby pushed heavily for a return to a "dual federalism" form of national-state relations in which the national government and the states were not only responsible for separate policies, but also gained revenue from different tax sources. Groups like the Chamber of Commerce and the National Association of Manufacturers promoted federal withdrawal from a variety of policy areas that the national government had first entered in the 1930s (including old-age assistance and unemployment compensation), alongside a withdrawal of the national government from various tax sources (most notably, estate and inheritance taxation). According to representatives of these groups, states would be able to assume responsibility for these areas of policy once they had complete access to the tax sources that were currently being heavily exploited by the national government. These devolutionary reforms were depicted as facilitating responsive democratic government: through separating state and national policy responsibility and tax sources, the reforms would clarify the roles and taxing powers of different levels of government in the minds of voters, thereby enhancing democratic accountability.

Members of the House Subcommittee on Intergovernmental Relations, who had read the business lobby's written statements and listened to its representatives' testimonies, greeted these arguments with a large degree of skepticism. To begin with, they questioned whether state governments would effectively step into the breach created by the withdrawal of the national government that was envisioned by the business groups. In doing so, they often emphasized that previous federal tax cuts on overlapping tax sources did not lead to state tax increases on those sources. House members repeatedly questioned business representatives regarding how their vision would be influenced by the dynamic of interstate tax competition. Their concerns were simple: properly funding many social welfare programs required high levels of tax revenue, but interstate competitive pressures might force states to keep taxes low, thereby resulting in less overall tax revenue for these programs.

As the business community promoted its twin fiscal federalism agenda of devolution and separation of tax sources, organized labor mobilized in opposition. Unlike the business community, whose interest in fiscal federalism issues stretched back to the New Deal Era and to some extent before, labor unions had not focused much of their attention on intergovernmental fiscal relations prior to World War II. Their voices were largely absent from the debate over fiscal coordination in the 1930s, for example. In the postwar era, however, labor groups began to engage in America's fiscal federalism debate much more intensely. In doing so, they promoted a new perspective on fiscal federalism that had not been previously expressed. This approach was rooted in a deep suspicion of state governments and a reflexive opposition to all federalism reforms that would decentralize either spending or taxing decisions at the state level.

Labor's fiscal federalism agenda was first and foremost oriented around protecting the complex system of conditional grants-in-aid that had arisen in the postwar era from attacks by business and conservative groups. Labor groups did not trust state governments, which they viewed as reactionary anachronisms controlled by conservative forces, with the responsibility of either formulating or administering the nation's social policies. Conditional grants with specific programmatic goals and instructions, in their view, were essential for ensuring that states comported with "national standards" in areas such as health care or welfare. But, just as importantly, labor groups did not trust state governments with increased taxation authority either. Indeed, over the course of the 1950s, groups like the AFL-CIO sounded increasingly loud alarms regarding the scale and growth of state-level regressive taxation, particularly as states expanded their sales taxes to meet new revenue needs. In its monthly publications, for example, the AFL-CIO routinely warned about the growth of regressive state and local taxes during the 1950s. "The rapid rise in state and local taxes is shifting more and more of the total tax burden to those least able to pay," wrote the editors of *Labor's Economic Review* in November 1956.[18]

Given labor's lack of faith in the ability of state governments to make wise taxing or spending decisions, the solution that national labor groups offered to the growing revenue needs of state governments was to further expand conditional grant programs. As a resolution from the AFL-CIO's Sixth Constitutional Convention stated, "Far greater federal aid to the states is imperative...Toward this end, the AFL-CIO urges a rapid increase in federal grant-in-aid programs."[19] Even as a national consensus that reforming the intergovernmental fiscal relationship required giving states greater flexibility in spending federal money began to emerge in the late 1960s to early 1970s, the unions never wavered from their underlying view that federal aid to the states should always be clearly directed and tightly monitored.

Walter Heller and the Emergence of a Fiscal Federalism "Third Way"

The general pattern of the 1950s—conservatives and business groups promoting the return to a "dual" form of fiscal federalism, with both taxation authority and policy responsibility strictly separated between national and state government, and progressives and labor unions doubling down on categorical grants-in-aid as the solutions to state revenue problems—was interrupted in the early 1960s by the emergence of a third approach to fiscal federalism. This approach, championed by liberal policymakers in the Kennedy and Johnson administrations, occupied a middle ground between

[18] "State and Local Taxes Hit Low-Income Families Hardest," *Labor's Economic Review*, Vol. 1, no. 10 (November 1956).

[19] "Revenue Sharing and the AFL-CIO: Selected Documents," Box 42, AFL-CIO Legislation Department Records, University of Maryland Libraries, College Park, MD.

the conservative, business-backed approach and the progressive, labor-backed approach. Its core premise was that existing grants-in-aid should not be rolled back, but that rather than expand the existing system, Congress should supplement it with a new program of general revenue support for state governments. This new program would be based on intergovernmental transfers not linked to specific, programmatic purposes defined by the national government. Instead, states would get federal money that they could use as they saw fit, a fiscal strategy that quickly came to be known by the moniker "revenue sharing."

The political figure primarily responsible for the formulation and promotion of this middle-ground approach to fiscal federalism was Walter Heller, the Chairman of the Council of Economic Advisors during parts of both the Kennedy and Johnson presidencies. A professor of economics at the University of Minnesota prior to entering government service, Heller had developed an early interest in intergovernmental fiscal relations as a graduate student at the University of Wisconsin, where he studied with Harold Groves, a leading early-twentieth-century scholar of subnational tax policy who also served in the Wisconsin Legislature.[20] Heller's studies with Groves helped inculcate in him the importance of preserving the vitality of state governments, a concern that would later distinguish him from the other, more nationally oriented policymakers in the Johnson and Kennedy administrations.

Heller understood the primary fiscal federalism problem the country was facing in the postwar era to be one of fiscal imbalance: whereas the national government was blessed with a powerful tax system generating far more revenue than it needed, state tax systems were simply not sufficiently robust to keep pace with the vastly increasing expenses they were accruing on an annual basis. This created a mismatch between the amount of revenue each level of government raised and the amount of money each level needed. As Heller stated, "prosperity gives the federal government the revenue, and the state and local governments the problems."[21]

In Heller's view, the first step to rectifying the fiscal imbalance in the American federal system was to cut the federal income tax. In classic Keynesian fashion, Heller theorized that a broad-based federal income tax cut would

[20] Walter Heller Oral History, Interview by David McComb, December 21, 1971, Lyndon Johnson Presidential Library. https://www.discoverlbj.org/item/oh-hellerw-19711221-2-83-10

[21] Walter W. Heller, *New Dimensions of Political Economy* (New York: Norton, 1967), 118.

redound in greater economic activity and higher average incomes; the latter would, over time, have a positive effect on state income tax revenues. Heller thus became a leading advocate of the income tax reduction passed by Congress in 1963. In a letter to Pierre Salinger, Lyndon Johnson's former press secretary who had just moved back to his native California, Heller joked that the "tax cut will be the greatest thing for California since the return of Pierre Salinger." This was because "California state and local tax revenues will grow with the increase in incomes. The full economic impact of the tax cut will mean some $198 million in additional California state tax revenues..."[22] The Treasury Department largely concurred with Heller's assessment, concluding that the reduction in income tax rates "would alleviate to a substantial degree the conditions which have forced state and local governments to raise their tax rates in the postwar era."[23]

But Heller was also convinced that cutting the federal income tax would not be sufficient to address the fiscal problems facing state governments. Even with lower income tax rates, the national government would still be receiving far more revenue than it needed (particularly if the tax cuts had their intended effect of boosting economic growth) while the states (especially those without income taxes or with very modest ones) would still be strapped for cash. More importantly, a federal income tax cut would do nothing to address a second problem afflicting subnational finance: profound inequalities in fiscal capacity between rich and poor states. As Heller pointed out, "large disparities in economic and hence taxable capacity among the states...lead to perverse ratios in both state-local service levels and tax efforts."[24] Despite often imposing a higher overall tax burden on their citizens, the five poorest states in the country raised less than half the per capita revenue of the five richest. In Heller's view, these sorts of gaps constituted "a serious indictment of the workings of our fiscal federalism" that threatened the American government's commitment to all its citizens.[25]

Fully rectifying the fiscal problems facing state government thus required a second step: creating a program for sharing "the federal riches" with state and local governments without "all of the strings that are attached to grants-in-aid." Heller suggested that funds from this program be distributed to states

[22] Walter Heller to Pierre Salinger, April 11, 1964, Box 13, Walter Heller Papers, John F. Kennedy Presidential Library, Boston, MA.

[23] Treasury Department, "Effect of the Tax Bill on State and Local Tax Revenues," September 1, 1963, Box 24, Walter Heller Papers.

[24] Heller, *New Dimensions of Political Economy*, 136.

[25] Ibid., 138.

on a per capita basis, which would have a limited equalization effect, but added that, if greater interstate equalization were desired, various economic factors like state personal income or poverty levels could be incorporated into its distribution formula as well.[26] Regardless of the exact formula it employed, however, a stand-alone revenue-sharing program would help "promote…[the] independence and vitality" of state and local governments while also reducing major inequalities in subnational fiscal capacity.[27]

In promoting this third-way approach to fiscal federalism, Heller was motivated by a vision of robust subnational government in mid-twentieth-century America that was highly controversial among his fellow liberal elites. As Heller later acknowledged, most of the major players in the Kennedy and Johnson administrations were very skeptical of the states, sharing the view of labor unions that they were unrepresentative anachronisms that impeded the promise of modern government. Heller disputed that contention, arguing that "the states are here to stay" and that they "play an indispensable role in our federal system of government." Citing de Tocqueville's famous claim that America was a regime of centralized government and decentralized administration, Heller argued that governing a continent-sized country like America entirely from the center was a project doomed to failure and that decentralization is ultimately "essential to a democracy."[28] Pushing back against the notion that states could not be productive policymaking centers in the modern United States, Heller pointed to numerous examples of mid-twentieth-century state governments innovating in positive ways. Furthermore, he argued, the Supreme Court's reapportionment decisions of the early 1960s (particularly *Reynolds v. Sims*, which mandated equal-population state legislative districts) would have the effect of democratizing the state governments and making them more representative to their citizens than the national government (which, despite the reapportionment revolution, would continue to feature an unrepresentative U.S. Senate). In defending states and their prerogatives, Heller intentionally sought to place himself between liberal Democrats who unapologetically promoted further centralization (the "Hamiltonians," as he called them) and Southern Democrats who, in Heller's view, advanced futile and outdated notions of states' rights.

[26] Ibid., 146–147.

[27] Walter Heller Oral History, Interview by David McComb, December 21, 1971, Lyndon Johnson Presidential Library. https://www.discoverlbj.org/item/oh-hellerw-19711221-2-83-10

[28] Heller, *New Dimensions of Political Economy*, 125.

Crucially, Heller's approach to revenue sharing was also informed by his understanding of state taxation politics. Having closely monitored state fiscal policies for over two decades, Heller saw how the constant need to raise new revenues made taxation a more central issue in state politics than in national politics. The salience of taxation policy in state political debates had the effect of making it especially difficult for state-level policymakers to raise taxes, since tax increases would inevitably draw the ire of voters and render incumbents vulnerable to their political opponents. As Heller wrote, "Again and again, good governors have been defeated by the higher taxes they have had to espouse to finance their innovations and expansion."[29] Heller also recognized that the difficulties states faced in raising taxes were compounded by the ever-present context of interstate competition for businesses and an increasingly mobile citizenry. Quoting the economist Laszlo Ecker-Raz, Heller wrote that "fear of losing business to another jurisdiction haunts the mind and stills the pen of the state and local lawmaker, and special pleaders have developed the skill of exploiting this fear to a high art."[30] Interstate tax competition was especially harmful to state efforts to adopt more progressive taxes, since the wealthy taxpayers were also often the most mobile. For all these reasons, Heller believed that "the states just cannot go it alone fiscally"[31]; securing the vitality of state governments in the twentieth century would require national fiscal assistance. Revenue sharing seemed like the optimal way of delivering that assistance while preserving the ability of state governments to independently make public policy.

Heller's efforts on behalf of revenue sharing kicked into high gear in early 1964, following the implementation of the 1963 federal income tax cuts. In a memo he wrote to President Johnson on May 27, 1964, Heller emphasized that "state-local taxes, debt, and spending have been rising by leaps and bounds" and that "the Federal government is not growing nearly as fast as State-local."[32] In another memo, Heller emphasized to Johnson that, thanks to the growth in economic activity spawned by the tax cuts, the national government had a tremendous amount of revenue on its hands and that "we ought to find some new way of sharing...the federal riches with the poorer state and local governments."[33] Johnson reportedly responded favorably to

[29] Ibid., 126.

[30] Ibid.

[31] Ibid. 125.

[32] Walter Heller to Lyndon Johnson, "Memorandum for the President," May 27, 1964, Box 6, Heller Papers.

[33] Walter Heller Oral History.

the general concept of revenue sharing and, with Heller's prodding, established a presidential task force to study the issue. The task force eventually settled on what came to be known as the Heller-Pechman Plan,[34] which called for distributing 1–2% of national income tax receipts to the states each year on a per capita basis.[35]

By the fall of 1964, it appeared that the Johnson Administration was preparing to publicly unveil a revenue-sharing proposal along the lines of the Heller-Pechman Plan. Johnson's advisors became especially favorable to the idea of releasing a proposal after Senator Barry Goldwater, Johnson's Republican opponent in the 1964 presidential election, announced his own revenue-sharing plan to a series of news magazines. Unlike Heller, Goldwater advocated returning national income tax revenues to the states based on their points of origin, and thus with no equalization component.[36] Responding to the Goldwater campaign's proposal, the White House Press Secretary released a statement providing the basic contours of Johnson's approach to "strengthen[ing] state and local government."[37] In this statement, the White House alluded to the fiscal imbalance that Heller had long emphasized: "at the state and local level, we see responsibilities rising faster than revenues, while at the Federal level and average annual revenue growth of some $6 billion provides a comfortable margin for Federal tax reduction." The statement went on to say that the national government should "help restore fiscal balance...by making available... some part of our great and growing Federal tax revenues" to state and local governments.[38]

But as the unveiling of an administration-backed revenue-sharing plan drew closer, a series of events led to its implosion. Due to an apparent miscommunication between Heller and members of President Johnson's inner circle, Heller mistakenly assumed that President Johnson had given his approval to the unveiling of an administration-backed revenue-sharing plan. According to Heller, he then spoke with *New York Times* fiscal policy reporter Edwin Dale in what was supposed to be an off-the-record

[34] Joseph Pechman was the head of the task force.

[35] Paul R. Dommel, *The Politics of Revenue Sharing* (Bloomington, IN: Indiana University Press, 1973), 43.

[36] "Goldwater's Economics," *Business Week*, September 26, 1964, 177.

[37] This was one of a series of statements outlining the administration's approach to the most pressing economic issues facing the country.

[38] Office of the White House Press Secretary, "Presidential Statement #6 on Economic Issues," October 28, 1964, Box 15, Heller Papers.

conversation. In this conversation, Heller conveyed to Dale that Johnson had given general approval for a revenue-sharing proposal, but that specific details were to be worked out later.[39] In what Heller would later allege to be a betrayal of confidence, Dale then published an article suggesting that Johnson had given support to a specific plan calling for $2–3 billion to be set aside into a trust fund whose proceeds would be annually distributed to the states on per capita basis.[40] The Dale article was a bombshell that immediately primed liberal interest groups skeptical of state governments into action. In a letter to President Johnson, AFL-CIO President George Meany wrote that he was "deeply disturbed" by Dale's reporting that Johnson had agreed to "unconditionally allocate up to $3 billion in federal funds annually to the states."[41] Meany argued that the inception of such funds transfers would undermine the national government's new commitment to addressing the country's pressing urban problems (presumably because state governments could not be trusted to use the money to address problems besetting their large cities).

The Dale article and the subsequent reaction to it caused movement on the revenue-sharing proposal inside the Johnson administration to grind to a sudden halt. Labor's angry reaction apparently caused Johnson himself to have a change of heart, and the cautious steps that the administration was taking to advance a revenue-sharing package therefore ceased. The whole affair apparently soured the relationship between Johnson and Heller, who departed from Washington to return to his academic duties at the University of Minnesota not long afterward. Sometime after his departure, Heller wrote a memo to Johnson seeking to assure the president that he was no longer publicly promoting his revenue-sharing proposal. "The so-called 'Heller Plan' is not being talked up—or about—by Heller," he wrote. "In fact, ever since last November, I have simply refused to talk publicly—or conspire privately—on the revenue-sharing plan (I've turned down dozens of invitations to speak on it."[42]

[39] Walter Heller, interview by David McComb, December 21, 1971, *Lyndon B. Johnson Library Oral Histories.*

[40] Edwin L. Dale, Jr., "President Favors Giving the States a Share of Revenue," *New York Times*, October 28, 1964, 1.

[41] Text of George Meany letter to Lyndon Johnson from November 2, 1964, "Revenue Sharing and the AFL-CIO: Selected Documents," Box 42, AFL-CIO Legislation Department Records.

[42] Walter Heller to Lyndon Johnson, "Memorandum to the President," Box 15, Heller Papers.

The Intergovernmental Lobby Forces State (and Local) Fiscal Issues to the Fore

In the wake of the failure of Walter Heller's revenue-sharing proposal, many assumed that efforts to provide direct fiscal assistance to state governments were dead. In rejecting revenue sharing, President Johnson signaled his strong preference for continuing to grow the conditional grants-in-aid system over direct state and local assistance, and the eighty-ninth Congress (1965–1967) responded in kind by dramatically increasing the size and scope of conditional grant programs.[43] But the issue of direct federal assistance did not go away, in large part because an increasingly large community of advocates for subnational governments in Washington, D.C., continued to push for it.

Indeed, the rise of the so-called "Intergovernmental Lobby" in the mid twentieth century is probably the crucial factor explaining the ultimate success of the revenue-sharing efforts of the 1960s and early 1970s.[44] Without the Intergovernmental Lobby's extensive work and influence, Congress would have likely given up on intergovernmental fiscal reform and turned its attention to other issues—the same outcome as in the 1930s. But state government advocacy groups working on Capitol Hill during the 1960s were much more organized and capacious than they were in the 1930s. Additionally, local governments had by the 1960s organized their own advocacy groups that also sought increased fiscal support from the national government. The competing approaches of states and municipalities to intergovernmental fiscal reform made the task of finding an acceptable compromise even more complicated, but it also made it more pressing. That, coupled with the fact that Congress had more resources at its disposal in the 1960s, is probably what explains the difference in the outcomes between the two decades.

In terms of state government advocacy, the biggest difference between the 1930s and 1960s was that the nation's governors had a much larger role in the latter. As Chapter 2 recounts, during the 1930s, efforts to reform the national-state taxation relationship were spearheaded by a set of Chicago-based

[43] Jerome R. Hellerstein, "Current Issues in Fiscal Federalism: Federal Grants-in-Aid," *Florida Law Review* 20, no. 4 (1968): 510; "The 89th Congress alone adopted 21 new health programs, 17 new education programs, 15 new economic development programs, 12 new programs for the cities, and 4 new manpower programs."

[44] Donald H. Haider, *When Governments Come to Washington: Governors, Mayors, and Intergovernmental Lobbying* (New York: Free Press, 1974).

organizations including the American Legislators Association and the Interstate Assembly. These organizations were primarily led by state legislatures, not governors. While the nation's governors had their own longstanding interstate organization (called the Governor's Conference), it originally had no relationship to the Chicago-based organizations and made no effort to develop an intergovernmental fiscal reform strategy of its own.[45] According to Donald Haider, most early-twentieth-century governors maintained a "dual" vision of federalism that emphasized the separation of state and national responsibilities, which led them to reject or at least de-emphasize intergovernmental reform efforts.[46] As a result, governors largely ceded the responsibility for pushing intergovernmental fiscal reforms to state legislative leaders during the New Deal.

In the postwar era, however, governors gradually stepped up their advocacy efforts in the nation's capital. Their changed approach was a grudging response to the intervention of the national government into numerous areas of domestic policy in the 1950s and 1960s. This "Great Broadening" of national policymaking convinced governors that they could no longer afford to stay out of national politics.[47] Thus, routine discussions in the Governor's Conferences of the 1950s regarding how to separate national and state responsibilities gave way to discussions regarding "how governors could increase their influence on national policies that affect the states" by the mid 1960s.[48] Not long afterwards, the Governors' Conference relocated its headquarters from Chicago to Washington, D.C., a move clearly designed to gain greater access to national levers of power.[49]

While fiscal policy was not the only item on the governors' national policy agenda in the 1960s, it was likely the most important one. As discussed in Chapter 3, state governments throughout the 1950s and early 1960s were

[45] In 1936, the Governors' Conference did finally establish a relationship with the Council of State Governments, the most important Chicago-based intergovernmental organization at that point, but the relationship largely consisted of the latter providing resources and professional staff to the former. The role of other state government actors, especially legislatures but also other state constitutional officers, in the "Chicago Group" of intergovernmental organizations during the 1930s was far larger. Glenn E. Brooks, *When Governors Convene: The Governors' Conference and National Politics* (Baltimore, MD: Johns Hopkins University Press, 1961), 32–40.

[46] Haider, *When Governments Come to Washington*, 21.

[47] Bryan D. Jones, Sean M. Theriault, and Michelle Whyman, *The Great Broadening: How the Vast Expansion of the Policymaking Agenda Transformed National Politics*, (Chicago: University of Chicago Press, 2019).

[48] Jennifer M. Jensen, *The Governors' Lobbyists: Federal-State Relations offices and Governors Associations in Washington* (Ann Arbor, MI: University of Michigan Press, 2016), 69.

[49] Jennifer M. Jensen, *The Governors' Lobbyists*, 67.

consumed with the question of how to raise the necessary revenue to fund the enormous new social-service responsibilities they had incurred. During much of the 1950s, governors mostly aligned with business interests in arguing that shoring up state finances required that the national government relinquish certain tax fields to the states. By the mid 1960s, however, governors were singing a different tune. Now broadly aware of the possibility of revenue sharing thanks to Walter Heller's efforts, governors became entranced by the notion of a regular infusion of federal money with no strings attached.[50] Thus, one year after President Johnson shot down Heller's revenue-sharing plan, the Governor's Conference decided to go on record as endorsing the principle of revenue sharing. Soon thereafter, the Conference created a special committee led by Michigan Governor George Romney to generate a revenue-sharing plan that the Conference could endorse.[51] In its efforts, the Conference had an important ally in the National Legislative Conference (NLC), a group that emerged in 1948 to organize America's state legislatures. Like the Governor's Conference, the Legislative Conference strongly supported revenue sharing throughout the late 1960s and early 1970s.[52]

In working to advance a revenue-sharing bill through the halls of Congress, however, the Governor's Conference and NLC quickly realized that their efforts would not bear fruit without engaging with the newest players on the intergovernmental lobbying scene: local governments. Prior to the postwar era, local governments had very little presence in Washington, D.C. The notion that local governments could bypass the state governments that created them and appeal directly to the national government for fiscal assistance originated in the 1930s, but it had not yet taken hold as a general feature of American political life. Consequently, organizations like the American Municipal Association (AMA) dedicated most of their resources to assisting their state chapters' state-level lobbying efforts rather than focusing on Congress.[53] While big-city mayors did organize themselves into a new group—the United States Conference of Mayors—that set up shop in the nation's capital and forged close ties with the Roosevelt Administration, their efforts were primarily oriented toward facilitating a direct role for city

[50] Paul R. Dommel, *The Politics of Revenue Sharing*, 51.
[51] Haider, *When Governments Come to Washington*, 65.
[52] Richard E. Thompson, *Revenue Sharing: A New Era in Federalism*, (Washington, D.C.: Revenue Sharing Advisory Service, 1973), 52.
[53] Haider, *When Government Comes to Washington*, 3–6; Thompson, *Revenue Sharing: A New Era of Federalism*, 50–51.

governments in New Deal relief programs. Thus, in the 1930s, debates over intergovernmental fiscal relations in Congress were primarily about the relationship between the national government and the states. Localities, which were viewed largely as instrumentalities of the states, were mostly ignored in these debates.

In the postwar era, much like the Governors' Conference, the country's local government organizations changed their approach to the national government dramatically. This was particularly the case for organizations representing the nation's cities, many of which were facing dire financial straits due to deindustrialization and white flight. Fed up with the longstanding refusal of malapportioned, rural-dominated state legislatures to address urban issues, cities began turning to the national government, a venue that was almost as difficult to penetrate but that had many more resources to devote to urban problems. Thus, in 1954, the American Municipal Association relocated its headquarters from Chicago to Washington, D.C. It later changed its name to the National League of Cities and merged with the United States Conference of Mayors to create a truly powerful presence in the nation's capital. In addition to the National League of Cities/Conference of Mayors, America's counties had their own national organization—the National Association of Counties—that had also begun actively advocating for its preferred policies on Capitol Hill. All these organizations eventually took an active interest in the revenue-sharing issue.

Fiscal Federalism Reform Moves to the Top of the National Policy Agenda, 1965–1971

Thus, by the mid 1960s, many of the most important advocacy groups on Capitol Hill—labor unions, business interests, state governments, and local governments—had decided to make intergovernmental fiscal issues a key component of their policy agenda. In doing so, however, each of these groups had distinct interests and thus favored very different reforms. Cash-strapped state governments, which had once urged that Congress relinquish some of its tax sources to the states, had become enthusiastic supporters of revenue sharing between the national and state governments. Local governments, in even more dire fiscal conditions than states but skeptical that states would share federal riches with them, began to urge that the national government share its revenue directly with municipalities along with (and perhaps more than) states. Labor unions, which were suspicious of subnational government at all levels, rejected revenue sharing and instead favored enhancing subnational fiscal capacity by doubling down on conditional grant programs. Their adversaries in the business community rejected revenue sharing too, but for a completely different reason: clinging to the increasingly unattainable goal of unwinding national and state government authority, they continued to endorse the New Deal-era prescription of separating national and state tax sources.

Like the Johnson White House, the Democrats who controlled Congress in the mid 1960s responded to these interest group pressures by siding with their labor union allies and focusing on building up conditional grant programs in lieu of pursuing any major fiscal federalism reform. From their perspective, there was no reason to change course: the states and municipalities were divided about the best way to implement a revenue-sharing program, thereby limiting their political strength, and in any case they had relatively little leverage on members of Congress for the moment. Moreover, like President Johnson, congressional Democrats were not enamored of the idea of giving governors and mayors the opportunity to claim credit for local programs funded with federal money.

Congressional Republicans, on the other hand, responded to the growing interest in fiscal federalism reform in a markedly different way. Beginning in the eighty-ninth Congress, they began to sponsor many revenue-sharing bills, leading to a sudden upsurge in congressional attention to revenue-sharing proposals. Revenue-sharing bills were particularly common in the House of Representatives, where under the Constitution all revenue-related bills must originate.

The interest of congressional Republicans in revenue sharing as a fiscal federalism reform actually predated the efforts of Walter Heller in the Johnson Administration. Indeed, by the late 1950s, a handful of Republican House members (most notably, Rep. Melvin Laird of Wisconsin) had signaled their interest in the issue and begun sponsoring bills to create a revenue-sharing program.[54] These longstanding proponents of revenue sharing were joined by a much larger contingent of House Republicans in the mid 1960s. In the eighty-ninth Congress, for example, fifty different revenue-sharing bills were introduced in the House, of which thirty-eight were sponsored by Republicans.[55]

[54] 113 Cong. Rec. H1848 (January 30, 1967) (statement of Rep. Goodell).
[55] Dommel, *The Politics of Revenue Sharing*, 53–55.

Previous research has argued that the surge of support for revenue sharing among Republicans in the late 1960s was largely a reaction to the massive number of new conditional grants that congressional Democrats created to implement President Johnson's Great Society program. According to this argument, Republicans were appalled by the growth of conditional grants under the Great Society and promoted revenue sharing as a substitute for these grants. There is certainly some merit to this argument: in his classic work on the politics of revenue sharing, Paul Dommel considered the relationship between support for revenue sharing and roll-call voting on conditional grant programs and found "*a very strong disposition among Republicans favoring revenue sharing to oppose new or expanded grant programs.*"[56] At the same time, it seems clear that this is not the whole story. For example, the upsurge in revenue-sharing bill introduction began early in the eighty-ninth Congress, *before* many of the biggest Great Society programs were passed. Additionally, as Dommel himself shows, many of the bills proposed to implement revenue sharing as a *supplement* to conditional grants rather than as a *replacement* for them.[57]

A more nuanced assessment of Republicans' motivations for promoting revenue sharing would acknowledge that congressional Republicans understood revenue sharing as a viable alternative to the Great Society's conditional grants while also taking seriously the possibility that many of them were genuinely interested in revitalizing state governments and understood the struggles of the states to raise adequate revenue as an impediment to such revitalization. For example, in a speech he gave on the House floor on behalf of a revenue sharing bill he had just introduced, Rep. Charles Goodell (R-NY) made no secret of the fact that he envisioned his proposal as an "alternative to the philosophy of the Great Society which would meet [public] needs by massive expansion of Federal programs and by further proliferation of narrow categorical grant-in-aid programs."[58] At the same time, Goodell emphasized the longstanding concerns of progressives regarding the taxation capacities of state governments, including the fact that "interstate competition for industry limits the revenue-raising potential of the wealthiest States" and that "an inadequate tax base limits the poorer States."[59] Furthermore, his bill (along with many, though not all, of

[56] Dommel, *The Politics of Revenue Sharing*, 59.
[57] Ibid., 52–67.
[58] 113 Cong. Rec. H1850 (January 30, 1967) (statement of Rep. Goodell)
[59] Ibid.

the Republican-sponsored revenue-sharing bills) made equalizing the fiscal capacities of state governments an important priority.

Importantly, in promoting revenue sharing, congressional Republicans parted company from their traditional allies in the business community, who continued to be publicly on record as supporting a complete "unwinding" of national and state fiscal systems via the relinquishment of certain federal tax sources to the states. They did so in large part because, unlike business interests, they understood that unwinding national and state tax sources was effectively impossible.

The prominence of the revenue-sharing issue on Capitol Hill increased substantially following the 1966 midterm elections, in which Republicans picked up forty-seven House seats and thus gained substantial political power. By the time the Ninetieth Congress (1967–1969) was sworn in, support for revenue sharing had become a consensus view among Republican members of Congress, even as the specifics of a revenue-sharing program were a matter of substantial intraparty debate. Indeed, Republicans were so united on revenue sharing that the House and Senate Republican leaders felt comfortable issuing a series of joint press releases on the topic. In these statements, House Minority Leader Gerald Ford and Senate Minority Leader Everett Dirksen urged that the Democratic leadership in Congress take up the task of holding hearings on revenue sharing immediately.[60] In other speeches, Ford emphasized that revenue sharing was crucial to ensuring "responsive and responsible state governments," which were "essential to the workings of a truly *creative* federalism."[61] Even more to the point, an address to an organization of young Republicans, Ford argued that the 1966 reelections marked "a turning point in American political history" in which Americans "repudiated" the Democrats and "began looking to the Republican Party for answers." Ford went on:

> "The Republican answer is federal-tax sharing, giving the states and cities a percentage slice of the federal income tax take without strings. This is the way to rebuild state government."[62]

[60] Joint statement by the Republican Congressional Leadership, February 24, 1967, Box D5, Gerald Ford Congressional Papers, Gerald R. Ford Presidential Library, Ann Arbor, MI.

[61] Press Release by House Minority Leader Ford, April 20, 1967, Box D7, Gerald Ford Congressional Papers. The use of "creative federalism" was an attempt to coopt President Johnson's term for describing the Great Society's conditional grant programs.

[62] Address before Young Republican National Leadership Training School, February 15, 1967, Box D21, Gerald Ford Congressional Papers.

In short, by 1967, congressional Republicans believed they had found their signature domestic policy issue in revenue sharing. Not only did the issue resonate with the Republican ideological vision of a limited national government and vital states, but it also had potentially massive political benefits. Given the growing push for fiscal support for subnational government from the Intergovernmental Lobby, congressional Republicans saw support for revenue sharing as a way to curry favor with governors, state legislatures, and big-city mayors. Creating an alliance between state and local government officials and the national Republican Party could potentially advantage the latter in myriad ways.

By the Ninetieth Congress, therefore, national Democrats were beginning to feel pressure on the question of intergovernmental fiscal reform. While their traditional interest group allies (most especially Labor Unions) continued to express strong opposition to shared revenues, the strength of the Intergovernmental Lobby's pressure campaign combined with Republican efforts to advance revenue-sharing bills was beginning to have an effect. A number of Democrats in Congress therefore began to cautiously endorse revenue sharing as a concept. In particular, Rep. Henry Reuss (D-WI) sponsored a bill establishing block grants for the purposes of modernizing state governments; this was not quite a revenue-sharing bill in that it did not propose sending money to the states with absolutely no strings attached, but it was close.[63]

During the 1968 presidential campaign, the national Democratic Party moved toward expressing tacit approval of revenue sharing. Its presidential candidate, Sen. Hubert Humphrey, was advised on economic matters by his fellow Minnesotan and longtime revenue-sharing champion Walter Heller. Despite the skeptical views of many in his party, Humphrey publicly supported revenue sharing and helped secure a provision in the national Democratic Party platform stating that, "to help states and cities meet their fiscal challenges, we must seek new methods for states and local governments to share in federal revenues."[64] Meanwhile, the Republican presidential nominee Richard Nixon echoed the consensus in his party and fully endorsed revenue sharing as well. Following the lead of its standard-bearers, the Republican Party adopted a platform stating that "we propose the sharing

[63] "Proposals for Sharing Federal Revenues with State and Local Governments; Bills and Resolutions Introduced in the Ninetieth Congress for General State and Local Government Support," n.d., Box 6604, Ervin Papers.

[64] "1968 Democratic Party Platform," *The American Presidency Project*, https://presidency.ucsb.edu/documents/1968-democratic-party-platform, accessed April 9, 2023.

of federal revenues with state governments," a clearer statement of support than that of the Democrats.[65] Thus, as the 1968 presidential campaign unfolded, it appeared that revenue sharing might gain renewed attention in upcoming years, particularly if Richard Nixon were elected president.

The Backdrop to the Fight Over Revenue Sharing in the Nixon Presidency

Nixon's victory in the 1968 presidential election thus improved the prospects for revenue sharing substantially. For the first time, the United States had a president who was dedicated to the issue and determined to use his bully pulpit to advance it on the national stage. But even with Nixon's backing, passage of revenue sharing was far from assured. To begin with, Democrats maintained control of Congress and, notwithstanding their 1968 presidential nominee's endorsement of the policy, the party's congressional leaders continued to be highly skeptical of it. This was the case for two reasons: in addition to being very solicitous of their labor-union allies who maintained their strong opposition to revenue sharing, congressional Democrats were reluctant to relinquish their authority over the spending of federal revenue to states and localities. But an even more profound obstacle to the passage of revenue sharing was the fact that its supporters were internally divided over how the policy ought to be designed. Before a pressure campaign could be waged to break down the resistance of congressional Democrats to revenue sharing, its supporters had to unite around a common approach to the policy.

Internal divisions over the design of a revenue-sharing program centered on three basic areas of disagreement: whether revenue sharing should be a substitute for categorical grants or an "add-on" to them; whether revenue-sharing funds should be distributed to states, municipalities, or both levels of government; and finally, what the formula(s) for distributing revenue across states and localities should be. The first two of these areas, while surely controversial, nonetheless proved amenable to consensus once the Nixon Administration took the lead in advancing the revenue-sharing cause. But the allocation question proved extremely dicey and took much longer to resolve. The fact that it was the allocation issue that nearly scuttled Nixon-era revenue-sharing efforts is unsurprising given that the previous

[65] "Republican Party Platform of 1968," *The American Presidency Project, https://www.presidency.ucsb.edu/documents/republican-party-platform-1968*, accessed April 9, 2023.

major effort in Congress to adopt an intergovernmental revenue-sharing scheme—the alcohol tax revenue-sharing proposal of the 1930s, discussed in Chapter 2—died in Congress precisely because legislators could not agree on an allocation formula. And the amount of revenue involved in that proposal was a pittance compared with what was at stake in the revenue-sharing fights of the late 1960s/early 1970s.

How Competing Goals Impacted the Conflict Over the Revenue-Sharing Allocation Formula

The dilemma over the allocation of revenue-sharing funds started with the fact that significant disagreement among revenue-sharing supporters existed over what the purpose of the program should be. Revenue-sharing supporters were motivated by a variety of goals, and because each of these goals was best achieved via a different distributional strategy, the allocation question implicated deep-seated differences in philosophical vision among the supporters themselves. Moreover, much as in the 1930s, different distributional approaches inevitably advantaged certain states and communities and disadvantaged others, such that the foregoing philosophical visions became entangled with interest-based conflicts.

Setting aside the conservative goal of using revenue sharing as a way to dismantle categorical grant programs (discussed in the next section), there were four overarching goals that drove the revenue-sharing movement. These goals and their associated optimal basis for an allocation formula are summarized in Table 4.1. First, there was the technocratic goal of addressing

Table 4.1 Revenue-Sharing Goals and Their Optimal Bases for Distribution to States

Revenue-Sharing Goal	Optimal Base for Interstate Allocation Formula
Addressing "Fiscal Mismatch"	• State point of origin
Fiscal Equalization	• State population • State economic characteristics (per capita income, poverty level)
Addressing the National Urban Crisis	• Level of urbanization of the state
Incentivizing Greater State Taxation	• State tax effort metric • State income tax collections

the longstanding "fiscal mismatch" issue, *viz* the fact that, since the end of World War II, the national government had been raising far more revenue than it needed while states (and localities) were raising far less than they needed (or could conceivably raise on their own). Addressing fiscal mismatch was, of course, the primary though not exclusive goal espoused by Walter Heller for the program, and it was also regularly espoused by congressional Republicans in the mid 1960s. By the late 1960s, as the national government's fiscal situation began to deteriorate, this goal became less frequently invoked, but it nonetheless continued to feature occasionally in the rhetoric of some supporters. On its own, reducing "fiscal mismatch" did not require redistributing revenue across states or localities. All it required was redirecting national revenue to state governments, which could technically be accomplished simply by returning national revenue to the states that were its points of origin. This was, in fact, the allocation approach in many of the revenue-sharing bills that were sponsored by Republicans in the mid 1960s.

Of course, Heller also espoused a second goal for the revenue-sharing program: equalizing the fiscal conditions of state governments. Indeed, by the late 1960s, many Republicans and nearly all Democrats who supported revenue sharing agreed that the program needed to be oriented, at least in part, toward fiscal equalization. Unlike addressing the "fiscal mismatch" issue, fiscal equalization necessarily involved redistributing revenue across states and localities. As Heller had pointed out, a small amount of fiscal equalization could be achieved simply by returning nationally collected revenues to the states based on population rather than point of origin. A more aggressive strategy of fiscal equalization would involve considering economic characteristics, such as state per capita income or the percentage of the population living in poverty, when allocating nationally collected revenues to the states.

By the late 1960s, however, a third goal for revenue sharing surfaced: assisting the nation's fiscally distressed cities and ameliorating its urban crisis. This goal was elevated to national prominence by the nation's mayors, and in particular by their advocacy organizations (the National Conference of Mayors, etc.) in Washington, D.C. Over time, it became the most important goal for congressional Democrats as they gradually moved past their longstanding reluctance to embrace revenue sharing. The extent to which revenue sharing would be oriented toward addressing urban issues obviously bore upon the separate question of whether revenue should be shared with municipalities in addition to states, but it also affected the allocation question: if addressing the urban crisis was to be a goal of revenue sharing, then the degree of urbanization of a state needed to be incorporated into the revenue-sharing allocation formula in some way.

Finally, since the dawn of the revenue-sharing discussion in the late 1950s and early 1960s, some supporters had always articulated the goal of using revenue sharing as a way of incentivizing states to raise their own taxes. By linking revenue-sharing funds to some measure of state tax effort, Congress could give state legislatures an additional rationale for raising taxes that would help them overcome the political difficulties involved in doing so. Some supporters of revenue sharing, mindful of the fact that states had been disproportionately relying on regressive sales taxes to close budget gaps throughout the 1950s and early 1960s, wanted to go further and use revenue sharing as a way of incentivizing states to adopt or raise personal income taxes. This could be done by tying revenue-sharing funds to state income tax collections. In addition to making state tax systems more progressive, this approach would have the added benefit of reducing state tax competition, which seemed to center on the income tax. This rationale was frequently invoked by governors of states with high income tax rates who felt especially hamstrung in their revenue-raising capacity. As Gov. Nelson Rockefeller of New York said: "...the top ten...high-tax states, because of their competitive economic disadvantage, [have] virtually reached the end of their capacity to raise taxes to meet their needs and those of their local governments. The result of these growing disparities in state and local tax structures is a balkanization of America."[66] Incorporating state tax effort, particularly income tax effort, into the revenue-sharing allocation formula was seen as a way of facilitating the standardization of state tax systems and thereby ameliorating the "balkanization" to which Rockefeller referred.

Helping the States Help Themselves: An Alternative to Revenue Sharing Emerges

The drive to incorporate state tax effort into the revenue-sharing allocation formula was partly motivated by a minority view that the fiscal situations facing low-tax states were less dire than commonly believed. According to holders of this view, states were not as powerless to solve their fiscal

[66] Senate Subcommittee on Intergovernmental Relations, *Intergovernmental Revenue Act of 1971 and Related Legislation*, Ninety-Second Congress, 1st session, June and August 1971, 216.

problems as their governors and legislatures routinely claimed. Instead, they had a range of tools at their disposal (most notably, the personal income tax) that they were not using sufficiently due to a lack of political will. Indeed, for some who held this view, any revenue-sharing program (even one that incentivized states to raise their own taxes) represented an irresponsible giveaway to the states.[67] Rather than rely on federal assistance, these naysayers contended, states should learn to help themselves.

The most prominent expounder of the "states should help themselves" view was the powerful chair of the House Ways and Means Committee, Arkansas Democrat Wilbur Mills. A fiscal conservative, Mills was an ardent opponent of revenue sharing because he disliked the idea of separating taxing and spending authority; according to him, the link between spending and taxation was a "necessary discipline on any governmental authority" that revenue sharing would jeopardize.[68] But Mills was also convinced that numerous states had fiscal resources that they had not yet tapped into, and that they should attempt to right their own fiscal ships before begging Congress for an annual handout.

The argument that states had no business begging the national government for fiscal assistance when many had not implemented income taxes was repeated by opponents of revenue sharing who were both to the left and right of Mills. Writing in *The Progressive*, Melville J. Ulmer chided state governments for running to Congress "like...lovely damsel[s] in distress" when "it is simply not true that...[they] have exhausted the sources of tax revenue available to them." Pointing to the fact that one-third of states did not levy a personal income tax and that many others levied them at very low rates, Ulmer argued that "Until some of the lagging states are induced to employ the fiscal powers they already possess, it would seem premature to talk of tax-sharing."[69] Labor unions, the most consistent and ardent critics of revenue sharing, made similar arguments. Meanwhile, on the other end of the political spectrum, Rep. John Byrnes, a conservative Republican from Wisconsin, likewise argued that revenue sharing would allow officials in numerous states to avoid having to make difficult but necessary tax choices and that public officials should be "required to impose the taxes necessary to finance benefits they desire to provide."[70]

[67] Importantly, many of these individuals distinguished between the fiscal situations of states and those of municipalities, which they agreed could not be solved by municipalities on their own.

[68] Quoted in Thompson, *Revenue Sharing*, 67–68.

[69] Melville J. Ulmer, 1967, "The Tax-Sharing Fallacy," *The Progressive*, May issue, 17–20.

[70] "Tax-Sharing Alternative Proposed by Byrnes," *The Sunday Star* (Washington, D.C.), May 9, 1971, A-3.

If the laggard states could help themselves, why weren't they? The standard answer offered by conservatives and business groups like the Chamber of Commerce was that the national government had occupied too much of the income tax space, and that it needed to cut its income tax rates if it wanted the states to step up and raise their own taxes. But this answer was met with obvious suspicion and derision by liberal interest groups like the AFL-CIO, who well understood that state income tax increases would be far smaller than the federal income tax cuts preceding them. It also appeared to be contradicted by the outcome of the national government's income tax cuts in the early 1960s, which were not immediately followed by state income tax adoptions or rate increases.

For the strange panoply of supporters of the "states should help themselves" theory, an alternative to both the ascendant revenue sharing concept as well as the business-backed federal tax cut concept emerged. This approach drew from a longstanding intergovernmental tax coordination strategy that the national government had first employed decades earlier: federal tax credits on state taxes paid. As discussed in Chapter 2, in the 1920s, Congress had enacted a credit on state inheritance taxes worth 80% of the federal inheritance tax as a way of suppressing interstate tax competition. By the late 1960s, the idea of adopting a similar type of tax credit for state income taxes had resurfaced, and opponents of revenue sharing seized upon it as an alternative. The premise behind the tax credit approach was that, rather than providing the states with free cash, the national government should attempt to use the federal income tax code to incentivize reluctant states to upgrade their tax systems. This approach would ameliorate state tax competition while also ensuring that state-level taxing and spending decisions would continue to be linked. For these reasons, according to its proponents, the tax credit was a more fiscally responsible means of assisting states than any revenue-sharing scheme could be.

The Long and Winding Road to Revenue Sharing's Final Passage

The ultra-complex terrain surrounding the revenue-sharing issue was not lost on Nixon and his advisors in the months following his election to the presidency. Based on his public statements in 1968 and early 1969, Nixon's personal goals for revenue sharing appear to have been broadly consistent with those of most congressional Republicans: to address the "fiscal mismatch" issue and more generally to decentralize power away from Washington, D.C. These goals would have been well-served by a revenue-sharing program exclusively supporting the states, in which federal money would have been distributed to the states on the basis of point of origin. Moreover, Nixon was likely sympathetic to the efforts of many congressional Republicans to use revenue sharing as a means of rolling back categorical grant programs (rather than establishing a revenue-sharing program as a supplement to existing grant programs).

But Nixon and his advisors also realized that, for revenue sharing to have any chance of passing, it would have to be designed very differently from what the president's ideal version of the program might look like. The Democrats who controlled Congress would under no circumstances agree to a revenue-sharing program that would substitute for the categorical grants that their party had developed and prized. Nor would they agree to any revenue-sharing program that was not oriented toward achieving some amount of fiscal equalization. Thus, from the outset, the Nixon administration understood that any revenue-sharing plan they introduced would have to adopt the "add-on" approach and include some sort of fiscal equalization component. More than that, however, administration officials knew that, to break down the stiff opposition to revenue sharing among many congressional Democrats, the president would have to unify revenue sharing's disparate supporters around a common proposal that they could all live with. This necessarily meant developing a compromise revenue-sharing proposal that diverged quite far from the traditional Republican vision for the program.

Soon after his election, therefore, Nixon began work on putting together the coalition that would underpin his revenue-sharing efforts for the next four years. In addition to convening several task forces exploring intergovernmental fiscal reform, Nixon put together a committee tasked with coming up with a revenue-sharing plan. His administration also convened numerous meetings with important stakeholders to try to unite the disparate strands of the pro-revenue-sharing coalition around a common framework. The most important dispute to resolve was that between the states and local governments (and in particular between governors and mayors), who disagreed over how the distribution of revenue-sharing funds going to state governments and municipalities should be determined.[71] The Nixon Administration's assumption was that, if states and localities could unite

[71] Dommel, *Politics of Revenue Sharing*, 79–82.

around a common approach, the political heft of the revenue-sharing coalition would be impossible for congressional Democrats to ignore. Importantly, as the Nixon administration was working on its revenue-sharing plan, the action on the revenue-sharing issue in Congress slowed considerably. This was particularly the case among congressional Republicans, who were the driving force behind revenue sharing during the preceding years. But with a president from their party at the helm, and one who had indicated significant interest in the issue, congressional Republicans in 1969 and 1970 mostly decided to stand down and wait and see what Nixon would do.[72]

By the middle of 1969, the meetings convened by the Nixon Administration were yielding fruit: representatives from both states and local governments (including the National Governors' Conference, National League of Cities, and National Association of Counties) had tentatively agreed on a general set of revenue-sharing principles, including that money would be allocated to the states but that states would be required to pass a share of the money to localities. The Nixon Administration hoped that this agreement would improve the prospects for revenue sharing in Congress by splitting congressional Democrats from big-city mayors, who were their longstanding allies.[73] Shorn of their traditional base of support, Democratic leaders in Congress would be forced to crack and eventually endorse revenue sharing.

As it turned out, however, the opportunity for a revenue-sharing breakthrough was not yet ripe. For one thing, though Nixon had committed to offering a revenue-sharing plan along the lines of what states and localities had accepted, he was hesitant to offer massive sums of money at a moment in which (unlike in the early 1960s, when Walter Heller proposed his revenue-sharing plan) the national government was running major deficits. When Nixon ultimately did unveil his plan in August of 1969, he proposed to share only $500 million of federal revenue, which was far too little for states and localities to get excited about.[74] At this point in its tenure, the Nixon Administration seemed to be emphasizing welfare reform over revenue sharing as its top domestic priority, so its officials did not immediately seek to appease the Intergovernmental Lobby when it did not greet the president's proposal with enthusiasm. With the intergovernmental groups (particularly the National Conference of Mayors) not fully in sync with the president,

[72] Ibid., 83–89.

[73] Ibid., 93; Richard P. Nathan, Allen D. Manvel, and Susannah E. Calkins, *Monitoring Revenue Sharing* (Washington, D.C.: Brookings Institution Press, 1975), 353.

[74] Haider, *When Governments Come to Washington*, 66.

congressional Democrats, despite their growing isolation on the issue, did not feel the need to change their approach. And as the 1970 midterm elections approached, everyone understood that revenue sharing would not be passed in the Ninety-First Congress.

Nonetheless, Nixon Administration officials kept meeting with the Intergovernmental Lobby, this time with an eye toward the Ninety-Second Congress that would begin in January 1971. By the end of 1970, the various parties to these meetings reached a more comprehensive agreement that would truly be a political game-changer. For their part, Nixon and his staff agreed to make revenue sharing their top priority in 1971 and to offer a much larger sum of money to states and localities in the second version of their plan.[75] States and localities agreed to a more specific set of rules for allocating funds, including a roughly 50–50 split nationally and a complex process for negotiating the precise distribution of the money within individual states.[76] With this agreement in hand alongside Nixon's commitment to a much larger sum of money, the Intergovernmental Lobby was prepared to wage a massive pressure campaign aimed at dismantling the wall of resistance to revenue sharing among congressional Democrats.[77]

The next step was for Nixon to publicly announce a revenue-sharing proposal, which he did to much fanfare on January 22, 1971. Following through on his commitments to the Intergovernmental Lobby, Nixon proposed a revenue-sharing package of $5 billion, ten times larger than his proposal from two years earlier. The plan (introduced in the House as HR 4187) proposed to set aside 1.3% of the personal income tax base to be returned to state and local governments. States and their local jurisdictions were treated as one fiscal system, with all funds going to states rather than directly to municipalities. Funds were to be distributed to the states according to a formula primarily based on population but with an adjustment for "tax effort" to reward those states making a greater effort to meet their needs from their own resources.[78] To assuage local governments concerned that states wouldn't pass on enough of the funds they received, a monetary incentive was included to incentivize each state to work out an agreement with its municipalities for distributing the revenue. If such an agreement were not reached, states would forfeit the incentive and also be required to pass 50%

[75] Ibid., 67–68.
[76] Thompson, *Revenue Sharing: A New Era of Federalism*, 63–64.
[77] Haider, *When Governments Come to Washington*, 68–69.
[78] Dommel, *Politics of Revenue Sharing*, 125.

of their funds to local governments. These intricate rules were broadly in line with the agreement upon which representatives of states and localities had settled several months before.

Following the unveiling of Nixon's proposal, the pressure campaign directed at Democrats in Congress began in earnest. The campaign was both sustained and multi-faceted, consisting of visits to Capitol Hill by hundreds of state and local elected officials, summits and conferences around the country to promote revenue sharing, letter-writing, and phone calls.[79] Congressional Democrats were clearly on the defensive, precisely what the pro-revenue-sharing coalition intended. Democratic leaders outside Congress grew increasingly worried that the split between the party's congressional wing and its allies in state and local government would cause long-term damage to the party. Eventually, Democratic leaders in Congress began to understand that they could no longer sit on the sidelines and refuse to engage with the revenue-sharing issue. Thus, in May of 1971, Sen. Edward Muskie, the chair of the Subcommittee on Intergovernmental Relations and a potential 1972 presidential aspirant, stepped up to the plate and put forward his own revenue-sharing plan in May of 1971.[80] With powerful congressional Democrats now promoting their own revenue-sharing plan in addition to the president, prospects for a breakthrough grew significantly.

Despite the foregoing political developments, one major barrier to the passage of a revenue-sharing law remained: House Ways and Means Committee Chairman Wilbur Mills. Unlike other congressional Democrats, Mills' opposition to revenue sharing seemed implacable. Following the release of Nixon's proposal, Mills announced that he would hold hearings on the President's revenue-sharing plan, but "for the purpose of killing it."[81] Little seemed to move Mills in the period between the plan's unveiling and the inception of those hearings four months later. Indeed, comments Mills made on the first day of the hearings in June strongly suggested he remained opposed to the entire revenue-sharing concept.

During the second week of the hearings, however, Mills made a rather stunning about-face. In a closed-door meeting with Democratic party leaders, he announced that he was considering a revenue-sharing package for

[79] Thompson, *Revenue Sharing: A New era of Federalism*, 68–69; Haider, *When Governments Come to Washington*, 69.

[80] Maureen McBreen, "History of Federal Revenue Sharing Proposals and Enactment of the State and Local Fiscal Assistance Act of 1972 (Public Law 92-512)," Congressional Research Service, November 16, 1972.

[81] Quoted in Thompson, *Revenue Sharing: A New Era in Federalism*, 67.

local governments only and exclusively on the basis of need. It is impossible to know what led to Mills' sudden change of heart. Paul Dommel speculated that two factors were involved: first, the ceaseless pressure campaign from the Intergovernmental Lobby simply became too great for Mills to ignore; second, Mills was (like Muskie) considering a presidential run and needed the support of the nation's big-city mayors within the still elite-dominated Democratic Party.[82] Importantly, however, while Mills was budging on the general principle of revenue sharing, his insistence on only providing revenue-sharing funds to local governments suggested that he was holding fast to the view that states (as opposed to municipalities) could and should help themselves. Indeed, Mills made that point clear in an appearance on William F. Buckley's TV show *Firing Line*, in which he publicly stated that he was moving toward offering a revenue-sharing proposal of his own but that it would be only for localities, which, unlike the states, were truly in dire need of assistance.

Eventually, however, Mills was forced to adjust his stance on revenue sharing for the states as well. This occurred gradually and in stages. Over the course of the summer and fall of 1971, Mills' office was overrun with communications from Democratic governors urging him to revise his stance on sharing revenue with the states. Typical of these communications was a letter from Washington Governor Daniel J. Evans in July, in which Evans urged Mills to "reconsider the needs of state government." In particular, Evans pointed to the dire fiscal situation facing his state, which was leading to service cuts, under-compensation of teachers, and unbearable property tax levies. Notably, Evans admitted that the problem ultimately lay with the fact that "Washington is not an income tax state," but argued that, since the state's voters had decisively rejected a referendum to impose an income tax in 1969, he and the state legislature had very few tools available with which to address the state's fiscal crisis in a reasonable way.[83] Reading this letter, Mills may well have felt validated in his longstanding view that the fiscal challenges facing state governments (as opposed to local governments) were essentially problems of political will, not an inability to raise revenue. Nonetheless, given his well-known political savvy, Mills likely also understood that the alliance hatched between states and localities on the revenue-sharing issue was strong and thus that, if he wished to maintain the

[82] Dommel, *The Politics of Revenue Sharing*, 138.

[83] Daniel J. Evans to Wilbur Mills, July 20, 1971, Box 134, Records of the U.S. House, Committee on Ways and Means, Ninety-Second Congress, RG 233, National Archives, Washington, DC.

support of his Democratic colleagues in the House while also currying favor with the mayors whose support counting on for a presidential bid, he would need to include the states in his revenue-sharing proposal.[84]

Thus, during the summer and early fall of 1971, the Ways and Means Committee convened a series of closed-door meetings to come up with an alternative plan that would satisfy the states, the cities, as well as Mills himself. The result was Mills' counter-proposal to the Nixon and Muskie plans, the Intergovernmental Fiscal Coordination Act of 1971, which Mills introduced on November 30. The Mills plan provided roughly the same overall amount of money toward revenue sharing as the Nixon plan, but the structure of the revenue-sharing program he proposed was very different. To begin with, unlike the Nixon Plan, the Mills Plan treated states and local governments separately and proposed independent funding streams to each. Second, the amount of funds to be distributed to local governments was roughly double the amount of state funds ($3.5 billion to $1.8 billion). Third, the Mills Plan explicitly identified distinct goals for the local and state components of revenue sharing, and these goals were reflected in the distribution formulas it proposed for the respective components. The goal of the local component was to help local governments "meet...high priority demands placed upon them," and local funds were therefore to be distributed via a formula incorporating measures of need (including urbanization and percentage of low-income families). The goal of the state component, on the other hand, was to induce states to "make appropriate use of individual income taxes to meet their revenue needs," and this was to be accomplished via giving each state an amount equal to 15% of its personal income tax receipts.[85] States without an income tax would receive an amount of revenue equal to 1% of federal income tax receipts from within their borders, but only for the first two years in which the law was in effect.

By pegging the amount of revenue-sharing funds states received to their personal income tax collections, Mills' proposal significantly benefited income tax states over non-income tax states. For example, under Mills' proposal, Oregon (population 2.1 million) would have received $34 million, while neighboring Washington (population 3.4 million) would have received

[84] Samuel H. Beer, "The adoption of General Revenue Sharing: A Case Study in Public Sector Politics," *Public Policy* 24, no. 2, 182.

[85] "Chairman Mills Introduces Proposed 'Intergovernmental Fiscal Coordination Act,'" Press Release, Office of Congressman Wilbur Mills, November 30, 1971, Box 641, Records of the Joint Committee of Taxation, RG 128, National Archives, Washington, DC.

$15.6 million.[86] Vermont (population 332,000) would have received $6.4 million, while neighboring New Hampshire (population 737,000) would have received $2.8 million. Not surprisingly, the Mills proposal sparked outrage among states with no income tax. In Texas, for example, the state's major newspapers published numerous official editorials inveighing against the proposal. The *Dallas Morning News*, for example, argued that the legislation was tantamount to a "bribe."[87] Various Texas public officials embarked upon a full-court press to convince Mills to rethink his approach. Lieutenant Governor Ben Barnes, for example, wrote a letter indicating he was "greatly concerned" about an approach that would use the concept of revenue sharing to "coerce states into adopting one form of taxation or another."[88]

Eventually, Mills decided to modify the income-tax inducement component of his plan (once again bowing to pressure from state officials). Scholars have speculated that this decision was directly related to his presidential ambitions. After all, one of the ten states without a personal income tax was New Hampshire, a state whose primary election would play a pivotal role in the Democrats' new nominee selection process. Indeed, while visiting New Hampshire to explore a presidential bid in early February 1972, Mills promised the state's legislature that his revenue-sharing bill would be changed "so that no state is penalized for acting as frugally as New Hampshire."[89] Several months later, a brand-new revenue-sharing bill (HR 14370—the State and Local Fiscal Assistance Act of 1972, hereinafter referred to as SLFAA) emerged from the House Ways and Means Committee. This bill largely adhered to the framework of HR 11950 (Mills' original proposal), but the formula for allocating revenue to states was changed to consider overall tax effort alongside state income tax receipts.[90] Additionally, the formula for distributing money to local governments was altered to benefit large cities. The House passed its version of SLFAA on a 275–122 vote. The bill was passed under a closed rule (i.e., a rule disallowing changes on the House floor) to prevent representatives with parochial interests from muddying up the already-complicated legislation. Importantly, the final vote was bipartisan, with Democrats supporting it 153–80 and Republicans

[86] James H. Symons to Laurence N. Woodworth, Memorandum, December 6, 1971, Box 641, Records of the Joint Committee on Taxation, RG 128, National Archives, Washington, DC.

[87] "Sharing—With Strings," *Dallas Morning News*, March 6, 1972.

[88] Ben Barnes to Wilbur Mills, March 9, 1972, Box 96, Records of the U.S. House, Ninety-Second Congress, RG 233, National Archives, Washington, DC.

[89] Quoted in Thompson, *Revenue Sharing: A New Era of Federalism*, 89.

[90] Beer, "The adoption of General Revenue Sharing," 182.

supporting it 122–42. This was remarkable given the origins of revenue sharing as a Republican issue. The final vote breakdown was also interesting in terms of ideology: while some liberals and conservatives in both parties voted for the legislation, the rate of liberal support was significantly higher than the rate of conservative support. As Dommel argues, support for revenue sharing among congressional conservatives (both Republicans and southern Democrats) declined over time as it became clear that revenue sharing would not be used as a substitute for categorical grant programs, but instead as an addition to them.[91]

After SLFAA passed the House, the action shifted to the Senate, where the political dynamics were very different. As is well-known, the equal representation of the states in the Senate—regardless of population—results in the disproportionate influence of rural states and communities in that chamber. In the case of revenue sharing, rural overrepresentation mattered because the House's bill (in an effort to address the financial problems plaguing the nation's cities) very clearly favored urban over rural areas. On top of that, Senate malapportionment also had the effect of giving states without a personal income tax (many of which, including Wyoming, South Dakota, Nevada, and New Hampshire, were lightly populated) somewhat greater influence than in the House. Senators from these states chafed at any advantage given to income tax states in the revenue-sharing funding formula, including the more limited advantage upon which the House had settled. Finally, there was widespread dissatisfaction with the complex approach for allocating revenue-shared funds upon which the House had settled.

Under the markup of the Senate Finance Committee, SLFAA was changed substantially. While keeping the one-third, two-thirds split in funds between state and local jurisdictions, the Committee opted to abandon the usage of separate distributional formulas for each level of government and, like the Nixon proposal, to treat states and their municipalities as part of a single system instead. The formula for distributing revenue-sharing funds across states that the Committee developed was a "three-factor one based on population, total tax effort, and needs as measured by per capita income."[92] Thus, the modest advantage given to income tax states in the version of SLFAA that ultimately passed the House was eliminated. On the other hand, the greater weight given to relative income and tax effort in the Senate version meant that its equalizing effect was somewhat larger as well, though this

[91] Dommel, *Politics of Revenue Sharing*, 153–155.
[92] Dommel, *Politics of Revenue Sharing*, 159.

does not appear to have been the main goal of the Committee. Instead, the Committee appears to have been motivated by the goal of "[making] the distributions more favorable to the central cities and rural areas, particularly in the south."[93]

After the Senate passed its version of SLFAA on September 12, 1972, House and Senate leaders appointed confreres to a conference committee whose purpose was to iron out the inter-chamber differences and develop a compromise bill that would pass both chambers. Two of the three main issues in the designing of a revenue-sharing program (whether it should be a substitute for categorical grants or an "add-on," and what the distribution of funds between state and local governments should be) were no longer issues: both chambers had already passed bills establishing an "add-on" approach and splitting funds such that local governments would get two-thirds of the money. The remaining issue to be hashed out, of course, was the formula for distributing the money across states. Ultimately, the conference committee settled on the Senate's approach of a single formula in which states and their municipalities were treated as a single unit. In deciding on the formula's specifics, the confreres split the difference between the House and Senate approaches. Both the Senate's three-factor formula and the House's more complicated formula for distributing funds across local governments would be considered, and states would receive an amount of money equal to whichever of the two formulas would lead to a higher allocation of funds.[94] This compromise formed the basis for the conference report that the committee produced. This report was quickly approved by both the House and Senate; not long afterwards, President Nixon signed the SLFAA, and revenue sharing was on the books.

The Murky Final Product

The passage of SLFAA was greeted effusively by many of its staunchest proponents. In signing the law, President Nixon triumphantly announced that "a new American revolution...is truly underway."[95] Similarly, the *New York Times* called the law's passage "the most fundamental change of this century

[93] Ibid.
[94] Ibid., 163.
[95] Richard Nixon Statement about the General Revenue Sharing Bill, *The American Presidency Project*, University of California-Santa Barbara, https://www.presidency.ucsb.edu/documents/statement-about-the-general-revenue-sharing-bill, accessed April 16, 2023.

in fiscal relationships between Federal, state, and local governments."[96] But were the grandiose claims of revenue sharing's supporters justified? Considering this question entails evaluating the goals that motivated revenue sharing's supporters alongside the details of the revenue-sharing law that was ultimately passed. And as already discussed, the goals motivating revenue-sharing proponents were legion.

Among its initial proponents in the late 1950s and early 1960s (most notably Walter Heller), an important overarching goal of revenue sharing was to revitalize the states. The notion that state governments had become lethargic, antiquated institutions, and that their lethargy was threatening the entire American federal system, was a widely expressed sentiment among political observers, politicians, and scholars alike during the mid twentieth century.[97] Though observers blamed the lassitude of the mid-twentieth-century states on a wide variety of factors (including legislative malapportionment/rural overrepresentation, corruption, the nationalization of the economy, and others), a common assertion they made was that the dynamism of the states was threatened by their constant revenue-raising difficulties and consequent inability to respond adequately to modern problems. From today's standpoint, this seems to be contradicted by the enormous increase in state own-source revenue that occurred between the 1930s and 1970s. Nonetheless, to many who lived through these decades, it was a compelling claim. Revenue sharing was thus seen as a way of providing states (particularly poorer ones) with a dependable source of revenue from the national government that would ease their fiscal burdens, facilitate their modernization, and reinvigorate their policymaking capacities.

SLFAA did not do much to facilitate this goal, however. This was largely because, by the late 1960s and early 1970s, signs were emerging that states were already revitalizing and that a revenue-sharing program oriented toward that purpose was therefore not necessary. The Supreme Court's reapportionment decisions, though much criticized by defenders of states' rights as an intrusion on state sovereignty, helped facilitate the resurgence of state governments by making them more responsive to the needs of large cities. At the same time as states reapportioned their legislatures, those legislatures began a decades-long process of professionalization that helped modernize

[96] "Updated Federalism," *New York Times*, October 17, 1972, 40.

[97] See, for example, Terry Sanford, *Storm over the States* (New York: McGraw-Hill, 1967).

state governments more generally.[98] These and other developments convinced members of Congress like Wilbur Mills that the states could rise to the challenges of modern governance without significant assistance from the national government. Thus, SLFAA did not focus primarily on the states, sending only one-third of revenue-sharing funds to them.

Closely related to the goal of revitalizing state governments was the nuts-and-bolts, technocratic goal of addressing the "fiscal mismatch" between national and subnational government. This goal, most clearly expressed by Walter Heller in the early 1960s, continued to be promoted by some revenue-sharing proponents in the late 1960s and early 1970s. Over time, however, it was sublimated in favor of other goals, like tackling the national urban crisis. It is difficult to assess the extent to which SLFAA addressed fiscal mismatch because of the basic indeterminacy of the term. In a certain sense, any revenue-sharing program, as a large-scale transfer of resources from national to subnational government, is a way of addressing the mismatch issue. That said, as the previous section made clear, SLFAA's distribution formula was clearly not oriented toward addressing the issue first and foremost.

Another goal that was frequently articulated by proponents of revenue sharing was fiscal equalization. Here, the main objects of interest were states rather than localities (or, perhaps more accurately stated, states as complete political systems including both the state governments as well as their municipal subdivisions), and the main concern was ameliorating regional inequalities in subnational fiscal capacity. As discussed in the previous section, fiscal equalization was weakly prioritized in the distribution formulas for both Wilbur Mill's HR 11950 and the original House version of SLFAA, but more heavily emphasized in the formula in the Senate version. The final, compromise version of SLFAA clearly did have an equalization impact. This is shown in Figure 4.1, which plots state per capita income in 1969 (x-axis) against a measure of per capita redistribution of funds wrought by SLFAA across state areas in 1972.[99] As the figure shows, wealthy states like New Jersey and Connecticut were net losers in the redistribution of

[98] James D. King, "Changes in Professionalism in U.S. State Legislatures," *Legislative Studies Quarterly* 25, no. 2 (2000): 327–343.

[99] The latter measure comes from Richard P. Nathan, Allen D. Manvel, and Susannah E. Calkins, *Monitoring Revenue Sharing* (Washington, D.C.: Brookings Institution Press, 1975). It is calculated by taking the total amount of funds allocated by SLFAA to state and local governments within a particular state area, and then subtracting from it the state's contribution to federal revenue between multiplied by 2.82%, the proportion of the 1972 federal budget dedicated to revenue sharing. See Nathan, Manvel, and Calkins, 70–72.

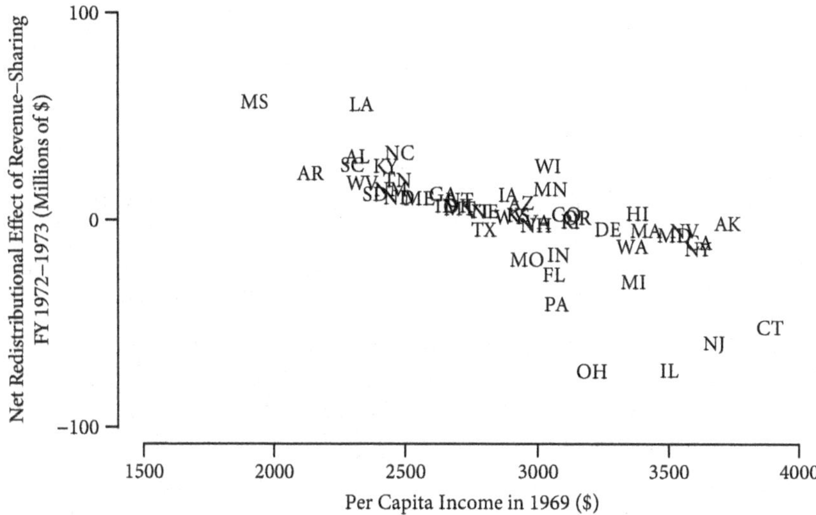

Figure 4.1 The Relationship between State Per Capita Income and the Net Redistributive Effect of Revenue Sharing

Sources: Richard P. Nathan, Allen D. Manvel, and Susannah E. Calkins, *Monitoring Revenue Sharing* (Washington, D.C.: Brookings Institution Press, 1975); U.S. Census, "Table S3: Per Capita Income by State," https://www2.census.gov/programs-surveys/decennial/tables/time-series/historical-income-states/state3.csv

funds through SLFAA (though, to be sure, their state and local governments received SLFAA funds as well), while poor states like Mississippi and Arkansas were clearly net gainers. But the figure also shows that per capita income does not come close to explaining all the variation in cross-state redistribution. For example, New Jersey and Connecticut were net losers to a much larger extent than states of similar wealth levels like Massachusetts, New York, and California. This disparity, of course, has to do with differences in the states' tax systems, which were also incorporated into the SLFAA distribution formula.

Additionally, it is important to emphasize that the redistributional effects of SLFAA, while significant, were nonetheless relatively small—particularly for state governments. This is shown in Figure 4.2, which includes two plots displaying the relationship between state per capita income and SLFAA funds as a percentage of own-source revenue for state governments (left plot) and local governments (right plot). The left plot shows that, even in the poorest states, revenue-sharing funds were less than one-tenth the size of state own-source revenue. The right plot, on the other hand, shows that

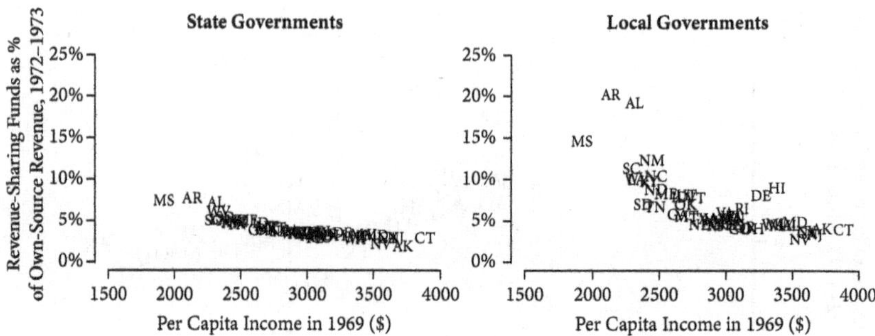

Figure 4.2 The Relationship between State Per Capita Income and the Importance of Revenue-Sharing Funds to State and Local Fiscal Systems

Sources: Richard P. Nathan, Allen D. Manvel, and Susannah E. Calkins, *Monitoring Revenue Sharing* (Washington, D.C.: Brookings Institution Press, 1975); U.S. Census, "Table S3: Per Capita Income by State," https://www2.census.gov/programs-surveys/decennial/tables/time-series/historical-income-states/state3.csv

SLFAA did have a more pronounced redistributional effect for some local governments: in poor states like Mississippi and Alabama, SLFAA funds were one-fifth the size of all local own-source revenues. Outside those states, however, revenue sharing provided a fairly limited budgetary boost to local governments as well as states.

Even when gauged in terms of the goal that seemed to gain the most support over the course of revenue sharing's journey from entry onto the policy agenda to final passage—providing support to America's cash-strapped large cities—SLFAA seems to have had a fairly limited impact. While the original House version of SLFAA would have oriented the program more toward this goal, the Senate eliminated urbanization as a factor in its own version and the final, compromise bill considered it only modestly. Thus, for the country's most economically depressed large cities (i.e., Detroit, Baltimore, St. Louis, etc.), SLFAA funds only added up to around 10% of their own-source revenues. For more prosperous cities, the percentage was far less.[100]

The last goal motivating many revenue-sharing supporters—incentivizing states to upgrade their own tax systems, particularly via adopting or raising income taxes—was also only weakly advanced by the final version of SLFAA. This goal would have been more strongly facilitated by the House version of

[100] Nathan, Manvel, and Calkins, *Monitoring Revenue Sharing*, 109.

SLFAA, which tied state revenue-sharing funds to tax effort and income tax collections, and even more so by Wilbur Mills' initial bill, which tied them only to income tax collections. But the Senate's decision to distribute state and local revenue-sharing funds according to a single formula (rather than establishing separate formulas for each level of government) and to make state tax effort only one-third of that formula, eliminating state income tax collections from it entirely, severely limited the bill's ability to incentivize the states. The final, compromise version of the bill diminished the importance of state taxation metrics even further. Thus, it is not surprising that state tax activity, so robust in the late 1960s and early 1970s, slowed down considerably after the passage of revenue sharing in 1972. Indeed, the best case that can be made for revenue sharing having an impact on state tax policy would focus on state tax changes *preceding* SLFAA's passage. As discussed in the previous chapter, several states (including Ohio, Pennsylvania, and Rhode Island) adopted income taxes in the year before SLFAA was passed. There is some evidence that the decisions of these states to enact income taxes was partly motivated by the beliefs of state policymakers that passage of a federal revenue-sharing law with incentives for state income taxation was imminent. Thus, revenue sharing may have had some role in changing state tax policy, but only in a roundabout way.

The End of an Era of Fiscal Federalism Debate

In the final analysis, despite its initial promise (and the boisterous language of SLFAA's designers), revenue sharing under the SLFAA did not come close to realizing the transformational potential that many once believed the policy could have. As this chapter has shown, the chief reason for this was that revenue sharing's supporters were internally divided over what they wanted the goals of the program to be, and these divisions reflected profoundly different visions of American federalism itself. Walter Heller's initial vision of vital states acting alongside a robust national government stood in stark contrast to the vision of congressional Republicans, who wanted to use revenue sharing as a way of rolling back national power. As time went on, revenue sharing was embraced by big-city mayors and their supporters among congressional Democrats; the federalism vision motivating them was of the national government in partnership with America's cities, with state governments generally cast aside. Still others, like Wilbur Mills, stood for a form of federalism in which the states maintained fiscal independence from the national government (though granting that the national government could use its fiscal powers to "help the states help themselves") while hard-pressed municipalities occasionally relied on the national government for fiscal assistance. These very different visions and their attendant goals resulted in numerous revenue-sharing proposals featuring wildly different distribution formulas. The final product of SLFAA was a classic congressional compromise that attempted to incorporate as many programmatic goals as possible. In doing so, however, SLFAA diluted all of them such that none were adequately achieved.

This chapter provides important new evidence for understanding why the United States is the world's only advanced federal democracy that lacks a fiscal equalization program. In their pioneering article examining the unique absence of such a program in the United States, Béland and Lecours argue that countries adopt regional equalization programs in response to the convergence of two conditions: a serious regional secessionist threat and a cultural commitment to equal access to government services for all citizens regardless of geography.[101] Because neither of these conditions obtained in the twentieth-century United States, the authors claim, little pressure existed within the American political system to implement an equalization scheme.[102] While Béland and Lecours concede that equalization was occasionally discussed in the United States and that SLFAA had an equalization component, they nonetheless argue that equalization was not at the forefront of the mid-century fiscal federalism reform agenda and took a backseat to other concerns (as reflected in the distributional formula that was ultimately agreed to in SLFAA).

The findings of this chapter, based on a much fuller examination of mid-century fiscal federalism developments in the United States are largely consistent with Béland and Lecours' argument but also suggest that some modifications to it should be made. Most fundamentally, Béland and Lecours are correct that state-level equalization was never the primary goal of revenue-sharing efforts in the mid-century United States. Additionally,

[101] Béland and Lecours, "Fiscal Federalism and American Exceptionalism," 303–329.

[102] Béland and Lecours go on to argue that, even if American policymakers had decided to pursue fiscal equalization efforts, they likely would have failed due to America's unique institutional arrangements (most notably the U.S. Senate, where overrepresented small-population states would have scuttled efforts to allocate national revenue on a per capita basis).

their notion that the absence of a regional secessionist threat in the postwar United States made a strict focus on equalization less likely is reasonable. But the issue of interstate fiscal inequality was given significantly more attention by the nation's leaders than they suggest. Particularly in the late 1950s and early 1960s, disparities in state tax systems and fiscal capacities were some of the chief problems being considered by America's intergovernmental institutions (most notably, the ACIR) as well as congressional subcommittees focused on intergovernmental relations. Policymakers in these bodies understood state fiscal inequality as threatening the nation's commitment to all its citizens and undermining national unity—a major aspiration in postwar America. In line with these concerns, fiscal equalization was one of two central goals of the original Heller-Pechman revenue-sharing plan of 1964 (the other being rectifying the "fiscal mismatch" between the national government and the states). Over the course of the 1960s, however, the revenue-sharing cause was taken over by conservatives eager to replace conditional grant programs, and concerns about state-level fiscal disparities declined as states converged in their tax structures and attention shifted to the crisis facing the nation's cities. By the time SLFAA was passed, fiscal equalization was indeed an afterthought in the nation's fiscal federalism debate. But it did not start this way.

It did not take long for the tensions within the coalition that had advanced the SLFAA to unravel after its passage. In 1973, President Nixon responded to the national government's growing deficits by proposing a budget for FY 1974 that featured major cuts to various conditional grants to state and local governments. In defending these cuts, the Nixon Administration emphasized that revenue-sharing funds could be used as substitutes for them, thereby reinforcing the suspicions of many on the left that conservatives favored revenue sharing largely as a means to abolish conditional grant programs.[103] This contretemps largely ended any prospect of expansion for the revenue-sharing program, and a series of developments in the late 1970s to early 1980s (described in the next chapter) led to the eventual elimination of the entire program.

With the passage of SLFAA, a twenty-year period of intense national conversation over intergovernmental fiscal relations effectively came to a close. This was likely not recognized at the time, but it would become clear in due course. Over the next decade, the fiscal circumstances of national, state, and

[103] Dommel, *Politics of Revenue Sharing*, 172–175.

local government, the politics of taxation, and the ideological orientation of the national government would all change enormously. These changes would set American fiscal federalism on a new path, one that would no longer feature the kind of robust debate over ideas such as tax coordination or intergovernmental fiscal cooperation that had featured so prominently in the early and mid twentieth centuries.

5

State Taxation in an Anti-Tax Era

The State Response to National Retrenchment during the Reagan Revolution

The late 1970s and 1980s were a profound period of rupture in the American political system. After decades of growth in both national and subnational government, American politics shifted in a decidedly anti-statist direction. This shift was initially felt at the state and local levels, where voters chafed against rising tax burdens in the so-called "Tax Revolt" of the late 1970s, but it became far more palpable with Ronald Reagan's landslide victory over Jimmy Carter in the 1980 presidential election. Reagan's presidential tenure—the period that both journalists and scholars have taken to calling "the Reagan Revolution"—changed the trajectory of American government and politics in numerous ways. Though he did not succeed in his deepest goal of thoroughly uprooting the domestic public sector, Reagan did succeed in arresting its growth and in changing collective assumptions about the domestic role of the national government. These successes yielded a wide range of consequences that have in many cases lasted until the present day.

Among the many long-lasting consequences of the Reagan presidency was a profound transformation in intergovernmental fiscal relations. However, much like its other consequences, the fiscal federalism transformation wrought by the Reagan presidency was substantively quite different from what Reagan and his lieutenants envisioned when Reagan entered the White House in 1981. As previous scholarship has demonstrated, Reagan and his top advisors believed that they could impose a comprehensive new order of limited government at all levels, state and local as well as national. This belief was based on the assumption that subnational governments had limited fiscal agency, relied on the national government for their vitality, and would therefore follow the national government and retrench once the mid-twentieth-century fiscal supports provided by Congress disappeared. But against the expectations of the Reaganites, state governments proved surprisingly fiscally resourceful and used their taxation powers to curb Reagan's

Coordination Failure. Adam S. Myers, Oxford University Press. © Oxford University Press (2026).
DOI: 10.1093/9780197831878.003.0006

all-out assault on the domestic public sector. To be sure, state governments did not suddenly become active agents of progressive policy innovation in the 1980s, but they did in many cases work to protect the status quo put into place during the 1960s against the Reagan onslaught. The end result was a new fiscal order in which the states took a more active role and state fiscal strength grew substantially vis-à-vis that of both national and local government.

This chapter details the complex interplay between fiscal policy struggles at the state and national levels from the late 1970s to the late 1980s, the ten-year period when the valence of American politics shifted in a decidedly anti-government direction. It begins with a brief discussion of the state-level Tax Revolt of the late 1970s, detailing its origins and effects on national politics in the Reagan Era that followed. The chapter then proceeds to consider the federalism philosophy of the Reagan administration, analyzing how Reagan and his economic advisors understood devolution to subnational governments as complementary to their paramount goal of dismantling the welfare state. A distinguishing characteristic of Reagan's approach to fiscal federalism, I argue, is the importance it placed on devolving substantive policy authority *as well as* revenue-raising responsibility to the states. In the minds of the Reaganites, pursuing both objectives was crucial to facilitating a truly "competitive federalism" in which states, concerned about the potential flight of businesses and taxpayers to other states in response to high taxes, would be disciplined into retrenchment.

From there, the chapter details Reagan's efforts to pursue his retrenchment-oriented goals through a reorientation of intergovernmental fiscal relations, as well as how states responded to these efforts. As I show, Reagan's efforts in this regard differed substantially between his two terms in office. In his first term, Reagan focused heavily on cutting intergovernmental grants and curtailing other forms of direct fiscal support to state and local government. The disappointment of the Reagan administration with the limited impact of these cuts on the subnational public sector led to another effort to undermine state government revenue streams in Reagan's second term. This time, rather than proposing to reduce financial support for intergovernmental programs, Reagan attacked the ability of states to raise their own revenue through various proposed changes to the federal tax code (most notably, by proposing to abolish the State and Local Tax Deduction). As I show, however, Congress did not accept Reagan's proposals; instead, it adopted a tax reform package in 1986 that actually expanded the capacity of state governments to raise revenue via their own income taxes. Largely content with the fiscal status quo, states responded to this reform by giving most, but not all, of their "windfall" back to their citizens. In sum, the unexpected outcome of the Reagan presidency was that, as the 1980s drew to a close, state governments had more diversified and capacious revenue systems than ever before. Relatedly, thanks to the 1986 federal tax reform, the personal income tax finally assumed a co-equal role with the general sales tax as a source of state government revenue.

Precursor to the Reagan Revolution: The 1970s "Tax Revolt" in the States

For the most part, the 1970s was a quiet time for state and local tax policy. Following the surge of state tax activity during the 1965–1972 period, the number of state tax actions fell dramatically and stayed low for much of the decade.[1] A variety of factors converged to create a rare reprieve from tax worries for state policymakers during these years. First, the many tax increases of the 1960s were having their intended effects, turning previously unused or hardly used taxes into major sources of revenue. The effects of these tax increases were compounded by the onset of inflation during the 1970s, which triggered a "bracket creep" that boosted personal income tax receipts. States were also assisted by the advent of federal revenue sharing in 1973, which (as intended) eased the fiscal pressures facing state and especially local governments. On the spending side, states were aided by the cresting of the post-World War II baby boom, which caused public school enrollments to stabilize after a twenty-year period of growth.[2]

But at the same time as state lawmakers were taking a collective deep breath after decades of wrestling nonstop with the tax dilemma, major changes were afoot in American politics that would soon revolutionize fiscal politics and policy at all levels of government for decades to come. Most importantly, frustration with activist government was beginning to

[1] On the unusually low rate of state tax activity during the mid 1970s, see: Leon Rothenberg, "Recent Trends in State Taxation," *Book of the States 1974–1975*, (Lexington, KY: Council of State Governments, 1974), 225; John Gambrill, "Recent Trends in State Taxation," *Book of the States 1976–1977* (Lexington, KY: Council of State Governments, 1976), 280; John Gambrill, "Recent Trends in State Taxation," *Book of the States 1978–1979*, 309.

[2] Leon Rothenberg, "Recent Trends in State Taxation," *The Book of the States 1974–1975* (Lexington, KY: Council of State Governments).

percolate among the American people. This frustration was borne of many factors, including growing economic anxieties fueled by deindustrialization and inflation, the widespread perception that government had become too big and unresponsive, the common view among White Americans that government was elevating the needs of racial minorities at their expense, and others.[3] For those who were growing disenchanted with "big government," particularly in the context of declining purchasing power due to inflation, the sting of high taxes was becoming a focal point for a new and significant movement in American politics.

Initial evidence of the emergence of an anti-tax movement in the United States could be seen in 1976, when grassroots activists put tax-limiting citizen initiatives on the ballots of four states.[4] The moment was not quite ripe for these initiatives, though, and all of them failed at the polls. Two years later, the anti-tax movement (which came to be known as the Tax Revolt) achieved its clear breakout moment when California voters passed Proposition 13. Considered one of the most influential ballot referendums in American history, Proposition 13 capped taxes on property in California at 1% of its assessed value and required a two-thirds legislative supermajority for all increases on non-property taxes in the state. According to David Sears and Jack Citrin, the passage of Proposition 13 was simultaneously a response to public anger over growing property tax burdens as well as the expression of a nascent anti-government populism that was spreading across the country. As evidence of the latter, Sears and Citrin point to the crucial role played by Howard Jarvis, the charismatic leader of California's anti-tax movement whose fiery anti-statist rhetoric helped build support for Proposition 13 among the state's voters.[5]

As a far-reaching tax limitation in the country's largest state, Proposition 13 drew national attention and had immediate national consequences. In particular, it energized anti-tax activists in other states and dramatically increased popular support for their efforts. By the end of 1978, voters in another five states had adopted various tax-limiting referenda.[6] Then, in 1979, state legislatures responded to the growing anti-tax fervor in the

[3] David O. Sears and Jack Citrin, *Tax Revolt: Something for Nothing in California* (Cambridge, MA: Harvard University Press, 1982), 8–22.

[4] Alvin Rabushka, "Tax and Spending Limits," In *The United States in the 1980s*, eds. Peter Duignan and Alvin Rabushka (Stanford, CA: Hoover Institution, 1980), 39.

[5] Sears and Citrin, *Tax Revolt.*

[6] Daniel A. Smith, *Tax Crusaders and the Politics of Direct Democracy* (New York: Routledge, 1998), 33.

American electorate by passing perhaps the largest number of state-level tax reductions in a single year since before the 1930s.[7] By 1980, however, the energy behind state-level anti-tax efforts was dissipating: of the five anti-tax referenda that made it to state ballots that year, all but one failed.[8] The slowing advance of these efforts seems to have been a result of growing public awareness of their excesses as well as a shift in the anti-tax movement's focus (spurred by Ronald Reagan's presidential candidacy) from the state and local to the national level.

Despite its short time frame, the subnational tax revolt of the late 1970s had several enduring consequences, not all of which its proponents anticipated or would have favored. In terms of fiscal policy, its most important consequence was a further centralization of subnational fiscal authority (and, in turn, political power) at the state level. This was because, while it did seek to limit other taxes, the primary target of the tax revolt was the property tax, the only significant revenue source exclusively levied by local governments in most states. Where they succeeded in restricting property tax growth, anti-tax activists thus inadvertently paved the way for future state government tax increases to provide greater support to local governments. Such increases inevitably led to greater state interference in local matters and the further erosion of local authority over time. This was the case in both California and Massachusetts, the two states that adopted the most consequential tax-restricting policy changes during the 1978–1980 period.[9]

But the effects of the subnational tax revolt went well beyond a recalibration of state-local fiscal relations. By tapping into a latent dissatisfaction with "big government" among a large segment of the American electorate, Howard Jarvis and his counterparts in other states awakened politicians, journalists, and political observers across the country to the growing potency of anti-statist appeals. In doing so, they changed the terms of American political debate, moving concerns about an overweening domestic public sector to the center of the national policy agenda.[10] Perhaps even more importantly, through demonstrating the power of their strident anti-tax

[7] John Gambrill, "Recent Trends in State Taxation," In *Book of the States 1980–1981* (Lexington, KY: Council of State Governments), 318–326.

[8] Sears and Citrin, 6.

[9] William H. Oakland, "Proposition 13: Genesis and Consequences," In *The Property Tax Revolt: The Case of Proposition 13*, eds. George G. Kaufman and Kenneth T. Rosen (Cambridge, MA: Ballinger Publishing Company, 1981), 31–64; Dennis Hale, "Proposition 2 ½ A Decade Later: The Ambiguous Legacy of Tax Reform in Massachusetts," *State and Local Government Review* 25, no. 2 (1993), 117–129.

[10] Sears and Citrin, 40–41.

message, the activists who led the tax revolt reshaped the American conservative movement. In place of the cautious conservatism of the Nixon era, which emphasized reform rather than retrenchment, the anti-tax activists promoted a more radical, no-holds-barred approach with the clear-eyed goal of dismantling the welfare state.[11] This approach would soon become the hallmark of conservatism during the Reagan presidency, with major implications for fiscal federalism.

The Demise of Revenue Sharing with the States in the Late 1970s

The improved fiscal condition of the states over the course of the 1970s overlapped with the growing deterioration of the national government's finances. Thanks to the increased fiscal burdens it assumed with the Great Society programs of the mid 1960s along with a recession in the early 1970s that reduced federal income tax receipts, the national government began to accumulate regular and significant annual deficits around 1975.[12] Thus, the fiscal conditions of the national government and the states, which had previously diverged following the end of World War II, reversed course substantially some thirty years later. This reversal in fiscal fortunes sharply undermined the case for revenue sharing with the states in the halls of Congress. As detailed in Chapter 4, Walter Heller originally promoted revenue sharing in the mid 1960s as a way to address the postwar "fiscal mismatch" between the national government (with its ample revenues) and the states (with their massive new spending needs). By the mid 1970s, this mismatch was largely a thing of the past, and the original justification for a revenue-sharing program thus disappeared.

Other factors also began to weaken support for SLFAA (the 1972 revenue-sharing law) on Capitol Hill during this period. Most importantly, the fundamental incoherence of the SLFAA's distributional formula meant that it failed to adequately deliver on the goals that the various proponents of revenue sharing envisioned for the program. For example, the incorporation of state tax effort and state income tax collections into the SLFAA

[11] Thomas Byrne Edsall and Mary D. Edsall, *Chain Reaction: The Impact of Race, Rights, and Taxes on American Politics* (New York: Norton, 1992).

[12] "Federal Surplus or Deficit," FRED Economic Data, Federal Reserve Bank of St. Louis, https://fred.stlouisfed.org/series/FYFSD, accessed June 19, 2023.

formula was meant to incentivize the states to increase their own taxes (and especially their income taxes), but as discussed above, states largely ceased to raise taxes in the years immediately following SLFAA's implementation. Clearly, then, the incentives for states to raise their own taxes in SLFAA were not strong enough to induce significant state tax action. To the contrary, when states began cutting their own taxes during the years of the Tax Revolt, members of Congress began to see the state component of SLFAA as a subsidy that enabled the tax cuts—precisely the opposite of what the law's designers intended.[13] Similarly, SLFAA's modest interstate equalization effect was simply not strong enough to secure durable support from legislators representing the country's poorest states.

Given SLFAA's failure to achieve many of its intended goals, it should not be surprising that efforts to scale back or even abolish the law began soon after it went into effect. Thus, a mere two years after SLFAA was passed, Wilbur Mills introduced a bill in the House to remove the states from the revenue-sharing program.[14] Though Congress ultimately approved reauthorization of the entire program in 1976, records from the congressional hearings and floor debates in which the authorization was considered demonstrate that numerous members of Congress were dissatisfied with the program, particularly its state component.[15] By 1980, congressional dissatisfaction with the state component of SLFAA had increased even further. As Andrew Karch and Shanna Rose document, members of Congress were particularly unhappy with efforts in the states during the late 1970s to advance a balanced-budget amendment to the U.S. Constitution. These efforts, a response to the national government's growing deficits, struck U.S. representatives and senators as hypocritical: at the same time as the states were trying to force Uncle Sam to trim its fiscal sails, they were happy to take federal money with no strings attached. When state government officials realized that Congress might retaliate by eliminating the state component of SLFAA, they mobilized to keep the state component, but with less gusto than one might expect. Essentially, numerous governors and state legislative

[13] Andrew Karch and Shanna Rose, *Responsive States: Federalism and American Public Policy* (New York: Cambridge, 2019), 119. While the distributional formula of SLFAA did modestly reward states for greater tax effort and income tax collections, these components were so watered down by the many other factors in the formula (as detailed in Chapter 4) that state legislators did not feel they provided enough of an incentive to keep their taxes high in the middle of the Tax Revolt.

[14] Advisory Committee on Intergovernmental Relations, *General Revenue Sharing: An ACIR Re-Evaluation*, Report # A-48, October 1974, 19.

[15] Karch and Rose, *Responsive States*, 118–122.

leaders tacitly agreed with Congress that the states, given their improved fiscal situations, could do without the SLFAA money.[16] Hence, in 1980, Congress reauthorized revenue sharing, but this time for local governments only. Not long afterwards, with the ascendancy of Ronald Reagan to the presidency, the local component of revenue sharing would also come under the federal chopping block. Thus would end the only stand-alone effort to equalize subnational fiscal conditions in American history.

Ronald Reagan's Fiscal Federalism Agenda

On the heels of the Tax Revolt, the poor economic conditions of the late 1970s, and general dissatisfaction with the state of the country, Ronald Reagan defeated incumbent President Jimmy Carter in the 1980 presidential election. Thus began the most consequential effort to change the trajectory of American government since the New Deal. In campaigning for president, Reagan made no secret of his desire to vastly shrink the size of government and cut taxes. Reagan reaffirmed these goals in his inaugural address, in which he uttered perhaps his most famous statement: "Government is not the solution to our problem; government is the problem." Somewhat less noticed in the same inaugural address was Reagan's equally emphatic statement of his intention to revive American federalism. As he said,

> "It is my intention to... demand recognition of the distinction between the powers granted to the Federal Government and those reserved to the States or to the people. All of us need to be reminded that the Federal Government did not create the States; the States created the Federal Government."[17]

As his inaugural address suggested, Reagan's agenda for reforming the domestic public sector rested on two pillars: domestic program retrenchment and devolution of responsibilities to the states. To begin with, Reagan and his allies were motivated by the goal of shrinking the domestic public sector, which they viewed as the primary source of the social, economic, and political problems plaguing America. The scholarly literature on Reagan's

[16] Ibid., 122–127.

[17] Ronald Reagan, "Inaugural Address of 1981," Ronald Reagan Presidential Library and Museum, https://www.reaganlibrary.gov/archives/speech/inaugural-address-1981, accessed July 20, 2023.

retrenchment-oriented agenda is vast and need not be extensively reviewed here, but a few important points do merit mention.[18] First, in targeting the domestic public sector, the Reaganites focused heavily on shrinking intergovernmental grants to states and local governments, particularly grants for programs to help the poor like Aid to Families with Dependent Children, Medicaid, food stamps, and others. Indeed, an estimated two-thirds of the cuts in Reagan's 1981 budget proposal targeted intergovernmental grants, even though aid to states and localities composed less than one-fifth of the national budget.[19] Second, the goal of shrinking the domestic public sector was closely linked to a more popular element of the Reagan agenda: cutting taxes. In the Reaganite vision, spending cuts and tax cuts had a mutually reinforcing relationship: on the one hand, less domestic spending would mean that taxes could be lowered, while on the other hand tax cuts would trigger deficits that would eventually necessitate cuts in domestic spending.[20]

Reagan's fiscal agenda for the national government was supplemented by a secondary goal of devolving fiscal authority to state governments. Like the business groups of the 1950s and 1960s (discussed in Chapter 4), Reagan justified his devolutionary vision by arguing that, in advancing it, he was seeking to restore the proper, dual form of American federalism, one in which the national government and the states operated separately in both the substantive and fiscal spheres.[21] Reagan also closely resembled the mid-century business groups in his actual fiscal federalism proposals. Like those of business groups, Reagan's proposals sought to transfer both substantive policy responsibilities *as well as* taxation authority to the states. It was the emphasis on reallocating tax authority that provided the clearest contrast between Reagan's approach to fiscal federalism and that of Richard Nixon. As Rich Williamson, the head of the Office of Intergovernmental Affairs (OIA) for much of the Reagan presidency, explained, Reagan "wanted to go

[18] Important works analyzing Reagan-era domestic policy include: Paul Pierson, *Dismantling the Welfare State? Reagan, Thatcher, and the Politics of Retrenchment* (New York: Cambridge University Press, 1994); Sean Wilentz, *The Age of Reagan: A History, 1974–1988* (New York: Harper Collins, 2008); Matt Guardino, *Framing Inequality: News Media, Public Opinion, and the Neoliberal Turn in U.S. Public Policy* (New York: Oxford University Press, 2019); Timothy Conlan, *From New Federalism to Devolution: Twenty-Five Years of Intergovernmental Reform* (Washington, D.C.: Brookings Institution Press, 1998).

[19] Conlan, *From New Federalism to Devolution: Twenty-Five Years of Intergovernmental Reform*, 113.

[20] Ibid., 128.

[21] Richard S. Williamson, *Reagan's Federalism: His Efforts to Decentralize Government*, (Lanham, MD: University Press of America, 1990), 1.

even further than bestowing revenue on the states [as Nixon had]; he wanted to return actual tax sources."[22]

The extent to which Reagan's devolutionary agenda was based on a genuine ideological commitment to dual federalism, as opposed to being simply a means to the end of a smaller domestic public sector, is debatable. Reagan's liberal critics at the time, as well as many scholars who have written about his presidency since, have charged that Reagan and his advisors only really promoted devolution when doing so helped advance their primary goal of shrinking government at all levels. According to these critics, the Reagan federalism vision was most certainly *not* one of a small national government alongside robust, energetic states.[23] To the contrary, Reagan's desire to restore authority to the states was matched by "strong opinions about how they should exercise that authority: they should join the federal government in its effort to reduce the size of the public sector."[24] In the view of these critics, Reagan's overarching goal of shrinking government regularly took precedence over his goal of restoring dual federalism and, when the two goals conflicted, the latter was "consistently sacrificed" in favor of the former.[25]

Reagan's defenders, on the other hand, contend that he was ideologically committed to devolution for its own sake, and not merely as a vehicle for advancing retrenchment. These defenders point to the fact that Reagan was preaching the virtues of dual federalism long before he entered the White House and fell under the influence of retrenchment-focused advisors like David Stockman, his Office of Management and Budget (OMB) head. Notably, in his pre-presidency encomia to federalism, Reagan nearly always discussed his goals in terms of reallocating fiscal authority to *states* and respecting their status as fiscal sovereigns with ultimate control over municipalities within their borders.[26] This approach, which contrasted sharply with the 1972 revenue-sharing law (which treated municipalities as entities to some degree independent of states), is consistent with a dual-federalism

[22] Ibid., 39.

[23] One can make the case that this was, indeed, the vision of many congressional Republicans, and perhaps President Nixon himself, during the late 1960s and early 1970s.

[24] Richard P. Nathan and Fred C. Doolittle, *Reagan and the States*, (Princeton, NJ: Princeton University Press, 1987), 6.

[25] Conlan, *From New Federalism to Devolution*, 109.

[26] For example, in television appearances and speeches throughout 1970s, Reagan regularly called for the devolution of responsibilities to lower level of government. See, e.g., Richard P. Nathan and Fred C. Doolittle, *Reagan and the States* (Princeton, NJ: Princeton University Press, 1987), 6; Williamson, *Reagan's Federalism: His Efforts to Decentralize Government.*

understanding of the U.S. Constitution holding that only the national government and the states are actors with constitutional authority. Perhaps the most convincing evidence that Reagan's commitment to dual federalism was genuine comes from his OIA chief, Williamson, who writes that in his many budget-related meetings with Reagan, he "never once" heard the president make the cynical argument that the real purpose of devolution was to shrink American government at all levels.[27] According to Williamson, Reagan's federalism agenda (including his drive to reallocate tax authority to the states) was premised on the assumption that the states—the rightful holders of much domestic policy authority under the Constitution—had by the 1980s become sufficiently capacious to step up to the plate in the areas where the national government would retreat.

Adjudicating between these two competing perspectives is difficult, but on balance, there is more evidence in favor of the view that Reagan (or at least the Reagan administration) viewed devolution primarily as a means to an end rather than an end in itself. The clearest evidence for this view comes from Reagan's second term, when the administration pursued policies that seemed clearly designed to sap the vitality of state governments. As will be shown, these policy moves seem likely to have been, at least in part, a reaction to the failure of state-level politicians to join in the Reagan Administration's crusade against the domestic public sector in the early part of the Reagan presidency.

Competitive Federalism: The Link Between Retrenchment and Devolution

While the Reaganites may have eventually come to recognize the tensions between the goals of retrenchment and devolution, evidence suggests that they saw these two goals as largely compatible during Reagan's first term. The supposed link between them lay in expectations regarding how states would respond to cutbacks in conditional grant programs and a restoration of their exclusive authority in many areas of taxation. These expectations were derived from a theory of federalism that had developed in various corners of academia and the business world during the mid twentieth century but that did not enter the mainstream of American life until it

[27] Williamson, *Reagan's Federalism*, 186.

was fully embraced by the Reaganites. This was the theory of *competitive federalism.*

Though some of the ideas underpinning competitive federalism can be found in the works of early-twentieth-century economists, the theory really began to take shape during the postwar era. Charles Tiebout's famous model of mobile citizens making their residential decisions based on the bundle of public goods and tax burdens offered by local jurisdictions, eventually resulting in an equilibrium in which local fiscal policies approximate resident preferences, inspired a great deal of mid-twentieth-century economists working in the area of intergovernmental fiscal relations.[28] Tiebout's central insight that citizen mobility creates a competitive dynamic among subnational jurisdictions became the basis for a more fully worked-out theory of competitive federalism among public choice scholars in the late twentieth century. Undoubtedly, the leading architect of this theory was the famed economist and Nobel Prize winner James Buchanan. Adopting a decidedly unsentimental view of politics, Buchanan understood all governments to be "leviathans" interested in maximizing the "revenue surplus" they could extract from taxpayers and using it to support the core constituencies that kept them in power.[29] While Buchanan saw national governments as relatively unencumbered in their pursuit of exploitative surplus, he viewed subnational governments (particularly those operating in a federal system) as limited in their surplus-generating capacity by the threat of exit from unhappy taxpayers and businesses.

Because federalism served as a restraint on leviathan-like government, Buchanan saw it as a "liberty-enhancing institution" and thus argued that "a coherent classical liberal must generally be supportive of federal political structures."[30] However, Buchanan also made clear that federalism's salutary characteristics could only be secured if there was a strict fiscal separation between national and subnational government. For this reason, Buchanan and his confreres understood the kind of federalism that was emerging in the United States of the 1960s and 1970s—that of a fiscally expansive national government sharing its revenue with subnational governments—as the worst possible type of intergovernmental fiscal relationship. In place of a

[28] Charles M. Tiebout, "A Pure Theory of Local Expenditures," *Journal of Political Economy* 64, no. 5 (1956): 416–424.

[29] Lars P. Feld, "James Buchanan's Theory of Federalism: From Fiscal Equity to the Ideal Political Order," *Constitutional Political Economy* 25 (2014): 236.

[30] James M. Buchanan, "Federalism and Individual Sovereignty," *CATO Journal* 15, no. 2–3 (1995–1996): 259–268.

competitive arrangement that served to discipline governments, Buchanan and his fellow competitive federalists argued, the United States was developing an intergovernmental "cartel" that restricted jurisdictional competition and empowered government at all levels.[31] For competitive federalists, then, the solution to America's fiscal problems necessarily entailed vastly shrinking the national government's fiscal footprint and simultaneously removing the fiscal supports that shielded states from competitive pressures. Eliminating conditional grant programs would force states to fend for themselves. Not wanting to lose residents and businesses to other states, the competitive federalists theorized, states and localities would follow the national government in retrenching.

Significant evidence exists that many of the economists serving in the Reagan administration were sympathetic to the basic tenets of competitive federalism, and there is at least some reason to believe that their policy proposals were motivated by the theory. For example, Robert W. Rafuse, Jr., the official in charge of the state and local finances unit in the Treasury Department for much of Reagan's presidency, wrote articles contesting the conventional wisdom among liberal economists that interjurisdictional tax competition is an "undesirable phenomenon." Downplaying the notion that the threat of business or taxpayer exit led states to undersupply public goods, Rafuse argued instead that variations in tax burdens across the states were largely attributable to differences in "public tastes" (i.e., that Tieboutian sorting was operative in late-twentieth-century America) and that "competition is healthy and should not be discouraged by the Federal government."[32] Similarly, when responding to the claim that reduced fiscal support from the national government would cause state and local governments to lower their own tax burdens, Assistant Treasury Secretary Ronald Pearlman commented: "That's as it should be."[33] Perhaps most notably, William A. Niskanen, a public choice economist who served as chairman of Reagan's Council of Economic Advisors (and, like Buchanan, earned his

[31] The use of the term "cartel" to describe the foregoing intergovernmental relationship was apparently pioneered by political scientist Michael Greve, not Buchanan. However, Greve was heavily influenced by the ideas of James Buchanan on these matters. See, e.g., Michael S. Greve, "Cartel Federalism: Antitrust Enforcement by State Attorneys General," *University of Chicago Law Review* 72, no. 1 (2005): 99–122; Michael S. Greve, *The Upside-Down Constitution* (Cambridge, MA: Harvard University Press, 2012).

[32] Robert W. Rafuse, Jr., "Modifying Deductibility: Impacts on States and Local Governments," *Proceedings of the Eighty-Second Annual Conference on Taxation held under the Auspices of the National Tax Association*, Denver, CO, October 13–16, 1985, 13.

[33] Conlan, *From New Federalism to Devolution.*

Ph.D. in economics from the University of Chicago in the mid twentieth century), lauded interjurisdictional competition for "[increasing] the range of choices available to citizens for the level, type, and production of public services."[34]

Implementing the Reagan Revolution in Fiscal Federalism, 1981–1983

Driven by the primary goal of retrenchment and the secondary (but, in their minds, related) goal of devolution, Reagan and his advisors successfully pushed a highly ambitious domestic policy agenda through Congress in the first year of his presidency. As many others have documented, the budget Reagan proposed to Congress in 1981 represented an unprecedented effort to roll back key pillars of the mid-twentieth-century welfare state. Ultimately, through tenacity and political skill, Reagan and his advisors got much of what they wanted out of Congress: the 1981 budget law that Congress passed and Reagan signed was a turning point in American domestic policy.

The many details of the 1981 budget need not detain us here, but several crucial points are worth mentioning. First and foremost, the massive spending cuts in the budget overwhelmingly targeted intergovernmental programs bearing directly upon state and local finances rather than purely national programs. This was accomplished in two ways. First, the budget made major changes in eligibility for intergovernmental programs benefiting the poor, including Aid to Families with Dependent Children, food stamps, child nutrition, and Medicaid.[35] Second, the budget consolidated eighty-five categorical grants into seven block grants in the areas of education, health care, social services, and others. In doing so, it gave states greater flexibility in administering numerous intergovernmental programs at the same time as it vastly reduced the federal funds states received for them.[36]

At the same time as Reagan pursued his steep domestic spending cuts in the 1981 budget, he also pursued the more popular component of his

[34] William A. Niskanen, "Protecting Citizens through Vigorous Competition and Limited Cooperation," *Interjurisdictional Competition in the Federal System: A Roundtable Discussion*, Advisory Commission on Intergovernmental Relations, Report # M-157, August 1988.

[35] As many others have documented, Reagan's budget did not target Medicare and Social Security, two nationally administered programs benefiting the elderly, a powerful and well-organized constituency. See, e.g., Nathan and Doolittle, *Reagan and the States*, 26.

[36] Nathan and Doolittle, *Reagan and the States*, 57–59.

domestic policy agenda: a substantial reduction in the federal tax burden. This was initially achieved in the Economic Recovery Tax Act of 1981, whose numerous components included across-the-board income tax rate cuts, a reduction in the maximum effective top tax rate from 70% to 50%, and hefty cuts in the federal estate and gift taxes.[37] One of the justifications for the tax cuts offered by Reagan and his advisors was that they helped facilitate a return to dual federalism. According to Reagan, the tax cuts were designed to "[address] the problem created by the Federal government usurping revenue sources which otherwise would have been available to State and local governments..."[38] Through combining the elimination of numerous intergovernmental grants with large tax cuts intended (at least publicly) to give states more "tax room," the Reagan administration successfully implemented much of the intergovernmental fiscal agenda promoted by business groups some twenty to twenty-five years earlier.[39] In doing so, the Reaganites also changed the ideological terrain on which American federalism battles were fought: some fifty years after it had been effectively dismissed as an operating principle of American government, dual federalism had returned as a theory motivating congressional action.

To say that dual federalism returned is not to say that it was fully re-embraced, however. Even with the 1981 reforms, the national government would remain the senior partner in many areas of domestic policymaking once reserved for the states and—equally important—federal tax revenues would continue to outstrip those of state and local governments. Reagan and his advisors fully understood this: to them, the intergovernmental fiscal reforms of 1981 were merely the first step in the much larger fiscal transformation they envisioned. As William Niskanen later acknowledged, the new block grants adopted in place of the old categorical grants were considered by most Reaganites to be "temporary measures, pending a more though

[37] Edward N. Delaney, "The Economic Recovery Tax Act of 1981," *American Bar Association Journal* 67, no. 10 (1981): 1266–1269.

[38] Ronald Reagan, "Message to the Transmitting Proposed Federalism Legislation," February 14, 1983, *Ronald Reagan Presidential Library and Museum, https://www.reaganlibrary.gov/archives/speech/message-congress-transmitting-proposed-federalism-legislation*, accessed June 18, 2023.

[39] In 1983, Reagan and his advisors attempted to build on their success in 1981 with a large-scale federalism proposal that attempted to reform the intergovernmental fiscal relationship even more explicitly. Stated simply, Reagan proposed to have consolidate even more categorical grants into block grants alongside cutting or eliminating a large number of federal excise taxes. The federalism link between the spending and taxing reforms was made especially clear: the national government was "turning back" both the substantive policies and the tax fields to the states. However, this didn't get very far....

sorting-out of government roles in our federal system."[40] In other words, the ultimate goal of the Reaganites was to end almost all fiscal support for state and local governments.[41] Much like James Buchanan and the other competitive federalists in the ivory tower, the Reaganites considered nearly all grants to state and local governments to be the building blocks of a massive and loathsome intergovernmental cartel. Hence, while block grants were preferable to categorical grants, neither was ideal; both, in the Reaganites' view, needed to be put on a path toward elimination.

The State Taxation Response to the Reagan Revolution, 1981–1983

The Reagan Revolution in fiscal policy hit statehouses around the country at a particularly inopportune time. After enjoying a decade of regular surpluses and relatively easy budget decisions, states suddenly found themselves facing the most difficult fiscal situations they had encountered in nearly two generations.[42] Several factors coalesced to create this situation. The overarching factor, of course, was the national recession—the worst economic downturn the country had experienced since the Great Depression—that had set in at the beginning of 1981 and which naturally caused state tax revenues to plummet.[43] The effect of the recession on state tax revenues was compounded by several other factors, including the tax cuts that many states had implemented during the Tax Revolt and the sudden decline in inflation during this same period (which reversed some of the "bracket creep" that had resulted in higher state income tax revenues during the 1970s). On top of that, the demise of the state component of revenue sharing in 1980 deprived the states of a revenue source that they had waved off earlier, but that would have been beneficial in a moment of fiscal distress.

The aforementioned factors would have been bad enough, but the steep cuts to intergovernmental grants in the 1981 national budget made state fiscal decisions even more challenging. This was, of course, by design: in

[40] William A. Niskanen, *Reaganomics: An Insider's Account of the Policies and the People* (New York: Oxford, 1988), 58.

[41] To be sure, Niskanen emphasized that a small number of national grants oriented toward a truly "national purpose" might be appropriate federal expenditures.

[42] Advisory Commission on Intergovernmental Relations, "For the States, A Time of Testing," *Intergovernmental Perspectives* 8, no. 3 (1982): 7.

[43] Tim Sablik, "Recession of 1981–1982," *Federal Reserve History*, https://www.federalreservehistory.org/essays/recession-of-1981-82, accessed July 9, 2023

justifying the cuts, President Reagan made it clear that it was now up to the states to determine whether to preserve the social programs jeopardized by them or not, but that preserving them would require states to use their own resources. As Thomas R. Swartz and John E. Peck put it, Reagan's essential message to state and local governments was: "Raise taxes to pay for your own public services, or do without them."[44] As discussed earlier, the evidence suggests that many of Reagan's advisors, motivated by the theory of competitive federalism, assumed that most states and localities would ultimately opt to "do without them." But ostensibly, at least, the choice was theirs to make.

In responding to the multipronged fiscal crisis they faced, states took a path that was in some ways similar to the one they took some fifty years earlier, when they faced a fiscal crisis of similar magnitude: after a period of adopting temporizing solutions, they finally acted. Initially, in the 1981 legislative sessions, states largely avoided making big fiscal changes. This was at least in part because they did not yet know the depth of the fiscal challenges they were facing. While the economic downturn was already cutting into state tax receipts, there was major uncertainty regarding how long the downturn would last. Additionally, the fate of President Reagan's budget proposal (which was being considered in Congress at the time state legislatures were in session) was unknown, so states did not have a good sense of how large cuts in intergovernmental spending would be. Thus, for the most part, state budgeting in 1981 was "a rather tame game of budget adjustment politics..."[45] Rather than making steep cuts or levying large tax increases, most states opted for modest belt-tightening alongside various accounting gimmicks to "[put] off the day of reckoning."[46]

By 1982, the full weight of the unpleasant fiscal reality was beginning to set in. The budget passed by Congress in the summer of 1981 ended up including many of Reagan's proposed cuts to intergovernmental programs, meaning that it would be up to state policymakers to decide whether and how much to cushion the blow of these cuts on needy populations. Additionally, the recession was proving to be far deeper and more long-lasting than the ones of previous decades, making painful structural decisions about state fiscal policy more likely. But mindful that the 1982 midterm elections were right around the corner, states put off making the hard choices during

[44] Thomas R. Swartz and John E. Peck, "The Changing Face of Fiscal Federalism," *Challenge* 33, no. 6 (1990): 41–46.

[45] Stephen L. Schechter, "The State of American Federalism: 1981," *Publius* 12 (1983): 1–17.

[46] Nathan and Doolittle, *Reagan and the States*, 11.

their regular legislative sessions. Instead, many balanced their budgets via administrative downsizing, including personnel cuts and hiring freezes.

It was only after November of 1982 (during special sessions at the very end of the year, but even more so in the regular sessions of 1983) that states finally began to make the painful budgetary decisions that they had repeatedly pushed back. In considering the outcomes of this crucial period, several contextual factors are important to keep in mind. The first is the overwhelming advantage that Democrats enjoyed in statehouses across the country in the early 1980s. Despite his large victory in the 1980 presidential election, Reagan had limited coattails in that year's state legislative contests: Republicans emerged from that election with full control of only seven states while Democrats controlled seventeen.[47] The situation got even worse for Republicans following the Democratic landslide in the 1982 midterms. In its aftermath, the number of Democrat-controlled states rose to twenty-four while the number of Republican-controlled states dropped to four. The fact that the vast bulk of states in the 1980s were either Democrat-controlled or featured divided government meant that Reagan Republicans had very few opportunities to implement their tax policy preferences at the state level.[48]

In addition to the partisan breakdown of state governments, interest-group influence also had a highly important impact on state responses to the 1982–1983 fiscal crises. The universe of interest groups operating inside statehouses had changed substantially since the 1950s and early 1960s, when (as described in Chapter 3) business groups, labor unions, and (to a lesser extent) groups representing teachers and state universities played a dominant role in shaping state fiscal policy. In the intervening period, as state governments professionalized and underwent a substantial fiscal expansion, the number of interest groups lobbying state governments mushroomed.[49] Many of these new interest groups represented vulnerable populations (e.g., the urban poor, African Americans, the mentally ill, and others) that had long been ignored by state governments. Despite their skepticism of the states and preference for national power, the leaders of these groups decided to organize in many state capitals during the late 1960s and 1970s

[47] George B. Merry, "Democratic Legislatures May Stymie GOP Ambitions to Control US House," *Christian Science Monitor*, December 1, 1980, 12.

[48] This would change dramatically in the 1990s and the twenty-first century, as Chapter 6 will show.

[49] James M. Strickland, "A Quiet Revolution in State Lobbying: Government Growth and Interest Populations," *Political Research Quarterly* 74, no. 4 (2021): 1181–1196.

because much was at stake in the way states implemented the Great Society's intergovernmental programs.

During the early 1980s, however, something unexpected happened: as the Reagan Revolution swept through the national government, social-welfare advocates found themselves in a stronger position in many state capitals than in Washington, D.C. As the leader of a national anti-poverty campaign told the *New York Times* in 1985, "The states were far more progressive than we expected..."[50] Recognizing that they could use the states as a crucial backstop against the Reagan Administration's efforts to dismantle the safety net, social-welfare groups kicked into high gear in the states where they held sway in an effort to prevent the most draconian program cuts being considered. In many cases, their efforts went beyond behind-the-scenes lobbying to direct action. In Illinois, for example, more than one hundred social-welfare organizations united to form the Emergency Campaign for Human Needs, which staged large protests throughout the state and led a march from Chicago to Springfield to highlight the potential consequences of major budget cuts for the state's most vulnerable communities. As a leader of the coalition emphasized, the goal was to reframe the state's fiscal crisis as a "human crisis."[51]

The outcomes of such efforts were complex and varied from state to state, but in many cases social-welfare advocates were able to save important programs from the budgetary axe. To be sure, state budget cuts were substantial, and intergovernmental programs serving the most vulnerable populations tended to fare the worst (programs serving broader populations, like Medicaid, were generally more protected than programs exclusively for the poor, like AFDC). Nonetheless, contemporary observers were impressed at the extent to which states succeeded in preserving social programs that many expected to either be drastically pared down or disappear completely.[52] These successes, combined with the decisions of many states to preserve high levels of education spending, resulted in overall fiscal approaches that were significantly more moderate than those emanating from Congress. And, most importantly, while Congress coupled its large spending cuts with massive tax cuts, states—constitutionally required in most cases to balance

[50] Robert Pear, "States Are Found More Responsive on Social Issues," *New York Times*, May 19, 1985, 1.

[51] "Coalition Plans counterpoint to Thompson 'State of the State,'" *The Times* (Streator, IL), February 8, 1983, 9; Don Thompson, "Marchers support social concerns," *The Pantagraph* (Bloomington, IL), May 15, 1983, 3.

[52] Nathan and Doolittle, *Reagan and the States*, 357.

Table 5.1 Number of Tax Rate Increases by States in the 1982–1983 Recession

	1982	1983
Personal Income Tax	9	12
General Sales Tax	11	12
Corporate Income Tax	6	13
Motor Fuel Tax	5	18
Cigarette Tax	9	13
Alcohol Beverage Taxes	5	11

Source: 1984–1985 *Book of the States* (Council of State Governments)

their budgets—supplemented more moderate spending cuts with substantial tax increases. The extent of state tax increases in 1982–1983 is shown in Table 5.1. As the table shows, states turned to nearly all the leading state tax sources to fill their budget gaps. Thus, unlike the 1950s and early 1960s, the early 1980s was clearly not a moment in which states opted to rely primarily on their more regressive taxes (i.e., general sales taxes, alcohol and tobacco taxes) and less on their more progressive ones (i.e., personal and corporate income taxes). Rather, it was a time in which the different taxes were, on the whole, raised at roughly equal levels.

These overall numbers, however, mask significant differences across states. As in other periods of major state tax activity (e.g., the 1930s and the 1960s), there was a great deal of variation in state tax choices in 1982–1983. And also much like those other periods, the state taxation decisions of the 1982–1983 period cannot be easily explained by the standard variables of political science research. For example, party control of state government accounts for almost none of the variation in state tax response. This is, of course, partially a result of the fact that Republicans controlled so few states during these years. However, even after taking into account the lopsided partisan balance in state government, it does not appear that partisanship significantly affected the state tax policy outcomes of this period. When Democrats controlled state government in 1982–1983, they raised personal income taxes 33% of the time, corporate income taxes 19% of the time, and general sales taxes 31% of the time.[53] Conversely, during the rare instances

[53] This is based on an analysis of state-years (i.e., Alabama in 1982, Alabama in 1983, Alaska in 1982, Alaska in 1983, etc.), so that the total number of observations is 100 (fifty states across two years).

when Republicans controlled state governments during this period, they raised personal income taxes 30% of the time, corporate income taxes 13% of the time, and general sales taxes 30% of the time. Clearly, greater Democratic representation in state government made it no more likely that major state tax increases would be passed, and greater Republican representation made it no more likely that they would be avoided.

Looking more carefully at the developments in individual states, one finds evidence of numerous types of partisan scenarios playing out. In states like Michigan, Minnesota, Ohio, and Rhode Island, Democratic legislatures worked with Democratic governors to push through income tax increases over the near-complete opposition of the Republican minority (this is perhaps the type of scenario that one might most expect to see). But there were also examples of Democrat-controlled state governments (for example, in Wisconsin) eschewing income tax increases to raise sales taxes, and likewise drawing uniform Republican opposition.[54] There were also Democrat-controlled state governments (like Massachusetts) that passed through the 1982–1983 period without making any major changes to the "Big Three" taxes. Likewise, among the small number of Republican-controlled states during this period, one can see a much wider range of tax actions than one would see in "red states" today. In both Indiana and Vermont, for example, Republican-controlled legislatures passed and Republican governors signed a package of income and sales tax increases. Finally, in states featuring divided government, deals were often worked out to have both parties share the burden of passing tax increases. This occurred in Illinois and Washington, where bipartisan coalitions in the Democrat-controlled legislatures passed tax increases promoted by moderate Republican governors.

In contrast to the state tax policy actions of the 1960s, those of the 1982–1983 period can only be weakly explained by path dependence. By the early 1980s, variations in tax usage among the fifty states had declined dramatically from what they were in the early 1960s, prior to the second critical juncture in state taxation. There were now only ten states without personal income taxes, seven states without corporate income taxes, and five states without general sales taxes left. The fact that most states had each of the "Big Three" taxes already on their books meant that it was much easier to turn to any of them in a moment of fiscal crisis. Thus, historical usage patterns did

[54] "Tax Bill Before Earl For Signing," *Stevens Point Journal* (Stevens Point, WI), January 6, 1983, 1.

not affect the tax choices of states to a great degree. Perhaps more surprising is the fact that historical tax *reliance* patterns did not affect them either. Some states that had traditionally relied heavily on personal income taxes (like Vermont) raised them further in 1983, while others (like Wisconsin) raised their sales taxes instead. The situation was similar with states that had traditionally relied on the sales tax: some responded to the fiscal crisis by making their sales tax rates even higher, while others decided to close their budget gaps by raising their income taxes.

Rather than partisanship or path dependence, the variable that matters most in explaining state tax outcomes during the 1982–1983 recession is region. Figure 5.1 presents a map showing which states raised at least one of the "Big Three" taxes during the 1982–1983 period, and which did not. As can be seen, all the industrial Midwestern states and many of the Mountain West states raised at least one of the "Big Three" taxes during this period, while Southern and Northeastern states were significantly less likely to raise any of them. The fact that all the industrial Midwestern states raised taxes during the 1982–1983 period can be explained by two factors. First, the recession hit these states especially hard, causing larger-than-average revenue losses.[55] Second, these states had by the 1980s accrued a long tradition of high social-service provisioning and featured strong public-sector unions, which meant that reducing expenses by cutting social services or reducing public employee benefits was less politically feasible than it was in other places.

Despite the fact that they were somewhat difficult to explain, the state tax increases of 1982–1983 garnered substantial national attention. National economic-policy journalists wrote articles expressing surprise that so many states, which had just a few years earlier been reeling from the Tax Revolt, were now raising their taxes. They further pointed out that the state-level tax increases weren't just relevant for state politics: given their direct interference with President Reagan's stated goals of lowering the nation's overall tax burden, the tax increases had national implications. As *New York Times* reporter Robert Hershey pointed out, their cumulative effect was such that "Despite President Reagan's tax cuts, the total tax burden on Americans is still going up."[56]

[55] Andrew H. Malcolm, "Midwest Struggling to Stem Deficit Tide," *New York Times*, March 5, 1983, 13.
[56] Robert D. Hershey, "Despite Reagan Cuts, Many Are Taxed More," *New York Times*, April 15, 1983, D1.

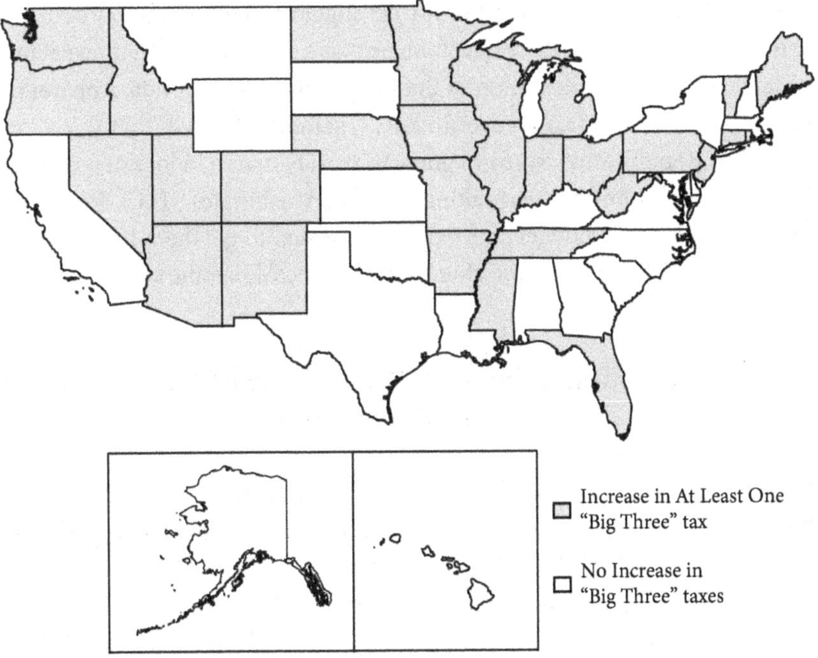

Figure 5.1 Increases in "Big Three" Taxes in 1982–1983
Source: State Tax Actions Dataset

This fact was not lost on the growing cadre of national anti-tax activists who were beginning to gain power in Washington, D.C. Following the recall of two state senators who had supported an income tax increase in Michigan, a young Grover Norquist and John Fund jointly penned an article in the *Wall Street Journal* in which they wrote that "voters in Michigan are boiling mad about taxes, and politicians nationwide should take heed if they value their electoral survival."[57] Similarly, in an official op-ed of the newspaper, the *Journal* profiled a 39-year-old automobile worker in Ohio who was angry about his state's tax increase, suggesting that a second-wave "Blue-Collar Tax Revolt" was in the works across the Midwest.[58] The extent to which this claim was true is debatable (Ohio voters ended up rejecting a citizen-initiated referendum to override the tax increase that November), but the fact that the nation's leading conservative newspaper offered such substantial coverage of

[57] John H. Fund and Grover Norquist, "Michigan Taxes Spark a Blue Flame," *Wall Street Journal*, January 25, 1984, 32.
[58] "The Blue-Collar Tax Revolt," *Wall Street Journal*, August 17, 1983, 22.

the state-level tax increases of 1982–1983 suggests that the country's conservative elites recognized these developments as a considerable (if unexpected) obstacle to the implementation of the Reagan domestic agenda. Apparently, they likely reasoned, state governments (including the few that were controlled by Republicans) were not going to readily march in lockstep with the Reagan Revolution that was taking place in Washington, D.C. Something more than the 1981 budget cuts would be needed to get them to fall in line. And that something was a big change in the federal income tax code.

Fiscal Federalism in Reagan's Second Term: The Fight Over the SALT Deduction

In 1984, as President Reagan was running for reelection, scholars and other interested observers took stock of what his first term had wrought for American federalism. Their overall verdict on the significance of Reagan's accomplishments was surprisingly nuanced. On the one hand, no one could deny the scale of the 1981 budget cuts and the profound changes in public finance that they triggered. But because state governments were able to preserve many of the intergovernmental programs targeted by Reagan (albeit in reduced form in many cases), these cuts proved to be less "disruptive" than many anticipated.[59] Moreover, following his success in the 1981 budget, Reagan embarked on a large-scale project (which he called New Federalism) to formally separate the *substantive* responsibilities of national and subnational government. But this project, which involved turning over welfare completely to the states while nationalizing Medicaid, languished in Congress. On balance, therefore, Reagan's biggest first-term, federalism-related accomplishment was in facilitating *fiscal* rather than substantive-policy separation. Through the cuts to intergovernmental programs that he successfully championed, Reagan ensured that the states would be less fiscally dependent on the national government in the 1980s than they had been in decades.

As it turned out, Reagan was not done with his efforts to fiscally separate national and state government. Indeed, the goal of intergovernmental fiscal separation would arguably feature even more prominently in Reagan's second term than in his first. Unlike in Reagan's first term, however, the vehicle

[59] George E. Peterson, "Federalism and the States: An Experiment in Decentralization," In *The Reagan Record*, eds. John L. Palmer and Isabel V. Sawhill (Cambridge, MA: Ballinger Publishing, 1984), 257.

for advancing fiscal separation would be the tax code rather than the federal budget. More specifically, soon after beginning his second term, Reagan proposed eliminating two federal tax subsidies upon which state and local governments had relied for nearly a century: the deduction on state and local taxes that Americans could claim in their federal income tax filings (hereinafter referred to as SALT, for "State and Local Tax Deduction), and the tax-exempt status of state and local bonds. Eliminating these two provisions of the federal tax code would have had the effect of almost completely delinking the federal tax system from those of the states. It also would have put considerable pressure on states to lower their tax burdens, which (as we shall see) was part of the point.

The changes in intergovernmental tax policy that Reagan pursued in his second term were part of a comprehensive tax reform package—what eventually became the Tax Reform Act of 1986. This package, the centerpiece of Reagan's second-term domestic policy agenda, was motivated by a different economic philosophy than his 1981 tax cuts: whereas the latter were based in supply-side principles and thus focused on lowering tax burdens for everyone, the tax reforms of Reagan's second term were meant to combine lower rates with a broader tax base and thus be "revenue neutral."[60] Unlike the supply-side approach, the base-broadening approach would inevitably yield losers (i.e., people and businesses who would see their taxes go up) in addition to winners, making it both more difficult to pass and more politically risky.[61] As a result, Reagan and his top economic policy advisers took over a year (from April of 1984 to May of 1985) to develop their tax reform proposal.[62] Over the course of that period, Reagan's advisors (including Treasury Secretaries Donald Regan and James Baker and Assistant Secretary Richard Darman) had to figure out how to broaden the tax base sufficiently

[60] Timothy J. Conlan, Margaret T. Wrightson, and David R. Beam, *Taxing Choices: The Politics of Tax Reform* (Washington, D.C.: CQ Press, 1990), 30–38.

[61] Given this reality, scholars and journalists have spent time trying to understand why Reagan and his advisors decided to pursue the so-called "base-broadening approach" to tax reform as their main domestic-policy item. While the answer remains somewhat murky, it appears that the decision was the result of several concurrent factors: economists in the Treasury Department promoted it, Reagan's advisers viewed it as politically beneficial (particularly if the tax reform resulted in a lower overall tax burden for those in the middle of the income distribution in addition to the wealthy), and Reagan himself was personally passionate about securing even lower income tax rates. On top of all this, Reagan and his advisors saw tax reform as an important goal of securing a smaller government, not just at the national level but at the state and local levels as well. Conlan, *From New Federalism to Devolution*, 136; Conlan, Wrightson, and Beam, *Taxing Choices*, 45–47.

[62] The ins-and-outs of this process have been described elsewhere. See, in particular, Conlan, *From New Federalism to Devolution*, and Wrightson, and Beam, *Taxing Choices*.

to pay for lower rates. Stated differently, they had to decide which preferences in the tax code would be eliminated and which would be kept.

In the end, the president's team came up with a plan that included a long list of tax expenditures to be repealed, but at or near the top of the list (in terms of the amount of revenue at stake) were the SALT deduction and the exemption of interest from state and municipal bonds. Importantly, SALT was the most controversial tax expenditure that the Reaganites decided to target (other politically sensitive and very costly tax preferences, such as the mortgage interest deduction and the deduction on charitable contributions, were not selected for elimination). Scholarly and journalistic accounts of the plan's formulation, which were based on numerous interviews conducted with involved personnel, show that the president's team needed to propose the repeal of at least one of the largest tax expenditures to finance the rate reductions Reagan wanted, and that of the largest expenditures, SALT was the most obvious candidate for elimination.[63] As Conlan, Wrightson, and Beam write, SALT was "viewed as fiscally unavoidable by [Treasury Secretary] Baker, economically inefficient by Treasury staff, and 'socialistic' by White House conservatives."[64] In other words, in the Reaganites' eyes, eliminating SALT was first and foremost fiscally necessary, but it also had a highly important policy benefit: removing this crucial federal subsidy upon which states had built their tax systems would help dismantle America's intergovernmental cartel and advance a truly competitive federalism, one in which the states would be disciplined into retrenchment. Indeed, the Reaganites did not really hide the goals motivating their decision to target the SALT deduction: as White House Communications Director Pat Buchanan told journalists at a press conference, while the main purpose of eliminating the SALT deduction was to recover foregone revenue, its secondary purpose was to rein in "neo-socialist" state governments and force them to cut spending.[65]

Because SALT was such a longstanding part of the federal tax code and because it benefited state and local governments (which continued to enjoy a big lobbying presence on Capitol Hill), Reagan and his advisors concluded that convincing Congress to abolish it would require mobilizing the American people to their side. The first step in their efforts to this effect

[63] Conlan, Wrightson, and Beam, *Taxing Choices*, 76–77; Jeffrey H. Birnbaum and Alan S. Murray, *Showdown at Gucci Gulch: Lawmakers, Lobbyists, and the Unlikely Triumph of Tax Reform* (New York: Vintage Books, 1988), 88.

[64] Conlan, Wrightson, and Beam, *Taxing Choices*, 76–77.

[65] Ronald Sullivan, "Cuomo angered by Reagan Aide," *New York Times*, June 9, 1985, 1.

occurred on May 28, 1985, when Reagan gave a primetime address introducing his tax plan to the public. In this address, Reagan called for a tax system that was "clear, simple, and fair to all" and argued that his proposal would "free us from the grip of special interests and create a binding commitment to the only special interest that counts—you, the people who pay America's bills." After summarizing his plan's rate cuts, he explained that they would be financed by "simplifying the complex system of special provisions that favor some at the expense of others." But while he alluded to a variety of such "special provisions," he mentioned only one by name: "the State and local tax deduction, which actually provides a special subsidy for high-income individuals, especially in a few high-tax States."[66] From an intergovernmental relations standpoint, the speech was striking. As many would later observe, Reagan was effectively treating state and local governments as "special interests," no different from the business sectors and other economic actors that had successfully inserted and defended benefits into the federal tax code over decades. No previous president had ever depicted America's subnational governments in this way. For students of federalism who were paying attention, this rhetoric could not be easily squared with the president's paeans to dual federalism and state sovereignty from just a few years earlier.

Reagan's address effectively functioned as the first shot in the battle over the SALT Deduction that would be fought over the course of the next sixteen months. In the wake of the address, the White House prepared for an intensive public relations blitz to sell the president's tax proposal—and especially the elimination of SALT—to the American people, while supporters of SALT quickly and rapidly countermobilized to save it. The White House's plan for winning the battle was to pit states against each other, i.e., to marshal public support for ending the deduction in the majority of states where relatively few people claimed the deduction and use it to isolate the small number of high-tax states in which SALT claims were high.[67] Thus, in stop after stop in his barnstorming tour of the country that summer, Reagan presented SALT as a giveaway to a few heavily taxed, fiscally irresponsible state governments. As he said at a rally in Oklahoma, "some state governments outside Oklahoma have not yet learned to say 'no' to special interest groups

[66] Ronald Reagan, "Address to the Nation on Tax Reform," May 28, 1985, The American Presidency Project, *https://www.presidency.ucsb.edu/documents/address-the-nation-tax-reform*, accessed July 6, 2023.

[67] Birnbaum and Murray, *Showdown at Gucci Gulch*.

and higher taxes...I just don't believe the good people of Oklahoma or other low-tax states...should be forced to pay for their lack of resolve."[68]

Organized efforts to save SALT were initially led by citizens of the state that stood to lose the most from the deduction's repeal—New York. As Jeffrey H. Birnbaum and Alan S. Murray document in their classic account of the tax reform fight, the Empire State's most powerful businessmen quickly responded to Reagan's plan by spearheading a well-funded lobbying campaign to convince Congress to keep the deduction. Recognizing the White House's strategy of isolating New York, the campaign's strategists decided to create a national group—the Coalition Against Double Taxation—to draw leaders of other states into the fight to save SALT. A crucial part of the Coalition's strategy was to pump out studies conveying the fiscal threat posed by the abolition of SALT to states and municipal governments across the country.[69] Meanwhile, New York Governor Mario Cuomo became a regular spokesperson on behalf of the deduction in national media, and members of the state's congressional delegation from both parties focused almost single-mindedly on preserving the deduction as the Reagan tax plan was being considered in congressional committees. Importantly, the New Yorkers framed the deduction as an important tax incentive for middle-class Americans, not just the wealthy Manhattanites that Reagan was fond of knocking in his speeches.[70]

Eventually, the foregoing strategy bore fruit as officials and sectoral interests from outside New York joined the effort to preserve SALT. Many of the largest intergovernmental lobbying groups as well as the National Education Association came out strongly against SALT's repeal.[71] The Northeast-Midwest Coalition, a caucus of 196 House members from relatively high-tax states in the country's Northeastern quadrant, announced its demand that SALT be maintained in full.[72] Eventually, even state and local officials from low-tax Southern states—whose residents would in theory have had the most to gain from SALT's elimination—began speaking out in favor of SALT (their argument was that its repeal would make raising taxes to pay for vital public services even harder in their jurisdictions than it already was).[73] Ultimately,

[68] "Reagan Criticizes High-Tax States," *New York Times*, June 6, 1985, D5.
[69] Birnbaum and Murray, *Showdown at Gucci Gulch*, 113–114.
[70] Nicholas F. Jacobs, "Economic Sectionalism, Executive-Centered Partisanship, and the Politics of the State and Local Tax Deduction," *Political Science Quarterly* 136, no. 2 (2021), 326.
[71] Ibid.
[72] Timothy B. Clark, "Taking a Regional Stand," *National Journal*, March 22, 1986, 699.
[73] Conlan, Wrightson, and Beam, *Taxing Choices*, 113.

then, the New Yorkers' strategy of creating allies among elites from different parts of the country proved more effective than the White House's strategy of marshaling public opinion against New York and a handful of other high-tax states.

The New Yorkers' outmaneuvering of the Reaganites became evident as the tax reform bill moved through the legislative process in the House of Representatives (where, under the Constitution, all revenue-related bills must originate). House Ways and Means Committee Chairman Dan Rostenkowski, an enthusiastic supporter of base-broadening tax reform who was initially open to SALT repeal, became increasingly convinced that the SALT issue was emboldening tax reform's opponents and had the potential to scuttle the entire legislation.[74] He thus directed a rewrite of the tax bill that ultimately preserved SALT (as well as several other controversial expenditures that the president proposed cutting) and paid for it by having a higher top federal income tax rate (38% to 35%) as well as slightly higher corporate income and capital-gains tax rates.[75] The rewritten bill caused a minor rebellion among conservative Republicans, thereby threatening its passage, but President Reagan urged them to support the bill despite its flaws and "keep the process alive" (he assured them that he would not sign any tax reform bill with tax rates as high as those in the House version).[76] Thus, on December 17, 1985, tax reform passed the House and moved to the Senate with SALT intact.

The dynamics in the Senate were considerably different than those in the House. Though controlled by Republicans, the Senate had a long tradition of being highly solicitous of tax expenditures, making a base-broadening approach a steeper climb there.[77] Equally important, Senate Finance Committee Chair Bob Packwood, who had a major influence on the chamber's fiscal policy bills, was a longtime supporter of various business tax breaks and was thus particularly skeptical of the base-broadening framework.[78] At first, Packwood tried to rally the Senate around a pragmatic, incremental approach to tax reform in which numerous tax expenditures—including SALT—would be downsized but not eliminated while tax rates would be lowered but not as much in the House bill. However, in attempting to please

[74] Birnbaum and Murray, *Showdown at Gucci Gulch*, 130–133.
[75] Conlan, Wrightson, and Beam, *Taxing Choices*, 265–266.
[76] Conlan, Wrightson, and Beam, *Taxing Choices*, 130–132.
[77] Conlan, Wrightson, and Beam, *Taxing Choices*, 137–138.
[78] Birnbaum and Murray, *Showdown at Gucci Gulch*, 188–191.

everyone, Packwood pleased no one: during the markup stage, the bill was fattened with so many amendments fully restoring various tax breaks that it quickly lost any semblance of being revenue-neutral. Chastened, Packwood started from scratch with a new and completely different premise: income tax rates would be trimmed in half (with a top rate of 25%, significantly lower than what even Reagan proposed) and nearly all the big tax expenditures would be eliminated. Gauging that members of the Finance Committee were surprisingly sympathetic to his framework, Packwood convened a bipartisan group of six fellow Finance Committee members to fill in the details of his plan. The group completed its work in just twelve days, and its bill was then passed unanimously by the committee.[79] The speed with which a transformational tax reform bill was making its way through the traditional lethargic Senate was nothing short of breathtaking.

For defenders of SALT, the quick advance of the Packwood bill through the Senate was greeted with mixed feelings. Though the bill proposed to completely eliminate many tax expenditures, it did not do so with SALT. Instead, the bill proposed to scale SALT back by no longer having it apply to state sales taxes (state and local income and property taxes could still be deducted). How and why the six-member group that designed the bill decided to restructure the deduction in this way is a bit of a mystery. It seems likely that the group considered the politics of SALT and concluded that eliminating the entire deduction was politically impossible, but that eliminating only the sales tax deduction was something that most members of Congress could accept. In contrast to deducting income and property taxes, deducting state sales taxes required that taxpayers keep numerous sales receipts. This was something relatively few Americans did: as of 1980, only 16% of taxes deducted through SALT were sales taxes (41% were income taxes and 44% were property taxes). Moreover, because high-tax states (i.e., ones where people would be more likely to claim the deduction) tended to rely on income taxes more than sales taxes, the share of SALT from sales taxes was on average even lower (14%) in the ten states with the largest share of taxpayers itemizing their returns.[80] The quintessential such state was New York, whose senior senator, Daniel Patrick Moynihan, told his colleagues in

[79] Conlan, Wrightson, and Beam, *Taxing Choices*, 154–172.

[80] These statistics were calculated using state-level data on SALT claims from: Albert J. Davis, "Closing the National Deficit with Higher Taxes—A Federalism Perspective," *Proceedings of the Seventy-Sixth Annual Conference on Taxation, National Tax Association—Tax Institute of America*, Seattle, WA, October 2–5, 1983, 129–151.

the group that eliminating the sales tax deduction was as far as he would be willing to go in altering SALT.[81]

As the Packwood plan moved through the legislative process in the Senate, the alliance of groups that had been defending SALT for a year began to split. SALT's most ardent defenders, including the Coalition against Double Taxation, had long argued that nothing short of full retention of SALT was acceptable. In their view, limiting SALT to only certain types of state and local taxes stood the very real chance of dividing the leaders of states with different tax systems, and state and local officials needed to remain as united as possible to ensure SALT's long-term survival. But other SALT supporters believed that base-broadening reform required shared sacrifice and that eliminating the sales tax deduction, while not optimal, was relatively unlikely to burden many taxpayers or harm state governments too abjectly. Thus, in the wake of the Packwood Plan's approval by the Senate Finance Committee, New York's previously united leadership began to fracture on the SALT issue: Gov. Cuomo and Sen. Alfonse D'Amato opposed the Senate bill on account of the elimination of the sales tax deduction, while Sen. Moynihan and State Comptroller Edward Regan said they supported the Senate bill despite the sales tax provision.[82] Importantly, Cuomo and Moynihan were Democrats while D'Amato and Regan were Republicans, demonstrating the extent to which views on SALT were only weakly associated with partisanship (even among politicians from the same state) at this time.

With New York's political leadership effectively laying down its arms (at least temporarily) on the issue of the sales tax deduction, the burden of fighting to maintain it largely fell to members of Congress from the small number of states for which sales taxes accounted for a high percentage of SALT claims. Nearly all these states, including Florida, Nevada, South Dakota, Tennessee, Texas, Washington, and Wyoming, were ones that had a sales tax but no personal income tax.[83] The legislators from these states did indeed put up a fight. On June 12, 1986, Washington Senators Dan Evans and Slade Gorton joined with Texas Senator Phil Gramm to propose an amendment allowing taxpayers to deduct *either* their sales taxes or their state income taxes, but not both, and to pay for it by prohibiting the deduction

[81] Conlan, Wrightson, and Beam, *Taxing Choices*, 171.

[82] Jeffrey Schmalz, "New York Leaders Split in Tax Debate," *New York Times*, May 7, 1986, D4.

[83] Other states with a high percentage of sales tax claims were Louisiana, Mississippi, Alabama, and New Mexico. These states all had personal income taxes in addition to sales taxes, but their rates were very low.

for interest paid on home-equity loans. The amendment evoked a spirited debate on the Senate floor. Senators from sales-tax-only states argued that the amendment would rectify a "gross inequity" that both unfairly targeted their constituents and violated federalism principles by attempting to coerce states into a particular tax policy.[84] But senators from Northeastern states with high housing costs argued that, in proposing to eliminate the deduction for home-equity loan interest instead, the amendment merely replaced the targeting of one group of states with the targeting of another.[85] Other senators—most notably, Bill Bradley of New Jersey, the original proponent of the base-broadening approach to tax reform—pointed to an important difference between the income and sales tax deduction: the latter was almost never claimed by low and middle-income taxpayers, despite the regressive nature of the sales tax. More than the income tax deduction, it was a give-away to the wealthy.[86] Sensing that the amendment did not have the votes, Sen. Evans withdrew it.

At this point, it looked like the sales tax deduction was dead in the water, but Senate Majority Leader Robert Dole was mindful that several members of his caucus who were facing tough reelection fights—most notably, Gorton of Washington and Jim Abdnor of South Dakota—came from sales-tax-only states and stood a good chance of losing if they appeared ineffectual in preventing the deduction's elimination. He thus helped to engineer a proposal to allow residents of sales-tax-only states to deduct as much as 60% of the sales taxes they paid. This compromise made it into the final bill that the Senate passed, allowing Gorton, Abdnor, and other senators from these states to temporarily breathe a sigh of relief. However, they were in for a rude awakening when the conference committee charged with ironing out differences between the House and Senate versions of the tax reform unveiled their proposal in mid-August. In the complicated back-and-forth between the House and Senate negotiators, the bill that eventually emerged once again proposed to eliminate, rather than scale back, the sales tax deduction.

The release of the conference committee's report split members of Congress from sales-tax-only states into two camps. One group, including Gorton and Gramm, insisted that the fight was not over and vowed to reinstate the sales tax deduction.[87] But others saw the writing on the wall:

[84] 132 Cong. Rec. S13590-13593 (June 12, 1986).
[85] Ibid., 13598–13600.
[86] Ibid., 13559–13560.
[87] "Dole, Gorton Say They'll fight to revive sales tax deduction," *Spokesman-Review* (Spokane, WA), August 19, 1986, 22; "Gramm Fights for Deduction," *San Angelo Standard-Times* (San Angelo, TX), September 10, 1986, 4.

after over a year of wrangling over tax reform, most members of Congress from both parties were anxious to pass a tax reform bill into law and were thus unlikely to support anything that would undermine the delicate compromise that the conference committee came up with. Acknowledging the likely disappearance of the deduction to local reporters in his state, Sen. Evans attempted to minimize its impact: "Probably less than a fourth of Washington state taxpayers will itemize, so the sales tax deduction would make no difference to three-fourths of those who file," he said.[88] And indeed, on September 25 and 27, the House and Senate passed the conference committee's conference report and sent the Tax Reform Act of 1986 to President Reagan's desk.

In the final analysis, the deduction for state income and property taxes survived the legislative process while that for sales taxes perished for a complex litany of reasons. First and foremost, because American taxpayers deducted income and property taxes far more often than they deducted sales taxes, the leaders of high-tax, heavily SALT-reliant states (particularly New York) perceived the elimination of the deduction for income and property taxes as an existential threat, but did not feel the same way about the sales tax deduction. As a result, New York's entire leadership class—crucially including its business community—worked in tandem to preserve the SALT deduction for income and property taxes, and its well-financed efforts brought leaders of many other state and local governments into the fight to save SALT. But when the Senate Finance Committee proposed to repeal the sales tax deduction alone, the pro-SALT coalition failed to stay united. Suddenly, it was not the high-tax states with robust income taxes but rather the low-tax states that relied on sales taxes that were being targeted, and with the pro-SALT coalition faltering, these states were isolated. Moreover, though they surely perceived the Finance Committee's proposal as arbitrary and unfair, the leaders of sales-tax-only states were just not as appalled by the possible elimination of the sales tax deduction as New York's leaders were by the possible elimination of the income and property tax deductions. Given the relatively low rates of SALT claims among their citizens, the issue did not galvanize elites in sales-tax-only states to the same degree. Thus, though senators from sales-tax-only states (especially those up for reelection in 1986) did attempt to save the sales tax deduction, their comparatively meager

[88] Robert L. Rose, "Evans Holds Little Hope for Sales Tax Deductions," *Spokane Chronicle* (Spokane, WA), September 10, 1986, C7.

efforts were ultimately overwhelmed by the growing desire on Capitol Hill to pass a bill into law.[89]

For President Reagan and his staff, the outcome of the fight over the SALT deduction in Congress must have been bittersweet. Clearly, the issue was an important one for both the President as well as his top economic advisors, who did not believe that the national government should subsidize state and local governments and desired to foster a more competitive federalism across the country. But at some point over the course of the tax reform struggle (perhaps when the House passed its initial bill with the entire SALT deduction intact), the Reagan White House likely recognized that it had been outmaneuvered by the pro-SALT coalition and decided to set aside its efforts to repeal SALT in service of its greater goal: comprehensive tax reform with lower rates. Tax reform was Reagan's top second-term domestic-policy priority, after all, and though Reagan was surely interested in revamping American federalism, he was more determined to secure his legacy through a major domestic policy reform. Additionally, as the battle over tax reform stretched on and the 1986 midterm elections drew closer, Reagan became increasingly aware that his time as a non-lame-duck president was drawing to a close and that he would soon have limited political capital with Congress. Thus, from the passage of the initial House bill onward, Reagan focused his efforts on facilitating final passage of tax reform rather than quibbling over its particular components. When the conference committee agreed upon a tax reform bill that was satisfactory to both the House and Senate negotiators. Reagan was ecstatic despite the fact that the bill differed in many ways from his original tax reform proposal (including on the SALT issue). Two months later, President Reagan signed that bill into law in a big ceremony on the White House South Lawn. The Tax Reform Act of 1986 (TRA) was now on the books.

The State Response to the 1986 Tax Reform

To everyone's surprise, the final version of TRA was, for the most part, highly favorable to state (and, to a lesser extent, local) governments. The two biggest hits that subnational governments took in the reform were new restrictions

[89] In fact, these senators did end up paying a political price for their failure to save the sales tax deduction. Both Sen. Gorton and Sen. Abdnor were voted out of office that November, and political commentators in Washington and South Dakota partly blamed their losses on the sales tax issue.

placed on the tax exemption for municipal bond interest and the elimination of the SALT deduction for sales taxes. The former was indeed a significant new burden (and one whose impact is beyond the scope of this book), but the latter was widely viewed as an insignificant loss for all but the small number of states that relied disproportionately on the sales tax. Moreover, for states with personal income taxes, the Tax Reform turned out to be a massive fiscal boon. Because most of them tied their income taxes to the federal income tax code, the elimination of so many exemptions and deductions in the Tax Reform meant that the base of many state income taxes had suddenly expanded substantially. According to one estimate, states stood to gain $6.3 billion in additional tax revenues in 1987 due to TRA—what became known as the state tax "windfall."[90] Ironically, then, it was the states that relied most heavily on income taxes—the very states that Reagan had spent many months attacking in his effort to repeal the entire SALT deduction in 1985—that ended up benefiting the most from his tax reform. Conversely, it was the low-tax states that relied heavily on sales taxes—the very states that Reagan unsuccessfully tried to enlist in the campaign to repeal the deduction—that suffered the most from it.

Given the enormous consequences of the 1986 Tax Reform for state tax systems, everyone expected the 1987 state legislative sessions to be focused intensely on tax policy, perhaps more so than for any previous year since the early 1970s. For the vast majority of states with personal income taxes, the big question concerned what to do with the "windfall" in state personal income tax revenue that they were expecting. Would states happily collect the windfall without changing their tax structures, or would they cut their own income taxes to return the new revenue to their citizens? For the small number of states with no income tax and/or that relied heavily on sales taxes, the question was quite the opposite: given that the tax overhaul clearly favored the state income tax and disfavored the state sales tax, activists in these states began to reprise the argument (last heard in the late 1960s and early 1970s) that the time had finally come to bite the bullet and adopt an income tax.[91] Would such arguments gain any traction?

[90] W. John Moore, "Tax Reform Ripples," *National Journal*, September 12, 1987, 2269.

[91] Robert Reinhold, "Thinking the Unthinkable in Texas: State Income Tax is On the Horizon," *New York Times*, April 6, 1987, A12; Tom Humphrey, "Reform May Spur State Income Tax," *Knoxville News Sentinel* (Knoxville, TN), August 25, 1986, 1; "Tax Reform; It's Time to Take a Look," *The Olympian* (Olympia, WA), July 24, 1987, 13.

By the end of the year, the answers to both questions were clear. With regard to state income taxes, 1987 did indeed end up featuring the highest amount of policy changes of any year in recent decades, but the policy changes did not result in a meaningful increase in the overall amount of revenue states collected.[92] Most states responded to the reform by either cutting their income tax rates or restructuring their income tax systems (through more generous deductions or credits, or higher personal exemptions) to reduce their citizens' income tax burdens. To be sure, there were exceptions: a minority of states maintained their existing income tax structures, effectively taking advantage of the federal tax reform to dramatically increase their revenues. But, on the whole, states were content to stick with the revenue amounts they already had and return most of the windfall from the federal tax reform to their citizens.[93]

How states did this is shown in Table 5.2, which arrays rate changes (the rows) against non-rate changes (the columns) to state income taxes in the 1987 legislative sessions. As the table shows, eleven states simultaneously cut their income tax rates while also making significant non-rate cuts (such as expanded deductions or credits, or higher personal exemptions). Notably, many of these were states with some of the highest income tax burdens, including New York, California, Minnesota, Wisconsin, and Oregon. Particularly notable were the changes in California and New York, which were "so large" as to "dwarf all other actions."[94] In New York, a nine-bracket income tax with rates ranging from 1% to 9% was changed to a two-bracket income tax with rates of 5.5% and 7%, but the standard deduction and the exemption for filers with dependents were raised as well.[95] Similarly, in California, legislators replaced an eleven-bracket rate system ranging from 1% to 11% with a six-bracket system ranging from 1% to 9.3%, and also increased the standard deduction as well as credits for dependents and child care.[96] Another eight states did not reduce their income tax rates but did cut their income taxes via higher exemptions, deductions, or credits. Only a handful of states raised income tax rates, and this was usually accompanied by some form

[92] As state tax policy expert Steven Gold observed, "Despite the plethora of activity, 1987 was not a year when the aggregate level of state taxation changed much." Steven D. Gold, "The Blizzard of 1987: A Year of Tax Reform Activity in the States," *Publius* 18 (Summer 1988): 18.

[93] Estimates suggest that states kept only 20% of the windfall. Gold, "The Blizzard of 1987."

[94] Gold, "The Blizzard of 1987," 19.

[95] Joel Benenson, "Legislature OKs $41 Billion Budget," *The Standard-Star* (New Rochelle, NY), April 11, 1987, 1

[96] "Highlights of State Income Tax Revision," *Los Angeles Times*, September 12, 1987, 29.

Table 5.2 Changes in State Personal Income Taxes in the 1987 Legislative Sessions

Changes in Tax Rates	Changes in Tax Structure other than Rates	
	Non-Rate Tax Cut	**No Change**
Rate Decrease	11 states (CA, CO, DE, IA, MN, NY, OR, VA, VT, WI, WV)	1 state (OH)
Rate Increase	4 states (ID, NE, ND, SC)	2 states (IN, MT)
No Change	8 states (AR, GA, HI, ME, MD, MI, MO, UT)	12 states (AL, AZ, IL, KS, LA, MA, MS, NC, NJ, NM, OK, PA)

Note: The nine states without a personal income tax as of 1987 (AK, CT, FL, NH, TN, TX, SD, WA, WY) are not included in this table. Source: Gold, "The Blizzard of 1987"
Source: State Tax Actions Dataset

of non-rate cut as well. Most strikingly, no state in 1987 attempted to raise revenue via non-rate tax increases.

Importantly, the large state income tax cuts of 1987 had the counterintuitive effect of making state tax systems more progressive, not regressive. This was because the non-rate tax cuts were primarily aimed at taxpayers at the lower end of the income scale. As alluded to above, one of the most common changes states made to their tax structures in 1987 was increasing personal and dependent credits or exemptions, which effectively made a higher share of citizens' initial income tax-free.[97] A number of states also began experimenting with newer forms of tax relief for the poor, such as the Earned Income Tax Credit (EITC). Thus, while the 1987 state income tax cuts tended to lower the tax burdens of all citizens, they were especially generous toward those with little income.

For states without income taxes (or ones whose income taxes were very modest), the enactment of TRA ended up having remarkably little impact on tax policy. In nearly all these states, discussions of the personal income tax as a solution to revenue problems percolated among fiscal-policy think tanks, public interest groups, and progressive state legislators, but these discussions inevitably went nowhere. Rather than adopt income taxes, the legislatures of these states either increased other taxes or pushed off difficult revenue decisions for another day. Clearly, the policy changes in TRA were not

[97] In doing this, states emulated TRA, which included similar provisions for the federal income tax.

sufficiently significant to make the income tax an attractive option in the eyes of the lawmakers of these states.

The inability of the personal income tax to gain traction in sales-tax-only states at this moment, when its benefits over the sales tax as a state revenue source were clearer than ever, is even more striking when one considers state fiscal conditions in 1987. While many states were in solid financial condition during this year, a disproportionate share of sales-tax-only states were facing major fiscal problems. Chief among them was Texas, the largest such state. Due to a collapse in oil markets, the Lone Star State faced a $5.8 billion deficit—the largest state deficit in American history up to that point.[98] This massive deficit was the backdrop to the 1987 Texas legislative session, in which Republican Gov. Bill Clements, who was adamantly opposed to any new taxes, squared off against Democratic Lieutenant Governor (and State Senate President) Bill Hobby, who made the case for tax increases in order to avoid draconian spending cuts.[99] In the end, Governor Clements relented and signed a revenue package that included rate increases to the sales tax, corporate franchise tax, and motor vehicle tax, but no action was taken on any income tax proposals.[100] Similar outcomes occurred in Washington and South Dakota. Even in Alaska, a state that—like Texas—was hard hit by the plunge in oil prices, legislators ultimately decided not to reinstate a personal income tax (which had been abolished in 1980) despite the public support for reinstatement of Gov. Steve Cowper.[101]

A close examination of journalistic coverage of income tax adoption efforts in sales-tax-only states in 1987 suggests that opposition to the income tax among policymakers in these states went beyond concerns about public disapproval or electoral backlash (though such concerns were certainly evident). To a significant degree, policymakers in these states had by the late 1980s come to see the lack of a personal income tax as a core state identity-marker or distinguishing characteristic, one that was worth keeping as part of their state's marketing strategy. In Tennessee, for example, state legislators quickly shrugged off calls to adopt a state income tax in the wake of the congressional agreement to eliminate the sales tax deduction. As one legislator told her local newspaper, the lack of an income tax "is one of our most

[98] Reinhold, "Thinking the Unthinkable in Texas."
[99] Ibid.
[100] Don McCarthy, "Texas Budget Approved with Record Tax Boost," *Washington Post*, July 22, 1987, https://www.washingtonpost.com/archive/politics/1987/07/22/texas-budget-approved-with-record-tax-boost/cd41bf17-3d56-44f1-9211-ae8ead516085/, accessed August 1, 2023.
[101] Reinhold, "Thinking the Unthinkable in Texas."

attractive inducements to get industry to come here, and for people to come and live in the state."[102] The TRA, in other words, did not change the perception of policymakers that the absence of an income tax gave their states a competitive advantage. As a result, all the states that entered the Reagan Era without an income tax also exited it without one.

Fiscal Federalism and State Taxation at the End of the Reagan Era

Subnational government finance in the United States underwent major changes over the course of the late 1970s and 1980s. These changes are depicted in Figure 5.2, which shows the total amounts of the three most important sources of subnational revenue: state government own-source tax revenue, local government own-source tax revenue, and fiscal transfers from the national government.[103] The amounts are divided by $1000 in national personal income to allow for standardization and cross-time comparison. As can be seen, the amount of revenue raised by local governments via taxes declined substantially in the late 1970s (largely due to the Tax Revolt, whose effects fell disproportionately on the property tax). Though it began to increase again in the mid 1980s, the volume of local own-source tax revenue was still considerably lower at the beginning of the 1990s than what it was in 1975. National government transfers to state and local governments likewise fell over this period, primarily in the early 1980s thanks to the 1981 budget cuts. Unlike revenue from both local taxes and national transfers, however, the amount of tax revenue raised by state governments was higher in 1990 than what it was in both 1975 and 1980. After a small, recession-induced decline in the early 1980s, its volume increased in the mid 1980s (thanks to the 1982–1983 tax increases and improved economic conditions). States, in other words, largely filled the gap left by the decline in both national transfers and local taxes. They thus emerged from the 1980s as more significant fiscal actors than they had been before.

Clearly, then, the goal of at least some in the Reagan administration of inducing state government retrenchment via national fiscal reform did not

[102] Alan Weston, "Tax Reform May Push State Income Tax Issue," *Kingsport Times-News* (Kingsport, TN), August 28, 1986, 7.

[103] Non-tax, own-source revenue for state and local governments (i.e., user fees, lottery revenue, etc.) is not shown in this graph.

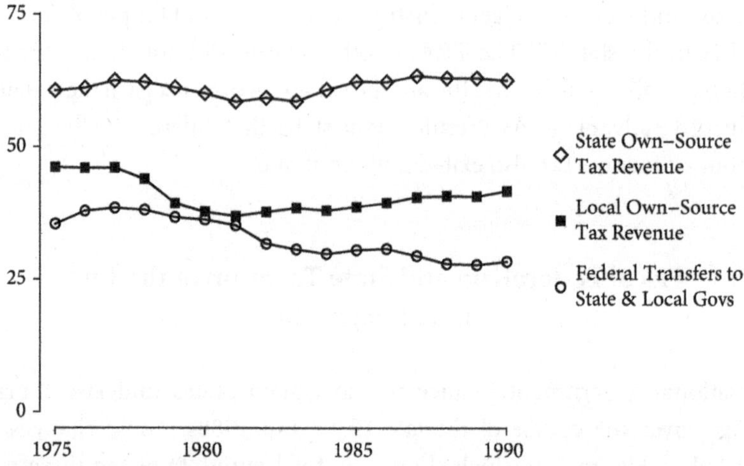

Figure 5.2 Subnational Government Revenue Sources (per $1000 of National Personal Income), 1975–1990
Source: U.S. Census, *Historical Finances of State Governments* dataset

succeed. But if states refused to join forces with the Reaganites and embrace mass retrenchment, neither did they pursue a path of major fiscal expansion. As Figure 5.2 also shows, state own-source tax revenue did not increase substantially following the passage of TRA in 1986, largely because states returned most of the windfall they stood to get from it to their citizens. The best way to describe the state tax response to the Reagan Revolution, therefore, is that states strove to maintain the pre-Reagan fiscal status quo. Where a plunge in revenue threatened to lead to a substantial decrease in the public services they offered, states stepped into the breach, but when handed the opportunity to increase their revenues and provide new services, they declined.

Still, the fact that the states did not embrace a thoroughgoing program of retrenchment in response to the intergovernmental budget cuts of the 1980s, as the competitive federalists in the Reagan Administration predicted, is an outcome that demands further explanation. One possible account of this unexpected outcome—the one that the Reaganites appear to have accepted as of the mid 1980s—is that those cuts were simply insufficient to unleash competitive pressures on the states on their own. Due to the existence of the SALT deduction, this account holds, states reasoned that they could raise taxes to replenish the funds lost from the cuts without feeling any major economic repercussions. The implication of this explanation is that a truly competitive federalism cannot materialize in the United States unless the federal tax code is reformed to completely separate the national government's tax system from those of the states.

Because such a form of intergovernmental fiscal separation has never been put into place, the foregoing account of why the states did not follow the national government in retrenching in the 1980s remains untested. But there is another, perhaps more compelling explanation for why state-level developments in the Reagan Era did not proceed as the Reaganites intended: an underappreciation of the states as distinct spheres of politics in which outcomes are affected partially, but not exclusively, by the workings of the larger federal system. Stated differently, the theory of competitive federalism envisioned the states as unitary actors making predictable demands on the national government and responding more or less mechanistically to its incentives or disincentives. But states, like the national government, are arenas of politics in which numerous actors and sectors contest for power. By the 1980s, groups that had come to depend on the intergovernmental programs of the New Deal and Great Society had become important players in many state capitals, and they successfully compelled state policymakers to avoid the retrenchment-oriented outcomes that the Reaganites assumed would come to pass.

Like subnational government finance overall, the structure of state tax systems also changed during the late 1970s and 1980s, though these changes were less noteworthy. Figure 5.3 plots the relevant contributions of various tax sources to total state tax revenue (per $1000 of National Personal Income) between 1975 and 1990. The figure shows that the modest increase in the volume of state tax revenue across this period was primarily driven by an increase in state personal income tax collections. State personal income tax revenue grew substantially at two points: between 1982 and 1984 (due to the 1983 state tax increases as well as an improved economy) and between 1986 and 1987 (due to the expansion of state income tax bases wrought by the TRA). By contrast, the amount of general sales tax revenue increased only slightly between 1975 and 1990, and the amount of alcohol/tobacco and motor vehicle tax revenue actually decreased over this period. Though relatively small, these changes meant that, by the late 1980s, the personal income tax had finally come to assume an equal status with the general sales tax as a source of state revenue.

Importantly, both the personal income tax and the general sales tax grew the most in the states where each tax was relatively recently adopted. In states

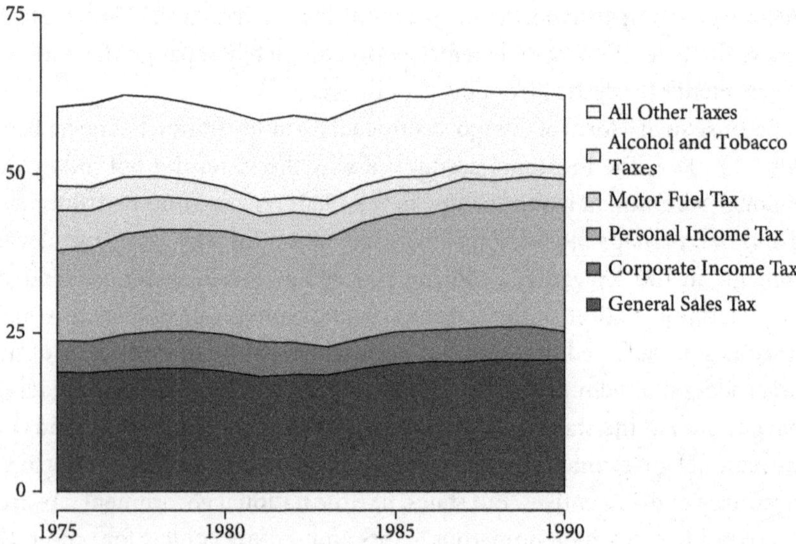

Figure 5.3 Sources of State Own-Source Tax Revenue (per $1000 of National Personal Income), 1975–1990

Source: U.S. Census, *Historical Finances of State Governments* dataset. Non-tax own-source revenues for state and local governments not included in the figure.

that adopted the personal income tax in the late 1960s or early 1970s, the share of state tax revenue from the personal income tax rose by an average of 65.5% between 1975 and 1990. By contrast, among states that adopted the personal income tax in the early twentieth century, it rose by only 37.7%. Likewise, among states that adopted the general sales tax in the late 1960s or early 1970s, the share of state tax revenue from that tax rose by an average of 21.6% between 1975 and 1990, but it actually fell by an average of 4.6% among states that adopted the general sales tax in the 1930s.[104] The fact that states were increasingly turning to taxes they had adopted rather late meant that longstanding historical variations in state tax systems were becoming less pronounced. The long shadow of the first critical juncture in state taxation was becoming considerably smaller. State tax systems were becoming more alike.

In sum, as the 1980s drew to a close and the final decade of the twentieth century was set to begin, states were in arguably their strongest fiscal position

[104] These data are based on analysis of Census Bureau's Historical Finances of State Government dataset.

since the 1930s. After a half-century of new tax adoptions and tax increases, the vast bulk of states had developed diversified tax systems underpinned in roughly equal proportions by the personal income tax and general sales tax. If Reagan is taken at his word in his numerous pre-presidency speeches in which he expressed hope that state governments would be fiscally capable of taking on the service responsibilities that would devolve upon them in the late twentieth century, the data suggest that Reagan's hope was borne out by the time he left the White House.

But it is crucial to reiterate two previously discussed factors that led state governments to unexpectedly take on a greater fiscal role in the 1980s. The first was that the large majority of state governments in the 1980s were controlled by Democrats, and the second was that state fiscal policy during this decade was not highly affected by party control of state government. Though Democrats and Republicans *in Congress* were beginning to polarize over fiscal policy, the same could not be said of their counterparts in state legislatures. Starting in the 1990s, however, both these factors would change. Not only would Republicans gain tremendous ground in statehouses across the country, but state-level Republicans would increasingly emulate the fiscal approaches of their co-partisans in Washington, D.C. As a result, state fiscal policy would become tightly linked to state government party composition for the first time in modern American history. How this happened, and what its consequences were, is the subject of the next chapter.

6

Red Tax, Blue Tax

The Polarization of State Tax Policy in an Era of Nationalized Politics, 1990–2020

> "We have got to have a pro-growth stance on taxes...You can't be a high-tax, high-regulation state and hope you can grow."
>
> —Kansas Sen. Sam Brownback (R), 2010 gubernatorial campaign speech

> "And we needed to lower taxes, and we needed to make our state more competitive. Ladies and gentlemen, this is not ideology; this is just the way the world works. You know, it is necessary to grow an economy and to create jobs by reducing that income tax."
>
> —Ohio Gov. John Kasich (R), 2013 State of the State Address

At the inception of the final decade of the twentieth century, the politics of U.S. fiscal policy looked substantially different at the national and subnational levels. At the national level, the political parties had taken on, and become identified with, distinct approaches to fiscal policy: the Republicans had, under Reagan, become the party of retrenchment and tax cuts, while the Democrats had become the party that stood for the preservation of the national social safety net and the progressive tax system that underpinned it. As discussed in the previous chapter, however, this national-level party divide did not (yet) extend to state politics. State-level politicians may have occasionally paid rhetorical lip service to the fiscal approaches of their national parties, but the policies they advanced and adopted were often at odds with them. This was especially the case for Republican governors and state legislators, who were not as enamored of tax cuts as their national-level counterparts and were particularly reluctant to implement them when doing so would have necessitated draconian cuts in state spending. As the previous chapter showed, the reluctance of Republican state politicians to follow the Reagan approach to fiscal policy, combined with the overall low

Coordination Failure. Adam S. Myers, Oxford University Press. © Oxford University Press (2026).
DOI: 10.1093/9780197831878.003.0007

levels of Republican state-level strength throughout the 1980s, is what ultimately scuttled the fiscal federalism vision of retrenchment across all levels of government that motivated the Reaganites.

Beginning in the mid 1990s, though, a long process ensued that would eventually lead to the ideological alignment of state parties with their national counterparts on fiscal policy. Over the course of several decades, state Republican parties began to prioritize reducing state tax burdens, and in particular cutting state income taxes, over maintaining previous levels of state spending. Democrats, meanwhile, fought to preserve levels of state tax revenue requisite to maintaining core services, while occasionally also advancing tax increases targeting the rich. The polarization of state parties over tax policy overlapped with a variety of other, more well-known trends in American politics during the early twenty-first century, including the ascendancy of Republicans in numerous state governments as well the increasingly pronounced electoral divide between states in the South and Great Plains (which were becoming more Republican) and states in the Northeast and West Coast (which were becoming more Democratic).[1] All these trends coalesced such that, by the second decade of the twenty-first century, a clear partisan divide in state fiscal policy was emerging: whereas coastal blue states were raising taxes on the rich and preserving social services, numerous Southern and inland red states embarked on a quest to transform their tax systems away from a reliance on progressive income taxation. For the first time in modern American history, state taxing and spending decisions were best explained not by region, fiscal circumstance, or path dependence, but rather by party control of state government. The bewildering variety of state taxation systems that had emerged in the 1930s was increasingly being reduced to a binary division between red-state taxes and blue-state taxes (even if, to be sure, certain longstanding historical distinctions between otherwise similar blue states or red states remained).

In this chapter, I demonstrate in great detail how party polarization in state fiscal policy gradually developed over the course of the thirty-year period between 1990 and 2020. In doing so, I link the underlying story to several well-known trends in American politics, including the rise of party polarization more generally and the nationalization of state politics.[2] As I

[1] On the ascendancy of Republicans in state governments, see: Matt Grossmann, *Red State Blues: How the Conservative Revolution Stalled in the states* (New York: Cambridge, 2019), 32–51.

[2] The polarization of American politics is a very well-known story, and the literature on it may be the most extensive of any topic in modern American politics. Two works that offer a thorough

show, the polarization of state fiscal policy can, from one vantage point, be understood as a representative case study in how Democrat-controlled and Republican-controlled state governments have diverged in many important matters of policymaking since the end of the twentieth century.[3] As with other state-level policies, for example, the partisan divergence in state fiscal policy was driven in part by the work of national and nationally affiliated interest groups that sought to turn state governments into "laboratories" of conservative or liberal policymaking.[4] But there were also distinctive features of the fiscal-policy story, in particular the efforts of twenty-first-century Republican politicians and libertarian activists to frame state tax policy within the competitive federalism vision that had been previously articulated by the Reaganites in the 1980s. As we shall see, a common, publicly stated refrain among Republicans throughout the twenty-first century was that the American states were in competition with each other for jobs and people, and that "red states"—through their low-tax, low-spending policies—were consistently outstripping "blue states" in the race for both. Thus, whereas competitive federalism in the 1980s was largely an elite-level political discourse that guided conservative policymakers in the Reagan Administration, by the twenty-first century it had become a public narrative used by Republican state-level politicians to simultaneously vindicate conservative fiscal policies and justify doubling down on them further. For their part, Democrats struggled to come up with a response to that narrative, a problem made more difficult by the fact that, by the 2010s, they controlled very few states and thus had few venues in which to promote an alternative set of fiscal policies.

synopsis of this literature are: James E. Campbell, *Polarized: Making Sense of a Divided America* (Princeton, NJ: Princeton University Press, 2018); Nolan McCarty, *Polarization: What Everyone Needs to Know®* (New York: Oxford University Press, 2019); The literature on the nationalization of state politics is more recent and far less vast. The two most important works in this area are: Daniel Hopkins, *The Increasingly United States* (Chicago: University of Chicago Press, 2018) (specifically on the nationalization of state-level mass opinion); Jacob Grumbach, *Laboratories against Democracy* (Princeton, NJ: Princeton University Press, 2022) (specifically on the nationalization of state policymaking).

[3] Two books that examine policy polarization among states across a wide range of policy areas include are: Grumbach, *Laboratories against Democracy*; Devin Caughey and Christopher Warshaw, *Dynamic Democracy: Public Opinion, Elections, and Policymaking in the American States* (Chicago: University of Chicago Press, 2022). Both these books note state-level polarization in tax policy, though they do not go into it in much detail in analyzing it.

[4] On the role of national interest groups in promoting conservative policies at the state level, see especially: Alexander Hertel-Fernandez, *State Capture: How Conservative Activists, Big Businesses, and Wealthy Donors Reshaped the American States—and the Nation* (New York: Oxford University Press, 2019).

One important note: unlike Chapter 5, this chapter focuses primarily on state-level fiscal policy developments, with the activities of national policymakers largely receding into the background. This is because, in contrast to the 1980s (or the 1960s or even the 1930s), the period covered in this chapter was one in which intergovernmental fiscal relations were, for the most part, not a major topic of debate in Congress. To be sure, Congress did infrequently intervene in state taxation matters, most notably through its very modest efforts to streamline state taxation of internet sales (a development this chapter covers, in a brief departure from the focus on state tax-policy polarization). In general, however, fiscal federalism debates—and, more specifically, discussions of the fiscal situations of the states—did not figure nearly as prominently into Congress's work as they did in previous decades. Thus, while certain congressional policies with important consequences for state budgets are mentioned, policymaking in Washington, D.C., is generally not emphasized. The focus instead is on state tax actions in an increasingly polarized and nationalized political environment.

The Early 1990s: A Little-Noticed Shift Begins at the State Level

The beginning of the 1990s witnessed an economic downturn that, while comparatively mild, nonetheless had substantial negative effects on state budgets, particularly in the most hard-hit regions including California and the Northeast.[5] These negative effects were compounded by the ongoing devolution of responsibilities from the national government to the states that had begun in the Reagan era, as well as spiraling costs in state Medicaid programs and new criminal justice costs associated with the prison boom of the 1980s.[6] As with the recession of the early Reagan presidency some ten years earlier, the recession of the early 1990s called for tough fiscal choices inside statehouses.

States responded to their fiscal problems by, in many cases, enacting substantial tax increases. To be sure, the amount of state tax activity in the

[5] Donald J. Boyd, "The Future of State Fiscal Conditions: Fiscal Boom, Fiscal Bust, Then What?," *Spectrum: The Journal of State Government* 75, no. 2 (2022): 5–8.

[6] Michael deCourcy Hinds, "States and Cities Fight Recession with New Taxes," *New York Times*, July 27, 1991, 1; Gwen Ifill, "Governors Seek $10 Billion in Increased Taxes," *New York Times*, April 18, 1991, B10.

1990–1991 period was not nearly as large as in the 1982–1983 period discussed in Chapter 5. For example, twelve states passed personal income tax rate increases in 1990–1991, much less than the twenty-one that did so in 1982–1983. Similarly, fifteen states passed sales tax rate increases in 1990–1991 as opposed to twenty-three that did so in 1982–1983.[7] Nonetheless, the influx of revenue due to state tax increases during this period was very substantial. Indeed, data from the National Conference on State Legislatures show that, as a percentage of total state tax revenue from the previous year, the increase in state revenue due to tax increases in 1991 was greater than for any year since then.[8]

Like in 1982–1983, variations in state tax activity in 1990–1991 were largely unrelated to patterns of party control of state government. Of the twelve states that raised personal income tax rates during this two-year period, eight featured divided government and the other four were controlled by Democrats. The proportion of Democrat-controlled states that raised personal income taxes during this period (25%) was nearly identical to the proportion of divided-government states that did so (26.7%).[9] The statistics are fairly similar for the corporate income tax and the general sales tax. As for states under Republican control, there were so few of them at this point (three in 1990 and four in 1991) that their own tax activity does not tell us much about underlying patterns of partisan policymaking.

The 1990–1991 period would, arguably, be one of the last moments in which major state tax activity occurred in a way that was largely unlinked to national party politics. Even so, specific events occurring during this period sowed some of the seeds that would grow into the tax-policy polarization that would typify state politics in later years. Perhaps the most important such event occurred in New Jersey, where Democratic Governor Jim Florio pushed for steep increases in both income and sales taxes to help close a large budget deficit. The Democrat-controlled state legislature agreed with him and narrowly passed those increases, and both Florio and legislative

[7] These counts are based on data from various editions of the *Book of the States*.

[8] See, e.g., Mandy Rafool, *State Tax Actions: 2013* (Denver, CO: National Conference of State Legislatures, 2014), p. 3. Figure 1 shows that, as a percentage of total tax collections in the previous year, the amount of new revenue collected via tax increases in 1991 exceeded even that collected via tax increases in 2009 (when numerous states raised taxes in response to the Great Recession). The table only shows data between 1991 and 2013, but it is highly unlikely that new revenue generated via state tax increases in any year since 2013 accounted for a larger share of the previous year's tax revenue.

[9] Much as in the early 1980s, a very small number of states (three in 1990, four in 1991) were controlled by Republicans, so the fact that no Republican-controlled state raised income taxes is not very noteworthy.

Democrats went on to pay a heavy political price for them. First, Republicans took control of the legislature in the 1991 off-year elections. Then, in 1993, Republican challenger Christine Todd Whitman defeated Florio in his bid for reelection, a result that was widely interpreted as a rejection of the tax increases.[10] During her first two years as governor, Whitman and the now Republican-controlled state legislature followed through on her pledge to cut the Garden State's income taxes. This earned her major national media coverage and acclaim among national Republican politicians and conservative pundits. Her success was widely seen as a model for Republican politicians in states across the country to follow.[11]

During the 1994 midterm elections, numerous Republican gubernatorial and state legislative candidates took their cue from Whitman and made taxation a major issue in their campaigns. In state after state, they promised to make deep cuts to state taxes if elected.[12] Moreover, in many states, legislative candidates signed "contracts" (modeled after Newt Gingrich's Contract with America for Republican congressional nominees) developed by state Republican parties in which candidates, among other things, vowed to cut or at least not to raise state taxes.[13] Importantly, the state-level Republican "contracts" were part of a coordinated effort by the Republican National Committee to align state Republican parties with the national party's approach to many issues, certainly including taxation.[14] Thus, in many respects, the 1994 campaign represents the first of many instances in which Republicans would seek to nationalize the state-level politics of taxation.

The result of the 1994 campaigns was a Republican landslide of historic proportions at the state level. Republicans picked up ten governorships, bringing the total number of Republican governors to thirty. They also gained a net total of 354 state legislative seats, giving them control of 49 legislative chambers—a larger number than Democrats for the first time since

[10] Joseph P. Fried, "Jim Florio, New Jersey Governor Undone by Tax Hike, Dies at 85," *New York Times*, September 26, 2022, https://www.nytimes.com/2022/09/26/nyregion/jim-florio-dead.html, accessed December 28, 2023.

[11] See, e.g., Gerald F. Seib, "Trimming Down: GOP Governors Push Big New Tax Revolt—at the State Level," *Wall Street Journal*, May 2, 1994, A1; Lucinda Harper, "Tax-Cut Fervor Rages among GOP Candidates for Governor, Despite Glitches in new Jersey," *Wall Street Journal*, October 13, 1994, A18; Edwin Chen, "Dole Asserts 'Tax Cuts Work,' Cites N.J.," *Los Angeles Times*, August 23, 1996, A22.

[12] Steven Malanga, "As Goes New Jersey...," *City Journal*, Winter 2010, https://www.city-journal.org/article/as-goes-new-jersey, accessed December 28, 2023.

[13] Thomas H. Little, "On the Coattails of a Contract: RNC Activities and Republican Gains in the 1994 State Legislative Elections," *Political Research Quarterly* 51, no. 1 (1998): 173–190.

[14] Ibid., 179.

1958.[15] The combined effect of GOP victories in gubernatorial and state legislative elections was that the GOP, as of early 1995, Republicans enjoyed unified control of government in fifteen states. Thus, for the first time since the beginning of the Reagan Revolution, Republicans could advance their agendas in numerous statehouses.[16] And on fiscal matters at least, Republican state parties were increasingly uniting around the core tenets of the national Republican party during the Reagan presidency. The stage was thus set for significant changes in fiscal policy across the American states, particularly in regard to taxation.

The Late 1990s Fiscal Boom and the Beginning of State Tax Cuts

The Republican ascendancy in statehouses across the country overlapped with a turnaround in the country's economic fortunes: following the recession of the early 1990s, the United States entered a period of strong economic growth buttressed by greater worker productivity, rising stock markets, and particularly large increases in capital gains. The economic upturn of the mid 1990s was a major boon for state governments for two reasons. Most crucially, the growth in capital gains redounded in expanded state income tax bases and greater tax receipts. Second, sales tax revenues were also surging as Americans responded to the growth income in their bank accounts by increasing their consumption levels.[17] In short, for both American families and governments, the second half of the 1990s was a true "fiscal boom."[18]

For the Republican governors and legislatures who assumed power in 1995, the suddenly favorable economic circumstances they inherited represented an exceptionally rare political opportunity. To a greater degree than at any point in living memory (even more than the mid-late 1970s, when state governments encountered favorable fiscal situations as well), states could now cut taxes significantly without causing revenue levels to plunge or jeopardizing core state services. And so they did: between FY 1995 and FY 2001, states implemented net tax reductions every year, resulting $30 billion in

[15] Ibid., 175.

[16] Paul Brace and Laura Langer, "Interpreting the 1994 State Legislative Elections," *Spectrum: A Journal of State Government* (Spring 1995), 6.

[17] Donald J. Boyd, "The Future of State Fiscal Conditions: Fiscal Boom, Fiscal Bust, Then What?" *Spectrum: The Journal of State Government* 75, no. 2 (2002): 5–8.

[18] Ibid.

lost revenue, while nonetheless managing to increase spending on core services.[19] For politicians from both parties, but especially the recently elected Republicans who promised to cut taxes, this was a dream scenario.

The tax cuts of the late 1990s provide us with the first evidence of an emerging partisan divide over state-level taxation policy, albeit in attenuated form. In Republican-controlled states like Arizona, Colorado, Iowa, and Michigan, GOP governors sought to emulate Christine Todd Whitman's strategy of using state tax cuts as a means of achieving national prominence. They thus worked in concert with GOP legislatures to implement large cuts in income tax rates. These steep income tax rate cuts tended to be opposed by minority Democrats, who offered either non-rate cuts oriented toward low-income taxpayers (e.g., expanded personal exemptions) or cuts to taxes besides the income tax as alternatives. Nonetheless, when bills cutting income tax rates were voted on for final passage, many Democrats ended up supporting them so as to avoid electoral reprisal.[20]

In states featuring divided government, Democratic legislatures or legislative chambers often tempered the tax-cut agendas of Republican governors. In Connecticut, for example, Gov. John Rowland entered office in 1995 publicly intending to phase out the state's recently enacted income tax, but the Democrat-controlled state House of Representatives scuttled his plans.[21] Ultimately, Rowland settled for the creation of a new, lower tax bracket for low-income earners. Similarly, in neighboring New York, Gov. George Pataki proposed a 25% across-the-board tax cut for all income earners, but eventually struck a deal with the Democrat-controlled State Assembly for a tax cut that provided a greater amount of relief to New Yorkers with modest incomes.[22]

The difference in the tax-cutting proclivities of Republican-controlled and Democrat-controlled states during the late 1990s can be seen in Figure 6.1, which presents two bar graphs showing how many Republican-controlled and Democrat-controlled states there were in each biennium of the late 1990s, as well as how many Republican-controlled and Democrat-controlled

[19] Ibid, 5–6.

[20] C. Patrick Cleary, "House Oks Bill to Cut Tax Permanently," *Daily Sentinel* (Grand Junction, CO), March 24, 1999, 1; Malcolm Johnson, "Republican Legislation Moves Into Fast Lane," *Lansing State Journal*, February 8, 1999, 3B.

[21] Jonathan Rabinovitz, "Connecticut's New Governor: The Overview," *New York Times*, January 5, 1995, A1.

[22] Kevin Sack, "Pataki in Accord with Lawmakers on Tax-Cut Plan," *New York Times*, May 21, 1995, A1.

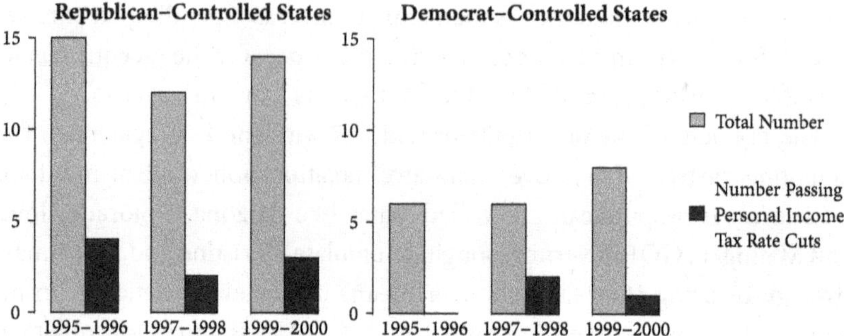

Figure 6.1 Personal Income Tax Rate Cuts among Democrat-Controlled and Republican-Controlled States, 1995–2000
Source: State Tax Actions Dataset

states passed income tax rate cuts in each biennium.[23] As the figure shows, there were a greater number of Republican-controlled states across this entire period, and states under Republican control were significantly more likely to pass income tax cuts. That said, Democrat-controlled states also cut income taxes during this period and the overall role of the party in shaping state tax decisions is not as great as it would become in future years.

The Interregnum: State Tax Choices during the Early and Mid 2000s

The tax cut fever sweeping through the country's statehouses in the late 1990s suddenly ended in 2001, when the United States entered the first recession of the twenty-first century. While this recession was relatively short (technically lasting for only eight months),[24] the national economy continued to be sluggish in its wake for several years. Moreover, the effect of the 2001 recession on state fiscal conditions was considerably larger than that of the recession of ten years prior, even though both recessions were similarly mild in terms of their effect on GDP.[25] The greater fiscal impact of

[23] No state raised income tax rates during the late 1990s.

[24] Kevin L. Kliesen, "The 2001 recession: How was it different and what developments may have caused it?," *Review-Federal Reserve Bank of Saint Louis* 85, no. 5 (2003): 23–38.

[25] Donald J. Boyd, "State Fiscal Conditions: 2003 and Beyond," *The Book of the States, 2003 Edition*, (Lexingon, KY: Council of State Governments, 2003).

the 2001 recession had much to do with the fact that it followed the "fiscal boom" of the late 1990s and thus resulted in a plunge in income and stock market positions relative to where they had been at their highest points just a few years earlier.[26] This plunge interacted with the income tax cuts of the "fiscal boom" to result in vastly lower income tax receipts and significant holes in state budgets.

States initially responded to the fiscal challenges they encountered in the early 2000s via their usual pattern of temporizing and looking for quick fixes before they turned to tax increases. Once they accepted the necessity of raising taxes, however, states en masse turned to a longstanding yet marginal tax source to fill their budget holes: the cigarette tax. As discussed in Chapter 1, state taxation of tobacco commenced in the 1920s and substantially grew during the first critical juncture of state taxation in the 1930s. Over the course of the next seventy years, states often raised taxes on tobacco products when they faced budget problems. Despite these increases, the taxation of tobacco and other sins (including alcohol products, gambling, etc.) never constituted a large share of state tax receipts; indeed, at the turn of the century, all forms of selective sales taxation besides the motor fuel tax together comprised only 9% of state tax revenue.[27]

With the arrival of the recession of 2001, however, states made tobacco tax increases a key component of their tax reform packages. An astonishing thirty-four states levied tobacco tax increases between 2001 and 2003, the vast majority of them via rate increases for the cigarette tax.[28] In 2022, cigarette and tobacco tax increases resulted in an influx of $3 billion in new state revenue, nearly double the influx due to personal income tax increases and over triple the influx from general sales tax increases.[29] For the first time in decades, the largest increase in new state tax revenue came from a tax other than one of the "Big Three."

This aberrational outcome was largely a result of the fact that the 2001 recession and the subsequent state budget gaps of 2002–2003 occurred at a moment when American attitudes toward the tobacco industry and tobacco use more generally were rapidly changing. Media coverage of the Master

[26] Ibid.

[27] This is based on calculations from the U.S. Census State Government Finance dataset.

[28] Calculations based on data from the annual *State Tax Actions* reports of the National Conference of State Legislatures.

[29] Mandy Rafool, *State Tax Actions 2002* (Denver, CO: National Conference of State Legislatures, 2003), 5.

Settlement between state attorneys general and the country's four largest tobacco companies in 1998 exposed Americans to much new information about the harmful effects of tobacco as well as the tobacco industry's "deceitful practices and tactics."[30] Increased public knowledge of the dangers of tobacco contributed to the growing popularity of public smoking bans, which spread across American cities and states over the course of the 1990s and 2000s.[31] The American public's growing antipathy toward tobacco products and the tobacco industry meant that raising tobacco taxes was a much more politically acceptable option for state legislatures than other potential tax increases were. This was even the case for Republican-controlled state legislatures: the increasingly anti-tax attitudes of state-level Republican parties notwithstanding, ten GOP-controlled state legislatures passed cigarette tax increases between 2001 and 2003. Despite these increases, however, the overall contribution of tobacco taxation to the revenue of state governments did not increase much in the long term, chiefly because tobacco use among Americans was going down at the same time as the taxes were going up. In other words, the very feature of tobacco taxes that made them so appealing to state legislators (i.e., the fact that increasing them could be publicly justified as a way of discouraging consumers from using tobacco products) made them ineffective revenue generators in the long run.

The large-scale use of tobacco tax increases to close state budget gaps in 2001–2003 substantially eased the pressure on state legislatures to increase other taxes, so in comparison to previous periods of state fiscal stress, relatively few states increased their income or general sales taxes. By 2004, steady economic growth had begun to ease the fiscal pressures states had faced immediately after the turn of the century. Between 2004 and 2008, state tax changes were relatively muted; some states cut taxes and others raised them, but in nearly all cases the tax changes were modest. States were likely cautious in their fiscal policy during these years because of general uncertainty over the country's long-term economic prospects, given both the country's challenges in its wars in the Middle East as well as emerging concerns over the health of the financial sector.

[30] Public Health Law Center, "Roadmap to a National Settlement Agreement," 2021, https://www.publichealthlawcenter.org/sites/default/files/resources/Juul-Roadmap-to-NSA.pdf, accessed December 26, 2023, 2.

[31] Charles R. Shipan and Craig Volden, "Bottom-up federalism: The diffusion of antismoking policies from US cities to states." *American Journal of Political Science* 50, no. 4 (2006): 825–843.

The Great Recession and the Intensification of Party Polarization in State Fiscal Policy

The period of fiscal limbo between 2004 and 2007 ended spectacularly in the late 2000s, when the United States entered a major economic downturn whose scope and consequences would be far greater than the recessions of the recent past. Sparked by the explosion of a bubble in an unsustainable real estate market, the downturn quickly spread to other sectors of America's economy and eventually threatened its entire financial system. For states, the impact of what became known as the Great Recession was devastating. Though state finances were in "superficially good health" prior to the recession, the Great Recession revealed major "inadequacies in [state] fiscal structures."[32] Indeed, after decades in which state tax revenue growth roughly matched GDP growth, states suddenly suffered a drop in tax revenues during the Great Recession that far exceeded the concomitant drop in GDP.[33] This enormous drop in tax revenues, combined with recession-induced demand for greater social services, led to unprecedented budget gaps.

The implications for state fiscal policy were enormous. Though most states had managed to navigate previous recessions (i.e., those of the early 1990s and 2000s) without major overhauls of their tax systems, this recession was of a far larger magnitude than those of recent memory. In terms of its overall impact on state budgets, it was probably more significant than any economic downturn since the pivotal decade of the 1930s. While the national government did step in to assist states through the American Recovery and Reinvestment Act (a.k.a. "The Stimulus") in 2009, the stimulus funds only covered 30 to 40% of state budget gaps.[34] Moreover, these funds did not last forever; after they dried up, states were forced to reckon with the structural imbalances in their fiscal systems that had been accruing for decades, most importantly in the form of vastly underfunded pension systems.[35]

[32] Andrea Louise Campbell and Michael W. Sances, "State Fiscal Policy during the Great Recession: Budgetary Impacts and Policy Reponses," *Annals of the American Academy of Political and Social Science* 650 (2013): 254.

[33] This was a result of the fact that, by exempting food and clothing from their sales taxes and making their income taxes more progressive over the course of the 1990s and 2000s, states inadvertently made their tax systems more volatile. Nathan Seegert, "The Performance of State Tax Portfolios during and After the Great Recession," *National Tax Journal* 68, no. 4 (2015), 901.

[34] Phil Oliff, Jon Shure, and Nicholas Johnson, "Federal Fiscal Relief is Working as Intended," *Center on Budget and Policy Priorities*, 2009, https://www.cbpp.org/research/federal-fiscal-relief-is-working-as-intended, accessed November 5, 2023; David Schleicher, *In a Bad State: Responding to State and Local Budget Crises*, (New York: Oxford University Press, 2023), 78.

[35] Schleicher, *In a Bad State*, 78–80.

In short, nearly every state in the union, regardless of its tax system or spending patterns, faced extremely difficult fiscal decisions as a result of the Great Recession.

In response to their budget problems, many states took major steps to increase their tax revenue: according to the National Council of State Legislatures, the tax changes made by states in 2009 resulted in $28.6 billion in new state revenue, an influx that was far higher than for any year in the previous two decades.[36] Importantly, this new revenue was a result of net increases in all the major taxes upon which states relied, demonstrating the extent to which states sought new revenue from all their traditional sources. Still, the net increase in state tax revenue in 2009 was somewhat lower than what might be expected given the depth of the challenges states faced. For example, as a percentage of total state tax revenue from the previous fiscal year, it was less than the corresponding percentage for 1991, despite the fact that state budget challenges in 2009 were greater than in 1991. State tax activity in the Great Recession looks even less impressive when compared to the surges in tax adoptions during the major critical junctures in state taxation—the 1930s (discussed in Chapter 1) and the 1960s (discussed in Chapter 3).

The relatively muted tax activity of states during the Great Recession can be explained by several factors, including the cushioning effects of the stimulus funds, concerns about the possibility that state tax increases would impede the national economic recovery, interstate competitive pressures, and others. But a crucial factor—one that was simply not present to any significant degree during previous moments of state fiscal distress—was growing party polarization in state fiscal policy. Stated simply, states run by Democrats—and particularly with Democratic legislatures—often turned to tax increases to close their budget gaps while Republican-controlled states did not. This is demonstrated in Table 6.1, which shows the mean net revenue effect of various state tax changes in 2009, as a share of total state tax revenue in fiscal year 2008, for state governments with different party compositions. Each column shows the revenue effect of changes for a different tax source. The third column, which considers the effect of all tax changes in 2009, shows that states with Democratic legislatures passed tax changes that led to far greater revenue intake than states with Republican legislatures.

[36] Bert Waisanen and Todd Haggerty, *State Tax Actions 2009* (Denver, CO: National Conference of State Legislatures, 2010).

Table 6.1 Mean Net Effect (across States) of 2009 Tax Actions as a Share of Total State Tax Revenue in FY 2008

Party Control Status	Number of States	Total Tax Changes	Personal Income Tax Changes	Business Taxes Changes	General Sales Tax Changes	Changes to All Other Taxes
Full Democratic control	17	3.47%	0.95%	0.65%	0.65%	1.21%
Democratic legislature, Republican governor	11	3.74%	1.32%	0.5%	0.41%	1.51%
Divided legislature, Democratic governor	6	1.21%	−0.05%	0.18%	0.18%	0.87%
Divided legislature, Republican governor	1	1.60%	−0.30%	0.00%	0.10%	1.80%
Republican legislature, Democratic governor	5	0.38%	0.08%	0.02%	0.06%	0.22%
Full Republican control	10	0.18%	−0.30%	−0.04%	−0.04%	0.57%

Sources: National Council of State Legislatures, *State Tax Actions 2009*; 2008 Census Survey of State Governments; Klarner, *State Partisan Division, 1937–2011*

The importance of legislative control clearly exceeded the importance of the party affiliation of governors, which exercised a negligible effect.

A closer look at the remaining columns in Table 6.1 reveals a variety of interesting patterns. First, states with Democratic legislatures were more likely to turn to taxes of all kinds than states with Republican legislatures, though (not surprisingly) the gap in net tax intake was largest for the personal income tax. Second, states under full Republican control on average actually implemented modest reductions in the personal income tax, business taxes, and general sales tax during the Great Recession. However, the total effect of tax changes in these states was, on average, an increase in tax revenue, largely due to increases in tobacco and motor fuel taxes.

As already mentioned, the starkest disparity between tax actions in Democrat- and Republican-controlled states during the Great Recession was in regard to the personal income tax. Of the fifteen states that raised their personal income taxes, all but one featured Democrat-controlled legislatures. In California, Connecticut, Delaware, Hawaii, North Carolina, New Jersey, New York, Oregon, and Wisconsin, these increases involved rate increases targeting high earners. In several other states like Colorado and Rhode Island, income tax statutes were changed so that capital gains were captured by state income taxes.[37] A few other states eliminated various deductions or exemptions in their income tax codes as a way of raising additional tax revenue.

The increased importance of parties in state tax decisions during the Great Recession was, to a significant degree, the result of the strengthening of alignments between state parties and state-level economic interest groups in preceding decades. In earlier eras like the 1930s and the 1960s (discussed in Chapter 1 and Chapter 3, respectively), state-level interest groups that focused on tax policy (such as labor unions, teachers' groups, and business groups) had loose ties to one party or the other but were not clearly aligned with either. Over the course of the late twentieth and early twenty-first centuries, however, labor unions became increasingly aligned with Democratic Parties while business groups and anti-government activists became increasingly aligned with Republicans.[38] To be sure, the extent of party-group alignment varied by state; in some states, Republicans maintained cordial relations with unions while Democrats kept a line of communication with the state business community. On the whole, however, the movement toward greater linkage between parties and interest groups was unmistakable, leading scholars of state politics to describe state-level party organizations in the early twenty-first century as "extended party networks" featuring complex connections between formal party organizations and the interest groups aligned with them.[39]

The role played by party-aligned interest groups in pushing policymakers toward their preferred tax outcomes during the Great Recession can be

[37] National Conference of State Legislatures, *State Tax Actions 2009*, (Denver, CO: 2010).

[38] Leslie K. Finger and Sarah Reckhow, "Policy Feedback and the Polarization of Interest Groups," *State Politics and Policy Quarterly* 22, no. 1 (2022): 70–95; Kevin Reuning, "Mapping Influence: Partisan Networks across the United States, 2000 to 2016," *State Politics and Policy Quarterly* 20, no. 3 (2019): 267–291.

[39] Kevin Reuning, *Party Coalitions, Party Ideology, and Party Action: Extended Party Networks in the United States* (Ph.D. Dissertation, Pennsylvania State University, 2018).

clearly seen among states in the Democratic Party's vanguard like California and New York. In New York, labor unions and social advocacy groups teamed up to exert major pressure on Democratic legislators to limit state budget cuts and pass a substantial income tax increase on the wealthy. Without the lobbying efforts of these groups, an income tax increase may not have passed the State Senate, where the margin for control was narrow and a number of legislative Democrats were very reluctant to vote for a tax hike. Similar dynamics were at play in California, New Jersey, and even North Carolina.[40]

In Republican-controlled states, on the other hand, interest groups aligned with the Democratic Party held much less sway. Far more important were groups representing the business community, such as state chapters of the Chamber of Commerce, as well as a new crop of national and nationally affiliated organizations that had come to assume great importance in state capitals across the country in the preceding decades. Chief among these was the American Legislative Exchange Council (ALEC), a national organization of conservative state legislators that produces and disseminates "model legislation" to its members across the country. Founded in 1973 as a counterweight to long-established interstate membership organizations like the National Conference of State Legislatures (which were perceived to have a liberal bias), ALEC quickly became a major force in Republican-controlled state capitals, particularly in its advocacy of retrenchment-oriented economic policies and punitive approaches to criminal justice.[41] In the 1990s and 2000s, ALEC's power in statehouses was amplified through its collaborations with local affiliates of the State Policy Network (SPN), a national network of state-level think tanks promoting libertarian social and economic policies. Importantly, a major focus of SPN-affiliated think tanks has been tax policy: according to one major study, tax reform was the second most common area of policy advocacy (exceeded only by education reform) among SPN affiliates in 2016.[42]

[40] On North Carolina, see: Rob Christensen and Benjamin Niolet, "Coalition Aims to Keep State Cuts at a Minimum," *Charlotte Observer*, February 25, 2009, 2B.

[41] Alexander Hertel-Fernandez, *State Capture: How Conservative Activists, Big Businesses, and Wealthy Donors Reshaped the American States—and the Nation* (New York: Oxford, 2019), 28–30.

[42] Hertel-Fernandez, *State Capture*, 152. Hertel-Fernandez argues that ALEC and SPN form part of a "right-wing troika" in state capitals that also includes the national advocacy organization Americans for Prosperity (AFP). In Hertel-Fernandez's view, each organization in the troika provides a key resource in service of conservative goals: ALEC gives state legislators model bills, SPN affiliates provide policy research, and AFP provides grassroots support. Because state tax policy generally (though with some very important exceptions) does not induce significant popular mobilization, the roles of ALEC and SPN affiliates in it are more important than that of AFP. For this reason, I do not discuss the latter much.

The role of ALEC and SPN affiliates in shaping state tax policy during the Great Recession could be seen in numerous states, though it was clearly more palpable in Republican-controlled ones. Two years before the crucial 2009 state legislative sessions, ALEC published the first edition of its now well-known text, *Rich States, Poor States*, co-written by the famed Reagan-era supply-side economist Arthur Laffer and *Wall Street Journal* economics writer Stephen Moore. In it, Laffer and Moore introduced a state-level Economic Competitiveness Index based on sixteen policy variables, ten of which involved taxes. They then argued that states that ranked higher on this index (generally speaking, states with less progressive tax systems and lower overall tax burdens) were consistently more likely to be economic "winners" with higher rates of population growth and interstate in-migration, while states ranked lower on the index were far more likely to be "losers" hemorrhaging both jobs and people. The authors also resurrected Reagan-era supply-side principles and applied them to the states, arguing that the best way for states to increase their revenues was to cut their taxes, particularly progressive income taxes targeting the rich.[43] At the same time as ALEC was promoting the findings of *Rich States, Poor States*, SPN affiliates churned out state-specific studies and op-eds arguing against recession-induced budget problems by raising taxes, particularly income taxes, and instead calling for major spending cuts to balance budgets.[44]

The effect of such efforts could be clearly seen in the Republican-controlled state of Arizona. Going into the 2009 legislative session, the Grand Canyon State faced a $4 billion budget deficit constituting over 40% of the previous fiscal year's budget—one of the largest budget gaps of any state in the country. But Arizona Republicans, who ruled the statehouse in Phoenix, were heavily influenced by ALEC and the local SPN affiliate, the Goldwater Institute. Since its founding in 1988, the Goldwater Institute had grown to become one of the largest state-level free-market think tanks in the country; according to Hertel-Fernandez, only four other SPN affiliates had larger budgets than the Goldwater Institute as of 2016, and three of these were in the far larger states of California, Texas, and New York.[45] Arizona Republicans were

[43] Arthur B. Laffer and Stephen Moore, *Rich States, Poor States: ALEC-Laffer State Economic Competitiveness Index*, 1st edition (Washington, DC: American Legislative Exchange Council, 2007), https://alec.org/wp-content/uploads/2016/01/RSPS-1st-Edition.pdf

[44] See, e.g., Jonathan Williams, "Kansas Becoming More Competitive," *Kansas City Star*, April 8, 2009, 14; Byron Schlomach, "Would a Flat Tax be Good for Arizona? Yes: State Revamp would Mean Creation of Jobs and Foster Economic Opportunities," *Arizona Republic*, July 5, 2009, B11.

[45] Hertel-Fernandez, *State Capture*, 154–155.

also heavily influenced by yet another national organization, the anti-tax group Americans for Tax Reform (ATR). Founded in 1985 by anti-tax activist Grover Norquist, ATR became famous for its pledge against tax increases that it pressured numerous Republican candidates for office to sign. As of 2009, 58% of Republicans in the Arizona Legislature had signed the ATR pledge.[46] The budget numbers, however, were so out of whack as to cause Gov. Jan Brewer, a conservative Republican and herself a pledge-taker, to propose a sales tax increase along with major spending cuts to close the state budget gap.

Brewer's proposal was a non-starter for most of her co-partisans, however, leading to an extended standoff over the budget that lasted over a year. Over the course of this standoff, Brewer attempted to compromise with legislative Republicans in ways that would have almost certainly caused Arizona's budget situation to deteriorate further. For example, in the middle of the summer, Brewer reached an agreement with legislative Republicans that would have paired a referendum on a *temporary* sales tax increase with a permanent transformation of the state income tax to a flat tax with a low rate.[47] Even this agreement, which would not have required the legislature to actually pass a sales tax increase (it only required them to put the issue to the voters), ended up collapsing on account of opposition from rank-and-file Republican lawmakers. The impasse continued until the early part of 2010, when legislative Republicans, having tired of the political brinksmanship and lacking good alternatives, abandoned their anti-tax pledge and voted in favor of proposing the sales tax referendum.[48] Arizona voters subsequently approved the sales tax, and the state's recession-induced budget crisis was finally over.

The extent of Arizona's budget struggles, though, was somewhat unusual for Republican-controlled states in 2009. On average, "red states" were in better fiscal positions than "blue states," a fact that did not go unnoticed by conservative pundits like Joel Kotkin and Ross Douthat.[49] In their articles

[46] According to the *Arizona Republic*, thirty-one Republican state legislators in Arizona as of February 2010 had taken the Taxpayer Protection Pledge. Mary Jo Pitzl, "Anti-Tax Pledge Hangs Over GOP," *Arizona Republic*, February 7, 2010, B1. According to the National Conference of State Legislatures, there were 53 Republican state legislators in Arizona during this time. National Conference of State Legislatures, "2010 State and Legislative Party Composition," https://documents.ncsl.org/wwwncsl/Elections/LegisControl_2010.pdf.

[47] Matthew Benson and Mary Jo Pitzl, "Budget Deal Calls for Tax Overhaul," *Arizona Republic*, June 27, 2009, 1

[48] Mary Jo Pitzl, "Tax was Rare Compromise," *Arizona Republic*, February 14, 2010, B1

[49] Whether the association between state partisanship and state fiscal outcomes in the Great Recession was evidence of a causal relationship was a topic of great dispute among economists.

and op-eds, these writers argued that the especially difficult finances of Democratic states owed to a failed "blue-state model" of political economy whose core pillars were high levels of public spending, strong public-sector unions, and high tax burdens on the rich.[50] Implicitly, if not explicitly, these pundits began to make the case that state-level prosperity in the twenty-first century would require dismantling these political-economic structures. Those arguments would be both mimicked and amplified by many others as the nation emerged from the Great Recession, with important consequences for state tax policy.

The Aftermath of the Financial Crisis: The Rise of the "Texas Model" and the Republican Takeover of State Governments

By the end of 2010, the national recession was beginning to fade, as were the state budget crises that accompanied it. To be sure, national economic conditions were far from ideal, with high unemployment rates and anemic job numbers persisting. For the states, fiscal conditions were beginning to stabilize, but long-term challenges, especially in the form of enormous pension liabilities, were still very much important topics for discussion.

The country's emergence from the Great Recession did not unfold evenly across its states or regions, however. On top of the variation in state fiscal conditions during the Great Recession, national macroeconomic data revealed large geographic disparities in state-level economic growth in the recession's aftermath. Specifically, the data showed that the nation's second-largest state—Texas—hovered above most others in the extent to which it had bounced back from the recession and was contributing to the country's economic recovery. In the two-year period between June 2009 and June 2011, for example, jobs created in Texas accounted for nearly half of the net increase in jobs created across the country, even though the state accounted for only 8% of the country's population.[51]

[50] Ross Douthat, "Blue-State Blues," *New York Times*, August 2, 2009, https://www.nytimes.com/2009/08/03/opinion/03douthat.html, accessed December 28, 2023; Joel Kotkin, "The Blue-State Meltdown and the Collapse of the Chicago Model," 2009, https://joelkotkin.com/0040-blue-state-meltdown-and-collapse-chicago-model/, accessed December 28, 2023.

[51] Richard W. Fisher, "Connecting the Dots—Texas Employment Growth; a dissenting vote; and the Ugly Truth (with Reference to P G Wodehouse)," address delivered at Midland Community Forum, Midland, TX, August 17, 2011, https://www.bis.org/review/r110822e.pdf, accessed November 10, 2023. In his speech, Fisher pointed out that a state's contribution to national job creation can be assessed in different ways. Another way to do it, he pointed out, is to "lop off those states have

Texas's undeniably impressive post-recession economic growth set off a major national debate among both economists and pundits regarding the sources and meaning of its success. Libertarian economists and small-government activists immediately latched onto the Texas numbers as evidence that the state's approach to fiscal policy—nicely encapsulated as "low taxes, low services," but increasingly invoked as "the Texas model"—was a key factor in its economic success. Richard Fisher, the president of the Federal Reserve Bank of Dallas and one of the state's most prominent boosters, made the connection clear in his many speeches and media appearances. As he said in one such speech:

> "Despite the fact that Texas has severely limited social services and [features] an education system that faces great challenges, people and businesses have been picking up stakes and moving to Texas in significant numbers...Jobs have been created for American workers in Texas in several different sectors, not just in the oil and gas and mining sectors...And yet Texas, like all states, is subject to the same monetary policy as all the rest...From this, I draw the conclusion that private sector capital and jobs will go to where taxes and spending and regulatory policy are most conducive to growth."[52]

Naturally, Fisher's conclusions were challenged by a plethora of liberal economists and political commentators. Writing in the *New York Times*, Paul Krugman argued that Texas's job numbers were a result of its high immigration rates and low housing costs, not its fiscal policies.[53] Others trotted out a variety of other arguments, including that the bulk of jobs being created in Texas were low-wage jobs, that the state's strict mortgage loan regulations cushioned it from the worst of the housing crisis, and that, on many other social-welfare metrics, Texas trailed much of the country.[54] The liberal commentariat's responses to conservative claims about the "Texas miracle" generated their share of conservative counter-responses, resulting

continued losing jobs and consider only those that have positive growth in employment." By this metric, Texas accounted for 29.2% of the country's job creation rather than 49.9%, still an impressive proportion.

[52] Fisher, "Connecting the Dots."

[53] Paul Krugman, "The Texas Unmiracle," *New York Times*, August 14, 2011, https://www.nytimes.com/2011/08/15/opinion/the-texas-unmiracle.html, accessed December 28, 2023.

[54] Merill Goozner, "Rick Perry and the Myth of the Texas Miracle," *Fiscal Times*, August 12, 2011, https://www.thefiscaltimes.com/2011/08/12/Rick-Perry-and-Myth-Texas-Miracle accessed December 28, 2023; Harold Meyerson, "The Sad Facts Behind Rick Perry's Texas Miracle," *Washington Post*, August 16, 2011, https://www.washingtonpost.com/opinions/the-sad-facts-behind-rick-perrys-texas-miracle/2011/08/16/gIQAxc3zJJ_story.html, accessed December 28, 2023.

in substantial media coverage over the course of 2010 and 2011. The "Texas model" narrative was further elevated in the national consciousness when Rick Perry, the state's brash governor, joined the 2012 presidential race. For a short time, the frontrunner in the Republican presidential primary contest, Perry based his campaign largely on Texas's economic record. In talking up the "Texas miracle," Perry reached millions of Americans who were previously not exposed to debates about the sources of Texas' growth rates in the opinion pages of the *New York Times* or *Wall Street Journal*. Thus, by the end of 2011, Texas's job-creation record was well-known among citizens across the country.

The rise of the "Texas model" narrative in the American political consciousness overlapped with another major shift in American state politics: the rise to power of the Republican Party in numerous statehouses across the country following the 2010 midterm elections. Fueled by voter anger with President Obama and supported by the newly formed Tea Party Movement, Republicans rode the 2010 campaign to unprecedented victories in the states, picking up 10 governorships, around 680 state legislative seats, and 18 state legislative chambers. These gains resulted in a level of Republican strength in American state governments that was even higher than what it was following the last major Republican state-level landslide in 1994. For example, after 1994, Republicans occupied 47.8% of the legislative seats chosen by partisan elections across the country; after 2010, that number was 53.8%.[55] According to one estimate, the total number of Republican state legislators across the country was higher than at any point since before the New Deal.[56] Moreover, because the 2010 elections occurred in the lead-up to a new redistricting cycle, the successes Republicans enjoyed facilitated their control of the legislative redistricting process in numerous states one year later. As a result, Republicans in closely divided states like Florida, Georgia, Michigan, Ohio, North Carolina, Pennsylvania, and Wisconsin were able to entrench their gains, leading the entire decade of the 2010s to feature the strongest level of Republican power in state governments in nearly a century.[57]

[55] These statistics are based on data on the total number of state legislators and the total number of Democratic/Republican state legislators from the 1996–1997 and 2011 editions of the *Book of the States*. The forty-nine members of the non-partisan Nebraska unicameral legislature were excluded from the data used to calculate these statistics.

[56] Michael Cooper, "Decisive Gains at State Level could Give Republicans a Boost for Years," *New York Times*, November 3, 2010, https://www.nytimes.com/2010/11/04/us/politics/04states.html, accessed December 28, 2023.

[57] Grossmann, *Red State Blues*, 40–41.

In state after state, Republicans in the 2010s used their newly gained power to advance efforts to emulate the "Texas model" of fiscal policy. The most important element of the "Texas model" was the lack of a state income tax, and numerous GOP politicians publicly announced that abolishing their state's personal income tax was their long-term goal, even if accomplishing it needed to be achieved incrementally via a series of cuts. In Louisiana, Gov. Bobby Jindal made the case that eliminating the state income tax was crucial to staunching the outmigration of residents from the Pelican State to nearby Dallas and Houston.[58] Likewise, in Ohio, Gov. John Kasich emphasized the importance of cutting income taxes so that the Buckeye State could compete in the "race to see who can create the best business climate."[59]

Two Republican-controlled states that featured especially impressive efforts at a complete redesign of their tax systems were Kansas and North Carolina. In Kansas, the efforts were led by Gov. Sam Brownback, a long-time U.S. Senator who won the state's governorship in 2010 on a campaign to transform the Sunflower State's government. Not long after assuming office, Brownback introduced his plan, which he openly touted as an effort to emulate Texas and generate a "real-life experiment" demonstrating the effect of "pro-growth" fiscal policy on the Kansas economy.[60] Central to Brownback's plan was a large proposed cut to the state's income tax, including both a steep cut in the top rate from 6.45% to 4.9% as well as a simplification of the tax's overall rate structure. Importantly, the plan was designed via close consultation with representatives from national organizations advancing conservative fiscal policy in the states, including both ALEC and AFP (indeed, Brownback hired a former AFP consultant as his budget director).[61] The state's fiscal experts warned that the plan, which was expected to cost Kansas $3.7 billion in tax revenue annually, was exceptionally risky at a moment when the state (like many others) was still struggling to emerge from the Great Recession. But Brownback justified the cuts on supply-side grounds, arguing that the economic growth generated by the cuts would,

[58] Aman Batheja, "Lack of Texas Income Tax Draws Out-Of-State Envy," *Texas Tribune*, May 24, 2013, https://www.texastribune.org/2013/05/24/lack-income-tax-texas-draws-envy/, accessed December 28, 2023.

[59] "Transcript of Gov. John Kasich's 2013 State of the State Address," *Canton Repository* (Canton, OH), February 19, 2013, https://www.cantonrep.com/story/news/state/2013/02/20/transcript-gov-john-kasich-s/42593286007/, accessed December 29, 2023.

[60] Chapman Rackaway, "Tax Cuts are a Roll of the Dice," *Wichita Eagle*, May 27, 2012, 15A; Brad Cooper and Brent Wistrom, "Brownback Says His Changes in Kansas are a Model for the Nation," *Kansas City Star*, December 30, 2012, A1, A12a.

[61] Cooper and Wistrom, "Brownback Says His Changes in Kansas are a Model for the Nation."

over time, lead to a revenue influx that would outweigh the initial drop in tax revenue. Despite some intraparty opposition, the state's conservative legislature eventually blessed the plan and the first part of Brownback's fiscal experiment went into effect.[62] One year later, Brownback requested a second round of tax cuts and the legislature largely acceded to his demands, dropping the top income tax in three steps to a final rate of 3.9% beginning in 2018.

Because of Brownback's national profile and his extensive efforts to promote his "experiment" through national media appearances and speeches across the country, the Kansas tax cuts of 2012 and 2013 received a great deal of national attention. By 2014 and 2015, as Kansas' fiscal situation further deteriorated and the job growth Brownback promised failed to materialize, liberal pundits across the country wrote columns and blog posts declaring the tax cuts a failure. Conservative commentators, however, responded by saying that the cuts had put Kansas on the right path but that their positive benefits would take time to accrue. Regardless of who was right, the deleterious short-term effects of the cuts—in particular, regular budget deficits, an inability to fund core social services, and a reduction in the state's bond rating—proved too much for the state's more moderate Republicans. In 2015, they joined forces with Democrats to freeze the top income tax rate at 4.6% while also increasing the state sales tax. Then, in 2017, a similar coalition of Republicans and Democrats passed a bill returning the income tax to a three-rate structure with a top rate of 5.7%. Thus, after a whipsawed process of rate cuts and (partial) restorations, Kansas emerged from the 2010s with a tax structure that was only slightly more oriented away from the income tax and toward the sales tax than that with which it started the decade.

Republicans saw greater success in institutionalizing their tax changes in North Carolina. Since the emergence of modern state tax systems in the New Deal Era, the Tar Heel State had featured one of the most progressive tax systems of any southern state, with a top income tax rate of at least 7% since 1937 and a comparatively low sales tax rate alongside it. But when Republicans took full control of North Carolina state government in 2013, GOP leaders in the State Senate announced an all-out effort to transform the state tax system into something that closely resembled the "Texas Model." First and

[62] Brad Cooper and Mark Davis, "Brownback Signs Big Tax Cut," *Kansas City Star*, May 23, 2012, A1.

foremost, Senate tax-writers proposed to abolish North Carolina's personal and corporate income taxes completely over time. To replace the estimated $12 billion in lost revenue, they offered a slew of consumption tax increases, including a sales tax rate increase, the extension of the sales tax to numerous services, the adoption of a hefty sales tax on groceries and pharmaceuticals, and a big increase in taxes on real estate transactions.[63] The authors of these proposals made no secret of the fact that their goal was to emulate Texas, at least in terms of its tax policies. As Senate President Phil Berger stated: "I wouldn't say we're in a position to replicate everything in Texas...We don't have much tumbleweed here."[64]

The proposal of North Carolina's Senate Republicans proved to be too much for their co-partisans in the other branches of state government. While the GOP leaders of the State House and Governor Pat McCrory also supported cutting personal and corporate income taxes, they were not fond of the revenue replacement proposals, particularly the extension of the sales tax to services and the new tax on groceries.[65] On top of that, the North Carolina Realtors Association waged an intensive campaign against increasing the taxes on real estate transactions. After a months-long stalemate between Republicans in the State House and Senate, they finally reached a deal in which the state's personal income tax would be reduced to a flat rate of 5.75% and its corporate income tax would be reduced to 5%. The revenue losses from these reductions would be counter-balanced by a modest extension of the sales tax to a few services.[66] While this proposal fell far short of what the most stridently anti-tax Republicans in the state had hoped for, it was nevertheless historic: in its eighty-three-year history, the North Carolina income tax had never been subjected to a rate cut before. Moreover, in cutting income tax rates in 2013, North Carolina Republicans helped pave the way for a series of additional cuts in the state income tax that would take place in 2014, 2015, 2017, and 2021.[67] The cumulative effect of these cuts was indeed to move the North Carolina tax system considerably closer to the "Texas Model."

[63] John Frank, "End N.C. income tax, GOP Suggests," *Charlotte Observer*, January 17, 2013, 1.

[64] Aman Batheja, "Lack of Texas Income Tax Draws Out-Of-State Envy," *Texas Tribune*, May 24, 2013, https://www.texastribune.org/2013/05/24/lack-income-tax-texas-draws-envy/, accessed November 22, 2023.

[65] Gary D. Robertson, "McCrory's Stance on Tax Plan Draws Rucho's Ire," *Charlotte Observer*, June 1, 2013, B3.

[66] Gary D. Robertson, "McCrory Supports Tax Deal," *News and Record*, July 16, 2013, 1.

[67] Katherine Loughead, "North Carolina Reinforces Its Tax Reform Legacy," *Tax Foundation*, https://taxfoundation.org/blog/north-carolina-tax-reform-2021/, accessed December 29, 2023.

The efforts of Republican leaders in both Kansas and North Carolina to overhaul their states' tax structures during the 2010s were perhaps extreme, but they were not unique. Figure 6.2 displays data on personal income tax changes made by Republican-controlled state governments in the ten biennia between 2001–2002 and 2019–2020. Each biennium features a cluster of three bars showing the total number of Republican-controlled state governments, the number of such governments that passed personal income tax rate increases, and the number of such governments that passed personal income tax rate decreases, respectively. The left bars in each cluster demonstrate the large increase in the number of Republican-controlled state governments following the 2010 midterm elections. The middle bars demonstrate that Republican-controlled state governments have very rarely raised personal income tax rates throughout the twenty-first century. But the most important bars are the ones on the right end of each cluster. A close examination of these bars shows a large increase in the number of Republican-controlled state governments passing income tax rate cuts beginning in 2011–2012. To an extent not seen before, personal income tax cuts had become a regular legislative output of Republican-controlled state legislatures, regardless of state economic conditions or fiscal circumstances.

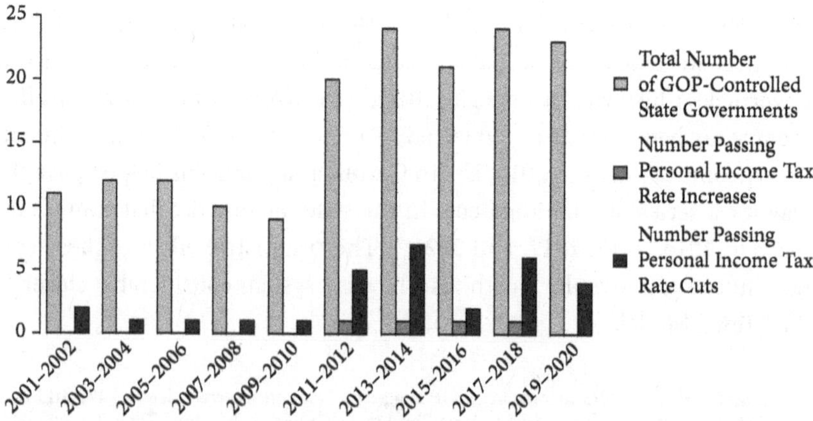

Figure 6.2 Personal Income Tax Rate Increases and Decreases for Republican-Controlled State Governments across Biennia, 2001–2002 to 2019–2020

Sources: State Tax Actions Dataset; Klarner, *State Partisan Division, 1937–2011*; data on state partisan control after 2011 collected from various sources by the author

The Blue-State Response to the Red-State Tax-Cutting Agenda

The Republican ascendancy in state governments during the 2010s put Democrats and progressive forces on the policy defensive in states across the country. While this was the case across a range of issues, it was especially true regarding taxation policy. Faced with ambitious plans to cut or eliminate income taxes and rely more heavily on sales taxation, progressive forces inside statehouses in the early 2010s struggled to come up with a coherent response. While the difficulties they faced stemmed partly from the truism that cutting taxes is always popular and arguing against tax cuts is always challenging, there were also a number of factors specific to state taxation in the early 2010s that made crafting a progressive response to the Republican tax-cutting agenda especially tricky. To begin with, because most state income taxes featured top tax brackets that applied to fairly low income levels, cutting the rates for those brackets (which nearly all Republican proposals sought to do) stood to result in reduced tax burdens for not just high-income households but for middle-income ones as well, making it more challenging for Democrats to depict the Republican proposals as a giveaway to the rich. Second, the precarity of the economic situation for many Americans in the early 2010s, when the country was gradually emerging from the Great Recession, made the prospect of tax cuts even more alluring than usual. Third, the prominence of the "Texas miracle" narrative in the media reinforced the popular notion that states were in competition with each other for jobs and that taxes were an important factor influencing state-level job growth. Stated differently, the Reaganite vision of competitive federalism (discussed in Chapter 5), once a largely elite-level discourse, had (thanks to media coverage of the "Texas model") become an important frame of reference for many ordinary Americans. This proved a vexing problem for many state-level Democrats and progressives, who struggled to answer the question of how their states could remain "competitive" in the battle for jobs and residents against states whose tax burdens were lower or declining.

In places where they were out of power, Democrats experimented with a variety of arguments against Republican tax cut plans, mostly to little avail. First, they made the conventional argument that the proposed cuts represented an effort to shift the tax burden from the wealthy to the middle class or poor. As alluded to above, this argument failed to gain much traction given that most of the proposed tax cuts stood to ease the tax burdens of nearly all taxpayers (even if the wealthy were to gain the most). Progressive state legislators and advocacy groups also made the argument that the best way for their states to maintain a competitive edge against other states was to maintain strong education systems and a well-educated workforce, and that both these goals would be threatened by large tax cuts that would deprive school districts of much-needed revenue. These arguments, however, were undercut by the increasingly common narrative, discussed above, that exorbitant spending on teacher salaries and pensions was at the heart of the failed "blue-state model" of governance.

In the few states featuring Democratic governors and Republican legislatures, the former were able to stave off the most ambitious Republican tax-cut plans by organizing the public education sector against those efforts, at least for a time. For example, in Missouri, Republican leaders in the state legislature made cutting their state's income tax a top priority, arguing that the state needed to remain competitive with neighboring Kansas, which was receiving national attention for its tax-cut experiment.[68] The push to cut Missouri's income tax was bolstered by a large-scale publicity campaign bankrolled by some of the state's wealthiest citizens and run by the state's SPN affiliate, the Show-Me Institute, which published studies claiming that income tax reduction would trigger economic growth.[69] But Democratic Governor Jay Nixon opposed cutting the income tax, arguing that it would reduce state funding for education and mental health over time. Nixon went on a barnstorming tour of the state over the summer of 2013 to bring the state's voters to his side; joined by local education leaders in community after community, Nixon argued that Missouri's income tax was already low and that reducing it further would result in "devastating cuts to our public schools and institutions of higher learning."[70] During the fall and winter, Nixon's strategy appeared to have worked, as Republican leaders, despite commanding a potentially veto-proof supermajority, were unable to muster the votes among their own members to override Nixon's veto of their tax-cut bill. A year later, however, the legislature passed another tax-cut bill, and this time Republicans were able to stay united and pass the bill into law over Nixon's objections.

[68] David A. Leib, "Gov. Nixon Vetoes Income Tax Cut Legislation," *St. Joseph News-Press* (St. Joseph, MO), June 6, 2013, A1.

[69] Kevin Collison, "High Taxes, Good Economy Can Co-Exist," *Kansas City Star*, January 15, 2013, C4.

[70] Kevin R. Jenkins, "Governor Warns of HB 253's Effect on Education," *The Daily Journal* (Flat River, MO), August 23, 2013, A1.

Progressives were only able to advance a coherent alternative to the Republican vision of state-level tax cuts and enhanced "competitiveness" in a very small number of states. All these states were ones in which Democrats managed to maintain unified control of government despite the 2010 Republican landslide. By far the most prominent such state was the nation's largest, California, where former Gov. Jerry Brown returned to the governor's mansion after a twenty-eight-year hiatus in 2011. During the Great Recession, the Golden State was beset with massive fiscal problems that garnered national attention and greatly contributed to the "failed blue-state model" media narrative. In his campaign for the governorship in 2010, Brown cast himself as a budget-balancer who would right California's fiscal ship, but he also promised that all tax increases passed during his governorship would require voter approval. After being sworn into office, Brown began making the case that tax increases—along with steep spending cuts—had to be part of the solution to California's fiscal crisis. He proposed a $6.9 billion tax-increase package including a 0.25% hike in the state sales tax rate and temporary new income tax brackets for Californians making over $250,000 a year.[71]

In keeping with his campaign promise, Brown sought the blessing of California voters for his proposed tax increase via the ballot initiative process.[72] In the lead-up to the ballot referendum in November 2012, Brown campaigned hard, warning that the referendum's defeat would lead to massive cuts in education spending.[73] Voters accepted his argument, passing the tax increase referendum by a vote of 55%–43%. This pivotal outcome allowed Brown and state legislative Democrats to stabilize the state's budget while also delivering on a variety of other priorities, including a new statewide education funding formula, in the ensuing years.[74] Reflecting on Brown's second stint as governor as he was stepping down from the office in 2019, many analysts argued that it was the success of the tax-increase initiative that defined his governorship and made it a success.

[71] Adam Nagourney, "Californians Asked for $6.9 Billion in New Taxes," *New York Times*, January 6, 2012, A14.

[72] Ben Adler, "The Make-or-Break Moment of Jerry Brown's Second Governorship," *capradio* (Sacramento, CA), 2019, https://www.capradio.org/articles/2019/01/03/the-make-or-break-moment-of-jerry-browns-second-governorship, accessed December 29, 2023. To be sure, passing a tax increase through the California Legislature would have been very difficult given the state's supermajority requirement for tax increases.

[73] Adam Nagourney, "Governor in High Gear over a Tax Initiative," *New York Times*, November 4, 2012, 16.

[74] William Chen, "What Has Proposition 30 Meant for California," *California Budget and Policy Center*, 2016, https://calbudgetcenter.org/resources/what-has-proposition-30-meant-for-california/, accessed December 29, 2023.

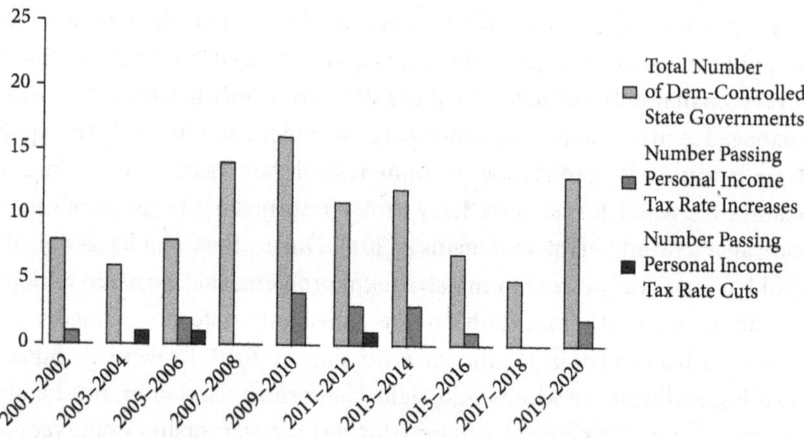

Figure 6.3 Personal Income Tax Rate Increases and Decreases for Democrat-Controlled State Governments across Biennia, 2001–2002 to 2019–2020

Sources: State Tax Actions Dataset; Klarner, *State Partisan Division, 1937–2011*; data on state partisan control after 2011 collected from various sources by the author

What happened in California was not entirely unprecedented, but neither was it the normal course of affairs for Democrat-controlled states in the 2010s. Figure 6.3 is the Democratic counterpart to Figure 6.2; it displays frequencies of personal income tax changes for Democrat-controlled state governments between 2001–2002 and 2019–2020. The figure shows both the decline in the total number of Democrat-controlled state governments in the 2010s (relative to the late 2000s), as well as the relatively low number of personal income tax changes made by Democrat-controlled states throughout both decades. Comparing Figure 6.3 to Figure 6.2, it is clear that the major changes in state personal income taxes of the 2010s occurred in states controlled by Republicans rather than Democrats.

State Sales Taxation in the Twenty-First Century: The Rise of E-Commerce and the Failure to Coordinate a Response

The focus of this chapter has thus far largely been on policy developments in state income taxation. General sales taxation has received little attention, largely because relatively few states passed major sales tax overhauls during the 1990–2020 period. Relatedly, and in clear contrast to the state-level polarization of income tax policy, polarization in sales tax policy during this period was low to non-existent. This difference can be explained by two main factors. First, because the United States lacks a federal general sales tax, America's national parties did not and have not taken clear policy positions on sales tax policy, limiting their absorption into the dynamic of nationalized party polarization that this chapter has described. Relatedly, the party-aligned interest groups that played such a large role in shaping tax policy inside statehouses during the 1990–2020 period were, and continue to be, far less energized by sales taxes than by income taxes. Groups like ALEC and SPN simply did not and have not encouraged Republican-controlled state legislatures to cut sales taxes to nearly the same degree as they have for income taxes, probably because their business-sector funders have always been far less opposed to sales taxation. For their part, labor unions and state-level progressive groups aligned with Democratic parties preferred income to sales taxation, but they also recognized the importance of the latter to state fiscal systems and did not wish to hamper the fiscal capacities of their states by advocating for major sales tax cuts. Thus, for the most part, a cross-party consensus existed in many statehouses during the 1990–2020 period to maintain sales taxes where they had been.

The paucity of party conflict over sales taxes during the 1990–2020 period does not mean that sales taxation was off the radar of state and national policymakers during these years, however. In fact, sales taxes were very much on the minds of policymakers, though not because of any large-scale reform agenda or due to the forces of national party politics. Rather, from the last decade of the twentieth century and into the first decades of the twenty-first, policymakers were concerned about sales taxes because technological developments were increasingly threatening the very viability of state sales taxation. With the rise of the internet, Americans were purchasing ever more products via e-commerce websites like Amazon, but prior judicial rulings made it exceptionally challenging for states to collect taxes on such transactions. The revenue implications of these developments were staggering (particularly for states that were highly reliant on sales taxes), but states struggled to develop a coherent response to them before the U.S. Supreme Court ultimately stepped in to save them in 2018. In this section, I recount how state and national efforts to respond to the threats posed by e-commerce to state sales taxes consistently floundered before the Supreme Court finally intervened. While the saga of state e-commerce taxation is a highly complex story that merits much greater detail than this book can give, I highlight it here as a rare twenty-first-century example of the recurrent pattern at the heart of this book: the consistent failure of state legislatures and Congress to coordinate on an effective response to an intergovernmental taxation problem.

The origins of the online sales tax conundrum that states began to face in the 1990s can be traced to two Supreme Court decisions: *National Bellas Hess, Inc. v. Department of Revenue of Illinois* (1967), and *Quill Corp. v. North Dakota* (1992). In these rulings, the Supreme Court established and then reaffirmed a basic rule that a state seeking to tax sales by an out-of-state company to an in-state resident must establish that the company has a "physical presence" in the state itself.[75] The Court's rationale in these decisions was that state nexus laws for the taxation of interstate sales had become far too complex and variegated, and were thus imposing an "undue burden" on interstate commerce. In the *Quill* decision, however, the Court emphasized that Congress's constitutional power to regulate interstate commerce gave it the ability to set a more flexible standard for state taxation of interstate sales than the one established by the Court. As Justice Stevens wrote in the majority opinion: "Congress is now free to decide whether, when, and to what extent the States may burden interstate mail-order concerns with a duty to collect use taxes."[76]

During the 1990s and early 2000s, as states began to lose out on enormous amounts of sales tax revenue because of their inability to meet the Court's physical-presence standard for internet sales, the search for potential solutions gained full force. The most obvious solution was for Congress to act, but much as in its previous tax coordination efforts, Congress failed to rise to the occasion. Congress's most notable effort to address the interstate sales tax conundrum was via the passage of the Internet Tax Freedom Act of 1998. In this legislation, Congress simultaneously prohibited states from taxing internet access while also taking very modest steps toward the development of a streamlined process through which states would tax internet sales. It accomplished the latter through returning to the oft-used strategy of passing off a difficult intergovernmental relations dilemma to an advisory commission—in this case, the newly created Advisory Commission on Electronic Commerce (ACEC).[77] Not surprisingly, the Commission's work

[75] R. Lainie W. Harris, "Did the Supreme Court do Congress's Dirty Work When It Killed Quill? State Sales Tax on Remote Sellers and Wayfair," *The Tax Lawyer* 74, no. 4 (2019): 671.

[76] *Quill Corp. v. North Dakota*, 504 U.S. 298 (1992).

[77] John A. Swain and Walter Hellerstein, "The Political Economy of the Streamlines Sales and Use Tax Agreement," *National Tax Journal* 58, no. 3 (2005): 605–619.

was beset by bickering between members who sought to find a solution that would facilitate state taxation of e-commerce and anti-tax activists determined to stymie such a solution.[78] In the end, the ACEC never even made recommendations for Congress to consider.

In the absence of congressional action to solve the e-commerce taxation dilemma, states explored a variety of other solutions, none of which proved successful. First, the states attempted a coordinated response of their own in the form of the Streamlined Sales Tax Project (SSTP), an intergovernmental forum formed in 2000 in which representatives of state governments worked to craft an agreement to simplify the administration of interstate sales taxes in a way that would pass muster with the Supreme Court. In an effort to achieve consensus across states, SSTP intentionally skirted difficult political issues, focusing on "administrative simplification" while mostly avoiding discussions about interstate uniformity in sales tax bases or rates.[79] The result of the SSTP was the Streamlined Sales and Use Tax Agreement (SSUTA), a voluntary agreement for sales tax simplification that would go into effect once at least ten states constituting at least 20% of the American population signed onto it.[80] In agreeing to enact the SSUTA, states pledged to make a variety of efficiency reforms, including centralizing their sales tax collections, requiring local governments to have the same sales tax base as that of the state, and requiring all local jurisdictions across a state to have the same local sales tax rate.

Predictably, however, even the limited framework of SSUTA ultimately failed to generate sufficient state buy-in to solve the coordination problems created by subnational e-commerce taxation. In the three-year period following the inception of SSUTA in October 2005, twenty states signed onto it, but interest in SSUTA declined substantially after this initial burst.[81] As of 2019, twenty-six states constituting nearly 65% of the American population had still not become SSUTA members, severely limiting the agreement's effectiveness.[82] The inability of SSUTA to spread beyond the initial rump of

[78] John B. Judis, "Taxing Issue," *New Republic*, October 11, 1999, https://newrepublic.com/article/92333/internet-sales-tax, accessed March 25, 2025.

[79] Swain and Hellerstein, "The Political Economy of the Streamlines Sales and Use Tax Agreement," 609.

[80] Streamlined Sales Tax Governing Board, "Streamlined Sales and Use Tax Agreement," November 12, 2002, https://www.streamlinedsalestax.org/docs/default-source/agreement/ssuta/ssuta-as-amended-through-5-25-22.pdf?sfvrsn=669c138_8, accessed April 1, 2025.

[81] Whitney B. Afonso, "The Barriers Created by Complexity: A State-By-State Analysis of Local Sales Tax Laws in Light of the Wayfair Ruling," *National Tax Journal* 72, no. 4 (2019): 777–800.

[82] This includes the four states (Delaware, Montana, New Hampshire, and Oregon) without general sales taxes. However, even excluding those states, the states that had not ratified the SSUTA constitutes over 62% of the population.

states that signed onto it was due to a host of reasons, most notably SSUTA's requirement that states implement a destination-based sourcing rule for local sales taxes (which aroused substantial opposition among municipal governments in key states like California and Illinois).[83]

States that refused to sign onto SSUTA often attempted a second solution to their e-commerce taxation conundrum: adopting new nexus definitions that they hoped would satisfy the Supreme Court and allow for the collection of sales taxes from out-of-state sellers. These laws, which became known in the e-commerce world as "Amazon tax laws," often sought to meet the Court's "physical presence" standard by linking out-of-state sellers to an in-state affiliate that performed some business functions for them.[84] Unfortunately, such laws generally fell short of delivering their expected revenue, in some cases because they were declared unconstitutional but more often because they caused out-of-state sellers to sever ties with their in-state affiliates.[85] In the final analysis, the main effect of state Amazon tax laws was not to solve the fiscal problems created by the rise of e-commerce, but to make state tax codes even more diverse and difficult for interstate businesses to navigate than they had been before.[86]

In the end, it was not congressional intervention or multi-state coordination that saved the state sales tax, but rather the Supreme Court's decision to reverse its earlier rulings. In its 2018 decision, *South Dakota v. Wayfair*, the Court upheld a South Dakota law imposing a requirement on most out-of-state sellers to collect sales taxes for purchases from South Dakota residents, even when those sellers did not have any "physical presence" in the state. In so doing, the Court overturned the standard it set in *Bellas Hess* and *Quill* and thus provided a "constitutional pathway" for all states to tax internet sales.[87] Writing for the majority, Justice Anthony Kennedy stated that "*Quill* was wrong on its own terms when it was decided in 1992" but that the rise of the internet—by making the virtual presence of a company within a state

[83] Swain and Hellerstein, "The Political Economy of the Streamlines Sales and Use Tax Agreement," 613.

[84] Geoffrey Propheter, "Political Determinants of State E-Commerce Sales Tax Policy," *Politics and Policy* 40, no. 4 (2012): 657–679.

[85] Propheter, "Political Determinants of State E-Commerce Sales Tax Policy," 662. Some Amazon tax laws also mandated that out-of-state sellers notify consumers that they must pay sales taxes on out-of-state purchases, but these provisions also failed to generate revenue due to low consumer compliance rates. Harris, "Did the Supreme Court do Congress's Dirty Work When It Killed Quill?," 686.

[86] Harris, "Did the Supreme Court do Congress's Dirty Work When It Killed Quill?," 673.

[87] Afonso, "The Barriers Created by Complexity," 777.

just as, if not more important than, its physical presence—made "*Quill*'s original error all the more egregious and harmful."[88] But in his dissent, Chief Justice John Roberts pointed out that—as *Quill* made clear—the Constitution allows Congress to supersede the Court's decisions on most matters of interstate commerce and that it, not the Court, was the proper venue for addressing "this important question of economic policy."[89]

In the wake of the *Wayfair* decision, nearly all sales tax states updated their sales tax codes to match the nexus definition adopted by South Dakota and blessed by the Supreme Court.[90] Thus, in 2019, states across the country began collecting sales taxes on most online purchases, saving the retail sales tax—a longstanding pillar of most state tax systems—from oblivion. What is noteworthy here is that the institutions charged with setting the country's tax policy—Congress and the state legislatures—were unable to coordinate to save the sales tax on their own. It ultimately took the U.S. Supreme Court—by a narrow, 5–4 majority—to rescue state sales taxation.

Tracking the Polarization of State Tax Policy Over Time

Returning to this chapter's primary focus on the polarization of state tax policy, this section uses historical data on state tax rates and receipts to track the divergence of Democrat-controlled and Republican-controlled states on matters of tax policy over the course of the 1990–2020 period. I begin by examining tax-rate divergence: Figure 6.4 includes three graphs showing mean tax rates for the "Big Three" state taxes for Democratic states and Republican states for every year between 1950 and 1970. States are classified as Democratic and Republican based on six-year rolling averages of Ranney Index values. The Ranney Index is a longstanding and widely used political science statistic used to measure partisanship in state government.[91] Based on four indicators (the partisan composition of each state legislative chamber, gubernatorial election outcomes, and the length of time in which

[88] *South Dakota v. Wayfair, Inc.*, 585 U.S. ___ (2018).

[89] *South Dakota v. Wayfair.*

[90] Kirk J. Stark, "*Wayfair* in Constitutional Perspective: Who Sets the Ground Rules in US Fiscal Federalism?," *National Tax Journal* 74, no. 1 (2021): 221–256.

[91] Austin Ranney, "Parties in State Politics," In *Politics in the American States: A Comparative Analysis*, eds. Jacobs and Vines (Boston: Little, Brown, 1965); Paul T. David, "How Can an Index of Party Competition Best Be Derived?," *Journal of Politics* 34, no. 2 (1972): 632–638; Gregory Shufeldt and Patrick Flavin, "Two Distinct Concepts: Party Competition in Government and Electoral Competition in the American States," *State Politics and Policy* 12, no. 3 (2012): 330–342.

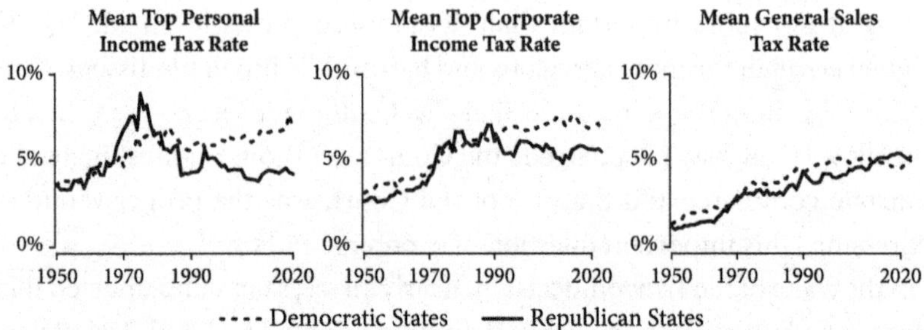

Figure 6.4 Mean Tax Rates for Democratic and Republican States (Based on Six-Year Ranney Index Values), 1950–2020

Sources: State Tax Actions Dataset; Klarner, *State Partisan Division, 1937–2011*; data on state partisan control after 2011 collected from various sources by the author

one party or the other has had unified control of state government), it ranges from 0 to 1, where 0 indicates complete Republican control and 1 indicates complete Democratic control. For the purposes of this figure, states with a value of greater than 0.5 are considered Democratic states, while states with a value of less than 0.5 are considered Republican states.[92]

As Figure 6.4 shows, Democratic and Republican states did not vary substantially and durably in their mean top rates for any of the "Big Three" Taxes until around 1990. The aberrational results for the late 1970s and early 1980s, when the mean personal income tax rate was higher for Republican than Democratic states, are largely explained by the fact that the number of Republican states during this period was unusually low (i.e., only 11 states had 6-year Ranney Index scores below 0.5 in 1977), and that this group included many rural northern states with historically high personal income tax rates (e.g., Idaho, Iowa, North Dakota, Vermont, etc.). It is only around 1990 that a substantial and durable partisan gap in mean tax rates opens up; crucially, this is only for the personal income tax and (to a lesser extent) the corporate income tax. The partisan gap in mean sales tax rates remains tiny or non-existent throughout the period at hand, consistent with the earlier finding that the polarization in state tax policy largely concerns income taxation, not sales taxation.

[92] Six-year Ranney Index scores for all states from 1950–2010 come from: Klarner, Carl, "Other Scholars' Competitiveness Measures," 2013, https://doi.org/10.7910/DVN/QSDYLH, Harvard Dataverse, V1, UNF:5:we2ixYigyI3GVaDGKsU58A== [fileUNF]. The remainder of Ranney Index scores (from 2011–2020) were calculated by the author. Nebraska is excluded from these analyses since its legislature is non-partisan.

The results displayed in Figure 6.4 raise an important question of causality regarding the observed increase in polarization in state tax policy since 1990. The question can be stated as: is the emergence of a partisan gap in income tax rates primarily a result of changes in the tax policies pursued by Democratic and Republican states (i.e., party control of state government increasingly affects state tax policy), or is it more a function of previously low-tax states becoming more Republican and previously high-tax states becoming more Democratic over the course of this period? There is good reason to suspect that the latter explanation is at least part of the story. After all, between 1990 and 2020, many southern state governments historically controlled by Democrats transitioned to Republican rule, and southern states (with the exception of North Carolina) have traditionally had low-rate income taxes or no income taxes at all.[93]

To analyze the extent to which each of these potential causes has contributed to the growth of the partisan gap in income taxation, I present Figure 6.5, which shows the size of the partisan gap over time (i.e., the mean tax rate for Democratic states minus the mean tax rate for Republican states) for each of the "Big Three" taxes using the actual tax rate figures for each year since 1990 (the solid lines) and substituting the 1990 tax rates for the actual tax rates for the entire period between 1990 and 2020 (the dotted line). The latter is meant to represent a hypothetical world in which no state made any

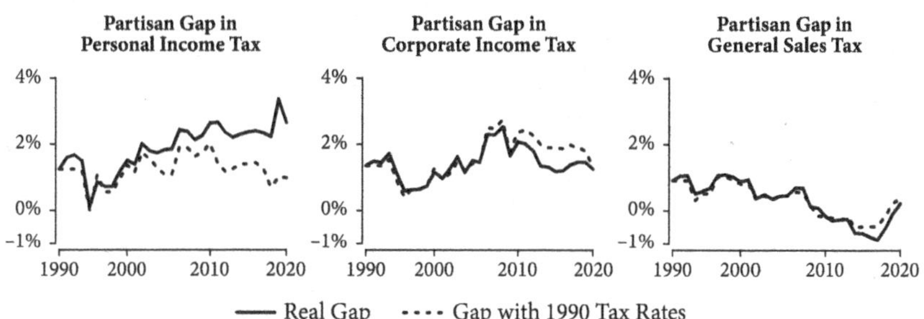

Figure 6.5 Partisan Gaps in Mean Tax Rates for Big Three Taxes using Real Tax Rates and 1990 Tax Rates, 1990–2020

Sources: State Tax Actions Dataset; Klarner, *State Partisan Division, 1937–2011*; data on state partisan control after 2011 collected from various sources by the author

[93] On the belated southern realignment at the state legislative level during the twenty-first century, see: Adam Myers, "Electoral Incongruence and Delayed Republican Gains in Southern State Legislatures," *American Review of Politics* 35, no. 2 (2016): 73–102; Adam S. Myers, "Changing Patterns of Uncontested Seats in Southern State Legislative Elections, 1984–2012," *Social Science Quarterly* 99, no. 2 (2018): 583–598.

tax rate changes since 1990 (i.e., a world in which any partisan gap in tax rates since 1990 could only be attributed to changes in party representation in state governments in the ensuing years). The graph for the personal income tax shows that the real gap and hypothetical gap for this tax were largely the same until the early 2000s, when the hypothetical gap remained relatively steady while the real gap generally grew in size. In other words, since the turn of the century, the growth of the partisan gap in personal income tax rates is largely attributable to changes in tax rates by Democratic and Republican states, not to changes in party strength in state governments by themselves. Once again, this is also the case (though to a lesser degree) for the corporate income tax.

The growing partisan polarization in state personal income taxation between 1990 and 2020 has had real and tangible effects on state finances. This is demonstrated in Figure 6.6, which tracks total state own-source tax revenue as a share of total state personal income (in $1000s of dollars) from 1990–2020 for Democratic and Republican states. Importantly, unlike Figures 6.4 and 6.5, Figure 6.6 does not use rolling averages of Ranney Index values to determine whether a state is Democratic or Republican. Instead, only the 2020 6-year Ranney Index is considered; the 19 states with values above 0.5 are considered Democratic states while the thirty states with Ranney Index values below 0.5 are considered Republican states across the

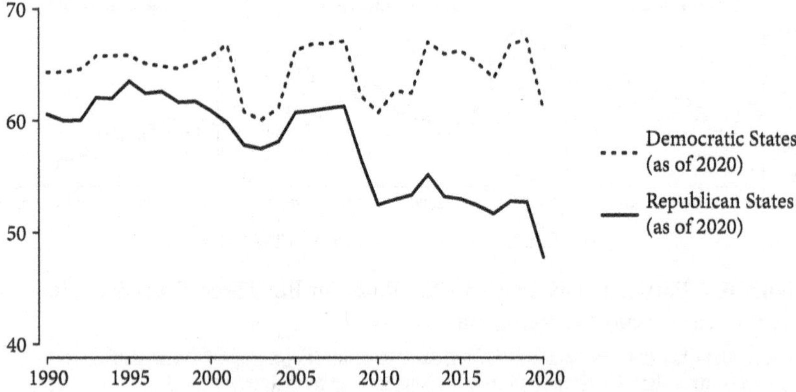

Figure 6.6 Total State Own-Source Tax Revenue (per $1000 of Personal Income) for Democratic and Republican States, 1990–2020

Sources: U.S. Census, *Historical Finances of State Governments* dataset; U.S. Census, *Annual Survey of State and Local Finances* (for tax revenue data post-2008); St. Louis Federal Reserve, Federal Reserve Economic Data (FRED) website (for state personal income post-2008)

entire time period (Nebraska is excluded from the analysis due to its nonpartisan legislature). This allows for an examination of the extent to which the same two sets of states have diverged in their tax revenue intake over the thirty-year time span.[94]

As the figure shows, there was a major difference in the fiscal trajectories of Democratic and Republican states between 1990 and 2020. In Democratic states, total state tax revenue (as a share of personal income) has largely been steady over the entire stretch of time: while these states have experienced dips in state tax revenue during periods of economic downturn (i.e., the early 2000s recession, the Great Recession of 2009, and the COVID downturn of 2020), their revenue levels bounced back to what they were when the periods were over. In Republican states, on the other hand, there has been a continuous decline in tax revenue levels since the late 1990s that has been amplified during periods of economic downturn but tends to persist even in periods of economic growth.

State Taxation and Fiscal Federalism at the Beginning of the Twenty-First Century

In addition to affecting state finances, the partisan polarization in state tax policy described in this chapter has had important effects on intergovernmental fiscal relations. To see how, I present Figure 6.7, which shows trends in the amount of state government own-source revenue, local government own-source revenue, and fiscal transfers from the national government to the states across the 1990–2020 period.[95] As in Figure 6.6, the amounts are presented as shares of $1000s of national personal income to facilitate standardization and cross-time comparison. The figure shows that, while local own-source revenue has held steady between 1990–2020 and federal transfers have increased, state government own-source revenue has been declining since the turn of the century. This is in marked contrast to the trends in the same sources of subnational government revenue between 1975

[94] The thirty Republican states (as of 2020) are: AK, AL, AR, AZ, FL, GA, IA, ID, IN, KS, KY, LA, MI, MO, MS, MT, NC, ND, NH, OH, OK, PA, SC, SD, TN, TX, UT, WI, and WY. The nineteen Democratic states (as of 2020) are: CA, CO, CT, DE, HI, IL, MA, MD, ME, MN, NJ, NM, NV, NY, OR, RI, VA, VT, and WA.

[95] Figure 5.2 (in Chapter 5) is a companion figure showing trends for the same three variables for the 1975–1990 period.

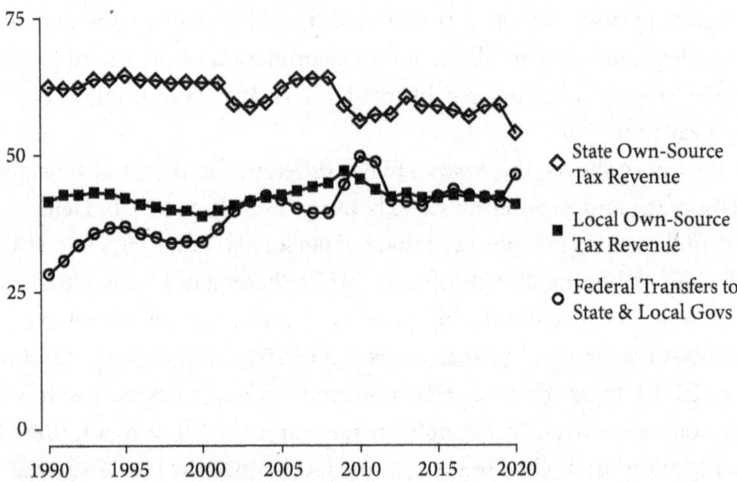

Figure 6.7 Sources of Subnational Government Revenue (per $1000 of National Personal Income), 1990–2020

Non-tax own-source revenues for state and local governments not included in the figure

Sources: U.S. Census, *Historical Finances of State Governments* dataset; U.S. Census, *Annual Survey of State and Local Finances* (for revenue data post-2008); St. Louis Federal Reserve, Federal Reserve Economic Data (FRED) website (for national personal income post-2008)

and 1990 (shown in Figure 5.2 in Chapter 5); during that period, state government tax revenue held steady while local tax revenue and federal transfers declined. While the overall decline in state own-source tax revenue can be attributed to a variety of factors (the various economic downturns of the twenty-first century being perhaps the most important), there is no doubt that the Republican tax-cutting agenda in the states has been an important factor as well. As Figure 6.6 showed, Democratic states have experienced little to no overall decline in state tax revenue. The decrease in state tax revenue seen in Figure 6.7, therefore, is a product of developments in Republican states.

The fact that the growth in federal transfers to state and local governments is roughly coterminous with the decline in state own-source tax revenue over this period strongly suggests that these two trends are related. Clearly, part of the relationship here has to do with the immediate effects of economic downturns: nearly whenever these downturns have occurred, state tax revenue has fallen while national transfers have increased as part of a broader countercyclical fiscal policy. But there appears to be an underlying and long-term secular pattern at work here as well: stated simply, as the Republican state-level tax-cutting agenda has increasingly undermined state fiscal capacity, pressure has been slowly building on the national government to ease state and local fiscal problems. Ironically, then, the Republican Party—the traditional champion of federalism and states' rights—appears to have inadvertently paved the way for greater national involvement in state fiscal matters. The implications of this profound shift, with a focus on how it played out during the COVID-19 pandemic, are explored in the book's conclusion.

Conclusion

State Taxation and Fiscal Federalism in the Twenty-First Century

This book has traced and analyzed two concomitant histories: the history of state taxation systems since their modern emergence in the 1930s, and that of intergovernmental fiscal relations over the same ninety-year period. In this concluding chapter, I examine how these two interconnected histories shape the core challenges of American fiscal federalism in the present day. I begin the chapter by synthesizing the book's key findings regarding the development of state tax systems and the various efforts at intergovernmental fiscal reform that accompanied them, extending the book's historical coverage to the COVID pandemic in the early 2020s. I then consider how the interplay between state and national fiscal policy informs the competing fiscal federalism approaches of the country's two political parties in our polarized age. For its part, the modern Republican Party has largely united around a federalism agenda emphasizing interstate tax competition and limited subnational fiscal capacity as positive goods for the country. This has created a predicament for the Democratic Party, whose goal of a fiscal expansion of the domestic public sector can be (and has been) scuttled by state-level Republican politicians eager to advance a tax-cutting agenda. The fiscal federalism dynamic created by these two competing approaches, I argue, is causing growing harms for the American public welfare—particularly through the gaps in subnational fiscal capacity that it is fostering. I conclude the chapter (and the book) by suggesting modest policy reforms that could ameliorate some of this dynamic's most noxious effects, while also contending that more substantial reforms will only be possible if a political consensus emerges around the need to reduce competitive pressures within the American federal system. Even if this happens, however, the structural obstacles that have long prevented large-scale intergovernmental fiscal reform efforts in the United States will still be in place, likely dooming the prospects for the large-scale

Coordination Failure. Adam S. Myers, Oxford University Press. © Oxford University Press (2026).
DOI: 10.1093/9780197831878.003.0008

reforms that are truly needed. Thus, the most likely outcome is that the American government in the twenty-first century will muddle along without resolving its deepest intergovernmental fiscal challenges.

State Tax Systems: From Path Dependence to Partisan Polarization

This book began in the 1930s, when states reconstructed their tax systems in response to the fiscal crises they faced during the Great Depression. As shown in Chapter 1, state tax decisions during this crucial decade—the first critical juncture in state taxation—were often made hastily and in moments of crisis after long stretches of delay. The types of taxes that states enacted during these moments of crisis varied widely, and these variations were highly influenced by a complex array of obscure institutional factors and historical contingencies that render generalizable explanations elusive. If one focuses on state tax *reliance* rather than adoption, however, an important generalization is apparent: whenever states adopted sales taxes, they were far more likely to rely heavily upon them than upon income taxes. This greater reliance on sales taxes meant that the state tax systems established during the 1930s were, on the whole, highly regressive.

The terrain of state taxation policy changed substantially during the 1950s and early 1960s, when state revenue needs surged once again in response to rapidly increasing public school enrollments and rising public demands for social services. As Chapter 3 showed, the states of this period featured distinct patterns of taxation politics based on the range of taxes they already had in place—a product of the decisions made in the 1930s. These differences led state tax actions to be highly path-dependent throughout the 1950s and early 1960s, with sales-tax-only states expanding sales taxation and income-tax-only states expanding income taxation. In the late 1960s and early 1970s, a variety of circumstances converged to create a major opening in many states: for the first time in three decades, significant new tax adoptions suddenly became politically possible. During this second critical juncture in state taxation, many states finally adopted whichever of the "Big Three" taxes they had avoided enacting up until then, leading to a convergence in the shape of state tax systems. Additionally, the personal income tax approached the general sales tax as a leading source of state revenue at this stage. Despite the increased uniformity in state tax systems, significant historical differences remained, with state reliance on particular taxes being closely related to the length of time since the taxes had been enacted.

Throughout the 1970s, variations in state tax systems continued to be closely tied to historical and regional differences, with political factors being of much lower importance. Even during the 1980s, as the Reagan domestic policy agenda wrought profound partisan divisions over national fiscal policy, the impact of party control of state government on state tax policy remained highly limited. Between the mid 1990s and 2020, however, the state-level politics of taxation underwent a major transformation across the country. As national politics gradually found its way into state political systems, the national party divide over fiscal issues reproduced itself in statehouses around the country. The new partisan politics of state taxation found its clearest expression in the many states in which Republicans gained control throughout the 1990s and 2000s. In nearly all these states, ascendant Republicans actively pursued a tax-cutting agenda in line with the supply-side economic philosophy that national Republicans had adopted during the Reagan presidency. The chief target of state-level Republicans was the personal income tax, particularly its top rates for higher incomes. In the few Democrat-controlled states that remained, on the other hand, Democratic leaders mostly avoided the opposite approach of levying income tax increases, and in the rare instances in which such increases were adopted, they were almost always targeted at a tiny sliver of ultra-high-income taxpayers. Still, the growing divide between red-state and blue-state approaches to taxation was plain for all to see, and during the early and mid 2010s, it became the object of national media attention as countless articles and blog posts made comparisons (with varying degrees of rigor and accuracy) on the divergent economic trajectories of high-tax blue states and low-tax red states. The so-called "Texas model" of low taxes and low services (later also ascribed to other large Republican-controlled states like Florida) became the central theme of Governor Rick Perry's ultimately failed (but initially quite serious) Republican presidential campaign in 2012 and continued to influence the tax choices of Republican-controlled states in the mid and late 2010s.

Divisions in taxation policy between red and blue states have only increased in the 2020s. This was especially evident in the years of the COVID-19 pandemic. The pandemic had a whipsawed effect on state finances: after an initial plunge in tax revenues driven by a dramatic slowdown in economic activity in 2020, state budgets quickly recovered and then experienced major surpluses thanks to a combination of increased consumer spending (which enhanced sales tax revenue), a surging stock market (which enhanced income tax revenue), and a glut of aid from the national government.[1] In response to these surpluses, nearly all states cut taxes between 2021 and 2023. The tax-cutting approach chosen by states varied dramatically, however, and party control of government was unsurprisingly the chief factor influencing state tax decisions. For their part, Republican-controlled states doubled down on their now-longstanding inclination to cut personal income tax rates, particularly for top brackets: of the twenty-three states that cut personal income tax rates during the 2021–2023 period, seventeen were Republican-controlled.[2] Democrat-controlled states, on the other hand, focused on expanding state-level Earned Income Tax Credits (EITC), a tax policy designed to help the poor that progressive states had begun to embrace in the late 1990s and that became increasingly popular throughout the 2000s and 2010s.[3] The pronounced role of partisanship in shaping state tax decisions during the COVID-19 pandemic is especially evident when the pandemic era is compared to the late 1990s, the previous period when the vast majority of states adopted large tax cuts. During the latter, the partisan divide was just beginning to emerge and partisan patterns in state tax-cutting strategies are hard to locate, but in the former they are crystal-clear.

The partisan differences in state tax-cutting approaches during the pandemic concerned not only the method used to cut income taxes but the size of the tax cuts as well. Table C.1 shows the mean net revenue effect of the pandemic-era tax changes as a share of FY 2020 tax revenue for states primarily controlled by Democrats, states primarily featuring divided government, and states primarily controlled by Republicans.[4] As the table shows, the mean net effect of the pandemic-era tax cuts was far larger for Republican-controlled states than for Democrat-controlled states. Moreover, the differences were especially large for the personal income tax, the focus of most of the tax-cut efforts. Though many Democrat-controlled states lost income tax revenue through their EITC expansions, the revenue they lost paled in comparison to the revenue lost by Republican-controlled states due to their income tax rate cuts.

[1] Richard C. Auxier, "Reviewing Three Years of State Tax Cuts," *Tax Policy Center*, July 20, 2023, https://www.taxpolicycenter.org/taxvox/three-years-state-tax-cuts, accessed March 12, 2024.

[2] Ibid.

[3] David Neumark and Katherine Williams, "Do State Earned Income Tax Credits Increase Participation in the Federal EITC?," *Public Finance Review* 48, no. 5 (2020): 579–626.

[4] This table is analogous to Table 6.1 in Chapter 6, which featured similar data for tax changes made during the 2009 financial crisis.

Table C.1 Mean Net Effect (across States) of Pandemic-Era (2021–2023) Tax Actions as a Share of Total FY 2020 Tax Revenue

Party Control Status	Number of States	Total Tax Changes	Personal Income Tax Changes	Corporate Income Tax Changes	General Sales Tax Changes	Changes to All Other Taxes
Primarily Democrat-Controlled	14	−0.3%	−2.2%	0.2%	0.3%	1.3%
Primarily Divided Government	12	−4.1%	−7.3%	−6.4%	−1.7%	−2.1%
Primarily Republican-Controlled	23	−4.7%	−13.9%	−8.1%	−1%	0.7%

Sources: National Association of State Budget Officers (NASBO), *Fiscal Survey of* States, various editions; Census Survey of State Governments (for data on total state tax revenue); National Conference of State Legislatures (for party control data). Party control status is based on which party controlled a state government during a majority of the years (i.e., at least two out of three) between 2021 and 2023. Data from Ohio are excluded from the corporate income tax numbers due to a discrepancy between how the NASBO and the Census classify its business profits tax. Data from Nebraska are excluded from all calculations due to its non-partisan legislature.

Moreover, unlike in previous major state tax-cutting moments, it was not just relatively prosperous states like Texas and North Carolina that passed large-scale income tax cuts. Instead, many of the largest cuts in state income taxes were implemented in some of the poorest states in the country, including Mississippi, West Virginia, Kentucky, and Arkansas. In most of these states, Republican governors or legislative leaders promoted these cuts by making highly unrealistic claims about their potential to revive moribund state economies or facilitate population growth. In West Virginia, for example, Gov. Jim Justice stated that "The more we lower the taxes, the more people will come. That's all there is to it."[5] In Mississippi, Gov. Tate Reeves and legislative leaders successfully advanced a large income tax cut as their chief policy goal in 2022, even as they kept the state's highly regressive grocery sales tax on the books and despite the state business community's

[5] Charles Young, "West Virginia Revenue Officials Keeping an Eye on Tax Law Implementation," wvnews.com, May 8, 2023, https://www.wvnews.com/statejournal/news/west-virginia-revenue-officials-keeping-an-eye-on-tax-law-implementation/article_0cba16be-e9e0-11ed-b83a-4b77721d16a0.html, accessed February 10, 2026.

insistence that income tax relief was not among their top priorities.[6] These actions demonstrate the extent to which the power of income tax rate cuts had by the 2020s become akin to an article of faith among state-level Republicans by the 2020s, the economic needs of their states or even the advice of the business community notwithstanding.

The Eclipse of "Intergovernmental Fiscal Relations" in a Polarized Era

As this study has shown, between the 1930s and 1970s, state fiscal systems and the state-national fiscal relationship were regular matters of concern among national policymakers. A wide array of interests, starting with the state governments themselves, were displeased with the system of fiscal federalism that had developed in the early and mid twentieth century. Those dissatisfied with the system pointed to many problems, including the difficulties states faced in generating enough revenue for the services they provided, the pernicious effects of interstate tax competition, the inefficiencies created by a multi-level taxing structure, the deleterious economic consequences of "double taxation," and others. Thus, throughout the 1930s, calls for intergovernmental fiscal reform were frequent, and something that looked like a movement working toward it seemed to be gaining steam in Washington, D.C. In retrospect, however, it was apparent that the fiscal coordination movement of the New Deal Era was only a movement in the weakest sense of the term. United by dissatisfaction with the status quo but sharing no common vision of what the alternative to it should be (i.e., what a "coordinated" tax system would look like), the coordination movement quickly fizzled. In the wake of its failure to pass a revenue-sharing program for the alcohol sales tax, Congress set aside work on intergovernmental tax reform, likely reasoning that the issue was too complicated and politically contentious to solve.

But the issue did not go away: following World War II, as states and now localities faced ever-growing fiscal burdens, a much wider range of groups began to call for national reforms to the intergovernmental fiscal relationship. With states, cities, big business, and labor all demanding changes,

[6] Bobby Harrison, "Grocery Tax Cut Considered, but Never Acted Upon by State's Political Leadership," *Northside Sun* (Jackson, MS), April 18, 2022; Geoff Bender, "State Chamber: Businesses are Concerned with Workforce, not State Income Tax," *Clarksdale Press Register* (Clarksdale, MS), February 18, 2022.

Congress finally got to work. It nonetheless took Congress nearly four years to pass the ultimate outcome of this work—the SLFAA—into law. As discussed in Chapter 4, the long process of creating SLFAA resulted in a program that sought to address so many competing goals that it ultimately did not address any particularly well. Perhaps most crucially, SLFAA never developed a constituency that would lobby vociferously on its behalf like other national fiscal programs did.[7] By the late 1970s and early 1980s, SLFAA had lost the institutional support it had once enjoyed in Congress, and changing political and fiscal circumstances thus led to its demise.

Since the 1980s, intergovernmental fiscal reform has rarely appeared on the congressional agenda as a stand-alone issue, and almost never in reference to taxation. To be sure (and as discussed in Chapter 6), the rise of the internet did prompt Congress to create a commission tasked with, among other things, exploring how to streamline state taxation of e-commerce. Aside from its very peripheral engagement with the internet sales tax dilemma, however, Congress has largely avoided fiscal federalism matters in the last thirty years. Fundamental questions like what the national government and the states should tax, what role the national government should take to equalize state fiscal capacities, and how or to what extent Congress should act to suppress subnational tax competition are almost never discussed in congressional hearings. Stated another way, fiscal federalism as an independent issue is simply no longer a subject of discussion in Washington, D.C.

The decline of intergovernmental fiscal reform efforts since the 1980s can be understood as part of a larger shift in American federalism between the mid twentieth and early twenty-first centuries. As scholars have shown, the mid twentieth century was a period in which a wide range of intergovernmental institutions (most notably the Advisory Commission on Intergovernmental Relations [ACIR], but also various congressional subcommittees focused on federalism issues, the Office of State and Local Finance within the U.S. Treasury Department, and an intergovernmental grants division within the Office of Management and Budget) facilitated extensive discussion of (if not always action on) intergovernmental policymaking.[8] This era of institutionalized "intergovernmental relations" was made possible by a political

[7] Andrew Karch and Shanna Rose, *Responsive states: Federalism and American Public Policy*, (New York: Cambridge University Press, 2019).
[8] Paul L. Posner, "Scarcity and the Federal System," In *Intergovernmental Relations in Transition: Reflections and Directions*, eds. Carl W. Stenberg and David K. Hamilton (New York: Routledge,

context whose key features included low levels of party polarization, strong state party organizations, consensus around the progressive values of "scientific management" and "good government," and a general lack of emphasis on racial or cultural issues.[9] It was within this context that fora in which stakeholders from national, state, and local government debated the proper fiscal roles of each level of government could take root.

Starting in the 1980s, American politics experienced a series of changes that eroded the sociopolitical context underpinning the era of institutionalized intergovernmental relations. The most important of these changes was nationalized party polarization.[10] Though its impact was highly complex, the essential effect of polarization was to amplify the role of partisanship in contemporary national policy debates while diminishing the significance of countervailing institutions and forces. In the realm of fiscal policy, polarization has led the parties to adopt highly distinct approaches, with Republicans generally advocating retrenchment at all levels of government and Democrats generally advocating the expansion of the domestic public sector, particularly at the national level. The steep divide between the parties on fiscal issues has made policymakers reluctant to tackle complex structural issues, such as the intergovernmental fiscal relationship, because the chances that they could be addressed via an old-fashioned congressional compromise are extremely low.

Polarization also undermined the era of institutionalized intergovernmental relations by weakening one of the central forces that maintained it: the intergovernmental lobby. As discussed in Chapter 2 and especially Chapter 4, the groups that composed the intergovernmental lobby—the Governors' Conference, National Legislative Conference, American Municipal Association, U.S. Conference of Mayors, and the National Association of Counties—played a profound role in putting intergovernmental relations on the congressional agenda and keeping it there until a major reform—the SLFAA—was finally passed during the early and mid twentieth century. But in the modern era of polarized parties, the political power of these groups has waned considerably. Riven by internal disagreements between Democratic

2018), 77–91; John Kincaid, "The U.S. Advisory Commission on Intergovernmental Relations: Unique Artifact of a Bygone Era," *Public Administration Review* 71, no. 2 (2011), 181–189.

[9] Ibid.

[10] Kincaid, "The U.S. Advisory Commission on Intergovernmental Relations"; Donald J. Borut, "The Unraveling of the Intergovernmental System: A Practitioner's Observations," In *Intergovernmental Relations in Transition: Reflections and Directions*, eds. Carl W. Stenberg and David K. Hamilton (New York: Routledge, 2018), 241–254.

and Republican officeholders, these groups and their modern analogues are often unable to function as strong defenders of state and local government interests.[11] Because partisanship triumphs over all rival concerns, the fiscal conditions of state and local governments receive scant attention from Washington (except perhaps when focusing on those conditions serves a national partisan purpose).

Within the new context of nationalized hyperpartisan conflict and an internally divided intergovernmental lobby, the old institutions that served as the sites of intergovernmental dialogue and policy formulation lost political support and faded in significance. The ACIR—arguably the most important of the mid-century intergovernmental institutions—underwent a major downsizing alongside a reorientation toward Ronald Reagan's competitive federalism vision during the 1980s.[12] This led to growing concerns that the ACIR was becoming politicized, leading state and local government organizations to withdraw their staunch support for it. The weakened position of the ACIR led Congress to abolish the agency in 1996.[13] Other important intergovernmental institutions suffered roughly the same fate: the U.S. House and Senate's federalism subcommittees were renamed and reoriented away from an intergovernmental relations focus, and executive agencies with a similar focus within the Office of Management and Budget and the Government Accountability Office were eliminated as well.[14] By the late 1990s, it was clear that the decades-long effort to foster dialogue across levels of government over fiscal issues was a thing of the past.

When viewed from the vantage point of the experts at the National Tax Association of the 1930s (discussed in Chapter 2), who championed a managerial, technocratic approach to intergovernmental fiscal relations, the multi-level structure of American taxation in the twenty-first century looks more incoherent, inefficient, and ill-equipped to facilitate the country's goals than ever. Those experts, were they around today, would likely be unanimous in assessing that the efforts to coordinate taxation across America's governments that began in the 1930s were an abject failure. Moreover, there is little sign that a recrudescence of fiscal federalism discussions may

[11] Posner, "Scarcity and the Federal System," 88.

[12] Bruce D. McDowell, "Reflections on the Spirit and Work of the U.S. Advisory Commission on Intergovernmental Relations," *Public Administration Review* 71, no. 2 (2011): 161–166.

[13] Bruce D. McDowell, "Advisory Commission on Intergovernmental Relations in 1996: The End of an Era," *Publius* 27, no. 2 (1997): 111–127.

[14] McDowell, "Advisory Commission on Intergovernmental Relations"; Posner, "Scarcity and the Federal System," 87.

be upon us. Whether consciously or not, America's leaders appear to have decided that, due to the steep barriers to intergovernmental fiscal reform in American politics, there is not much to be gained from trying to create a more coordinated intergovernmental taxation system.

The Republican Party and the Ascendancy of Competitive Federalism in the Twenty-First Century

One of the most remarkable changes in the politics of American federalism over the past century has been the growth of a discourse and policy agenda emphasizing the value to the American political system of robust competition among states for businesses, jobs, and residents. As discussed in Chapters 2 and 4 in particular, the strong consensus in American politics during the three-decade period between the 1930s and 1960s was that interstate competition (especially in taxation policy) was harmful to both the states and the nation as a whole. A widely accepted premise among the political elites of this period was that such competition caused states to undersupply important public goods, and thus that it was the duty of the national government to take affirmative steps to curb the competitive pressures states faced. This premise was essentially unchallenged by forces that one might assume would be in favor of maintaining or facilitating high levels of interstate economic competition, such as the business community. As Chapter 4 discussed, while mid-century business groups sought to reduce the national government's fiscal powers and return taxation authority to the states, they presented their efforts as being motivated by a desire to restore the original, "dual-federalist" constitutional order rather than to promote interstate competition. Even when framed in this way, however, such efforts attracted support from only a small number of national policymakers; most members of Congress in the 1950s and 1960s, both Democrats and Republicans, had little interest in pursuing the sort of federalism counter-revolution envisioned by big business.

In the 1980s, however, the business community's longstanding goals of scaling back the national government's fiscal role and subjecting the states to greater competitive pressures experienced a major boost. For the first time, these goals enjoyed the clear support of a presidential administration. As Chapter 5 demonstrated, Ronald Reagan's top advisors repeatedly acknowledged that key aspects of their domestic policy agenda—in particular, the steep cuts to conditional grant programs and the separation of national and state tax systems—were intended to induce greater interstate economic competition, thereby forcing states to reduce their own fiscal imprints. The notion that government at all levels needed to be kept small, and that facilitating interstate competition was a crucial means of restraining subnational government, became a key area of agreement among conservative policy intellectuals. But there is little indication that Republican politicians publicly championed interstate competition or that it had otherwise entered popular political discourse during this period.

By the twenty-first century, the competitive federalist vision embraced by the Reaganite policy wonks of the 1980s had come to assume a far more prominent role in mainstream American politics, even if it was rarely acknowledged as such. As Chapter 6 showed, the notion that the American states were in competition with each other for jobs and people, and that Republican-controlled states were winning the interstate economic battle thanks to their low taxes and regulations, had become a common talking point among Republican politicians and pundits in the aftermath of the 2008–2009 Great Recession and beyond. The invocation of such claims by GOP politicians occurred alongside the rise of a larger discourse pitting "red-state America" against "blue-state America" in the national media, as well as the growing polarization of state tax policy and the uneven emergence of state economies from the recession itself. Among those who made these sorts of claims, the aspirational lodestar was Texas—the nation's preeminent red state, lacking both a personal and corporate income tax, and the site of a very large share of the nation's job growth in 2009–2011.[15] Following the lead of Texas Gov. Rick Perry, who made Texas' apparent triumph in the interstate competition for jobs and people the centerpiece of his 2010 book as well as his 2012 presidential campaign, numerous Republican governors publicly made the case that their states needed to emulate "the Texas model" in an effort to stay competitive with their neighbors.

The promotion of competitive federalism by GOP politicians, in both substantive policy and public communications, carried over into the years of Trump (I) and Biden presidencies. As discussed in the book's introduction,

[15] Richard W. Fisher, "Connecting the Dots—Texas Employment Growth; a dissenting vote; and the Ugly Truth (with Reference to P. G. Wodehouse).") address delivered at the Midland Community Forum, Midland, TX, August 17, 2011, https://www.bis.org/review/r110822e.pdf, accessed November 10, 2023.

Trump-era congressional Republicans self-consciously sought to introduce greater interstate competitive pressures into the American federal system by capping the State and Local Tax (SALT) Deduction at $10,000. Following the SALT cap's enactment, Republican-aligned groups like the Cato Institute published reports arguing that blue states should hurry up and cut their taxes, lest their wealthiest residents relocate to more low-tax jurisdictions.[16] Other GOP pundits claimed that the SALT cap had rapidly triggered increased job growth in low-tax red states.[17] The conservative media universe's interest in interstate economic competition spiked again during the years of the COVID-19 Pandemic, when numerous conservative websites and newspapers published pieces arguing that the pandemic induced a large-scale migration of wealthy Americans from high-tax blue states to low-tax red states.[18]

Thus, competitive federalism now forms a core part of both the policy agenda and public narrative promoted by the diffuse network of politicians, interest groups, and media outlets associated with the modern Republican Party.[19] These actors have simultaneously sought to advance a tax-cutting agenda in statehouses, an unwinding of various forms of fiscal support for state governments in Congress, and a full-throated promotion of interstate economic competition in the media. The GOP's consistent and full-throated embrace of competitive federalism over the course of the twenty-first century is remarkable given that, in its positions on many other policy areas and indeed in its very identity, the Republican Party has undergone a substantial

[16] Chris Edwards, "Tax Reform and Interstate Migration," *Cato Institute Tax and Budget Bulletin*, no. 84 (September 18, 2018), https://www.cato.org/tax-budget-bulletin/tax-reform-interstate-migration#, accessed May 9, 2024.

[17] Chuck DeVore, "SALT Deduction Cap Appears to be Shifting Job Creation to Low Tax States," *Texas Public Policy Foundation*, May 9, 2018, https://www.texaspolicy.com/salt-deduction-cap-appears-to-be-shifting-job-creation-to-low-tax-states/, accessed February 10, 2026.

[18] See, e.g., Editorial Board, "The Great Pandemic Wealth Migration," *Wall Street Journal*, June 3, 2022, https://www.wsj.com/articles/irs-taxes-low-high-state-migration-moving-pandemic-remote-work-cost-of-living-11654289927, accessed May 9, 2024; Mark J. Perry, "Top 10 Inbound vs. Top 10 Outbound US States in 2021: How Do They Compare on a Variety of Economic, Tax, Business Climate, and Political Measures?," *American Enterprise Institute*, December 29, 2021, https://www.aei.org/carpe-diem/top-10-inbound-vs-top-10-outbound-us-states-in-2021-how-do-they-compare-on-a-variety-of-economic-tax-in-business-climate-and-political-measures/, accessed May 9, 2024; Michael Lee, "Americans Flee Blue Cities for Red States during the Pandemic: Report," *Fox News*, May 31, 2022, https://www.foxnews.com/us/flee-blue-cities-red-states-pandemic, accessed May 9, 2024. There are many other examples.

[19] As many scholars of the American political parties have written, it is more useful to conceptualize the modern parties as akin to extended networks of a diverse array of organizations rather than as highly organized, centralized institutions. See, e.g., Seth Masket, "The Networked Party: How Social Network Analysis is Revolutionizing the Study of American Political Parties," In *New Directions in American Politics*, ed. Raymond J. La Raja, (New York: Routledge, 2013), 107–124.

shift during these decades (particularly since Donald Trump's ascension to the presidency in 2016).

To be sure, there have been two instances in the last twenty years in which the Republican Party's actions deviated somewhat from the competitive federalism approach. Both these instances were brought about by highly unusual circumstances, so they do not indicate any sort of general pattern. The first instance occurred in the early months of the COVID-19 Pandemic, when Republicans joined with Democrats in Congress to pass a series of laws (the largest of which was the CARES Act) that temporarily provided a vast infusion of national funds to state and local governments. The GOP's embrace of intergovernmental spending in these months occurred at "a politically exceptional moment" in which COVID lockdowns triggered an unusually sudden economic downturn and in which a Republican president worried about being blamed by the public for an insufficient response to the pandemic.[20] By the end of 2020, congressional Republicans had already returned to their now-longstanding fiscal federalism approach, rejecting Democratic efforts to send more money to the states as "blue-state bailouts."[21] The second of these instances was the increase in the SALT cap that was included in the One Big Beautiful Bill Act of 2025. As discussed in the introduction, were it not for Republicans' razor-thin majority in the U.S. House (and thus their dependence on a very small bloc of GOP representatives from high-tax states to pass their agenda), this increase in the SALT cap would certainly not have occurred.

Given the sensitivity of state-level politicians to competitive pressures, the aggressive efforts of Republican politicians and Republican-aligned groups to turn interstate economic competition into a national partisan issue over the past fifteen years seems likely to create difficult political challenges for both Democrat and Republican-controlled state governments whenever the next persistent economic downturn occurs.[22] In the states that they control, Democrats will surely face immense political pressure against raising taxes. But in Republican-controlled states, GOP leaders will have to balance

[20] Mariely López-Santana and Philip Rocco, "Fiscal Federalism and Economic Crises in the United States: Lessons from the COVID-19 Pandemic and Great Recession," *Publius* 51, no. 3 (2021): 377.

[21] Ibid.; John Kincaid and Wesley J. Leckrone, "Large-Scale but Temporary: How the Federal Government's Responses to the Great Recession and COVID-19 (Mostly) Maintained Continuity in American Federalism," *Cuadernos Manuel Giménez Abad*, Special Issue, no. 9 (2023): 216.

[22] The downturn induced by the COVID-19 Pandemic in mid 2020 was so short, and was counteracted by such a large national countercyclical program, that state responses to it are not particularly revealing here.

the desire to further advance a tax-cutting, "competitive" agenda against the further hollowing out of core social services that have long been neglected due to decades of tax cuts. Of course, how states respond to the next downturn will be heavily influenced by national intergovernmental fiscal policy, which will almost certainly continue to be influenced by patterns of partisan control at the national level. While a Republican-controlled national government seems very likely to reduce (or at a minimum not to increase) fiscal support for state governments, the Democratic Party's complicated recent track record in fiscal federalism matters makes its likely response to future economic downturns more difficult to predict.

State Tax Policy and the Democratic Party's Fiscal Federalism Dilemma

As the Republican Party has doubled down on competitive federalism at both the national and state levels over the course of the twenty-first century, the national Democratic Party has faced a profound dilemma in its approach to intergovernmental fiscal relations. On the one hand, Democratic leaders have clearly chosen a fiscal policy approach that prioritizes expanding intergovernmental aid, particularly during moments of economic downturn. But structuring that aid in a way that achieves its intended goals has proven difficult for Democrats, given that state-level Republicans have frequently used that aid to facilitate tax cuts rather than to preserve or grow the subnational public sector.

The Democrats' fiscal federalism dilemma can be seen clearly in their response to America's two most recent economic crises: the 2007–2009 Great Recession and the COVID pandemic of 2020–2022. In response to the Great Recession, a Democrat-controlled Congress passed and President Barack Obama signed the American Recovery and Reinvestment Act (ARRA, more commonly referred to at the time as "the stimulus"), the largest countercyclical fiscal package implemented by the national government since the Great Depression.[23] In designing ARRA, Democrats in Congress and the Obama White House self-consciously sought to follow the Keynesian strategy of "priming the pump" in order to revive consumer demand in an economic

[23] Gerald Carlino and Robert P. Inman, "Fiscal stimulus in economic unions: what role for states?," *Tax Policy and the Economy* 30, no. 1 (2016): 1–50. ARRA was, in fact, the very first item on President Obama's agenda after he took office in January 2009.

downturn. The issue of whether and how to support state governments, however, was a complicated one for them. On the one hand, Democrats knew that, without substantial aid from the national government, states would be forced to retrench, thereby neutralizing the effects of any countercyclical stimulus package. But the political consequences of state aid were unappealing: many of the most direct beneficiaries of state aid would be Republican governors, who would inevitably use the funds to avoid making difficult fiscal decisions while at the same time attacking D.C. Democrats for being profligate spenders.[24] As the journalist Michael Grunwald recounts, state aid was an especially bitter pill for congressional Democrats to swallow since many of the Republican governors who stood to benefit from it had aggressively advanced a tax-cutting agenda that had weakened their states' fiscal positions in previous years. Indeed, among congressional Democrats, the most vociferous opponents of including state aid as part of the stimulus package were those from red states featuring conservative Republican governors and legislatures. These state governments seemed far more likely to use the stimulus funds to cut taxes than to preserve vital social services, as Democrats intended.[25]

In the end, congressional Democrats decided that the importance of providing fiscal support for the subnational public sector outweighed the political costs of bolstering state-level Republican politicians: of the $796 billion that the national government ultimately spent through ARRA, $318 billion was directed to state and local governments.[26] What happened in the months and years following ARRA's passage largely confirmed many of congressional Democrats' worst fears about the law's intergovernmental spending component. To begin with, rather than use the ARRA funds to maintain social services and protect public sector jobs, state-level Republicans often used them to pay for tax cuts.[27] Then, during the 2010 campaign season, Republicans campaigned against the ARRA, calling it wasteful government spending, and these attacks likely contributed to the GOP's spectacular victory in the elections of that year. Finally, the recovery from the Great Recession over the course of the early 2010s was gradual and halting, a fact that many Democrats blamed on the inability of ARRA to staunch

[24] Michael Grunwald, *The New New Deal: The Hidden Story of Change in the Obama Era* (New York: Simon & Schuster, 2012), 63.

[25] Grunwald, *The New New Deal*, 134–135.

[26] ibid.

[27] As Chapter 6 noted, some red states actually managed to cut income taxes while passing balanced budgets in the middle of the 2009–2010 recession, a feat that was likely made possible by acceptance of ARRA funds.

recession-induced spending cuts by state and local governments. All these outcomes convinced Democrats that ARRA was flawed in its approach to state and local aid.

When Democrats retook control of the national government in 2021, they once again assumed power in the middle of a large-scale economic crisis, this one induced by the COVID pandemic. In their efforts to combat the downturn, they seemed determined not to repeat their perceived mistakes with ARRA. To begin with, they pumped a lot more money into state and local governments: through the American Rescue Plan Act (ARP), which was passed on a near party-line vote, Democrats in Congress sent $350 billion to state and local governments for the purpose of COVID recovery.[28] When combined with the $340 billion that Congress had appropriated for intergovernmental COVID aid in 2020, the total amount of COVID intergovernmental aid ($690 billion) dwarfed the corresponding amount ($318 billion) spent by Congress to combat the Great Recession through ARRA.[29] Through sending states such a large amount of money, Democrats sought to ensure that their stimulus efforts would not be undermined by state-level retrenchment, as their efforts to combat the Great Recession were.

Second, to prevent state-level Republican politicians from using ARP money to further advance their tax-cutting agenda, Democrats included an unusual stipulation in the law: states could not use their ARP funds to "offset a reduction in...net tax revenue...resulting from a change in law..."[30] Revealingly, the inclusion of this provision was made at the request of a pivotal Democratic senator from a red state—Joe Manchin of West Virginia—who was aware that his state's Republican Governor, Jim Justice, was preparing to push a major income tax cut through the state legislature.[31] While press reports regarding internal negotiations about this provision are lacking, the available evidence suggests that Manchin's request was readily agreed to by Democrats in the executive branch and Congress. Indeed, the White House

[28] U.S. Department of the Treasury, "State and local Fiscal Recovery Funds," https://home.treasury.gov/policy-issues/coronavirus/assistance-for-state-local-and-tribal-governments/state-and-local-fiscal-recovery-funds, accessed May 17, 2024.

[29] According to López-Santana and Rocco, Congress appropriated $340 billion in COVID-related intergovernmental aid in 2020. López-Santana and Rocco, "Fiscal Federalism and Economic Crises in the United States," 374.

[30] *American Rescue Plan Act of 2021*, Public Law 117-2 (2021), sec. 802(c).

[31] Patrick Gleason, "How senator Joe Manchin's Move to Block Tax Relief In His Own State Costs All U.S. Taxpayers," *Forbes*, May 16, 2021, https://www.forbes.com/sites/patrickgleason/2021/03/16/how-senator-joe-manchins-move-to-block-tax-relief-in-his-own-state-costs-all-us-taxpayers/?sh=4c17bbda6188, accessed April 25, 2024.

expressed broad support for it publicly: as Biden Press Secretary Jen Psaki told reporters, "the original purpose of the state and local funding was to keep cops, firefighters, other essential employees at work and employed, and it wasn't intended to cut taxes."[32]

The inclusion within ARP of the prohibition against states using COVID relief funds to cut their own taxes set off a firestorm of protest from Republicans at both the national and state levels. GOP members of Congress railed against the provision as a violation of state fiscal autonomy and sponsored bills to repeal it.[33] More serious were the actions of Republican state attorneys general. Less than a week after ARP was signed into law, twenty-one of them sent a letter to Treasury Secretary Janet Yellen asking for immediate clarification on how the provision would be implemented and declaring that it could potentially amount to "the greatest attempted invasion of state sovereignty by Congress in the history of our Republic."[34] Specifically mentioning fourteen tax cut proposals being debated in Republican-controlled state legislatures, the letter argued that a maximalist interpretation of the ARP provision would mean that states would not be able to pass any tax cuts during years in which they accepted ARP funds.

Even before the Treasury Department had the opportunity to respond to the letter, Ohio Attorney General Dave Yost filed a lawsuit in federal court arguing that the provision exceeded Congress's spending powers and violated the Supreme Court's well-known "anti-commandeering doctrine" forbidding the national government from coercing the states into making (or, in this case, not making) particular policy choices.[35] Soon thereafter, various Republican attorneys general filed five additional lawsuits challenging the provision in different federal trial courts throughout the country.[36]

[32] "Press Briefing by Press Secretary Jen Psaki," whitehouse.gov, March 15, 2021, https://www.whitehouse.gov/briefing-room/statements-releases/2021/03/15/press-briefing-by-press-secretary-jen-psaki-march-15-2021/, accessed May 17, 2024.

[33] These bills included S. 743 (State Fiscal Flexibility Act of 2021), https://www.congress.gov/bill/117th-congress/senate-bill/743/text; and H.R. 2002/S.730 (Let States Cut Taxes Act), https://www.congress.gov/bill/117th-congress/senate-bill/730/text.

[34] Mark Brnovich et al. to the Honorable Janet Yellen, "Re: Treasury Action to Prevent Unconstitutional Restriction on State's Fiscal Policy through American Rescue Plan of 2021," March 16, 2021, accessed from https://www.taxnotes.com/featured-primary-source/ags-ask-treasury-if-federal-covid-19-relief-restricts-state-tax-policy/2021/03/17/3thbf, accessed February 10, 2026.

[35] State of Ohio, "Combined Motion for a Preliminary Injunction and Memorandum in Support of the Motion," State of Ohio v. Janet Yellen, United States District Court for the Southern District of Ohio, Case No. 1:21-cv-181, accessed from https://www.cleveland.com/open/2021/03/ohio-attorney-general-dave-yost-sues-over-federal-rules-on-billions-in-state-funding-contained-in-stimulus-bill.html, accessed February 10, 2026.

[36] These were: West Virginia et. al. v. U.S. Dept. of the Treasury, Case No. 7:21-cv-00465; Missouri v. Yellen, Case No. 21-cv-02118; Arizona v. Yellen, Case No. 21-cv-00514-PHX-DJH; Commonwealth of Kentucky et al. v. Yellen, Case No. 3:21-cv-00017-GFVT-EBA; Texas et al. v. Janet Yellen et al., Case No. 2:21-cv-00079-Z.

While each of these lawsuits made slightly different legal arguments, they all alleged that the tax-cut prohibition in ARP created unconstitutional restrictions on state fiscal authority. Importantly, many of the amicus briefs filed by Republican-aligned groups in support of these lawsuits explicitly argued that competitive federalism was a basic principle of the American constitutional order, one that the tax-cut prohibition threatened. For example, in its supporting brief in *Arizona v. Yellen*, the Goldwater Institute (the Arizona affiliate of the Koch-backed State Policy Network, discussed in Chapter 6) included a section entitled "Tax Competition Is an Important Part of Federalism, which ARPA infringes upon."[37]

For the most part, the courts agreed with the states in these lawsuits: federal district judges ruled in favor of them four out of six times.[38] Over the course of 2022 and 2023, each of the six cases moved up the federal judicial hierarchy and, as of the summer of 2024, three federal circuit courts of appeals had ruled in favor of the states as well.[39] Though the most basic legal question at hand (whether or how the national government can condition intergovernmental aid on states making particular tax policy choices) has not yet been resolved by the U.S. Supreme Court, the lawsuits and the resulting federal court injunctions clearly succeeded in preventing the national government from implementing the tax-cut prohibition in practice (as the huge number of state tax cuts since 2021 demonstrate).[40]

The Democratic Party's fiscal federalism dilemma can thus be summarized as follows: given the importance of the subnational public sector to domestic policy in the United States, it is impossible to enact a major

[37] "Brief Amicus Curiae of Goldwater Institute in Support of Petitioner," On Petition for a Writ of Certiorari to the United States Court of Appeals for the Sixth Circuit, #22-880.

[38] Andrew Wilford and Joe Bishop-Henchman, "Where Things Stand on the ARPA State Tax Cut Provision," *National Taxpayers Union*, March 21, 2022, https://www.ntu.org/foundation/detail/where-things-stand-on-the-arpa-state-tax-cut-provision, accessed December 23, 2025.

[39] The 11th Circuit ruled in favor of West Virginia and its twelve state co-plaintiffs in *West Virginia v. Department of the Treasury*, the 6th Circuit ruled in favor of Kentucky and Tennessee in *Kentucky v. Yellen*, and the 5th Circuit ruled in favor of Mississippi, Texas, and Louisiana in *Texas v. Yellen*. In some of the other cases involving the tax-cut prohibition, federal circuits dismissed the lawsuits, but they did so on procedural rather than substantive grounds. On balance, therefore, the federal courts have been broadly sympathetic to the states' substantive arguments. Ilya Somin, "Eleventh Circuit Becomes Second Federal Appellate Court to Strike Down Tax Mandate Condition in 2021 Covid Stimulus Bill," reason.com, January 24, 2023, https://reason.com/volokh/2023/01/24/eleventh-circuit-becomes-second-federal-court-to-strike-down-tax-mandate-condition-in-2021-covid-stimulus-bill/, accessed May 21, 2024. Abir Mandal, "ARPA's Tax Mandate Ruled Unconstitutional by Appellate Court," *Tax Foundation*, July 11, 2024, https://taxfoundation.org/blog/arpa-tax-mandate-state-tax-cuts-unconstitutional/, accessed December 23, 2025.

[40] The U.S. Supreme Court denied certiorari to Ohio following the 6th Circuit's ruling in *Ohio v Yellen*, but in this case, the 6th Circuit dismissed the case as moot rather than ruling against Ohio's substantive claims.

domestic fiscal expansion—as twenty-first century Democrats clearly wish to do—without bringing the states along for the ride. But states are independent fiscal policymakers, as the federal courts have made clear, and the Republicans who control many state governments have shown that they will actively use state fiscal policy—particularly income tax cuts—to undermine the Democrats' national fiscal vision. More than that, the GOP's promotion of competitive federalism in a highly nationalized political environment means that all states in the twenty-first century—regardless of their political composition—are under pressure to keep their tax burdens low. Within this context, even "blue states" are limited in their ability to join the national government as full partners in a fiscal expansion program. Here, it is important to point out that the significant tax increases that Democrat-controlled states have passed in the previous decade have almost always targeted only their wealthiest taxpayers, and have often been paired with tax relief for others.[41] To a greater degree than in previous eras, modern states of all political stripes assiduously avoid passing tax increases affecting more than a sliver of their populations.[42]

For Democrats, there is no easy solution to this conundrum. One option is to focus intergovernmental spending on categorical grants for specific programs in lieu of more flexible fiscal transfers like those of ARP. Targeting intergovernmental spending toward the expansion of particular programs makes it somewhat more difficult for states to use those funds to offset revenue lost due to tax cuts.[43] But because money is fungible, any large infusion of funds from the national government can ultimately be used by states to reduce the tax burdens they impose on their citizens, regardless of how specific instructions for use of those funds are or even whether acceptance of those funds requires that states contribute their own funds toward

[41] For example, in 2019, New Jersey added a top new tax bracket of 10.75%, but only for annual incomes exceeding a staggering $5,000,000. Sheila Reynertson, "Road to Recovery: Reforming New Jersey's Income Tax Code," *New Jersey Policy Perspective*, June 9, 2020, https://www.njpp.org/publications/report/road-to-recovery-reforming-new-jerseys-income-tax-code/, accessed December 23, 2025.

[42] The only major exception to this rule appears to be Illinois, which faced massive fiscal problems in the 2010s and whose constitution prohibits a graduated income tax. State lawmakers were thus forced to raise the state's flat income tax rate, effectively raising taxes on all its taxpayers.

[43] Moreover, one can look to the gradual implementation of Medicaid expansion under the 2009 Affordable Care Act by the majority of states, both red and blue, to find evidence that opposition to the expansion of intergovernmental programs by state-level Republicans will eventually wither away. The lesson of Medicaid expansion is that state politicians opposed to a new intergovernmental program (or its expansion) for partisan reasons will eventually fall in line and take the federal money to implement the program.

a program. Given the political dynamics of our modern era, it can therefore be expected that, in the long run, increased intergovernmental spending by the national government will lead to reduced state own-source tax revenue, precisely the trend shown in Figure 6.7 in Chapter 6.

There is a limit to how far this trend can go, however. It is difficult to imagine the national government using federal funds to overwhelmingly or wholly replace state own-source tax revenue for the wide array of programs or policies for which the states are primarily responsible. Such a transformation, which would be tantamount to the United States adopting the Australian model of fiscal federalism (wherein the vast bulk of subnational government revenue is raised by the central government), seems inconceivable in the American political and institutional context. In the absence of such a transformation, however, the tax-cutting agenda of state-level Republicans and the competitive federalism dynamic more generally will likely hamper Democratic aspirations for a major expansion of the domestic public sector.

The Dangers That Lie Ahead

Regardless of which party controls the national government, the divergence in the tax policies of red and blue states will create profound challenges for America's future leaders. Perhaps the chief such problem is the growth in state fiscal inequality that it will foster. It is important to bear in mind that, irrespective of their tax systems, states vary substantially in their fiscal capacities due to economic differences: wealthy states like Connecticut and Massachusetts have significantly greater taxable resources than poor states like Mississippi and West Virginia. These differences, which create major gaps in the quality of public services and benefits that states provide to their citizens, have long existed but have probably increased in recent decades as America's regions have diverged in their economic fortunes.[44] Importantly, such gaps are only weakly remediated by intergovernmental aid from the national government, since the primary purpose of such aid is to support

[44] Robert A. Schapiro, "States of Inequality: Fiscal Federalism, Unequal States, and Unequal People," *California Law Review* 108, no. 5 (2020): 1531–1596; Tom Kemeny and Michael Storper, "The Fall and Rise of Interregional Inequality: Explaining Shifts from Convergence to Divergence," *Scienze Regionali* 19, no. 2 (2020): 175–198; Tom Kemeny and Michael Storper, "The Changing Shape of Spatial Income Disparities in the United States," *Economic Geography* 99 (2023): 1–30.

intergovernmental programs rather than address interstate fiscal inequalities per se. Ultimately, the reason these gaps persist is because of America's status as the only federal democracy without a major interstate fiscal equalization program. As discussed in the introduction and Chapter 4, this unique feature of American fiscal federalism is a byproduct of the larger failure of the United States to adopt a more coordinated intergovernmental taxation arrangement.

While inequality in state fiscal capacity has always been a troubling feature of American fiscal federalism, the partisan polarization of state tax policy is making the underlying problem far more serious. Scholars of American politics (as well as more casual observers) have long noticed that the red-blue maps depicting contemporary American electoral outcomes also evince an economic pattern: the bluest states tend to be wealthy, while the reddest tend to be poor.[45] And as we have seen in this book, the red-blue maps increasingly correlate with state taxation choices as well: red states have been eagerly cutting taxes, especially income taxes, while blue states have not (and have in some cases raised them). Until recently, however, the relationship between state wealth and state tax policy has not been as strong as that between either variable or state partisanship, largely because it was the wealthier rather than the poorer red states that were at the vanguard of the GOP tax-cut push. But, as discussed earlier in this chapter, that is no longer the case: in the 2020s, poorer red states like West Virginia, Arkansas, and Mississippi have been enacting large tax cuts as well. Meanwhile, the blue states that have managed to pass large income tax increases on their high-income residents (e.g., New Jersey, Massachusetts) tend to be among the wealthiest states overall.

This emerging pattern threatens to exacerbate state fiscal inequalities and make the uneven provision of public services across states and localities an even larger problem than it has historically been. As their income tax rates fall, poorer red states will almost certainly see their revenue levels decline, particularly during periods of economic downturn, thereby forcing them to

[45] As Gelman and his co-authors famously showed, the state-level relationship between greater wealth and higher Democratic partisanship has historically been inverted at the individual level: wealthier individuals have been more likely to vote Republican, not Democrat. Andrew Gelman, *Red State, Blue State, Rich State, Poor State: Why Americans Vote the Way They Do—Expanded Edition* (Princeton, NJ: Princeton University Press, 2009). However, in recent election cycles, the individual-level relationship between income and Republican voting has diminished considerably. See, e.g., Andrew Gelman and Julia Azari, "19 Things We Learned from the 2016 Election," *Statistics and Public Policy* 4, no. 1 (2017): 1-10.

routinely cut back on their already-meager spending for basic public services. Meanwhile, spending on service provision in wealthy blue states will likely remain fairly stable, even as these states reckon with regular budget problems caused by unsustainable pension obligations. At some point, it seems reasonable to expect that these interstate differences will become a national issue. Whenever this happens, the responses of both political parties will likely be influenced by competing motivations. Despite their professed commitment to uniform national social-welfare standards, D.C. Democrats may be less than enthusiastic to help Republican-controlled state governments overcome fiscal difficulties created by (in the minds of Democrats) their own irresponsible tax cuts. For their part, D.C. Republicans will encounter a conflict between the needs of hard-pressed red states and the demands of competitive federalist ideology.

Toward a More Coordinated Intergovernmental Tax System

The foregoing section of the book paints a rather dire future for American fiscal federalism, one of growing balkanization in subnational fiscal capacity, increased regional variation in the provisioning of basic public services, and a hapless national government unable to properly address subnational fiscal challenges. This leads to the important question of what, if anything, can be done to avert the worst possible outcomes of the trajectory that the American federal system has been on in the twenty-first century. Unfortunately, there is little reason for optimism that the United States can right its course in the near future. In addition to the structural barriers to intergovernmental fiscal reform posed by the U.S. Constitution (a topic to which I return later), the defining features of the current era of American politics—high levels of party polarization, deep regional divisions, little appetite for bipartisan compromise among policymakers—render prospects for a substantial overhaul of America's intergovernmental fiscal arrangements extremely remote. Still, even absent a major revamping of American fiscal federalism, there are smaller reforms that Congress or the states might undertake to facilitate a more well-functioning, well-coordinated intergovernmental taxation system. While not sufficient to address the deepest challenges the system faces, such reforms could potentially mitigate the worst outcomes of these challenges and create a framework for addressing deeper issues down the line (when political circumstances improve).

First, subnational governments and other key stakeholders should lobby Congress to establish a new forum in which policymakers from national, state, and local government meet regularly to discuss and potentially resolve intergovernmental fiscal conflicts and dilemmas. Such a forum would ameliorate the various problems caused by the absence of formalized dialogue between fiscal policymakers at different levels of American government in the twenty-first century. One important such problem is the well-documented lack of understanding of, or interest in, the fiscal challenges facing state and local governments among contemporary members of Congress.[46] This ignorance and inattentiveness harms not just the states and localities, but the nation as well. Despite the efforts of various presidential administrations since the 1980s to impose greater fiscal separation between national and subnational government, America's national and state fiscal systems remain highly interconnected and it is very doubtful that they will be further separated in the future. Given this reality, implementing a successful national fiscal policy necessarily requires congressional attention to subnational fiscal circumstances. The (re-)establishment of an intergovernmental fiscal forum would help facilitate a greater awareness of these circumstances among national policymakers, potentially leading to improved policy output. It would likely also lead to improved fiscal policymaking at the subnational level, since subnational leaders would make fiscal decisions with a clearer understanding of Congress's vision and agenda.

The forum proposed here would be quite different from the robust network of institutions dedicated to establishing intergovernmental dialogue that existed in the mid twentieth century. As discussed previously, that network came about in a profoundly different political context, and it is highly unlikely that such a network could be rebuilt in this one. What is being envisioned here is something narrower: a single forum exclusively devoted to taxing and spending matters and composed of a mix of elected officials and tax administrators from each level of government, similar to the composition of the stillborn Tax Revision Council of the 1930s (discussed in Chapter 2). Importantly, there are analogues to this proposed forum in other federal democracies. In Canada, for example, the Federal-Provincial Committee on Taxation facilitates periodic consultation between policymakers in the Canadian federal and provincial governments over matters of taxation.

[46] Borut, "The Unraveling of the Intergovernmental System: A Practitioner's Observations," 251.

Regular meetings of the committee help to ensure that proposed tax policy changes at the federal level are "nationally effective and appropriate."[47]

One should not be too optimistic when predicting the outcomes that might result from the creation of such a forum in the United States. After all, the existence of the intergovernmental institutions described above in an earlier era did not lead to the sorts of reforms that the experts of the time believed the United States needed, though they certainly contributed to more limited ones like the SLFAA. We should therefore not expect that the establishment of an intergovernmental policy forum will help facilitate transformative policy change. Likewise, given the highly polarized nature of modern national policymaking, we should not expect that the proposed forum would assist policymakers in resolving issues that become entangled in national party conflict. Where the forum may be useful is in facilitating intergovernmental consultation and establishing intergovernmental comity and respect. Through regular intergovernmental meetings and interactions, national fiscal policymakers would hopefully learn to see their subnational counterparts as policymaking partners rather than obnoxious interest groups, while subnational policymakers would hopefully be able to better anticipate national policy changes when designing their budgets and engaging in long-term planning.

There are also modest steps that state governments could take without congressional action to facilitate a more unified intergovernmental tax system. One such step involves updating state income tax codes to conform more closely with that of the national government. Currently, the vast majority of states with personal income taxes (36 out of 41) opt for employing state-defined personal exemptions and deductions for determining taxable income rather than using federal taxable income as their starting point.[48] Aligning state tax bases with federal taxable income, or (even better) computing state income tax liability as a direct proportion of a taxpayer's

[47] Paul Berg-Dic, Michel Carreau, Deanne Field, and Mireille Ethier, "Tax Coordination under the Canadian Tax System," *Fiscal Federalism and Political Decentralization: Lessons from Spain, Germany, and Canada* (Cheltenham, UK: Edward Elgar, 2009), 175. Importantly, this committee is embedded within a larger edifice of federal-provincial meetings that forms a much more coordinated tax system than that which exists in the United States overall.

[48] Five of these states do not even use the federal government's definition of adjusted gross income, meaning that their income tax systems are ostensibly unrelated to that of the national government. Ronald C. Fisher, *State and Local Public Finance*, 5th edition (New York: Routledge, 2023), 336–337. However, as Ruth Mason points out, most of these states nonetheless rely on various federal tax forms and concepts and can therefore by described as "facially nonconforming." Ruth Mason, "Delegating Up: State Conformity with the Federal Tax Base," *Duke Law Journal* 62, no. 7 (2012): 1278.

federal liability,[49] would yield a wide array of benefits for taxpayers, states, and the country as a whole. Some of these benefits, such as greater state tax progressivity, more efficient income tax administration, and greater clarity regarding the tax implications of financial decisions for taxpayers have long been promoted by code-conformity proponents and will not be dwelt upon here.[50] But one crucial benefit of code conformity that has not been extensively discussed by other scholars relates to its implications for democratic governance. Political scientists have long noted that federal systems of government can impede democratic accountability by burdening voters with the need to separately monitor the policies of multiple levels of government.[51] This is certainly the case regarding tax policy in the United States: American voters who are concerned with taxation need to separately monitor the income tax policies set by Congress alongside those set by their state legislature. This is a heavy burden that few other countries expect of their citizens, and while empirical evidence on Americans' knowledge of state and federal tax policy is lacking, it seems likely that most voters are not up to the task. Conforming state tax codes to that of the national government (while maintaining state discretion regarding the setting up of income tax rates) would help simplify America's highly complex tax system for voters, making it easier for them to hold state governments accountable for their tax policy decisions.

To be sure, for states, the decision to conform state tax codes to those of the national government comes with important trade-offs. Most obviously, states that opt for tax-code conformity effectively "cede control" of the structure of their income taxes to the national government, with several potentially adverse consequences.[52] First, such conformity means that state income taxes automatically change whenever federal income tax structures do, thereby significantly increasing the revenue volatility of the former.[53]

[49] Currently, no state calculates its income tax as a percentage of the federal income tax, but several states (including Nebraska, Rhode Island, Vermont, and Washington) did so for many decades.

[50] For an extensive discussion of these benefits, see: Otto G. Stolz and George A. Purdy, "Federal Collection of State Individual Income Taxes," *Duke Law Journal* 59 (1977): 92–113.

[51] Christopher Wlezien and Stuart N. Soroka, "Federalism and Public Responsiveness to Policy," *Publius* 41, no. 1 (2011): 31–52; Sara Hobolt, James Tilley, and Susan Banducci, "Clarity of Responsibility: How Government Cohesion Conditions Performance Voting," *European Journal of Social Research* 52 (2013): 164–187; John Kennedy, Anthony Sayers, and Christopher Alcantara, "Does Federalism Prevent Democratic Accountability? Assigning Responsibility for Rates of COVID-19 Testing," *Political Studies Review* 20, no. 1 (2022): 158–165; Steven Rogers, *Accountability in State Legislatures* (Chicago: University of Chicago Press, 2023).

[52] Ruth Mason, "Delegating Up," 1289.

[53] Indeed, the desire to have a less volatile state income tax structure is what prompted a number of states to delink their income tax code from that of the national government in the past (RI, VT).

Linking state income tax codes to those of the national government also means that states largely lose the ability to independently use their income tax structures as a form of social policy (for example, by creating certain deductions or exemptions as a way of incentivizing particular behaviors), or to tailor their tax systems to local needs and conditions. For these reasons and others, the legal scholar Ruth Mason argues that state piggybacking off the federal tax code "represents a democratic loss for state residents."[54]

While these concerns should not be dismissed out of hand, they need to be considered with the highly nationalized context of twenty-first-century American politics (including state politics) in mind. As many scholars have pointed out, the resurgence of state governments in the twenty-first century has occurred not because of a renewed interest among Americans in their local communities, but rather because state governments have become venues of national party conflict in which, unlike the national government, one party or the other often dominates.[55] The existence of long stretches of unified party control in many states has allowed the parties to implement many aspects of their national domestic-policy visions at the state level, and (as this book has shown) this has certainly been the case for taxation. It seems hard to argue, however, that the fracturing of an essentially national debate over tax policy across fifty state governments has been a democracy-enhancing development for the United States. If contemporary American voters are only dimly aware of the budget fights happening in their state capitals,[56] the growing divergence in the tax policies produced in those capitals cannot be interpreted as a win for democracy.

To the contrary, since modern state tax policies reflect a nationalized politics, it would arguably be more of a democratic gain for states to shift decision-making over their income tax codes to the site of governance that is commanding the bulk of voter attention: that of the national government. In doing so, states would not be giving up all the discretion they currently enjoy regarding the structure of their income taxes, but rather limiting their discretion to those aspects of state income tax policy (i.e., the setting of tax rates and/or the overall degree of the tax burden) that are most visible to voters. Moreover, through piggybacking off the federal tax code, states would be

[54] Mason, "Delegating Up," 1301.

[55] Jessica Bulman-Pozen, "Partisan Federalism," *Harvard Law Review* 127, no. 4 (2013), 1077–1146; Jacob M. Grumbach, "From Backwaters to Major Policymakers: Policy Polarization in the States, 1970–2014," *Perspectives on Politics* 16, no. 2 (2018): 416–435.

[56] For much evidence of low public attention to state politics, see Daniel J. Hopkins, *The Increasingly United States: How and Why American Political Behavior Nationalized* (Chicago: University of Chicago Press, 2022).

able to more effectively fulfill the contemporary role they have taken on as sites of partisan opposition to the national government.[57] For example, if all states simply calculated their income taxes as a percentage of federal tax liability, blue states could relatively quickly respond to a federal income tax cut passed by a Republican-controlled Congress by raising their state percentages, while red states could relatively quickly respond to a federal income tax levy passed by a Democrat-controlled Congress by decreasing theirs. Under this scenario, states would retain discretion over how much income tax revenue they raise, but their own income tax changes would be more clearly understood by the public as interventions in a national tax-policy debate.

Moving Beyond Competitive Federalism

In the long run, the United States will need to implement reforms that are more far-reaching than those discussed above to tackle the challenges facing the country's intergovernmental tax system in the twenty-first century. For this to happen, however, fiscal federalism must return to the center of the national policy agenda—a place it has not been at since the 1980s. This book's case studies of intergovernmental fiscal reform efforts in earlier eras suggest that increased national attention to fiscal federalism issues has always been accompanied by the emergence of at least a rough consensus regarding the need to solve a particular fiscal federalism problem (federal-state tax conflicts in the 1930s, inadequate subnational fiscal capacity in the 1960s, and an overweening subnational public sector in the 1980s). A similar consensus regarding the core fiscal federalism problem to be addressed in the early twenty-first century will therefore need to emerge before robust discussions of intergovernmental fiscal reform can begin once again.

The final chapters of this book have pointed to what this core problem is: the deleterious influence of competitive federalism on the contemporary intergovernmental fiscal system.

In saying this, I am not making a comprehensive claim about the value (or lack thereof) of competitive federalism for the United States in all circumstances. Whether competition between state governments promotes the general welfare of American citizens, as evangelists of competitive federalism have long contended, is a highly complex question whose answer likely

[57] See Bulman-Pozen, "Partisan Federalism," for a full explication of this interpretation of the role of the states in twenty-first-century of American government and politics.

varies across policy domains as well as political contexts. What does seem evident, though, is that interstate tax competition—the specific form of competitive federalism that has been the focus of this book—has exacerbated rather than helped solve some of the biggest economic challenges in the contemporary United States. For example, the well-documented gap between the economic fortunes of America's "superstar" coastal metro areas and its stagnant inland regions has grown despite the best efforts of Republican politicians from the latter to attract business investment to their localities via tax cuts and deregulation.[58] This strongly suggests that, in the contemporary United States, interstate economic competition does not produce the degree of capital mobility necessary to reduce regional economic gaps, as theorists of competitive federalism have sometimes imagined.[59] Instead, it seems that the GOP's promotion of competitive federalist policies has amplified differences in subnational government fiscal capacity without reducing underlying regional economic disparities—the worst possible outcome.

When applied to intergovernmental fiscal relations in twenty-first-century America, the normative theory of competitive federalism suffers from two important shortcomings. The first is that it relies on empirical assumptions that, as a general matter, do not withstand scrutiny. As discussed in Chapter 5, competitive federalism assumes that Americans regularly "vote with their feet" in response to state tax policies, moving to states with the tax burdens they prefer, and that resulting interstate migration patterns ultimately serve to align state tax policies with citizen preferences—a purported win for popular rule. This basic claim has been the subject of many economic studies over the course of decades, and their highly contradictory findings suggest that the effect of state tax policies on migration patterns (and economic growth more generally) is fairly minimal and highly context-dependent.[60]

[58] On the growing divergence of regional economic circumstances in the United States, see, e.g., Mark Muro and Jacob Whiton, "America Has Two Economies—And They're Diverging Fast," *Brookings Institution*, September 19, 2019, https://www.brookings.edu/articles/america-has-two-economies-and-theyre-diverging-fast/, accessed February 10, 2026; Kemeny and Storper, "The Fall and Rise of Interregional Inequality: Explaining Shifts from Convergence to Divergence."

[59] Anwar Shah, "Comparative Conclusions on Fiscal Federalism," In *The Practice of Fiscal Federalism: Comparative Perspectives*, ed. Anwar Shaw (Montreal: McGill-Queen's University Press, 2007), 389.

[60] Important studies concluding that state taxation has little effect on interstate migration include: Cristobal Young, Charles Varner, Ithai Z. Lurie, and Richard Prisinzano, "Millionaire Migration and Taxation of the Elite: Evidence from Administrative Data," *American Sociological Review* 81, no. 3 (2016): 421–446; Karen Smith Conway and Jonathan C. Rork, "State 'Death' Taxes and Elderly Migration—The Chicken or the Egg?," *National Tax Journal* 59, no. 1 (2006): 97–128; Cristobal Young and Charles Varner, "Millionaire Migration and State Taxation of Top Incomes: Evidence from a Natural Experiment." *National Tax Journal* 64, no. 2 (2011): 255–283. Important studies

But regardless of the extent to which state tax policy actually influences migration patterns and economic growth rates, this book has clearly shown that state policymakers *perceive* that it does. It has also shown that such perceptions have occasionally caused state policymakers to subvert popular movements for tax increases, in some cases even when those movements enjoyed clear majority support.[61] This seems like a democratic loss, not a democratic gain.

Second, the logic underpinning claims regarding the value of competitive federalism—a theory that was largely developed in the 1970s and 1980s—appears flawed in the context of twenty-first-century American politics. To reiterate, competitive federalism imagines subnational politicians as ambitious "leviathans" seeking to maximize the revenues under their control as a way of increasing their power. A competitive fiscal constitution is meant to restrain such politicians (or to reduce their "surplus," in competitive federalist parlance), leading to a more efficient and accountable subnational public sector.[62] But the political landscape of the contemporary American states does not remotely resemble this vision. Rather than endlessly searching for new revenues, many (perhaps most) state-level politicians in today's America seem far more interested in finding ways to *reduce* the ones at their disposal. The theoretical premises of competitive federalism, which suggest that state policymakers always seek to aggrandize the positions they hold, cannot account for this reality. In fact, what seems to motivate contemporary state politicians in their tax-cutting zeal is a factor absent from traditional

coming to somewhat different conclusions include: Mark Gius, "The Effect of Income Taxes on Interstate migration: an Analysis by Age and Race," *Annals of Regional Science* 46, no. 1 (2011): 205–218; Roger Cohen, Andrew Lai, and Charles Steindel, "State Income Taxes and Interstate Migration," *Business Economics* 49, no. 3 (2014): 176–190; Traviss Cassidy, Mark Dincecco, and Ugo Antonio Troiano, "The Introduction of the Income Tax, Fiscal Capacity, and Migration: Evidence from US States," *American Economic Journal: Economic Policy* 16, no. 1 (2024): 359–393. In their comprehensive meta-analysis of studies examining the effect of state tax policies on various socioeconomic outcomes (including interstate migration), Rickman and Wang find that "the vast majority of the academic studies...found little or no effect" and that studies "have increasingly recognized hetereogeneity across geography and time..." Dan Rickman and Hongbo Wang, "US State and Local Fiscal Policy and Economic Activity: Do We Know More Now?," *Journal of Economic Surveys* 34, no. 2 (2020): 447, 448.

[61] A recent example of this occurred in Arizona in 2020, when the state's voters approved Proposition 208, which would have created a 2.5% income tax surcharge on high-income Arizonans to fund public education. The GOP-controlled state legislature responded to the ballot initiative's passage by filing suit to prevent the tax increase from going into effect. The state supreme court ultimately agreed with the legislature, striking down the initiative a year later. Mary Jo Pitzl, "Judge Deals Fatal Blow to Proposition 208, Ending 2-Year Battle over K-12 Funding," *Arizona Republic*, March 11, 2022, https://www.azcentral.com/story/news/politics/arizona-education/2022/03/11/proposition-208-tax-increase-arizonas-k-12-schools-struck-down/9433246002, accessed February 10, 2026.

[62] Michael Greve, *The Upside-Down Constitution*, (Cambridge, MA: Harvard University Press, 2012), 189–191.

competitive federalist theory: the political need to demonstrate fealty to a national party ideology. If competitive federalist policies in twenty-first-century America are largely a smokescreen for partisan political imperatives, as seems to be the case, it is hard to see how the normative theory of competitive federalism advances the public good in the way its proponents claim.

To truly promote the general welfare in today's America, policymakers must pursue a different fiscal federalism approach—one that secures adequate fiscal resources to subnational governments in every part of the country rather than pitting those governments against each other. Importantly, reducing the competitive pressures operating within American fiscal federalism does not require that the country resolve the deeper ideological disagreement with which questions of federalism in America have long been entangled—that which regards the size and scope of the entire domestic public sector, national and subnational—in favor of the "big government" vision of progressives. Though theorists of competitive federalism have long assumed that diminished subnational tax competition leads to greater overall public spending, decades of studies by economists have not conclusively confirmed the link: as a survey of the extant literature states, "little consensus has emerged on the effect of fiscal decentralization and the size of government."[63] The relationship between these two variables seems to be modulated by a wide array of confounding factors, rendering a clear association elusive. Moreover, in scanning the globe, one finds cases—such as Australia—of federal systems in which very low levels of interjurisdictional tax competition exist alongside a fairly limited welfare state, demonstrating that it is possible (if not common) to restrain interjurisdictional competitive pressures while also maintaining a fairly limited government.[64] In the final analysis, because the debate over the size and scope of the domestic public sector in twenty-first-century America is fundamentally a *national* debate, it would be better if it were contested squarely on its own terms, without the confusing side issue of competitive federalism accompanying it.

[63] Silvia Golem, "Fiscal Decentralisation and the Size of Government: a Review of the Empirical Literature," *Financial Theory and Practice* 34, no. 1 (2010): 53–69.

[64] Francis Castles and John Uhr point out that Australia exhibits a highly centralized tax system—with the vast bulk of taxes uniformly assessed by the national government and the Australian states largely dependent on the national government for their revenues—alongside public spending levels that are "very low by international standards," belying the common assumption that "centralized fiscal powers leads to high levels of public spending." Francis G. Castles and John Uhr, "Federalism and the Welfare State: Australia," unpublished paper, https://openresearch-repository.anu.edu.au/server/api/core/bitstreams/c5a0a234-6b52-4a09-97a3-9ab7bc0d61b6/content, accessed July 28, 2025, 3.

As previously suggested, moving beyond competitive federalism will likely only be possible if the Republican Party—competitive federalism's longtime champion—reexamines its commitment to that approach. One might hope that the changing makeup of the Republican electoral coalition in the Trump era has made such an outcome more likely. As much recent media commentary has emphasized, the GOP under Trump has gained political support from working-class Americans and increased its electoral strength in many of the country's poorest regions and states.[65] Since competitive federalism seeks to reduce federal intergovernmental transfers that disproportionately benefit the poorest states on the one hand, while also seeking to limit the ability of those states to raise their own revenue to fund social-service programs on the other, it seems to run counter to the interests of many Trump-era Republican voters. Indeed, a number of Republican politicians have arguably recognized this, even if they have not expressed their observations in federalism terms. For example, during the debate over the One Big Beautiful Bill Act in 2025, Sen. Josh Hawley of Missouri took to the pages of the *New York Times* to caution his Republican colleagues against making deep cuts to the nation's largest intergovernmental transfer program: Medicaid. As Sen. Hawley pointed out, cutting Medicaid substantially would lead to steep drops in health insurance coverage as well as hospital closures in his relatively poor home state. As he stated, "Republicans need to open their eyes: Our voters support social insurance programs. More than that, our voters depend on these programs."[66]

That said, the actions taken by Congress as well as Republican-controlled state legislatures in 2025 suggest that, Sen. Hawley's sentiments aside, the GOP's support for competitive federalism has not yet been diminished in any material way by the increasingly working-class composition of the party's electoral base. For example, nearly all Republicans in Congress (including Sen. Hawley) ended up supporting passage of a version of the Big Beautiful Bill that included steep cuts to Medicaid and other intergovernmental programs like SNAP. And while the bill did increase the SALT cap, it did so temporarily and (as noted previously) only because the margin of control in the U.S. House was so narrow. At the state level, Republicans in

[65] See, e.g., Yasmeen Abutaleb, Dan Keating, Sabrina Rodriguez, and Josh Dawsey, "Trump Coalition Marks a Transformed Republican Party," *Washington Post*, November 4, 2024, https://www.washingtonpost.com/politics/2024/11/06/trump-coalition-republicans-realignment/, accessed February 10, 2026; Henry Olsen, "The New Republican," *American Compass*, November 18, 2024, https://americancompass.org/the-new-republican/, accessed February 10, 2026.

[66] Josh Hawley, "Don't Cut Medicaid," *New York Times*, May 12, 2025, https://www.nytimes.com/2025/05/12/opinion/josh-hawley-dont-cut-medicaid.html, accessed February 10, 2026.

the Trump 2.0 era have clearly continued along the well-worn path of cutting income taxes, usually with the goal of ultimately abolishing them, in a bid to improve business competitiveness.[67] It thus appears that a broad reassessment of competitive federalism within the Republican Party is not on the verge of transpiring.

But even if such a reassessment were to come to pass at some point, and a robust discussion over broad-based intergovernmental fiscal reform in the halls of Congress ensued as a consequence, the resulting policy changes would likely fall short of truly transforming America's intergovernmental fiscal arrangements. To see why, consider the previous efforts to reform America's intergovernmental fiscal system that this book has documented. At each of the key moments that have been covered, national leaders had grand visions for reconstructing American fiscal federalism that they attempted to actuate in ostensibly favorable circumstances. In every instance, however, their visions were only partly implemented. Rather than wholly displacing the old system, these leaders at best managed to add a thin new institutional layer atop a largely robust if unwieldy apparatus. It is therefore likely that the nation's response to its fiscal federalism challenges in the twenty-first century will be only modestly shaped by the federalism visions of its future leaders. The heavy hand of history will overwhelm their political skills and will.

Thus, the most we can safely predict about the future is that America's complex intergovernmental taxation arrangement—wherein the states enjoy significant tax autonomy, numerous taxes are levied at both the national and state levels, and little coordination between national and state tax systems exists—will likely persist, though perhaps with some peripheral reforms to its workings. The institutional barriers to changing this system are too high, and the politics of renegotiating national and state taxation roles too challenging, for a transformational overhaul to be plausible at any point. American policymakers at both the national and state levels learned to live with this system as it developed haphazardly across the early and mid twentieth centuries, and there is little reason to believe that policymakers in the twenty-first century will be unable to muddle through it as they have before.

[67] As of mid-July, states that have implemented income tax rate cuts in 2025 include Indiana, Iowa, Louisiana, Mississippi, Missouri, and Oklahoma. Kelley R. Taylor, "State Tax Changes for 2025: Key Reforms and What They Mean for Your Finances," *Kiplinger*, March 22, 2025, https://www.kiplinger.com/taxes/several-states-announce-new-year-tax-changes, accessed February 10, 2026; Hicham Raache, "Gov. Stitt Signs Oklahoma Personal Income Tax Cut into Law," *Oklahoma Business Voice*, May 29, 2025, https://okbusinessvoice.com/2025/05/29/gov-stitt-signs-oklahoma-personal-income-tax-cut-into-law/, accessed February 10, 2026.

Index

For the benefit of digital users, indexed terms that span two pages (e.g., 52–53) may, on occasion, appear on only one of those pages.

Page numbers followed by *f* and *t* refer to figures and tables, respectively.